Participate

in a transformative

moment in history!

When students undertake a

Critical Mission,

they learn to read and analyze

sources, interpret maps and

timelines, and think like a

historian.

>> In this Critical Mission, students play a role in the impeachment of Andrew Johnson. They need to advise Edmund G. Ross, who represents the crucial swing vote in Congress, on how to vote.

<< A brief video provides students with context by reviewing the historical events leading up to the impeachment.

<< Students then read documents and examine maps to gather evidence and choose themes before writing their opinion for or against conviction.

⌃ Part 2 of the mission brings students to modern times by asking them to consider how Johnson's impeachment impacted more recent impeachment controversies.

Connect *to success in history*

<< Connect's **LearnSmart**, an adaptive learning system, provides students with remediation based not just on right or wrong answers, but also the confidence they feel in answering the question.

>> All Connect activities are linked to learning objectives, such as helping students understand the **geographical context** for historical events.

<< Students learn to **analyze cartoons and images** to extract key historical insights.

Independent research shows that students' grades improve with **Connect**, a learning platform that shows them what they know and what they still need to learn.

Linked to the "Then and Now" feature in the text, these comparisons help students make the **connection between past and current events.**

Dueling Documents

provide practice in analyzing and comparing primary source accounts of the same historical event.

Historian's Toolbox helps students learn how to examine an artifact or image from the past in the way a historian would.

We would like to express our deep appreciation to the following individuals who contributed to the development of this program:

Reviewers of U⋆S: A Narrative History

Mary Adams,
City College of San Francisco

Chris Bell,
Edmonds Community College

Roger Bowerman,
Glendale Community College

Jeffrey Brown,
New Mexico State University

Ann Chirhart,
Indiana State University

Patty Colman,
Moorpark College

Clarissa Confer,
California University of Pennsylvania

Cara Converse,
Moorpark College

Aaron Cowen,
Slippery Rock University

David Dalton,
College of the Ozarks

Brandon Franke,
Blinn College

Christos Frentzos,
Austin Peay State University

George Gastil,
Grossmont College

Frank Gilbert,
Southeastern Oklahoma State University

Jim Good,
Lone Star College, North Harris

Patricia Gower,
University of the Incarnate Word

Debbie Hargis,
Odessa College

Tom Heiting,
Odessa College

Carol Keller,
San Antonio College

Dennis Kortheuer,
California State University, Long Beach

Mary Lewis,
Jacksonville College

Tammi Littrel,
Chadron State College

Bob McConaughy,
Austin Community College

Russell Mitchell,
Tarrant County College, Southeast

Michael Namorato,
University of Mississippi

Bret Nelson,
San Jacinto College, North

Alison Ollinger-Riefstahl,
Mercyhurst Northeast College

Edward Richey,
University of North Texas

Joaquin Riveya-Martinez,
Texas State University, San Marcos

Stephen Rockenbach,
Virginia State University

Michele Rotunda,
Rutgers University, Newark

Steven Short,
Collin College

Maureen Melvin Sowa,
Bristol Community College

Rita Thomas,
Northern Kentucky University

Richard Trimble,
Ocean County College

Salli Vargis,
Georgia Perimeter College

William Wantland,
Mount Vernon Nazarene University

Chad Wooley,
Tarrant County College

Connect History Board of Advisors

Charles Ambler,
University of Texas, El Paso

Tramaine Anderson,
Tarrant County College

Mario Bennekin,
Georgia Perimeter College

Cassandra Cookson,
Lee College

Nancy Duke,
Daytona State College

Wendy Gunderson,
Collin County Community College

Aimee Harris,
El Paso Community College

Stephen Lopez,
San Jacinto College

Jan McCauley,
Tyler Junior College

Mark Newell,
Ramapo College of New Jersey

Jessica Patton,
Tarrant County College

Penne Restad,
University of Texas, Austin

Manfred Silva,
El Paso Community College, Northwest

Richard Straw,
Radford University

David Stricklin,
Dallas Baptist University

Paddy Swiney,
Tulsa Community College, Southeast

Teresa Thomas,
Austin Community College

Armando Villarreal,
Tarrant County College

Roger Ward,
Collin County Community College

Connect History and LearnSmart Subject Matter Experts

Jeff Bowersox, Chris Brooks, Rachel Burstein, Beatrice Burton, Rebecca Cerling, Javier Collazo, Maura Cunningham, Zachary Doleshal, Nancy Duke, Shennette Garrett-Scott, Patricia Goldsworthy, Drew Gonrowski, Amanda Guidotti, Lawrence Gutman, Aimee Harris, Giovanni Hortua, Jonathan Hunt, Michael Johnson, Sara Kimble, Aki Maehara, Suzanne McFadden, Brian McNeil, Aragorn Storm Miller, Rebecca Nykwest, Emily Pace, Marc Palen, Andrew Peterson, Michelle Reeves, Linda Scherr, Kimberly Shepard, Xia Shi, Richard Straw, David Villarreal, Ingrid Wilkerson, Scott Williams, Chad Wooley, David Yeatts

U*S

A NARRATIVE History

Volume 1

JAMES WEST DAVIDSON

BRIAN DeLAY
University of California, Berkeley

CHRISTINE LEIGH HEYRMAN
University of Delaware

MARK H. LYTLE
Bard College

MICHAEL B. STOFF
University of Texas, Austin

McGraw Hill

*Connect
Learn
Succeed*

U.S.: A Narrative History

AUTHORS

James West Davidson   **Brian DeLay**

Christine Leigh Heyrman   **Mark H. Lytle**   **Michael B. Stoff**

VICE PRESIDENT AND EDITOR IN CHIEF **Michael J. Ryan**

PUBLISHER **Christopher Freitag**

SPONSORING EDITOR **Matthew Busbridge**

DIRECTOR OF DEVELOPMENT **Nancy Crochiere**

DEVELOPMENT EDITOR **Cynthia Ward**

CONNECT DEVELOPMENT EDITOR **Laura Wilk**

EDITORIAL COORDINATOR **Jaclyn Mautone**

EDITORIAL INTERN **Megan Ruggiero**

MARKETING MANAGER **Stacy Ruel**

MARKETING SPECIALIST **Jen Nelson**

PRODUCTION EDITOR **Mel Valentin**

MANUSCRIPT EDITOR **Stacey Sawyer**

ART MANAGER **Robin Mouat**

COVER DESIGNER **Cassandra Chu**

INTERIOR DESIGNER **Maureen McCutcheon**

PHOTO RESEARCH COORDINATOR **Nora Agbayani**

PHOTO RESEARCHERS **Deborah Bull, NY; Jullie Chung**

MEDIA PROJECT MANAGER **Sarah B. Hill**

BUYER **Laura Fuller**

The McGraw·Hill Companies

US/A Narrative History, Volume 1

Published by MCGraw-Hill, and imprint of The McGraw-Hill Companies, Inc. 1221 Avenue of the American, New York, NY, 10020. Copyright © 2012 by The McGraw-Hill Companies, Inc. All rights reserved. No part of this publication may be reproduced or distributed in any form or by any means or stored in a database or retrieval system, without the prior written consent of The McGraw-Hill Companies, Inc., including, but not limited to, in any network or other electronic storage or transmission, or broadcast for distance learning.

Some ancillaries including electronic and print components may not be available to customer outside the United States.

Printed in the United States of America.
4 5 6 7 8 9 0 QVS/QVS 9 8 7 6 5 4 3

ISBN: 978-0-07-338566-2
MHID: 0-07-338566-2

This text was set in 10/12 Celeste Book by Laserwords Private Limited, and printed on acid-free 45# Orion Gloss by Quad/Graphics.

Cover image credits (clockwise): Ocean Photography/Veer; Library of Congress, Prints & Photographs Division, LC-DIG-cwpb-05664; Dirk Morla/PlainPicture; Library of Congress, Prints & Photographs Division, LC-USZ6-2032; (back cover): Purestock/Getty Images.

Because this page cannot legibly accommodate all acknowledgment for copyrighted material, credits appear at the end of the book, and constitute an extension of this copyright page.

Library of Congress Cataloging in Publication Data

Davidson, James West.
   US : a narrative history / James West Davidson, Brian DeLay, Christine Leigh Heyrman.—6th ed.
      p. cm.
   Includes bibliographical references and index.
   ISBN-13: 978-0-07-742076-5 (alk. paper)
   ISBN-10: 0-07-742076-4 (alk. paper)
   ISBN-13: 978-0-07-338566-2 (v. 1)
   ISBN-10: 0-07-338566-2 (v. 1)
   [etc.]
   1. United States—History. I. DeLay, Brian, 1971– II. Heyrman, Christine Leigh. III. Title.
   E178.1.D23 2011
   973—dc22

                                                                                  2011016596

www.mhhe.com

WHAT'S NEW IN U★S

HIGHLIGHTS IN VOL. 1:

>> **HISTORIAN'S TOOLBOX** is a new feature box appearing in many chapters. Historical images and artifacts—including a political cartoon, souvenir gloves, an African mask, a woman's cupboard, and paper money, among others—show how historians analyze visual clues and material culture.

>> **REVIEW QUESTIONS** immediately following each section within the chapter help students retain information by asking them to reconstruct what they've read.

>> **EXPANDED COVERAGE OF ENVIRONMENTAL HISTORY** in most chapters shows both how the environment has shaped American history—from the smallpox pandemics to army worm plagues—and how Americans have shaped their environments—from the Columbian exchange and razorback hogs to the watersheds serving Lowell mills and the environmental effects of the Civil War.

>> **EXPANDED CONTINENTAL COVERAGE OF EIGHTEENTH CENTURY AMERICA** in Chapter 5 provides greater coverage of New Spain, the contested ground of Texas, the rise of the Comanche empire, a comparison of women's legal status in Spanish and British North America, and New France's settlements in the St. Lawrence River Valley, the *pays d'en haut*, and in French Louisiana.

>> **CHAPTER 6**, now retitled "Imperial Triumph, Imperial Crisis, 1754–1776," begins with a new introduction focusing on young George Washington's encounter with the French at Jumonville Glen which helps set the imperial crisis of the 1760s and 1770s within the larger continental context of the Seven Years' War.

>> **CHAPTER 12**, now retitled "Afire with Faith, 1820–1850," has been extensively rewritten to provide superior coverage of evangelical religion. A new section on Roman Catholicism in antebellum America details the growth of a Catholic population in the United States, the contrast (and often enmity) between Catholic and evangelical outlooks, but also the adoption of Catholic symbols and architecture by an increasing number of Protestant churches.

U★S
BRIEF CONTENTS

Contents

4 COLONIZATION AND CONFLICT IN THE NORTH 1600–1700

5 THE MOSAIC OF EIGHTEENTH-CENTURY AMERICA 1689–1768

6 IMPERIAL TRIUMPH, IMPERIAL CRISIS 1754–1776

7 THE AMERICAN PEOPLE AND THE AMERICAN REVOLUTION 1775–1783

8 CRISIS AND CONSTITUTION 1776–1789

9 THE EARLY REPUBLIC 1789–1824

10 THE OPENING OF AMERICA 1815–1850

11 THE RISE OF DEMOCRACY 1824–1840

12 AFIRE WITH FAITH
1820–1850

13 THE OLD SOUTH
1820–1860

15 THE UNION BROKEN 1850–1861

14 WESTERN EXPANSION AND THE RISE OF THE SLAVERY ISSUE 1820–1850

Features

About the Authors

James West Davidson

Received his Ph.D. from Yale University. A historian who has pursued a full-time writing career, he is the author of numerous books, among them *After the Fact: The Art of Historical Detection* (with Mark H. Lytle), *The Logic of Millennial Thought: Eighteenth-Century New England,* and *Great Heart: The History of a Labrador Adventure* (with John Rugge). He is co-editor with Michael Stoff of the *Oxford New Narratives in American History,* in which his own most recent book appears: *'They Say': Ida B. Wells and the Reconstruction of Race.*

Brian DeLay

Received his Ph.D. from Harvard and is an Associate Professor of History at the University of California, Berkeley. He is a frequent guest speaker at teacher workshops across the country and has won several prizes for his book *War of a Thousand Deserts: Indian Raids and the U.S.-Mexican War.*

Christine Leigh Heyrman

Is the Robert W. and Shirley P. Grimble Professor of American History at the University of Delaware. She received a Ph.D. in American Studies from Yale University and is the author of *Commerce and Culture: The Maritime Communities of Colonial Massachusetts, 1690–1750.* Her book *Southern Cross: The Beginnings of the Bible Belt* was awarded the Bancroft Prize. She is currently writing a book about evangelical views of Islam in the early nineteenth century.

Mark H. Lytle

A Ph.D. from Yale University, is Professor of History and Chair of the Environmental Studies Program at Bard College. He has served two years as Mary Ball Washington Professor of American History at University College, Dublin, in Ireland. His publications include *The Origins of the Iranian-American Alliance, 1941–1953, After the Fact: The Art of Historical Detection* (with James West Davidson), *America's Uncivil Wars: The Sixties Era from Elvis to the Fall of Richard Nixon,* and most recently, *The Gentle Subversive: Rachel Carson, Silent Spring, and the Rise of the Environmental Movement.* He is also co-editor of a joint issue of the journals *Diplomatic History* and *Environmental History* dedicated to the field of environmental diplomacy.

Michael B. Stoff

Is Associate Professor of History and Director of the Plan II Honors Program at the University of Texas at Austin. The recipient of a Ph.D. from Yale University, he has been honored many times for his teaching, most recently with election to the Academy of Distinguished Teachers. He is the author of *Oil, War, and American Security: The Search for a National Policy on Foreign Oil, 1941–1947,* co-editor (with Jonathan Fanton and R. Hall Williams) of *The Manhattan Project: A Documentary Introduction to the Atomic Age,* and series co-editor (with James West Davidson) of the *Oxford New Narratives in American History.* He is currently working on a narrative of the bombing of Nagasaki.

1 The First Civilizations of
North

From the air, this serpentine mound fashioned thousands of years ago still stands out in bold relief. Located in southern Ohio, it extends from the snake's coiled tail at the left of the photo to the open mouth at the top right, which is pointed in the direction of the summer solstice sunset. The snake's tail points toward the winter solstice sunrise.

America

>> AN AMERICAN STORY

THE POWER OF A HIDDEN PAST

Stories told about the past have power over both the present and the future. Until recently most students were taught that American history began several centuries ago—with the "discovery" of America by Columbus, or with the English colonization of Jamestown and Plymouth. History books ignored or trivialized the continent's precontact history. But the reminders of that hidden past are everywhere. Scattered across the United States are thousands of ancient archaeological sites and hundreds of examples of monumental architecture, still imposing even after centuries of erosion, looting, and destruction.

Man-made earthen mounds, some nearly 5,000 years old, exist throughout eastern North America in a bewildering variety of shapes and sizes. Many are easily mistaken for modest hills, but others evoke wonder. In present-day Louisiana an ancient town with earthworks took laborers an estimated five million work hours to construct. In Ohio a massive serpent effigy snakes for a quarter-mile across the countryside, its head aligned to the summer solstice. In Illinois a vast, earthen construct covers 16 acres at its base and once reached as high as a 10-story building. >>

Observers in the colonial and revolutionary eras looked on such sites as curiosities and marvels. George Washington, Thomas Jefferson, and other prominent Americans collected ancient artifacts, took a keen interest in the excavation of mounds, and speculated about the Indian civilizations that created them. Travelers explored these strange mounds, trying to imagine in their mind's eye the peoples who had built them. In 1795 the Reverend James Smith traced the boundaries of a mound wall that was strategically placed to protect a neck of land along a looping river bend in the Ohio valley. "The wall at present is so mouldered down that a man could easily ride over it. It is however about 10 feet, as near as I can judge, in perpendicular height. . . . In one place I observe a breach in the wall about 60 feet wide, where I suppose the gate formerly stood through which the people passed in and out of this stronghold." Smith was astonished by the size of the project. "Compared with this," he exclaimed, "what feeble and insignificant works are those of Fort Hamilton or Fort Washington! They are no more in comparison to it than a rail fence is to a brick wall."

⌃ Some nineteenth-century Americans noted that these Mandan bull boats resembled Welsh boats called coracles—evidence, they thought, suggesting that King Madoc came to North America half a millennium earlier.

But in the 1830s and 1840s, as Americans sought to drive Indians west of the Mississippi and then confine them on smaller and smaller reservations, many began thinking differently about the continent's ancient sites. Surely the simple and "savage" people just then being expelled from American life could not have constructed such inspiring monuments. Politicians, writers, and even some influential scientists dismissed the claim that North America's ancient architecture had been built by the ancestors of contemporary Indians and instead attributed the mounds to peoples of Europe, Africa, or Asia—Hindus, perhaps, or Israelites, Egyptians, or Japanese. Many nineteenth-century Americans found special comfort in a tale about King Madoc from Wales, who supposedly shipwrecked in the Americas in the twelfth century and had left behind a small but ingenious population of Welsh pioneers who built the mysterious mounds before being overrun by Indians. The Welsh hypothesis seemed to offer poetic justice, because it implied that nineteenth-century Indians were only receiving a fitting punishment for what their ancestors had done to the remarkable mound builders from Wales.

These fanciful tales were discredited in the late nineteenth and early twentieth centuries. In recent decades archaeologists working across the Americas have discovered in more detail how native peoples built the hemisphere's ancient architecture. They have also helped to make clear the degree to which prejudice and politics have blinded European-Americans to the complexity, wonder, and significance of America's history before 1492. Fifteen thousand years of human habitation in North America allowed a broad range of cultures to develop, based on agriculture as well as hunting and gathering. In North America a population in the millions spoke hundreds of languages. Cities evolved as well as towns and farms, exhibiting great diversity in their cultural, political, economic, and religious organization. «

A CONTINENT OF CULTURES

Most archaeologists agree that the Western Hemisphere's first human inhabitants came from northeastern Asia. At least 15,000 years ago B.P.[1] during the most recent Ice Age, small groups of people began crossing the Bering Strait, then a narrow bridge of land connecting Siberia to Alaska. Gradually these **nomads** filtered southward, some following the Pacific coastline in small boats but most making their way down a narrow, glacier-free corridor along the eastern base of the Rocky Mountains and onto the northern Great Plains. There they found and hunted a stunning array of huge mammals, so-called megafauna. These animals included mammoths that were twice as heavy as elephants, giant bison, sloths that were taller than giraffes, several kinds of camels, and terrifying, 8-feet long lions. Within a few thousand years the descendants of these Siberians, people whom Columbus would wishfully dub "Indians," had spread throughout the length and breadth of the Americas. (Some evidence has led a few archaeologists to suggest that at least some Europeans also managed to cross into the Americas during antiquity. But thus far that evidence is slight.)

> **nomad** a member of a group of people who have no fixed home and who move about, usually seasonally, in pursuit of food, water, and other resources.

As the new world of the Americas was settled, it was changing dramatically. The last Ice Age literally melted away as warmer global temperatures freed the great reservoirs of water once locked in glaciers. A rise in sea levels inundated the Bering Strait, submerging the land bridge and creating new lakes and river systems. The emergence of new **ecosystems**—climates, waterways, and land environments in which humans interacted with other animals and plants—made for ever greater diversity. The first human inhabitants of the Americas had fed, clothed, warmed, and armed themselves by hunting megafauna, but few of these giants survived the end of the Ice Age. As the glaciers receded, later generations had to adapt to changing conditions. They

> **ecosystem** a community and/or region studied as a system of functioning relationships between organisms and their environments.

adjusted by hunting smaller animals with new, more specialized kinds of stone tools and by learning to exploit particular places more efficiently.

So it was that between 10,000 and 2,500 years ago distinctive regional cultures developed among the peoples of North America. Those who remained in the Great Plains turned to hunting the much smaller descendants of the now-extinct giant bison; those in the deserts of the Great Basin survived on small game, seeds, and edible plants; those in the Pacific Northwest relied mainly on fishing; and those east of the Mississippi, besides fishing and gathering, tracked deer and bear and trapped smaller game animals and birds. Over these same centuries, distinct groups developed their own languages, social organizations, governments, and religious beliefs and practices. Technological and cultural unity gave way to regional diversity as the first Americans learned how to best exploit their particular environments.

Cultures of Ancient Mexico >>

To the south, pioneers in **Mesoamerica** began domesticating plants 10,000 years ago. Over the next several thousand years farmers added other crops, including beans, tomatoes, and especially corn, to an agricultural revolution that would transform life through much of the Americas. Because many crops could be dried and stored, agriculture allowed these first farmers to settle in one place.

> **Mesoamerica** the area stretching from present-day central Mexico southward through Honduras and Nicaragua, in which pre-Columbian civilizations developed.

By about 1500 B.C.E. farming villages began giving way to larger societies, to richer and more advanced cultures. As the abundant food supply steadily expanded their populations, people began specializing in certain kinds of work. While most continued to labor on the land, others became craftworkers and merchants, architects and artists, warriors and priests. Their built environment reflected this social change as humble villages expanded into skillfully planned urban sites that were centers of trade, government, artistic display, and religious ceremony.

The Olmecs, the first city builders in the Americas, constructed large plazas, pyramidal structures, and sculpted enormous heads chiseled from basalt. The Olmec cultural influence gradually spread throughout Mesoamerica, perhaps as a result of their trade with neighboring peoples. By about 100 B.C.E. the Olmecs' example had inspired the

---

[1] Before the Present, used most commonly by archaeologists when the time spans are in multiple thousands of years. This text will also use C.E. for Common Era, equivalent to the Christian Era or A.D.; B.C.E. is Before the Common Era, equivalent to B.C.

^ Aztec merchants, or pochtecas, spoke many languages and traveled on foot great distances throughout Mesoamerica and parts of North America. This one carries a cane and bears a sack of trade goods, topped off by a parrot.

flowering of Teotihuacán from a small town in central Mexico into a metropolis of towering pyramids. The city had bustling marketplaces, palaces decorated with mural paintings that housed elite warriors and priests, schools for their children, and sprawling suburbs for commoners. At its height, around 650 C.E., Teotihuacán spanned more than 10 square miles and had a population of perhaps a quarter million—larger even than that of Rome at the time.

More impressive still were the achievements of the Mayas, who benefited from their contacts with both the Olmecs and Teotihuacán. In the lowland jungles of Mesoamerica they built cities filled with palaces, bridges, aqueducts, baths, astronomical observatories, and pyramids topped with temples. Their priests developed a written language, their mathematicians discovered the zero, and their astronomers devised a calendar more accurate than any then existing. In its glory, between the third and ninth century C.E., the Mayan empire boasted some 50 urban centers scattered throughout the Yucatán Peninsula, Belize, Guatemala, and Honduras.

But neither the earliest urban centers of the Olmecs nor the glittering city-state of Teotihuacán survived. Even the enduring kingdom of the Mayas had collapsed by 900 C.E. Like the ancient civilizations of Greece and Rome, they thrived for centuries and then declined. Scholars still debate the reasons for their collapse. Military attack may have brought about their ruin, or perhaps their large populations exhausted local resources.

Mayan grandeur was eventually outdone in the Valley of Mexico. In the middle of the thirteenth century the Aztecs, a people who had originally lived on Mesoamerica's northern frontiers, swept south and settled in central Mexico. By the end of the fifteenth century they ruled over a vast empire from their capital at Tenochtitlán, an island metropolis of perhaps a quarter of a million people. At its center lay a large plaza bordered by sumptuous palaces and the Great Temple of the Sun. Beyond stood three broad causeways connecting the island to the mainland, many other tall temples adorned with brightly painted carved images of the gods, zoological and botanical gardens, and well-stocked marketplaces. Through Tenochtitlán's canals flowed gold, silver, exotic feathers and jewels, cocoa, and millions of pounds of maize—all trade goods and tribute from the several million other peoples in the region subjugated by the Aztecs.

Unsurpassed in power and wealth, in technological and artistic attainments, theirs was also a highly stratified society. The Aztec ruler, or Chief Speaker, shared governing power with the aristocrats who monopolized all positions of religious, military, and political leadership, while the commoners—merchants, farmers, and craftworkers—performed all manual labor. There were slaves as well, some captives taken in war, others from the ranks of commoners forced by poverty to sell themselves or their children.

Cultures of the Southwest >> Mesoamerican crops and farming techniques began making their way north to the American Southwest by 1000 B.C.E. At first the most successful farmers in the region were the Mogollon and Hohokam peoples, two cultures that flourished in New Mexico and southern Arizona during the first millennium C.E. Both tended to cluster their dwellings near streams, which allowed them to adopt the systems of irrigation as well as the maize cultivation of central Mexico. The Mogollon came to be the master potters of

Opinion

If your outstretched arm represented North America's human history, contact with Europe would happen around the second knuckle of your index finger, with the fingertips being the present. Why do you think students learn so little about the Americas before 1492?

Cultures of the Eastern Woodlands

East of the Mississippi, Indian societies prospered in valleys near great rivers (Mississippi, Ohio, Tennessee, and Cumberland), the shores of the Great Lakes, and the coast of the Atlantic. Everywhere the earliest inhabitants depended on a combination of fishing, gathering, and hunting—mainly deer but also bear, raccoon, and a variety of birds. Around 2000 B.C.E. some groups in the temperate, fertile Southeast began growing the gourds and pumpkins first cultivated by Mesoamerican farmers, and later they also adopted the cultivation of maize. But unlike the ancient peoples of the Southwest, most Eastern Woodland peoples continued to subsist largely on animals, fish, and nuts, all of which were abundant enough to meet their needs and even to expand their numbers.

Indeed, many of the mysterious earthen mounds that would so fascinate Europeans were built by peoples who did not farm. About 1000 B.C.E. residents of a place now known as Poverty Point in northeastern Louisiana fashioned spectacular earthworks—six semicircular rings that rose nine feet in height and covered more than half a mile in diameter. Although these structures might have been sites for studying the planets and stars, hundreds of other mounds—built about 2,000 years ago by the Adena and the Hopewell cultures of the Ohio and Mississippi valleys—served as the burial places of their leading men and women. Alongside the corpses mourners heaped their richest goods—headdresses of antlers, necklaces of copper, troves of shells and pearls—rare and precious items

the Southwest. The Hohokam pioneered vast and complex irrigation systems in arid southern Arizona that allowed them to support one of the largest populations in precontact North America.

Their neighbors to the north, in what is now known as the Four Corners of Arizona, Colorado, New Mexico, and Utah, are known as the Anasazi. The Anasazi adapted corn, beans, and squash to the relatively high altitude of the Colorado Plateau and soon parlayed their growing surplus and prosperity into societies of considerable complexity. Their most stunning achievements were villages of exquisitely executed masonry buildings—apartment-like structures up to four stories high and containing hundreds of rooms at places such as Mesa Verde (Colorado) and Canyon de Chelly (Arizona). Scores of sites in Chaco Canyon (New Mexico), the largest center of Anasazi settlement, were linked to the wider region by hundreds of miles of wide, straight roads.

> All these mounds attest powerfully not only to the skill and sheer numbers of their builders but also to the complexity of these ancient societies.

Besides their impressive dwellings, the Anasazi filled their towns with religious shrines, astronomical observatories, and stations for sending signals to other villages. Their craftworkers fashioned delicate woven baskets, beautiful feather and hide sashes, decorated pottery, and turquoise jewelry that they traded throughout the region and beyond. For nearly a thousand years Anasazi civilization prospered, reaching its zenith between about 900 and 1100 C.E. During those three centuries the population grew to approximately 30,000 spread over 50,000 square miles, a total area larger than present-day California.

imported from as far north as Canada, as far west as Wyoming, and as far east as Florida. All these mounds attest powerfully not only to the skill and sheer numbers of their builders but also to the complexity of these ancient societies, their elaborate religious practices, and the wide scope of their trading networks.

Even so, the most magnificent culture of the ancient Eastern Woodlands, the Mississippian, owed much of its prominence to farming. By the twelfth century C.E. these peoples had emerged as the premier city-builders north of the Rio Grande, and their towns radiated for hundreds of miles in every direction from the hub of their trading

Legend:

- Bering land bridge
- Extent of ice cap during most recent glaciation
- Adena cultures
- Hopewell cultures
- Primary Mississippian cultures
- → Possible migration routes of early Indians
- ◆ Adena/Hopewell Site
- ■ Mississippian Site
- ● Mayan Site
- ● Olmec Site
- ● Southwestern Sites

Map labels: Bering Strait, Mississippi R., Missouri R., Ohio R., Mesa Verde, ANASAZI, Canyon de Chelly, Chaco Canyon, HOHOKAM, MOGOLLON, Poverty Point

EARLY PEOPLES OF NORTH AMERICA

Migration routes across the Bering Strait from Asia were taken by peoples whose descendants created the major civilizations of ancient Americans. The influence of Mesoamerica is most striking among the cultures of the Southwest and the Mississippians.

network at Cahokia, a port city of several thousand located directly across from present day St. Louis at the confluence of the Missouri and the Mississippi rivers. Cahokia's many broad plazas teemed with farmers hauling their corn, squash, and beans and with craftworkers and merchants plying their wares. But what commanded every eye were the structures surrounding the plazas—more than 100 flat-topped pyramidal mounds crowned by religious temples and elite dwellings.

Cultures of the Great Plains >> Cahokia's

size and power depended on consistent agricultural surpluses. Outside the Southwest and the river valleys

of the East, agriculture played a smaller role in shaping North American societies. On the Great Plains, for example, some people did cultivate corn, beans, squash, and sunflowers, near reliable rivers and streams. But more typically Plains communities depended on hunting and foraging, migrating to exploit seasonally variable resources. Plains hunters pursued game on foot; the horses that had once roamed the Americas became extinct after the last Ice Age. Sometimes large groups of people worked together to drive bison over cliffs or to trap them in corrals. The aridity of the Plains made it a dynamic and unpredictable place to live. During times of reliable rainfall, bison populations boomed, and hunters flocked to the region. But sometimes centuries passed with lower-than-average precipitation, and families abandoned the plains for eastern river valleys or the foothills of the Rocky Mountains.

Cultures of the Great Basin >> Some
peoples west of the Great Plains also kept to older ways of subsistence. Among them were the Numic-speaking peoples of the Great Basin, which includes present-day Nevada and Utah, eastern California, and western Wyoming and Colorado. Small family groups scoured their stark, arid landscape for the limited supplies of food it yielded, moving with each passing season to make the most of their environment. Men tracked elk and antelope and trapped smaller animals, birds, even toads, rattlesnakes, and insects. But the staples of their diet were edible seeds, nuts, and plants, which women gathered and stored in woven baskets to consume in times of scarcity. Several families occasionally hunted together or wintered in common quarters, but because the desert heat and soil defied farming, these bands usually numbered no more than about 50 people.

Cultures of the Pacific Northwest >>
The rugged stretch of coast from the southern banks of present-day British Columbia to northern California has always been an extraordinarily rich natural environment. Its mild climate and abundant rainfall yield forests lush with plants and game; its bays and rivers teem with salmon and halibut, its oceans with whales and porpoises, and its rocky beaches with seals, otters, abalone, mussels, and clams. Agriculture was unnecessary in such a bountiful place. From their villages on the banks of rivers, the shores of bays, and the beaches of low-lying offshore islands, the ancestors of the Nootkans, Makahs, Tlingits, Tshimshians, and Kwakiutls speared or netted salmon, trapped sea mammals, gathered shellfish, and launched canoes. The largest of these craft, from which they harpooned whales, measured 45 feet bow to stern and nearly 6 feet wide.

By the fifteenth century these fecund lands supported a population of perhaps 130,000. They also permitted a culture with the leisure time needed to create works of art as well as an elaborate social and ceremonial life. The peoples of the Northwest built houses and canoes from red cedar; carved bowls and dishes from red alder; crafted paddles and harpoon shafts, bows, and clubs from Pacific yew; and wove baskets from bark and blankets from mountain goat wool. They evolved a society with sharp distinctions among nobles, commoners, and slaves, the last group being mainly women and children captured in raids on other villages. Those who were free devoted their lives to accumulating and then redistributing their wealth among other villagers in elaborate potlatch ceremonies in order to confirm or enhance their social prestige.

Cultures of the Subarctic and the Arctic >> Most of present-day Canada and Alaska
were inhospitable to agriculture. In the farthest northern reaches—a treeless belt of Arctic tundra—temperatures fell below freezing for most of the year. The Subarctic, although densely forested, had only about 100 frost-free days each year. As a result, the peoples of both regions survived by fishing and hunting. The Inuit, or Eskimos, of northern Alaska harvested whales from their umiaks, boats made by stretching walrus skin over a driftwood frame and that could bear more than a ton of weight. In the central Arctic they tracked seals. The inhabitants of the Subarctic, both Algonquian-speaking peoples in the East and Athapaskan speakers of the West, moved from their summer fishing camps to berry patches in the fall to moose and caribou hunting grounds in the winter.

 REVIEW

How did native cultures differ region to region, and what accounts for these differences?

INNOVATIONS AND LIMITATIONS

The first Americans therefore expressed, governed, and supported themselves in a broad variety of ways. And yet they shared certain core characteristics, including the desire and ability to reshape their world. Whether they lived in forests, coastal regions, jungles, or prairies, whether they inhabited high mountains or low deserts, native communities experimented constantly with the resources around them. Over the course of millennia nearly all the hemisphere's peoples found ways to change the natural world in order to improve and enrich their lives.

America's Agricultural Gifts >> No inno-
vation proved more crucial to human history than native manipulation of plants. Like all first farmers agricultural pioneers in the Americas began experimenting accidentally. Modern-day species of corn, for example, probably derive from a Mesoamerican grass known as teosinte. It seems that ancient peoples gathered teosinte to collect its small grains. By selecting the grains that best suited them and bringing them back to their settlements, and by returning the grains to the soil through spillage or waste disposal, they unintentionally began the process of domestic cultivation. Soon these first farmers began deliberately saving seeds from the best plants and sowing them in gardens. In this way over hundreds of generations,

⌃ Theodore de Bry, *Florida Indians Planting Maize.* De Bry claimed that this image, produced and published in 1591, was based on a colonist's direct observation. Recently, however, scholars have noted that the image likely contains a variety of inaccuracies. Except for the digging stick, the baskets and tools are all European in design. Moreover, the image suggests that men and women shared agricultural labor, whereas in most American societies this work fell primarily to women and children.

American farmers transformed the modest teosinte grass into a staple crop that would give rise to the hemisphere's mightiest civilizations.

Indeed, ever since contact with Europe, the great breakthroughs in Native American farming have sustained peoples around the world. In addition to corn, the first Americans gave humanity scores of varieties of squash, potatoes, beans, and other basic foods. Today plants domesticated by indigenous Americans account for three-fifths of the world's crops, including many that have revolutionized the global diet. For good or ill, a handful of corn species occupies the center of the contemporary American diet. In addition to its traditional forms, corn is consumed in chips, breads, and breakfast cereals; corn syrup sweeteners are added to many of our processed foods and nearly all soft drinks; and corn is fed to almost all animals grown to be consumed, even farmed fish.

Other Native American crops have become integral to diets all over the world. Potatoes revolutionized northern European life in the centuries after contact, helping to avert famine and boost populations in several countries. Ireland's population tripled in the century after the introduction of potatoes. Beans and peanuts became prized for their protein content in Asia. And in Africa, corn, manioc, and other new-world crops so improved diets and overall health that the resulting rise in population may have offset the population lost to the Atlantic slave trade.

Landscapers ≫

Plant domestication requires the smallest of changes, changes farmers slowly encourage at the genetic level. But native peoples in the precontact Americas transformed their world on grand scales as well. In the Andes Peruvian engineers put people to work by the tens of thousands, creating an astonishing patchwork of terraces, dykes, and canals designed to maximize agricultural productivity. Similar public-works projects transformed large parts of central Mexico and the Yucatan. Even today, after several centuries of disuse, overgrowth, and even deliberate destruction, human-shaped landscapes dating from the precontact period still cover thousands of square miles of the Americas.

Recently scholars have begun to find evidence of incredible manipulation of landscapes and environments in the least likely of places. The vast Amazon rainforest has long been seen by westerners as an imposing symbol of untouched nature. But it now seems that much of the Amazon was in fact made by people. Whereas farmers elsewhere in the world domesticated plants for their gardens and fields, farmers in the Amazon cultivated food-bearing trees for thousands of years, cutting down less useful species and replacing them with ones that better suited human needs. All told there are more than 70 different species of domesticated trees throughout the Amazon. At least one-eighth of the non-flooded rainforest was directly or indirectly created by humans. Likewise, native peoples laboriously improved the soil across as much as a tenth of the Amazon, mixing it with charcoal and a variety of organic materials. These managed soils are more than 10 times as productive as untreated soils in the Amazon. Today farmers in the region still eagerly search for the places where precontact peoples enriched the earth.

Native North Americans likewise transformed their local environments. Sometimes they moved forests. Anasazis cut down and transported more than 200,000 trees to construct the floors and the roofs of the monumental

It now seems that much of the Amazon was in fact made by people.

buildings in Chaco Canyon. Sometimes they moved rivers. By taming the waters of the Salt and Gila Rivers in present-day Arizona with the most extensive system of irrigation canals anywhere in precontact North America, the Hohokam were able to support large populations in a desert environment. And sometimes they moved the land itself. Twenty-two million cubic feet of earth were moved to construct just one building in the Mississippian city of Cahokia.

Indians also employed fire to systematically reshape landscapes across the continent. Throughout North America's great eastern and western forests, native peoples periodically set low fires to consume undergrowth and fallen trees. In this way the continent's first inhabitants managed forests and also animals. Burning enriched the soil and encouraged the growth of grasses and bushes prized by game animals such as deer, elk, beaver, rabbit, grouse, and turkey. The systematic use of fire to reshape forests helped hunters in multiple ways: it increased the overall food supply for grazing animals, it attracted those animal species hunters valued most, and, by clearing forests of ground debris, fire made it easier to track, kill, and transport game. Deliberate burns transformed forests in eastern North America to such an extent that bison migrated from their original ranges on the plains and thrived far to the east. Thus, when native hunters from New York to Georgia brought down a buffalo, they were harvesting a resource that they themselves had helped to create.

The Shape of a Problem >> No matter how great their ingenuity, the first Americans were constrained by certain natural realities. One of the most important is so basic that it is easy to overlook. Unlike Eurasia, which stretches across the northern hemisphere along an east-west axis, the Americas fall along a north-south axis, stretching nearly pole to pole. Consequently, the Americas are broken up by tremendous geographic and climactic diversity, making communication and technology transfer far more difficult than it was in the Old World.

Consider the agricultural revolution in Eurasia. Once plants and animals were first domesticated in the Fertile Crescent around 10,000 years ago, they quickly began spreading east and west. Within 1,500 years these innovations had been adopted in Greece and India. A thousand years later the domesticated plants and animals of the Fertile Crescent had reached central Europe, and from there it took perhaps 200 years for them to be embraced in present-day Spain. Eurasia's east-west axis facilitated these transfers. Locations at roughly the same latitude share the same seasonal variation, have days of the same length, and often have similar habitats and rates of precipitation, making it relatively easy for plants and animals to move from one place to the next.

In contrast, the north-south orientation of the Americas erected natural barriers to plant and animal transfer.

Mesoamerica and South America, for example, are about as far apart as the Balkans and Mesopotamia. It took roughly 2,000 years for plants and animals domesticated in Mesopotamia to reach the Balkans. But because Mesoamerica and South America are separated by tropical, equatorial lowlands, it took domesticated plants such as corn several thousand years to jump between the two regions. Sometimes the transfer never happened at all before European contact. South American potatoes would have thrived in central Mexico, but the tropics stopped their northward migration. Equatorial jungles also denied Mesoamerican societies the llama and the alpaca, domesticated more than 5,000 years ago in the Andes. One wonders what even greater heights the Olmec, Toltec, Mayan, and Aztec civilizations would have achieved if they had had access to these large creatures as draft animals and reliable sources of protein.

What are these Ancient Ruins?

—Journal of the Reverend James Smith, November 18, 1795

"I have often observed while travelling thro' this country, a number of round hillocks, raised from 15 feet high and under and from 50 to 100 yards around them. It seems evident that those places are not natural, but the work of man. The only question seems to be, 'What were they made for?' Some have supposed that they were once places of defence. But the most probable opinion is, that they are burying places of the former inhabitants of this country."

Dramatic variations in climate likewise delayed the transfer of agriculture from Mexico to regions north of the Rio Grande. Archaeologists have recently discovered evidence of 10,000-year-old domesticated squash in a cave in southern Mexico, an indication that agriculture began in the Americas nearly as early as anywhere else in the world. Yet squash and corn were not cultivated in the present-day American Southwest for another 7,000 years, and the region's peoples did not embrace a fully sedentary, agricultural lifestyle until the start of the Common Era. Major differences in the length of days, the growing season, average temperatures, and rainfall between the Southwest and central Mexico meant that farmers north of the Rio Grande had to experiment for scores of generations before they had perfected crops suited to their particular environments. Corn took even longer to become a staple crop in eastern North America, which is why we do not see major urban centers arise there until approximately 1000 C.E.

By erecting barriers to communication and the spread of technology, then, the predominantly north-south orientation of Americas made it more difficult for the hemisphere's inhabitants to build on one another's successes. Had American innovations spread as quickly as innovations in Eurasia, the peoples of the Western Hemisphere would likely have been healthier, more numerous, and more powerful than they were when Europeans first encountered them in 1492.

Animals and Illness >>

One other profound difference between the Eurasian world and the Americas concerned animals and disease. Most diseases affecting humans originated from domesticated animals, which came inevitably into frequent and close contact with the humans who raised them. As people across Eurasia embraced agriculture and started living with one another and with domesticated animals in crowded villages, towns, and cities, they created ideal environments for the evolution and transmission of infectious disease. For example, measles, tuberculosis, and smallpox all seem to have derived from diseases afflicting cattle.

The north-south orientation of the Americas erected natural barriers to plant and animal transfer.

Eurasians therefore paid a heavy price for living closely with animals. Yet in the long run the continent's terrible illnesses hardened its population. Victims who survived into adulthood enjoyed acquired immunity to the most common diseases: that is, if they had already encountered a particular illness as children, their immune systems would recognize and combat the disease more effectively in the event of reinfection. By the fifteenth century, then, Eurasian bodies had learned to live with a host of deadly communicable diseases.

But Native American bodies had not. With a few important exceptions, including tuberculosis, pneumonia, and possibly herpes and syphilis, human populations in the western hemisphere seem to have been relatively free from major communicable pathogens. Insofar as most major diseases emerge from domesticated animals, it is easy enough to see why. Indigenous Americans domesticated turkeys, dogs, Muscovy ducks, and Guinea pigs but raised only one large mammal—the llama or alpaca (breeds of the same species).

This scarcity of domestic animals had more to do with available supply than with the interest or ability of their would-be breeders. The extinction of most species of megafauna soon after humans arrived in the Americas deprived the hemisphere of 80 percent of its large mammals. Those that remained, including modern-day bison, elk, deer, and moose, were more or less immune to domestication because of peculiarities in their dispositions, diets, rates of growth, mating habits, and social characteristics. In fact, of the world's 148 species of large mammals, only 14 were successfully domesticated before the twentieth century. Of those 14 only one—the ancestor to the llama/alpaca—remained in the Americas following the mass extinctions. Eurasia, in contrast, was home to 13—including the five most common and adaptable domestic mammals: sheep, goats, horses, cows, and pigs.

With virtually no large mammals to domesticate, Native Americans were spared the nightmarish effects of most of the world's major communicable diseases—until 1492. After that date European colonizers

⌃ Fewer large mammal species were available for domestication in the Americas, perhaps because the first wave of humans on the continent contributed to mass extinctions. Native Americans did domesticate dogs, shown here in a watercolor-and-ink sketch of a Mandan dog sled painted by Karl Bodmer in 1834.

INDIANS OF NORTH AMERICA, CIRCA 1500

Establishing the location of native groups in maps of precontact America is always problematic, since many peoples undertook major migrations in the contact period, boundaries between groups were fluid, and many of the names applied to native communities differ from what those communities called themselves before colonization. Nonetheless, this map depicts the rough location of important native peoples and their main modes of subsistence on the eve of contact.

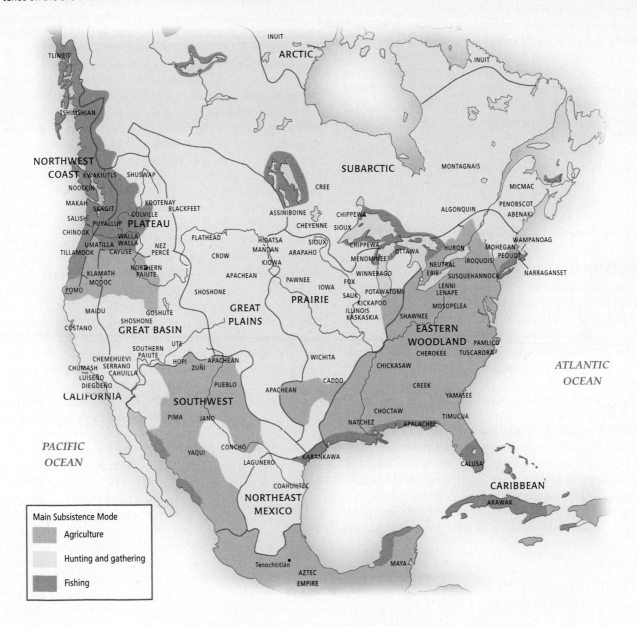

Main Subsistence Mode

- Agriculture
- Hunting and gathering
- Fishing

discovered the grim advantage of their millennia-long dance with disease. Old-world infections that most colonizers had experienced as children raged through indigenous communities, usually doing greatest damages to adults whose robust immune systems reacted violently to the novel pathogens. Often native communities came under attack from multiple diseases at the same time. Combined with the wars that attended colonization and the malnutrition, dislocation, and despair that attend wars, disease would kill native peoples by the millions while European colonizers increased and spread over the land. Despite their ingenuity and genius at reshaping plants and environments to their advantage, native peoples in the Americas labored under crucial disadvantages compared to Europe—disadvantages that would contribute to disaster after contact.

 REVIEW

How did the native inhabitants of the Americas transform their environments? What natural constraints put them at a disadvantage to Europeans?

CRISIS AND TRANSFORMATION

With its coastal plains, arid deserts, broad forests, and vast grassy plains, North America has always been a place of tremendous diversity and constant change. Indeed, many of the continent's most dramatic changes took place in the few centuries before European contact. Because of a complex and still poorly understood combination of ecological and social factors, the continent's most impressive civilizations collapsed as suddenly and mysteriously as had those of the Olmecs and the Mayas of Mesoamerica. In the Southwest the Mogollon culture went into eclipse around the twelfth century, the Hohokam and the Anasazi by about the fourteenth. In the Eastern Woodlands the story was strikingly similar. Most of the great Mississippian population centers, including the magnificent city of Cahokia, had faded by the fourteenth century.

Enduring Cultures >> The survivors of these crises struggled to construct new communities, societies, and political systems. In the Southwest descendents of the Hohokam withdrew to small farming villages that relied on simpler modes of irrigation. Anasazi refugees embarked on a massive, coordinated exodus from the Four Corners region and established new, permanent villages in Arizona and New Mexico that the Spaniards would collectively call the Pueblos. The Mogollons have a more mysterious legacy, but some of their number may have helped establish the remarkable trading city of Paquime in present-day Chihuahua. Built around 1300 Paquime contained more than 2,000 rooms and had a sophisticated water and sewage system unlike any other in the Americas. The city included 18 large mounds, all shaped differently from one another, and three ballcourts reminiscent of those found elsewhere in Mexico. Until its demise sometime in the fifteenth century Paquime was the center of a massive trading network, breeding macaws and turkeys for export and channeling prized feathers, turquoise, sea shells, and worked copper throughout a huge region.

The dramatic transformations remaking the Southwest involved tremendous suffering. Southwesterners had to rebuild in unfamiliar and oftentimes less productive places. Although some of their new settlements endure even to this day, many failed. Skeletal analysis from an abandoned pueblo on the Rio Grande, for example, indicates that the average life expectancy was only 16.5 years. Moreover, drought and migrations increased conflict over scarce resources. The most successful new settlements were large, containing several hundred people, and constructed in doorless, defensible blocks, or else set on high mesas to ward off enemy attacks. These changes were only compounded by the arrival of Athapaskan-speaking peoples (known to the Spanish as Apaches and Navajos) in the century or two before contact with Europeans. These hunters and foragers from western Canada and Alaska moved in small bands, were sometimes friendly, sometimes hostile toward different Pueblos, and eventually became key figures in the postcontact Southwest.

In the Eastern Woodlands the great Mississippian chieftainships never again attained the glory of Cahokia, but key traditions endured in the Southeast. In the lower Mississippi valley the Natchez maintained both the temple mound-building tradition and the rigid social distinctions of Mississippian civilization. Below the chief, or "Great Sun," of the Natchez stood a hereditary nobility of lesser "Suns" who demanded respect from the lowly "Stinkards," the common people. Other Muskogean-speakers rejected this rigid and hierarchical social model and gradually embraced a new, more flexible system of independent and relatively **egalitarian** villages that forged confederacies to better cope with outsiders. These groupings would eventually mature into three of the great southeastern Indian confederacies: Creek, Choctaw, and Chickasaw.

egalitarian exhibiting or asserting a belief in the equality of humans in a social, political, or economic context.

To the North lived speakers of Iroquoian languages, roughly divided into a southern faction including Cherokees and Tuscaroras, and a northern faction including the powerful Iroquois and Hurons. Like Muskogeans to the South, these Iroquoian communities mixed farming with a hunting/gathering economy and lived in semipermanent towns. The distinctive feature of Iroquois and Huron architecture was not the temple mound but rather the longhouse (some stretching up to 100 feet in length). Each sheltered as many as 10 families.

Point of View

Wilderness America?

"At the time of Columbus the Western Hemisphere had been thoroughly painted with the human brush. Agriculture occurred in as much as two-thirds of what is now the continental United States, with large swaths of the Southwest terraced and irrigated. Among the maize fields in the Midwest and Southeast, mounds by the thousand stippled the land. The forests of the eastern seaboard had been peeled back from the coasts, which were now lined with farms . . . When disease swept Indians from the land, this entire ecological *ancien regime* collapsed."

CHARLES C. MANN, *1491: New Revelations of the Americas before Columbus*

The Algonquians were the third major group of Eastern Woodlands people. They lived along the Atlantic seaboard and the Great Lakes in communities smaller than those of either the Muskogeans or the Iroquois. By the fifteenth century the coastal communities from southern New England to Virginia had adopted agriculture to supplement their diets, but those in the colder northern climates with shorter growing seasons depended entirely on hunting, fishing, and gathering plants such as wild rice.

Cultures of equal and even greater resources persisted and flourished during the fifteenth century in the Caribbean, particularly on the Greater Antilles—the islands of present-day Cuba, Haiti and the Dominican Republic, Jamaica, and Puerto Rico. Although the earliest inhabitants of the ancient Caribbean, the Ciboneys, probably came from the Florida peninsula, it was the Tainos, later emigrants from northern South America, who expanded throughout the Greater Antilles and the Bahamas. Taino chiefs known as *caciques,* along with a small number of noble families, ruled island tribes, controlling the production and distribution of food and tools and exacting tribute from the great mass of commoners, farmers, and fisherfolk. Attending to these elites were the poorest Taino peoples—servants who bedecked their masters and mistresses in brilliant diadems of feathers, fine woven textiles, and gold nose and ear pieces and then shouldered the litters on which the rulers sat and paraded their finery.

North America on the Eve of Contact ››

By the end of the fifteenth century, 5 to 10 million people lived north of the Rio Grande—with perhaps another million living on the islands of the Caribbean—and they were spread among more than 350 societies speaking nearly as many distinct languages. (The total precontact population for all of the Americas is estimated at between 57 and 112 million.)

These millions lived in remarkably diverse ways. Some peoples relied entirely on farming; others on hunting, fishing, and gathering; still others on a combination of the two. Some, such as the Natchez and the Iroquois, practiced matrilineal forms of kinship, in which women owned land, tools, and even children. Among others, such as the Algonquians, patrilineal kinship prevailed, and all property and prestige descended in the male line. Some societies, like those of the Great Plains and the Great Basin in the West, the Inuit in the Arctic, and the Iroquois and Algonquians in the East, were roughly egalitarian, whereas others, like many in the Caribbean and the Pacific Northwest, were rigidly divided into nobles and commoners and servants or slaves. Some, such as the Natchez and the Taino, were ruled by powerful chiefs; others, such as the Algonquians and the Pueblos, by councils of village elders or heads of family clans; still others in the Great Basin, the Great Plains, and the far North looked to the most skillful

hunter or the most powerful shaman for direction. Those people who relied on hunting practiced religions that celebrated their kinship with animals and solicited their aid as guardian spirits, whereas predominantly agricultural peoples sought the assistance of their gods to make the rain fall and the crops ripen.

When Europeans first arrived in North America the continent north of present-day Mexico boasted an ancient and rich history marked by cities, towns, and prosperous farms. At contact it was a land occupied by several million men, women, and children speaking hundreds of languages and characterized by tremendous political, cultural, economic, and religious diversity. This diversity was heightened by the north/south orientation of the Americas rather than the east/west orientation of Eurasia, since the spread of crops and animals in temperate regions was impeded by the tropical zones of the equator. The isolation from European diseases would make their arrival after 1492 even more devastating. Before 1492, though, the civilizations of North and South America remained populous, dynamic, and diverse.

 REVIEW

What was life like in the Americas on the eve of European contact?

For most of our nation's short history we have not wanted to remember things this way. European Americans have had a variety of reasons to minimize and belittle the past, the works, even the size of the native populations that ruled North America for 99 percent of its human history. In 1830, for example, President Andrew Jackson delivered an address before Congress in which he tried to answer the many critics of his Indian removal policies. Although "humanity has often wept over the fate of the aborigines of this country," Jackson said, the Indians' fate was as natural and inevitable "as the extinction of one generation to make room for another." He reminded his listeners of the mysterious mounds that had so captivated the founding fathers. "In the monuments and fortresses of an unknown people, spread over the extensive regions of the West, we behold the memorials of a once powerful race, which was exterminated, or has disappeared, to make room for the existing savage tribes." Just as the architects of the mounds supposedly met their end at the hands of these "savage tribes," the president concluded, so, too, must Indians pass away before the descendents of Europe. "What good man would prefer a country covered with forests and ranged by a few thousand savages, to our extensive republic, studded with cities, towns, and prosperous farms; embellished with all the improvements which art can devise, or industry execute; occupied by more than twelve millions of happy people, and filled with all the blessings of liberty, civilization, and religion!"

Indeed, stories told about the past have power over both the present and the future. Jackson and many others of his era preferred a national history that contained only a few thousand ranging "savages" to one shaped by millions of indigenous hunters, farmers, builders, and inventors. Yet every generation rewrites its history, and what seems clear from this latest draft is the rich diversity of American cultures on the eve of contact between the peoples of Eurasia, Africa, and the Americas. We are still struggling to find stories big enough to encompass not only Indians from across the continent but also people who have come from all over the world to forge this complex, tragic, and marvelous nation of nations.

CHAPTER SUMMARY

During the thousands of years after bands of Siberian nomads migrated across the Bering Strait to Alaska, their descendants spread throughout the Americas, creating civilizations that rivaled those of ancient Europe, Asia, and Africa.

- Around 1500 B.C.E. Mesoamerica emerged as the hearth of civilization in the Western Hemisphere, a process started by the Olmecs and brought to its height by the Mayans and Aztecs.

- These Mesoamerican peoples devised complex ways of organizing society, government, and religious worship and built cities remarkable for their art, architecture, and trade.
- Both commerce and migration spread cultural influences throughout the hemisphere, notably to the islands of the Caribbean basin and to North America, an influence that endured long after these empires declined.
- The adoption of agriculture gave peoples in the Southwest and the Eastern Woodlands the resource security necessary to develop sedentary cultures of increasing complexity. These cultures eventually enjoyed great achievements in culture, architecture, and agriculture.
- Inhabitants of the Great Plains, the Great Basin, the Arctic, and the Subarctic evolved their own diverse cultures, relying for subsistence on fishing, hunting, and gathering.
- Peoples of the Pacific Northwest boasted large populations and prosperous economies as well as an elaborate social, ceremonial, and artistic life.
- The native inhabitants of the Americas transformed their environments in a variety of ways, from pioneering crops that would eventually feed the world to terraforming mountains and jungles.
- Nonetheless, natural constraints would leave Native Americans at a disadvantage compared to Europe. The continent's north-south orientation inhibited the

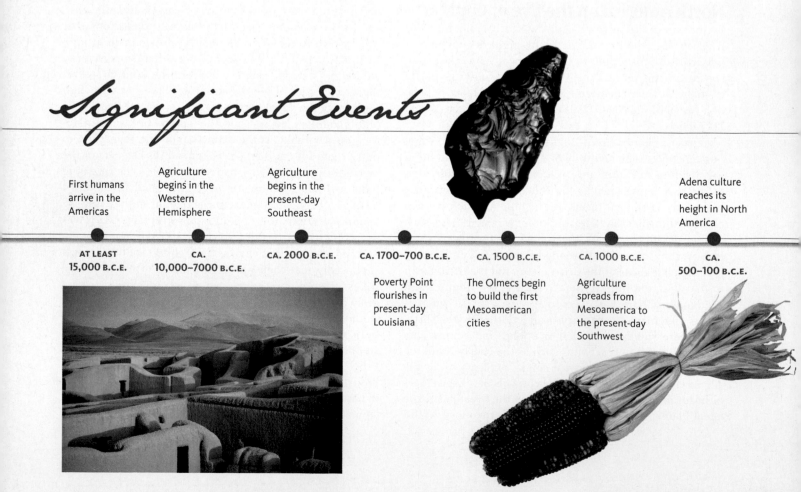

Significant Events

First humans arrive in the Americas	Agriculture begins in the Western Hemisphere	Agriculture begins in the present-day Southeast				Adena culture reaches its height in North America
AT LEAST 15,000 B.C.E.	**CA. 10,000–7000 B.C.E.**	**CA. 2000 B.C.E.**	**CA. 1700–700 B.C.E.**	**CA. 1500 B.C.E.**	**CA. 1000 B.C.E.**	**CA. 500–100 B.C.E.**
			Poverty Point flourishes in present-day Louisiana	The Olmecs begin to build the first Mesoamerican cities	Agriculture spreads from Mesoamerica to the present-day Southwest	

spread of agriculture and technology, and a lack of domesticatable animals compared to Europe left Native Americans with little protection against disease.

- For reasons that remain unclear, many of North America's most impressive early civilizations had collapsed by the end of the fifteenth century. In their wake a diverse array of cultures evolved across the continent.
  - In the Southwest, Pueblo Indians were joined by Athapaskan speaking hunters and foragers in an arid landscape.
  - In much of eastern North America, stratified chiefdoms of the Mississippian era gave way to more egalitarian confederacies of independent villages subsisting on farming and hunting.
- Although Americans in the nineteenth, twentieth, and even twenty-first centuries have been slow to recognize the fact, the societies of precontact America were remarkably populous, complex, and diverse. Their influence would continue to be felt in the centuries after contact.

Additional Reading

The best descriptions of ancient American civilizations are offered by Brian M. Fagan, *Kingdoms of Gold, Kingdoms of Jade: The Americas before Columbus* (1991); and, especially, Charles C. Mann, *1491: New Revelations of the Americas before Columbus* (2005). For North America specifically, see Alice Beck Kehoe, *America before the European Invasions* (2002). For the Southwest, see Stephen H. Leksar, *A History of the Ancient Southwest* (2009). For the Eastern Woodlands, see George R. Milner, *The Moundbuilders: Ancient Peoples of Eastern North America* (2005). Roger G. Kennedy, *Hidden Cities: The Discovery and Loss of Ancient North American Civilization* (1994), gives a fascinating account of how white Americans responded to the ruins of ancient American cultures. For the consequences of axis alignment and of domesticated animals, see the captivating work by Jared Diamond, *Guns, Germs, and Steel: The Fates of Human Societies* (1998).

For the cultures of precontact Mexico, see Michael D. Coe and Rex Koontz, *Mexico: From the Olmecs to the Aztecs* (5th ed., 2002). For exhaustive surveys of all regional cultures in North America, see William C. Sturtevant, general editor, *Handbook of North American Indians,* 20 volumes projected (1978–). Carl Waldman, *Atlas of the North American Indian* (1985), is also an excellent source of information, offering much more than good maps.

The Mayan civilization flourishes on the Yucatán Peninsula

Mogollon culture flourishes in present-day New Mexico

Hohokam, Anasazi, and Mississippian civilizations decline; Apache and Navajo peoples enter the Southwest from Canada

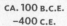

CA. 100 B.C.E.–400 C.E.   **CA. 200–800 C.E.**   **CA. 200–900 C.E.**   **CA. 800–1200 C.E.**   **CA. 900–1100 C.E.**   **CA. 1300 C.E.**   **CA. 1325–1500 C.E.**

Hopewell culture thrives in the Ohio and Mississippi valleys

Mississippian civilization reaches its height

Anasazi civilization reaches its height

Aztec empire rises in Mesoamerica

With sails bellying in a gale, the Dutch ship in this painting has furled the rest of its canvas to prevent the masts from being blown off. Sailors from western Europe risked much as they crossed the Atlantic in search of fish, silver, gold, and other commodities to trade.

2
Old Worlds

>> AN AMERICAN STORY

FISHING NETS AND FAR HORIZONS

All the world lay before them. Or so it seemed to mariners from England's seafaring "West Country" coasts, pushing toward unknown lands in the far Atlantic.

The scent of the new land came first—not the sight of it, but the smells, perhaps the scent of fir trees wafted from beyond the horizon, delicious to sailors who had felt nothing but the rolling sea for weeks on end. Straightaway the captain would call for a lead to be thrown overboard to sound the depths. At its end was a hollowed-out socket with a bit of tallow in it, so that some of the sea bottom would stick when the lead was hauled up. A good sailing master could tell where he was by what came up—"oozy sand" or perhaps "soft worms" or "popplestones" as big as beans. >>

New Worlds

1400–1600

Through much of the fifteenth century the search for cod had drawn West Country sailors north and west, toward Iceland. In the 1480s and 1490s a few English tried their luck farther west. They returned with little to show for their daring until the coming of an Italian named Giovanni Caboto, called John Cabot by the English. Cabot, who hailed from Venice, obtained the blessing of King Henry VII to hunt for unknown lands. From the port of Bristol his lone ship set out to the west in the spring of 1497.

This time the return voyage brought news of a "new-found" island where the trees were tall enough to make fine masts and the codfish were plentiful. After returning to Bristol, Cabot marched off to London to inform His Majesty, received 10 pounds as his reward, and with the proceeds dressed himself in dashing silks. The multitudes of London flocked after him, wondering over "the Admiral"; then Cabot returned triumphantly to Bristol to undertake a more ambitious search for a northwest passage to Asia. He set sail with five ships in 1498 and was never heard from again.

By the 1550s Cabot's island, now known as Newfoundland, attracted 400 vessels annually, fishermen not only from England but also from France, Portugal, and Spain. The harbor of present-day St. John's, Newfoundland, served as the informal hub of the North Atlantic fishery. Sailors from three kingdoms dropped anchor there, to take on supplies in the spring, trade with native peoples, or to prepare for the homeward voyage in autumn. There was eager conversation at this meeting place, for these seafarers knew as much as anyone—if not more—about the new world of wonders that was opening to Europeans. They were acquainted with names such as Cristoforo Colombo, the Italian from Genoa whom Cabot might have known as a boy. They listened to Portuguese tales of sailing around the Horn of Africa in pursuit of spices and to stories of Indian empires to the south, rich in gold and silver that Spanish treasure ships were bringing home.

Indeed, Newfoundland was one of the few places in the world where so many ordinary folk of different nations could gather and talk, crammed aboard dank ships moored in St. John's harbor, huddled before blazing fires on its beaches, or crowded into smoky makeshift taverns. When the ships sailed home in autumn, the tales went with them, repeated in the tiniest coastal villages by those pleased to have cheated the sea and death one more time. Eager to fish, talk, trade, and take profits, West Country mariners were almost giddy at the prospect of Europe's expanding horizons.

Most seafarers who fished the waters of Newfoundland's Grand Banks remain unknown today. Yet it is well to begin with these ordinary fisherfolk, for the European discovery of the Americas cannot be looked on simply as the voyages of a few bold explorers. Adventurers such as Christopher Columbus and John Cabot were only the most visible representatives of a much larger expansion of European peoples and culture that began in the 1450s. That expansion arose out of a series of gradual but telling changes in the fabric of European society—changes reflected in the lives of ordinary seafarers as much as in the careers of explorers decked out in silks.

Some of these changes were technological, arising out of advances in the arts of navigating and shipbuilding and the use of gunpowder. Some were economic, involving the development of trade networks such as those linking Bristol with ports in Iceland and Spain. Some were **demographic,** bringing

> **demographic** factors relating to the characteristics of populations. Demography is the study of populations, looking at such aspects as size, growth, density, and age distribution.

about a rise in Europe's population after a devastating century of plague. Other changes were religious, adding a dimension of devout belief to the political rivalries that fueled discoveries in the Americas. Yet others were political, making it possible for kingdoms to centralize and extend their influence across the ocean. Portugal, Spain, France, and England—all possessing coasts along the Atlantic—led the way in exploration, spurred on by Italian "admirals" such as Caboto and Colombo, Spanish *conquistadores*—"conquerors"—such as Hernán Cortés and Francisco Pizarro, and English sea dogs such as Humphrey Gilbert and Walter Raleigh. Ordinary folk rode these currents, too. The great and the small alike were propelled by forces that were remolding the face of Europe—and were beginning to remold the face of the world. **‹‹**

EURASIA AND AFRICA IN THE FIFTEENTH CENTURY

In 1450, however, the Western European kingdoms that would one day dominate much of the world still sat at the fringe of an international economy that revolved around China. By a variety of measures Ming China was the richest, most powerful, and most advanced society in the world. All Eurasia sought Chinese goods, especially spices, ceramics, and silks, and Chinese ships sped these goods to faraway ports. Seven times between 1405 and 1433 China's "treasure fleet"—300 ships manned by 28,000 sailors and commanded by Zheng He (pronounced "Jung Huh")—unfurled its red silk sails off the south China coast and traveled as far as the kingdoms of eastern Africa. The treasure fleet's largest craft were nine-masted junks measuring 400 feet long, sporting multiple decks and luxury cabins. By comparison, Columbus's largest ship in 1492 was a mere 85 feet long, and the crew aboard all three of his ships totaled just 90 men. Political turbulence led Chinese leaders to ground their trading fleet and end the long-distance voyages. But Chinese luxuries, most transported overland, continued to be Eurasia's most sought-after commodities.

The next mightiest powers in the Old World were not European kingdoms but rather huge Islamic empires, especially the Ottomans in the eastern Mediterranean. The Ottomans rose to prominence during the fourteenth and fifteenth centuries, gaining control of critical trade routes and centers of commerce between Asia and Europe. Their greatest triumph came in 1453, when the sultan Mehmed II conquered Constantinople (now Istanbul), the ancient and supposedly impregnable Christian city that straddled Europe and Asia. Mehmet's stunning victory sounded alarms throughout Europe.

Europe's Place in the World

» Europe's rulers had good reason for alarm. Distant from Asia's profitable trade and threatened by the Ottomans' military might, most of the continent remained fractious and vulnerable. During the fourteenth and the fifteenth centuries 90 percent of Europe's people, widely dispersed in small villages, made their living from the land. But warfare, poor transportation, and low grain yields all created food shortages, and undernourishment produced a population prone to disease. Under these circumstances life was, to paraphrase the English philosopher Thomas Hobbes, nasty, brutish, and usually short.

One-quarter of all children died in the first year of life. People who reached the age of 40 counted themselves fortunate.

It was also a world of sharp inequalities, where nobles and aristocrats enjoyed several hundred times the income of peasants or craftworkers. It was a world with no strong, centralized political authority, where kings were weak and warrior lords held sway over small towns and tiny fiefdoms. It was a world of violence and sudden death, where homicide, robbery, and rape occurred with brutal frequency. It was a world where security and order of any kind seemed so fragile that most people clung to tradition, and more than a few used witchcraft in an attempt to master the chaotic and unpredictable world around them.

But Europe was changing, in part because of a great calamity. Between the late 1340s and the early 1350s bubonic plague—known as the Black Death—swept away one quarter of Europe's population. Some urban areas lost 70 percent of their people to the disease. The Black Death disrupted both agriculture and commerce, and provoked a spiritual crisis that resulted in violent, unsanctioned religious movements, scapegoating of marginal groups, even massacres of Jews. Although Europeans seem to have met recurrent outbreaks of the disease with less panic, the sickness continued to disrupt social and economic life.

Yet the sudden drop in population relieved pressure on scarce resources. Survivors of the Black Death found that the relative scarcity of workers and consumers made for higher wages, lower prices, and more land. These changes promoted an overall expansion of trade. In earlier centuries Italian merchants had begun encouraging commerce across Europe and tapping into trade from Africa, the Middle East, and, when able, from Asia. By the late fifteenth century Europe's merchants and bankers had devised more efficient ways of transferring the money generated from manufacturing and trade, and established credit in order to support commerce across longer distances. Wealth flowed into the coffers of traders, financiers, and landlords, creating a pool of capital that investors could plow into new technologies, trading ventures, and, eventually, colonial enterprises.

<< As bubonic plague and other epidemic diseases wracked Europe, they brought the possibility of sudden death closer than ever. This skull pendant dating from the 1600s was designed as jewelry to hang from the wearer's breast. When opened, it revealed a skeleton in a coffin. In England, before the coming of the Black Death, funeral monuments usually portrayed deceased lords and ladies in their finest clothing. Afterward, the monuments increasingly featured death masks, contorted corpses, or skeletons with serpents slinking among their bones.

Historian's TOOLBOX

A Witch Bottle

Known as a "Bellarmine jar." Why? (Do a little web research!)

Pins and needles. Why might these have been deliberately bent?

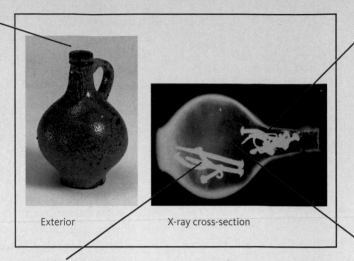

Exterior   X-ray cross-section

Fingernail clippings: well manicured, suggesting someone of higher social standing

Liquid: analysis shows it to be urine.

Historians often find clues about a culture from material artifacts discarded long ago. A Bellarmine jar was dug up in a cellar in England in 2004. Archaeologists recognized it as a "witch bottle," so called because some English folk used such items to defend against the perceived ill-will of witches. "The whole rationale for these bottles was sympathetic magic—so you put something intimate to the bewitched person in the bottle and then you put in bent pins and other unpleasant objects which are going to poison and cause great pain to the witch," explained historian Owen Davies. When shaken, this bottle splashed and rattled. An X-ray showed the objects inside, whose contents were examined in a laboratory. Among other items the bottle included hair, navel fluff, and a heart-shaped piece of leather with a nail through it. The liquid also contained traces of sulphur (popularly called brimstone in the seventeenth century). An estimated 40,000–60,000 witches were hanged and burned in early modern Europe, demonstrating that despite the Reformation's disdain for "Popish superstitions," supernaturalism and magic remained potent religious strains.

THINKING CRITICALLY

Why might brimstone have been added to the witch bottle? What social factors help explain why fifteenth-century Europeans saw witchcraft as a significant part of the way the world worked? Would illnesses such as the plague contribute to attitudes about witchcraft?

The direction of Europe's political development also laid the groundwork for overseas colonization. After 1450 strong monarchs in Europe steadily enlarged their power at the expense of warrior lords. Henry VII, the founder of England's Tudor dynasty, Francis I of France, and Ferdinand and Isabella of Spain began the trend, forging modern nation-states by extending their political control over more territory, people, and resources. Such larger, more centrally organized states were able to marshal the resources necessary to support colonial outposts and to sustain the professional armies and navies capable of creating and protecting overseas empires.

Africa and the Portuguese Wave >>

European expansion began with Africa. For centuries African spices, ivory, and gold had entered the Eurasian market either through ports on the Indian Ocean or through the Sahara Desert and into the Mediterranean Sea. Powerful African kingdoms controlled the routes through which these prized commodities moved, while Islamic expansion in the fifteenth century made competition all the more intense. European merchants yearned to access West African markets directly, by ship. But navigational and shipbuilding technology was not yet up to the challenge of the Atlantic's prevailing currents, which sped ships south along Africa's coast but made the return voyage virtually impossible.

Portugal was the first to solve this problem and tap directly into West African markets, thanks in large part to Prince Henry "the Navigator," as he became known. An ardent Catholic and a man who dreamed of turning back Islam's rising tide, Henry understood that direct commerce with West Africa would allow his kingdom to circumvent the costly trans-Sahara trade. To forward his vision Henry funded exploratory voyages, established a maritime school, and challenged sailors and engineers to conquer the problem of the current. The Portuguese responded by developing the caravel, a lighter, more maneuverable ship that could sail better against contrary winds and in rough seas. More seaworthy than the lumbering galleys of the Middle Ages, caravels combined longer, narrower hulls—a shape built for speed—with triangular lateen sails, which allowed for more flexible steering. The caravel allowed the Portuguese to regularly do what few Europeans had ever done, sail down Africa's west coast and return home. Other advances, including a sturdier version of the Islamic world's astrolabe, enabled Portugal's vessels to calculate their position at sea with unprecedented accuracy.

As the Portuguese pressed southward along the Atlantic rim of sub-Saharan Africa, they began to meet peoples who had never encountered Europeans or even possessed any knowledge of other continents. On catching their first sight of a Portuguese expedition in 1455, villagers on the Senegal River marveled at the strangers' clothing and their white skin. As an Italian member of that expedition recounted, some Africans "rubbed me with their spittle to discover whether my whiteness was dye or flesh."

But the Portuguese were wrong to mistake such acts of innocence for economic or political naïveté. Formidable African chiefdoms and states were eager to trade with Europeans but intent on protecting already established commercial networks. Portugal could not simply take what it wanted from West Africa. With few exceptions, it proved impossible for European powers to colonize territory in West Africa before the nineteenth century, because the region's people were too many and too organized. Furthermore, malaria would kill between one-fourth and one-half of all Portuguese unwise enough to try and stay. To succeed, the newcomers had to seek partners. As the Portuguese built forts and trading houses on the coast they gave tribute or taxes to local powers in return for trading privileges. The Portuguese offered textiles, especially, but also raw and worked metal goods, currency (in the form of cowry shells), and beads. In return Africans gave up prized commodities such as gold, ivory, and malaguetta pepper. Portuguese traders also expressed interest in another commodity, one that would reshape the wider Atlantic world: slaves.

Sugar and the Origins of the Atlantic Slave Trade >>
Unfree labor has existed in nearly all human societies. Although the norms, characteristics, and economic importance of slavery have varied widely over time and place, men, women, and children have been held as slaves from before recorded history to the present.

⌃ The rich, volcanic soils of the Azores, the Canaries, and Madeira proved ideal for growing sugar. These islands in the eastern Atlantic were a stepping-stone to later plantations in the Americas, such as the one pictured in this engraving by Theodore de Bry from 1596.

(U.S. and international organizations estimate that today there are as many as 27 million people held in some form of labor bondage and that nearly 1 million unfree people are sold across international borders every year.)

By the Middle Ages elites in Europe had largely abandoned the slave culture of the Roman Empire and relied instead on serfs or peasants for labor. Slaves became more important as status symbols than as workers, and most were young white women. Indeed, the word "slave" comes originally from "Slav"; Slavic girls and women from the Balkans and the coasts of the Black Sea were frequent targets of slave raids.

But European slavery began to change again following the Crusades. In 1099 Christian forces captured Jerusalem from the Seljuk Turks and discovered sugar plantations that the Turks had cultivated in the Holy Land. Crusaders recognized sugar's economic potential. But because sugar required intense work during planting and close tending during the growing season, they found it a difficult commodity to produce. On maturity the crop had to be harvested and processed 24 hours a day to avoid being spoiled. In short, sugar demanded cheap, pliable labor, and the newly arrived crusaders relied in part on slaves.

When Islamic forces under the famed leader Saladin reconquered Jerusalem in the twelfth century, European investors established new plantations on eastern Mediterranean islands. In addition to being labor intensive, though, sugar was a crop that quickly exhausted soils and forced planters to move operations regularly. Plantations spread to new islands, and by the early 1400s sugar was even being grown in Portugal. As production expanded planters had to work harder than ever to obtain the necessary labor because of the Black Death and because Turkish conquests restricted European access to the traditional slaving grounds of the eastern Mediterranean and the Balkans.

Thus by the fifteenth century the Portuguese were already producing sugar on slave-run plantations, but they were seeking new crop land and new sources of slaves. Once again Prince Henry's vision enhanced his kingdom's economic interests. While Portugal's merchants were establishing trading posts along the west coast of Africa, Iberian mariners were discovering or rediscovering islands in the eastern Atlantic: the Canaries, Madeira, and the Azores, islands with rich, volcanic soils ideally suited to sugarcane. By the late 1400s sugar plantations were booming on the Atlantic islands, staffed by West African slaves. By 1550 people of African descent accounted for 10 percent of the population of Lisbon, Portugal's capital city.

Now convinced that they could reach coveted Asian markets by sea, ambitious Portuguese mariners sailed their caravels farther and farther south. In 1488 Bartolomeu Dias rounded the Cape of Good Hope on the southern tip of Africa, sailing far enough up that continent's eastern coast to claim discovery of a sea route to India. Ten years later Vasco da Gama reached India itself, and Portugal's interests ultimately extended to Indochina and China.

Portuguese geographers had long felt certain that travel around Africa was the shortest route to the Orient, but an Italian sailor disagreed. Cristoforo Colombo had spent a decade gaining experience from Portugal's master mariners. He also threw himself into research, devouring Lisbon's books on geography and cartography. Columbus (the Latinized version of his name) became convinced that the fastest route to China lay west, across the uncharted Atlantic Ocean. He appealed to Portugal's king to support an exploratory voyage, but royal geographers scoffed at the idea. They agreed that the world was round but insisted (correctly, as it turns out) that the globe was far larger than Columbus had calculated, making any westward route impractical. Almost a decade of rejection had grayed Columbus's red hair, but—undaunted—he packed up in 1485 and took his audacious idea to Spain.

> **Columbus coasted along Cuba and Hispaniola, expecting at any moment to catch sight of gold-roofed Japanese temples or fleets of Chinese junks.**

REVIEW

Why did Europeans begin to develop commercial networks in the Atlantic, and how did the Portuguese operate in Africa?

SPAIN IN THE AMERICAS

He arrived a few years too early. Spain's monarchs, Ferdinand and Isabella, rejected Columbus's offer because they were engaged in a campaign to drive the Muslims out of their last stronghold on the Iberian Peninsula, the Moorish kingdom of Granada. But in 1492 Ferdinand and Isabella took Granada and completed their reconquest of Spain, or *reconquista*. Flush with victory, the pair listened to Columbus argue that a westward route to Asia would allow Spain to compete with Portugal and generate enough revenue to continue the reconquest, even into the Holy Land itself. Ignoring the advice of their geographers, the monarchs agreed to his proposal.

reconquista military reconquest of the Iberian peninsula from Islamic Moors of Africa by European Christian rulers.

Columbus's first voyage across the Atlantic could only have confirmed his conviction that he was destiny's darling. His three ships, no bigger than fishing vessels that sailed to Newfoundland, plied their course over placid seas, south from Seville to the Canary Islands and then due west. On October 11, a little more than two months after leaving Spain, branches, leaves, and flowers floated by their hulls, signals that land lay near. Just after midnight a sailor spied cliffs shining white in the moonlight. On the morning of October 12, the *Niña*, the *Pinta*, and the *Santa Maria* set anchor in a shallow sapphire bay, and their crews knelt on the white coral beach. Columbus christened the place San Salvador (Holy Savior).

The Spanish Beachhead in the Caribbean >> Like many men of destiny, Columbus mistook his true destination. At first he confused his actual location, the Bahamas, with an island near Japan. He coasted along Cuba and Hispaniola (today's Haiti and Dominican Republic), expecting at any moment to catch sight of gold-roofed Japanese temples or fleets of Chinese junks. He encountered instead a gentle, generous people who knew nothing of the Great Khan but who welcomed the newcomers profusely. Columbus's journals note that they wore little clothing, but they did wear jewelry—tiny pendants of gold suspended from the nose. He dubbed the Taino people "Indians"— inhabitants of the Indies.

Explorers' Routes
— Columbus (Spanish)
— Other Spanish
Other European
— French
— English

NORTH AMERICA

Hudson Bay

Missouri River

Mississippi River

Colorado River

Arkansas River

Ohio River

LABRADOR

GILBERT 1583

NEWFOUNDLAND

CARTIER 1534–35

St. Lawrence River

JOHN CABOT 1497

RALEIGH 1585

VERRAZANO 1524

Roanoke

ATLANTIC OCEAN

1492

CORONADO 1540–42

Cibola

DE VACA 1528–36

Rio Grande

DE SOTO 1539–42

PONCE DE LEÓN 1513

FLORIDA

DE NARVÁEZ 1528

Mississippi River

1493

Cuba

Hispaniola

Puerto Rico

1493

La Paz

Gulf of Mexico

CORTÉZ 1518–21

Chichen Itza

Jamaica

1502

1498

Veracruz

YUCATAN PENINSULA

Mexico City (Tenochtitlan)

AZTEC EMPIRE

MAYA

Caribbean Sea

BALBOA 1513

PACIFIC OCEAN

0   250   500 mi
0   500   1000 km

DRAKE 1577–80

ISTHMUS OF PANAMÁ

1502

Panamá

Orinoco River

RALEIGH 1595

PIZARRO 1531–33

Quito

INCA EMPIRE

SOUTH AMERICA

PRINCIPAL ROUTES OF EUROPEAN EXPLORATION

It would take some years before other mariners and geographers understood clearly that these newfound islands and the landmasses beyond them lay between Europe and Asia. One of the earliest geographers to do so was the Florentine Amerigo Vespucci, who first described Columbus's Indies as *Mundus Novus,* a "New World." Rather than dub the new lands "Columbia," a German mapmaker called them "America" in Vespucci's honor. The German's maps proved wildly successful, and the name stuck.

Unlike the kingdoms of West Africa the Taino chiefdoms lacked the military power to resist European aggression. And Europeans decided that the societies they encountered were better suited to be ruled than partnered with. Moreover, while the newfound islands eventually presented their own threats to European health, they seemed a good deal more inviting than the deadly coast of West Africa. Hints of gold, a seemingly weak and docile population, and a relatively healthy climate all insured that Columbus's second voyage would be one of colonization rather than commerce. During the 1490s and early 1500s Spanish colonizers imposed a brutal regime on the Tainos, slaughtering native leaders and forcing survivors to toil in mines and fields.

Only a few Spaniards spoke out against the exploitation. Among them was Bartolomé de las Casas, a man who spent several years in the Caribbean, participating in conquests and profiting from native labor. Eventually Las Casas renounced his conduct and, as a Dominican friar, became a tireless foe of Spanish cruelties toward Indians. He railed against the "unjust, cruel, and tyrannical" war waged to force the native peoples into "the hardest, harshest, and most heinous bondage to which men or beasts might ever be bound into." Las Casas's writings, translated throughout Europe and illustrated with gruesome drawings, helped give rise to the "Black Legend" of Spanish atrocities in the Americas.

The warnings had some effect, but not for decades. Within a generation of Columbus's landfall, the Taino population had nearly collapsed from war, overwork, malnutrition, despair, and strange new Eurasian diseases. Ambitious Spaniards began scouring the Caribbean basin, discovering new lands and searching for new populations of Indians to subjugate or enslave in place of the vanishing Tainos. Soon the Bahamas were depopulated by Spanish slavers, and conquests had done to present-day Cuba, Jamaica, and Puerto Rico what they first had done to Hispaniola.

Conquest of the Aztecs >>

Would-be conquistadors turned their eyes to the mainland. In 1519 an expedition led by the impetuous Hernán Cortés made contact with native peoples on Mexico's gulf coast. They spoke of an oppressive imperial people who occupied a fantastic city to the West. These were the Aztecs.

Aztecs had much in common with Spaniards. Both societies were predominantly rural, with most inhabitants living in small villages and engaging in agriculture. In both places merchants and specialized craftworkers clustered in cities, organized themselves into guilds, and clamored for protection from the government. Aztec noble and priestly classes, like those in Europe, took the lead in politics and religion, demanding tribute from the common people. Finally, both societies were robustly expansionist, bent on bringing new lands and peoples under their control.

Yet critical differences between these two peoples shaped the outcome of their meeting. The Aztecs lacked the knowledge of ocean navigation, metal tools and weaponry, and firearms. Equally important, the relatively young Aztec empire had not yet established total control over central Mexico. Formidable peoples remained outside Aztec domination, and conquered city-states within the empire bitterly resented Aztec rule. Cortés exploited that weakness. Massing an army of disgruntled native warriors, he and his men marched inland to the mighty Aztec capital Tenochtitlán, home to more people (roughly a quarter million) than any city then existing in Europe. When the emperor Moctezuma's ambassadors met Cortés on the road and attempted to appease him with gold ornaments and other gifts, an Indian witness noted that "the Spaniards . . . picked up the gold and fingered it like monkeys. . . . Their bodies swelled with greed." The newcomers were welcomed into the city as honored guests but soon seized Moctezuma and took him captive. For months Cortés ruled the empire indirectly, but the Aztecs drove the Spanish out after Moctezuma's death.

In the midst of this victory the city encountered another foe—smallpox. Geographically isolated from Eurasia and its complex disease environment, the Aztecs and all other native peoples in the Americas lacked the acquired immunity that gave Europeans a degree of protection against Old-World pathogens. The resulting **virgin soil epidemics**—so called because the victims had no previous exposure—took a nightmarish toll. Smallpox claimed millions in central Mexico between 1520 and 1521. This, too, presented Cortés with opportunities. Supported by a massive Indian force, he put Tenochtitlán to siege, killing tens of thousands before the ragged, starving survivors surrendered in August of 1521. The feared Aztec empire lay in ruins. Conquistadors fanned out from central Mexico, overwhelming new populations and eventually learning of another mighty kingdom to the South. Again relying on political faction, disease, technological advantages, and luck, by 1532 Spaniards under Francisco Pizzaro and his brothers had conquered the Incan empire in South America, which in certain regards outshone even the Aztecs.

virgin soil epidemic epidemic in which the populations at risk have had no previous contact with the diseases that strike them and are therefore immunologically almost defenseless.

WITNESS
A Conquistador
in the Aztec Markets

"We were astounded at the great number of people and the quantities of merchandise, and at the orderliness and good arrangements that prevailed, for we had never seen such a thing before . . . dealers in gold, silver, and precious stones, feathers, cloaks, and embroidered goods, and male and female slaves who are also sold there."

—Bernal Díaz, *The Conquest of New Spain* (1632)

⌃ Both the Aztecs and the Spanish tried to understand the new in terms of the familiar. Hence an Aztec artist portrayed Cortés as an Indian with strange clothes and a stranger beard (*left*), whereas a European artist depicted Moctezuma in the style of a Greco-Roman warrior (*right*).

The Columbian Exchange >> Virgin soil
epidemics, which contributed to the collapse of many Indian populations, were only one aspect of a complex web of interactions between the flora and fauna of the Americas on the one hand and those of Eurasia and Africa on the other. Just as germs migrated along with humans, so did plants and animals. These transfers, begun in the decades after Columbus first landed in the Caribbean, are known by historians as the **Columbian Exchange,** and they had far-reaching effects on both sides of the Atlantic. Europeans brought a host of American crops home with them, as seen in Chapter 1 (pages 4–19).

> **Columbian Exchange** transition of people, plants, insects, and microbes between the two hemispheres, initiated when Columbus reached the Americas in 1492.

They also most likely brought syphillis, an American disease that broke out across Europe in more virulent form than ever before. Europeans brought to the Americas the horses and large dogs that intimidated the Aztecs; they brought oranges, lemons, figs, and bananas from Africa and the Canary Islands. Escaped hogs multiplied so rapidly that they overran some Caribbean islands, as did European rats.

The Columbian exchange was not a short-lived event. In a host of different ways it reshaped the globe over the next 500 years as travel, exploration, and colonization brought cultures ever closer. Instead of smallpox, today bird flu from Asia or the West Nile virus threatens populations worldwide. But the exchanges of the sixteenth century were often more extreme, unpredictable, and far-reaching, because of the previous isolation of the two hemispheres.

The Crown Steps In >> Proud conquistadors
did not long enjoy their mastery in the Americas. Spain's monarchs, who had just tamed an aristocracy at home, were not about to allow a colonial nobility to arise across the Atlantic. The Crown bribed the conquistadors into retirement—or was saved the expense when men such as Francisco Pizarro were assassinated by their own followers. The task of governing Spain's new colonies passed from the conquerors to a small army of officials, soldiers, lawyers, and Catholic bishops, all appointed by the Crown, reporting to the Crown, and loyal to the Crown. Headquartered in urban centers such as Mexico City (formerly Tenochtitlán), an elaborate, centralized bureaucracy administered the Spanish empire, regulating nearly every aspect of economic and social life.

Few Spaniards besides imperial officials settled in the Americas. By 1600 only about 5 percent of the colonial population was of Spanish descent, the other 95 percent being Indian, African, or of mixed heritage. Even by 1800

SPANISH AMERICA, CA. 1600

By 1600 Spain was extracting large amounts of gold and silver from Mexico and South America, as well as profits from sugar plantations in the Caribbean. Each year Spanish treasure ships ferried bullion from mines such as the one at Potosí to the Isthmus of Panama, where it was transported by land to the Caribbean coast and from there to Spain. An expedition from Acapulco sailed annually to the Philippines as well, returning with Asian spices and other trade goods.

only 300,000 Spanish immigrants had come to live in the Americas. Indians often remained on the lands that they had farmed under the Aztecs and the Incas, now paying Spanish overlords their taxes and producing livestock for export. More importantly, Indians paid for the new order through their labor, sometimes as slaves but more often through an evolving administrative system channeling native workers to public and private enterprises throughout the Americas. The Spanish also established sugar plantations in the West Indies; these were worked by black slaves who by 1520 were being imported from Africa in large numbers.

Spain's colonies returned even more spectacular profits by the 1540s—the result of huge discoveries of silver in both Mexico and Peru. Silver mining developed into a large-scale capitalist enterprise requiring substantial investment. European investors and Spanish immigrants who had profited from cattle raising and sugar planting poured their capital into equipment and supplies used to mine the silver deposits more efficiently: stamp mills, water-powered crushing equipment, pumps, and mercury. Whole villages of Indians were pressed into service in the mines, joining black slaves and free European workers employed there.

By 1570 the town of Potosí, the site of a veritable mountain of silver, had become larger than any city in either Spain or its American empire, with a population of 120,000. Local farmers who supplied mining centers with food and Spanish merchants in Seville who exported European goods to Potosí profited handsomely. So, too, did the Spanish Crown, which claimed one-fifth of all extracted silver. During the sixteenth century, some 16,000 tons of the precious metal were exported from Spanish America to Europe.

The Search for North America's Indian Empires >> Riches and glory radicalized Spanish expectations. Would-be conquistadors embarked on an urgent race to discover and topple the next Aztec or Incan Empire, a race to become the next Cortés or Pizarro. The prevailing mood was captured by the portrait of a Spanish soldier that adorns the frontispiece of his book about the West Indies. He stands with one hand on his sword and the other holding a pair of compasses on top of a globe. Beneath is inscribed the motto "By compasses and the sword/More and more and more and more."

Some of the most ambitious adventurers felt certain that more lands and riches would be found in the North. The Spanish had probed the North American coast up to present-day South Carolina, looking for slaves. But Juan Ponce de León, the conquerer of Puerto Rico, launched the first official expedition to the mainland, which he named Florida in 1513. Everywhere he met armed resistance and was repulsed, because the inhabitants had come to despise Spaniards as slave raiders. Eight years later, he returned, only to be mortally wounded in a battle with Calusa Indians.

Still, the dreams of northern Indian empires persisted. In 1528 Pánfilo de Narváez, a red-bearded veteran from the conquest of Cuba, led a major expedition back to Florida. Ignoring advice from his second-in-command, Alvar Núñez Cabeza de Vaca, Narváez separated from his main force near Tampa Bay and led 300 men on a harrowing march in search of riches. For months Narváez plundered his way through Florida, while the men fell ill or fell victim to Indian archers, whose longbows could bury an arrow six inches into a tree. Disillusioned and desperate, 242 survivors lashed together makeshift rafts and tried to sail along the Gulf Coast to Mexico. Weeks later proud Narváez and most of his men had disappeared at sea, whereas Cabeza de Vaca and a handful of survivors washed up on islands off the Texas coast.

Local Indian groups then turned the tables and made slaves of the Spaniards. After years as prisoners Cabeza de Vaca and three others, including an African slave named Esteban, escaped to make an extraordinary trek across Texas and northern Mexico. Somewhere in present-day Chihuahua they passed through what had been the trading hinterland of Paquime, and Cabeza de Vaca noted an enduring regional commerce in feathers and "green stones"—turquoise. Finally, in July 1536 a shocked party of Spanish slavers stumbled across the four rag-tag castaways and brought them to Mexico City.

The stories the four men told of their ordeal inspired two more massive expeditions to the north. The first, led by Hernán de Soto, scoured the southeast's agricultural villages searching for gold and taking whatever he wanted: food, clothing, luxury goods, even young women whom he and his men "desired both as servants and for their foul uses. . . ." De Soto's men became the first and last Europeans to glimpse several declining Mississippian chiefdoms, echoes of Cahokia's ancient majesty. Some native communities resisted, inflicting substantial losses on the expedition. Others feigned friendship and sent de Soto to hunt gold in neighboring villages, thus ridding themselves of a great danger and directing it at enemies instead. De Soto's men never found the treasures they sought as they traveled through much of the present-day South (see the map, page 25). But the expedition's cruel and destructive foray did hasten the transformation of the southeastern chiefdoms into decentralized confederacies.

Spanish ambition met a similar fate in the West. In 1539, 29-year-old Francisco Vázquez de Coronado led 300 Spaniards and 1,000 Mexican Indian warriors north into the present-day American Southwest. Coronado was emboldened by tales of cities more wondrous than Tenochtitlán, but his brash confidence began to fail him when instead he found only mud and straw pueblos inhabited by modest farmers. Desperate to turn his hugely expensive expedition to advantage, Coronado sent men in all directions. To the west his scouts were blocked by the vastness of the Grand Canyon. Others traveled east, forcing themselves on the Pueblo peoples of the Upper Rio Grande, descendants of the Anasazi. Finally Coronado followed an Indian he dubbed the Turk out onto the Great Plains in search of a rumored kingdom called Quivira. Perhaps the Turk had in mind one of the easternmost Mississippian chiefdoms, but the frustrated conquistador became convinced he had been deceived. He had the Turk strangled somewhere in present-day Kansas and in 1542 returned to Mexico, where crown authorities tried him for inflicting "great cruelties" on Indians.

Such North American expeditions ruined conquistadors such as Coronado and de Soto, but Spain could afford

Disillusioned and desperate, 242 survivors lashed together makeshift rafts and tried to sail along the Gulf Coast to Mexico. Weeks later proud Narváez and most of his men had disappeared at sea.

these blunders. It had taken vast wealth from the Americas, conquered the hemisphere's mightiest peoples, and laid claim to the bulk of the new world. Yet for most of the sixteenth century rival European powers took little interest in the Americas. England's fishermen continued to explore the North Sea, Labrador, and Newfoundland. Portugal discovered and laid claim to Brazil. France launched expeditions along North America's eastern shoreline (Giovanni da Verrazano, 1524) and the St. Lawrence River Valley (Jacques Cartier, 1534, 1535, and 1541). These efforts proved important in the long run, but for most of the century Spain could treat the Americas as their own.

They owed that luxury, in part, to religious upheaval in Europe. During the second decade of the sixteenth century—the same decade in which Cortés laid siege to Tenochtitlán—religious changes of enormous significance began spreading through Europe. That revolution in Christianity, known as the Protestant Reformation, occupied European attentions and eventually figured as a crucial force in shaping the history of the Americas.

 REVIEW

How did the Spanish respond to the discovery of a "new world"?

RELIGIOUS REFORM DIVIDES EUROPE

During the Middle Ages, the Roman Catholic Church defined what it meant to be a Christian in western Europe. Like other institutions of medieval society the Catholic Church was a hierarchy. At the top was the pope in Rome, and under him were the descending ranks of other church officials—cardinals, archbishops, bishops. At the bottom of the Catholic hierarchy were parish priests, each serving his own village, as well as monks and nuns living in monasteries and convents. But medieval popes were weak, and their power was felt little in the lives of most Europeans. Like political units of the era, religious institutions of the Middle Ages were local and decentralized.

Between about 1100 and 1500, however, as the monarchs of Europe grew more powerful so, too, did the popes. The Catholic Church acquired land throughout Europe, and its swelling bureaucracy added to church income from tithing (taxes contributed by church members) and from fees paid by those appointed to church offices. In the thirteenth century church officials also began to sell "indulgences." For ordinary believers who expected to spend time after death purging their sins in purgatory, the purchase of an indulgence promised to shorten that punishment by drawing on a "treasury of merit" amassed by the good works of Christ and the saints.

By the fifteenth century the Catholic Church and the papacy had become enormously powerful but increasingly indifferent to popular religious concerns. Church officials meddled in secular politics. Popes and bishops flaunted their wealth, while poorly educated parish priests neglected their pastoral duties. At the same time, popular demands for religious assurance grew increasingly intense.

The Teachings of Martin Luther >> Into this climate of heightened spirituality stepped Martin Luther, who abandoned studying the law to enter a monastery. Like many of his contemporaries Luther was consumed by fears over his eternal fate. He was convinced that he was damned, and he could not find any consolation in the Catholic Church. Catholic doctrine taught that a person could be saved by faith in God and by his or her own good works—by leading a virtuous life, observing the sacraments (such as baptism, the Mass, and penance), making pilgrimages to holy places, and praying to Christ and the saints. Because Luther believed that human nature was innately evil, he despaired of being able to lead a life that "merited" salvation. If men and women are so bad, he reasoned, how could they ever win their way to heaven with good works?

Luther finally drew on the Bible to break through his despair. It convinced him that God did not require fallen humankind to earn salvation. Salvation, he concluded, came by faith alone, the "free gift" of God to undeserving sinners. The ability to live a good life could not be the *cause* of salvation but its *consequence:* once men and women believed that they had saving faith, moral behavior was possible. Luther elaborated that idea, known as "justification by faith alone," between 1513 and 1517.

Luther was ordained a priest and then assigned to teach at a university in Wittenberg, Germany. He became increasingly critical, however, of the Catholic Church as an institution. In 1517 he posted on the door of a local church 95 theses attacking the Catholic hierarchy for selling salvation in the form of indulgences.

The novelty of this attack was not Luther's open break with Catholic teaching. Challenges to the church had cropped up throughout the Middle Ages. What was new was the passion and force behind Luther's protest. Using the blunt, earthy Germanic tongue, he expressed the anxieties of many devout laypeople and their outrage at the church hierarchy's neglect. The "gross, ignorant asses and knaves at Rome," he warned, should keep their distance from Germany, or else "jump into the Rhine or the nearest river, and take . . . a cold bath."

The pope and his representatives in Germany at first tried to silence Martin Luther, then excommunicated him. But opposition only pushed Luther toward more radical positions. He asserted that the church and its officials were not infallible; only the Scriptures were without error. Every person, he said, should read and interpret the Bible for himself or herself. In an even more direct assault on church authority, he advanced an idea known as "the priesthood of all believers." Catholic doctrine held that salvation came only through the church and its clergy, a privileged group that possessed special access to God. Luther asserted that every person had the power claimed by priests.

Although Luther had not intended to start a schism within Catholicism, independent Lutheran churches were forming in Germany by the 1520s. During the 1530s Luther's ideas spread throughout Europe, where they were eagerly taken up by other reformers.

The Contribution of John Calvin »

Luther's most influential successor was John Calvin, a French lawyer turned theologian. Calvin agreed with Luther that men and women could not merit their salvation. But, whereas Luther's God was a loving deity who extended his mercy to sinful humankind, Calvin conceived of God as awesome, all-knowing and all-powerful—the controlling force in human history that would ultimately triumph over Satan. To bring about that final victory, to usher in his heavenly kingdom, God had selected certain people as his agents, Calvin believed. These people— "the saints," or "the **elect**"—had been "predestined" by God for eternal salvation in heaven.

> **elect** in theology, those of the faithful chosen, or "elected" by God for eternal salvation.

ʌ Protestants such as Luther and Calvin placed greater emphasis on the Word of Scripture rather than church rituals controlled by priests and bishops. In this seventeenth-century portrait of John Calvin, sacred words from scripture literally help define him.

Calvin's emphasis on predestination led him to another distinctively Protestant notion—the doctrine of calling. How could a person learn whether he or she belonged to the elect who were saved? Calvin answered: strive to behave like a saint. God expected his elect to serve the good of society by unrelenting work in a "calling," or occupation, in the world. In place of the Catholic belief in the importance of good works, Calvin emphasized the goodness of work itself. Success in attaining discipline and self-control, in bringing order into one's own life and the entire society, revealed that a person might be among the elect.

Calvin fashioned a religion to change the world. Whereas Luther believed that Christians should accept the existing social order, Calvin called on Christians to become activists, reshaping society and government to conform with God's laws laid down in the Bible. He wanted all Europe to become like Geneva, the Swiss city that he had converted into a holy commonwealth in which the elect regulated the behavior and morals of everyone else. And unlike Luther, who wrote primarily for a German audience, Calvin addressed his most important book, *The Institutes of the Christian Religion* (1536), to Christians throughout Europe. Reformers from every country flocked to Geneva to learn more about Calvin's ideas.

French Huguenots and the Birth of Spanish Florida »

The Protestant Reformation shattered the unity of Christendom in Western Europe. Spain, Ireland, and Italy remained firmly Catholic. England, Scotland, the Netherlands, Switzerland, and France developed either dominant or substantial Calvinist constituencies. Much of Germany and Scandinavia opted for Lutheranism. As religious groups competed for political power and the loyalties of believers, brutal wars swept sixteenth-century Europe. France experienced some of the worst violence. An influential group of Huguenots (Calvin's French followers) saw in North America a potential refuge from religious persecution. Under Jean Ribault 150 Huguenots in 1562 established a simple village on Parris Island off present-day South Carolina. That experiment ended in desperation and cannibalism, but two years later Ribault led another, larger group to a site south of present-day Jacksonville, Florida. Here, at Fort Caroline, the Huguenots nurtured a cordial relationship with the local Timucua Indians. It seemed a promising start.

But Spanish authorities in the Caribbean took the Huguenots for a triple threat. First, French pirates had long tried to siphon silver from the Americas by waylaying Spanish galleons as they rode the Gulf Stream up the southeastern coast of North America before turning east toward Spain. With good reason, Spanish administrators feared that Fort Caroline would entrench the threat of piracy. Second, Spain worried that France would take a broader interest in the Americas, perhaps eventually planting colonies in all of North America. Finally, many Spanish Catholics saw Protestantism as a loathsome contagion, to be expunged from Europe and barred from the Americas.

These interlocking concerns prompted Spain to found a permanent colony in Florida under the direction of a focused and unforgiving man named Pedro Menéndez de Avilés. In 1565 Menéndez established a settlement on the coast called Saint Augustine (still the United States' oldest continuously occupied, non-Indian settlement). Next he and 500 soldiers slogged through the rain and marsh until they found Fort Caroline. In battle and through later executions the attackers killed Ribault and about 500 of his Huguenots. Flush with victory Menéndez established several more outposts on Florida's Atlantic and Gulf coasts and in 1570 even encouraged a short-lived Jesuit mission just miles from where English colonists would establish Jamestown a generation later. As for the Huguenots, the calamity at Fort Caroline dashed hope that the New World would be their haven. Most had to resign themselves to intensifying persecution in France.

The English Reformation >> While the Reformation racked northern Europe, King Henry VIII of England labored at a goal more worldly than those of Luther and Calvin. He wanted a son, a male heir to continue the Tudor dynasty. When his wife, Catherine of Aragon, gave birth to a daughter, Mary, Henry petitioned the Pope to have his marriage annulled in the hope that a new wife would give him a son. This move enraged the king of Spain, who also happened to be Catherine's nephew. He persuaded the pope to refuse Henry's request. Defiantly, England's king proceeded with the divorce nonetheless and quickly married his mistress, Anne Boleyn. He then went further, making himself, not the pope, the head of the Church of England. Henry was an audacious but practical man, and he had little interest in promoting reformist doctrine. Apart from discarding the Pope, the Church of England remained essentially Catholic in its teachings and rituals.

England's Protestants gained ground during the six-year reign of Henry's son Edward VI but then found themselves persecuted when Edward's Catholic half-sister Mary became queen in 1553. Five years later the situation turned again, when Elizabeth I (Anne Boleyn's daughter) took the throne, proclaiming herself the defender of Protestantism. Elizabeth was no radical Calvinist, however. A vocal minority of her subjects were reformers of that stripe, calling for the English church to purge itself of bishops, elaborate ceremonies, and other Catholic "impurities." Because of the austerity and zeal of such Calvinist radicals, their opponents proclaimed them "Puritans."

Radical Protestants might annoy Elizabeth as she pursued her careful, moderate policies, but radical Catholics frightened her. She had reason to worry that Spain might use English Catholics to undermine her rule. More ominously, Elizabeth's advisors cautioned that Catholic Ireland to the west would be an ideal base from which Spain or France could launch an invasion of England. Beginning in 1565 the queen encouraged a number of her elite subjects to sponsor private ventures for subduing the native Irish and settling loyal English Protestants on their land. As events fell out, this Irish venture proved to be a prelude to England's bolder attempt to found colonies across the Atlantic.

REVIEW

What were the major branches of Protestant reform, and how did the religious wars affect the Americas?

ENGLAND'S ENTRY INTO AMERICA

Among the gentlemen eager to win fame and fortune were Humphrey Gilbert and Walter Raleigh, two adventurers with conquistador appetites for more and more. The pair were like most of the English who went to Ireland, ardent Protestants who viewed the native Catholic inhabitants as superstitious, pagan savages: "They blaspheme, they murder, commit whoredome," complained one Englishman, "hold no wedlocke, ravish, steal. . . ." Thus the English found it easy enough to justify their conquest. They proclaimed it their duty to teach the Irish the discipline of hard work, the rule of law, and the truth of Protestant Christianity. And, while the Irish were learning these civilized, English ways, they would not be allowed to buy land or hold office or serve on juries or give testimony in courts or learn a trade or bear arms.

Opinion

Do you think religion is only a surface justification or a primary motivation for the religious wars and rivalries of the sixteenth century?

When the Irish rebelled at that program of "liberation," the English ruthlessly repressed them, slaughtering not only combatants but civilians as well. Most English in Ireland, like most Spaniards in America, believed that native peoples who resisted civilization and proper Christianity should be subdued at any cost. No scruples stopped Humphrey Gilbert, in an insurgent country, from planting the path to his camp with the severed heads of Irish rebels.

The struggle to colonize and subdue Ireland would serve as a rough model for later English efforts at expansion. The approach was essentially military, like that of the conquistadors. It also set the ominous precedent that Englishmen could treat "savage" peoples with a level of brutal cruelty that would have been inappropriate in wars between "civilized" Europeans. Finding "neither reputation, or profytt" in Ireland, Gilbert, Raleigh, and other West County gentry took their ambition and their Irish education to North America.

The Ambitions of Gilbert, Raleigh, and Wingina >>

In 1578 Gilbert got his chance for glory when Elizabeth granted him a royal patent—the first English colonial charter—to explore, occupy, and govern any territory in America "not actually possessed of any Christian prince or people."

> **charter** document issued by a sovereign ruler, legislature, or other authority creating a public or private corporation.

The vague, wildly unrealistic charter ignored the Indian possession of North America and made Gilbert proprietor of all the land lying between Florida and Labrador. In many ways his dreams looked backward. Gilbert hoped to set up a kind of medieval kingdom of his own, where loyal tenant farmers would work the lands of manors, paying rent to feudal lords. Yet his vision also looked forward to a utopian society. He planned to encourage England's poor to emigrate by providing them free land and a government "to be chosen by consent of the people." Elizabeth had high hopes for her haughty champion, but a fierce storm got the better of his ship, and the Atlantic swallowed him before he ever set foot in his American dominions.

Meanwhile Gilbert's stepbrother Walter Raleigh had been laying the groundwork for a British American empire. Raleigh enlisted the talents of Richard Hakluyt, a clergyman, to write an eloquent plea for the English settlement of America, titled *A Discourse Concerning Westerne Planting*. North America's temperate and fertile lands, Hakluyt argued, would not only grow profitable crops,

>> John White's sensitive watercolor *Indian Elder or Chief* may well be of Wingina. The portrayal includes the copper ornament worn hanging from his neck, indicating high social status and the presence of an active trade network, since copper is not found on the island. Just as Raleigh had to gauge his strategy in dealing with the Indians, Wingina had to decide how to treat the strange newcomers from across the Atlantic.

they would also make an excellent base from which to harry the Spanish, search for a Northwest Passage to Asia, and spread Protestantism. Finally, Hakluyt predicted that because the "Spaniardes have executed most outragious and more then Turkishe cruelties in all the west Indies," that Indians would greet Englishmen as liberators.

By the summer of 1584 Raleigh had dispatched an exploratory voyage to the Outer Banks of present-day North Carolina. Expedition leaders made friendly contact with a people known as the Roanoke and ruled by a "weroance," or chief, named Wingina. The enthusiastic Hakluyt envisioned a colony that would become the Mexico of England, full of plantations producing sugar and silk and mountains yielding gold. Elizabeth knighted Raleigh and allowed him to name the new land "Virginia," after his virgin queen.

But Raleigh was not the only one with grand plans. Almost certainly Wingina had encountered or at least heard of Europeans before 1584. Like most coastal groups in the region, his people would have obtained prized European tools and commodities through indirect trade or by scouring wrecked ships. Eager to fortify his own and his people's power, Wingina recognized that friendly relations with the English would give him access to their trade and influence. Perhaps he believed he would act as patron to the newcomers. After all, they knew little of the region, spoke no Indian languages, and even lacked the skills necessary to survive in the area without native assistance. In short, Wingina seems to have welcomed the English because he believed that they could be useful and

> ## No scruples stopped Humphrey Gilbert, in an insurgent country, from planting the path to his camp with the severed heads of Irish rebels.

EUROPEAN EXPLORATION: FIFTEENTH AND SIXTEENTH CENTURIES

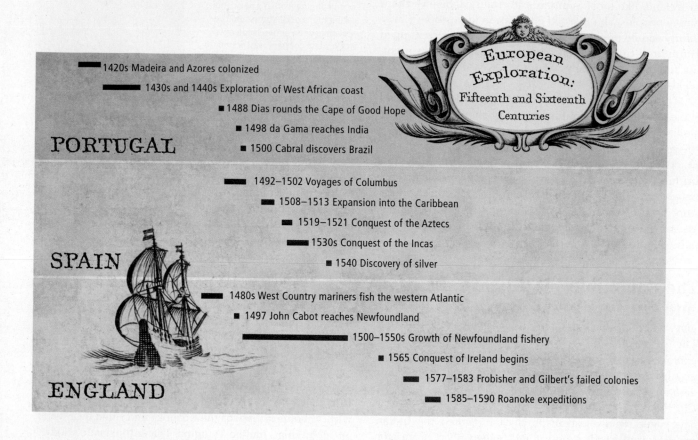

European Exploration: Fifteenth and Sixteenth Centuries

PORTUGAL
- 1420s Madeira and Azores colonized
- 1430s and 1440s Exploration of West African coast
- 1488 Dias rounds the Cape of Good Hope
- 1498 da Gama reaches India
- 1500 Cabral discovers Brazil

SPAIN
- 1492–1502 Voyages of Columbus
- 1508–1513 Expansion into the Caribbean
- 1519–1521 Conquest of the Aztecs
- 1530s Conquest of the Incas
- 1540 Discovery of silver

ENGLAND
- 1480s West Country mariners fish the western Atlantic
- 1497 John Cabot reaches Newfoundland
- 1500–1550s Growth of Newfoundland fishery
- 1565 Conquest of Ireland begins
- 1577–1583 Frobisher and Gilbert's failed colonies
- 1585–1590 Roanoke expeditions

that they could be controlled. It was a tragic if understandable miscalculation—one that Indian leaders would make again and again in colonial America.

Raleigh apparently aimed to establish on Roanoke a mining camp and a military garrison. In a stroke of genius he included in the company of 108 men a scientist, Thomas Hariot, to study the country's natural resources, and an artist, John White, to make drawings of the Virginia Indians. *A Briefe and True Reporte of the New Found Land of Virginia* (1588), written by Hariot and illustrated by White, served as one of the principal sources about North America and its Indian inhabitants for more than a century. Far less inspired was Raleigh's choice to lead the expedition—two veterans of the Irish campaigns, Sir Richard Grenville and Ralph Lane. Even his fellow conquistadors in Ireland considered Lane proud and greedy. As for Grenville, he was given to breaking wineglasses between his teeth and then swallowing the shards to show that he could stand the sight of blood, even his own.

The bullying ways of both men quickly alienated the natives of Roanoke. Wingina found the newcomers disrespectful, haughty, and cruel: when a local stole a cup, the English tried to teach everyone a lesson by torching his village and destroying its corn stores. As suspicions and resentments mounted on each side, Wingina tried to regain control of the situation the following summer by meeting with Lane to improve relations. But the meeting was a trap. Lane's men opened fire at the Indian envoys, killed Wingina, and hacked the head from his body. All that averted a massive counterattack was the arrival of England's preeminent privateer, Sir Francis Drake, fresh from freebooting up and down the Caribbean. The settlement's 102 survivors piled onto Drake's ships and put an ocean between themselves and the avenging Roanokes.

A Second Roanoke—and Croatoan »

Undaunted, Raleigh organized a second expedition to plant a colony farther north, in Chesapeake Bay. He recruited 119 men, women, and children, members of the English middle class, and granted each person an estate of 500 acres. He also appointed as governor the artist John White, who brought along a suit of armor for ceremonial occasions.

White deplored Lane's treachery toward Wingina and hated the senseless violence that had characterized the entire endeavor. The artist had spent his time on Roanoke closely observing native peoples, their material cultures, and their customs. His sensitive watercolors, especially those featuring women and children, indicate a genuine respect and affection. White believed that under prudent, moral leaders an English colony could indeed coexist peacefully with American Indians.

Despite his best intentions, everything went wrong. In July of 1587 the expedition's pilot insisted on leaving the colonists at Roanoke Island rather than the Chesapeake. Understandably, the Roanokes took no pleasure in seeing the English return. Sensing that the situation on Roanoke could quickly become desperate, the colonists sent White home to fetch reinforcements.

He returned to England in 1588 just as the massive Spanish navy, the Armada, was preparing an assault on England. Elizabeth enlisted every seaworthy ship and able-bodied sailor to stave off invasion. The Armada was defeated, but White was unable to return to Roanoke Island until 1590. There, he found only an empty fort and a few cottages in a clearing. The sole clue to the colony's fate was an inscription carved on a post: CROATOAN. It was the name of a nearby island off Cape Hatteras.

Had the Roanoke colonists fled to Croatoan for safety? Had they moved to the mainland and joined Indian communities? Had they been killed by Wingina's people? The fate of the "lost colony" remains a mystery, though later rumors suggest that the missing colonists merged with native societies in the interior. His dream of a tolerant, cooperative colony dashed, White sailed back to England, leaving behind the little cluster of cottages, which would soon be overgrown with vines, and his suit of armor, which was already "almost eaten through with rust."

 REVIEW

Why did Elizabeth agree to charter a colony in America, and how successful were the first attempts?

All the world lay before them. Or so it had seemed to the young men from England's West Country who dreamed of gold and glory, conquest and colonization. True, they lived on the fringe of the civilized world in the fifteenth and sixteenth centuries. China remained the distant, exotic kingdom of power and wealth, supplying silks and spices and other luxurious goods. Islamic empires stood astride the land routes from Europe to the east. Nations on the western edge of Europe thus took to the seas. Portugal sent slave and gold traders to Africa, as well as merchants to trade with the civilizations of the Indies. Spanish conquerors such as Cortés toppled Indian empires and brought home mountains of silver. But England's West County sea dogs— would-be conquistadors—met only with frustration. In 1600, more than a century after Columbus's first crossing, not a single English settlement existed in the Americas.

What was left of the freebooting West Country world? Raleigh, his ambition still afire, sailed to South America in quest of a rich city named El Dorado. In 1603, however, Elizabeth's death brought to the English throne her cousin James I, the founder of the Stuart dynasty. The new king arrested the old queen's favorite for treason and imprisoned him for 15 years in the Tower of London. Set free in 1618 at the age of 64, Raleigh returned to South America, his lust for El Dorado undiminished. Along the way he plundered some Spanish silver ships, defying King James's orders. It was a fatal mistake, because England had made peace with Spain. Raleigh lost his head.

James I did not want to harass the king of Spain; he wanted to imitate him. The Stuarts were even more determined than the Tudors had been to enlarge the sphere of royal power. There would be no room in America for a warrior nobility of conquistadors, no room for a feudal fiefdom ruled by the likes of Raleigh or Gilbert. Instead, there would be profitable plantations and colonies managed by loyal, efficient bureaucrats. America would strengthen English monarchs, paving their path to greater power, just as the dominions of Mexico and Peru had enlarged the authority of the Spanish Crown. America would be the making of kings and queens.

Or would it? For some Europeans, weary of freebooting conquistadors and sea rovers, the security that Crown rule and centralized states promoted in Western Europe would be enough. But others, men and women who were often desperate and sometimes idealistic, would cast their eyes west across the Atlantic and want more.

CHAPTER SUMMARY

During the late fifteenth century, Europeans and Africans made their first contact with the Americas, where native cultures were numerous and diverse.

- During the fourteenth and early fifteenth centuries, Western Europeans were on the fringes of an international economy drawn together by Chinese goods such as spices, ceramics, and silks.
- A combination of technological advances, the rise of new trade networks and techniques, and increased political centralization made Europe's expansion overseas possible.
- Led by Portugal, European expansion began with a push southward along the West African coast, in pursuit of spices, ivory, and gold. As sugar plantations were established in the islands of the eastern Atlantic, a slave trade in Africans became a part of this expansive commerce.
- Spain took the lead in exploring and colonizing the Americas, consolidating a vast and profitable empire

of its own in the place of Aztec and Inca empires. Divisions within Indian empires and the devastating effects of European diseases made Spanish conquest possible.

- The conquistadors who led the Spanish occupation were soon replaced by an elaborate, centralized royal bureaucracy, which regulated most aspects of economic and social life. The discovery of silver provided Spain with immense wealth, while leading to sharply increased mortality among the native population.

- Spanish conquistadors also explored much of the present day southeastern and southwestern United States. They found no empires, silver mines, or rich empires and were thwarted by the Indian peoples they encountered.

- The Protestant Reformation was inaugurated by Martin Luther in 1517 and carried on by John Calvin, whose more activist theology spread from his headquarters in Geneva outward to England, Scotland, the Netherlands, and the Huguenots in France.

- England, apprehensive of Spain's power, did not turn its attention to exploration and colonization until the 1570s and 1580s. By the time it did, European rivalries were heightened by splits arising out of the Protestant Reformation.

- England's merchants and gentry lent support to colonizing ventures, although early efforts, such as those at Roanoke, failed.

Additional Reading

For a description of the entrepreneurs, mariners, and ordinary folk who participated in the era of exploration and discovery, see Kenneth R. Andrews, *Trade, Plunder, and Settlement: Maritime Enterprise and the Genesis of the British Empire, 1480–1630* (1985). For Portugal's initial expansion, see Malyn Newitt, *A History of Portuguese Overseas Expansion, 1400–1668* (2004). John Thornton's *Africa and Africans in the Making of the Atlantic World 1400–1680* (1992) is a detailed analysis of West Africa's role in the changing international economy. For sugar as an engine of expansion, see Philip D. Curtin, *The Rise and Fall of the Plantation Complex: Essays in Atlantic History* (2nd ed., 1998). The demographic catastrophe that followed contact is explored in Massimo Livi Bacci, *Conquest: The Destruction of American Indios* (2008). For a contemporary classic that puts European expansion in global perspective, see Jared Diamond, *Guns, Germs, and Steel: The Fates of Human Societies* (1998).

For Spain in the Caribbean, see Carl Ortwin Sauer, *The Early Spanish Main* (Rev. ed., 1992). See also David Abulafia, *The Discovery of Mankind* (2008). For Indians in central Mexico after Cortés, see James Lockhart, *The Nahuas after Conquest: A Social and Cultural History of the Indians of Central Mexico, Sixteenth through Eighteenth Centuries* (1992).

Significant Events

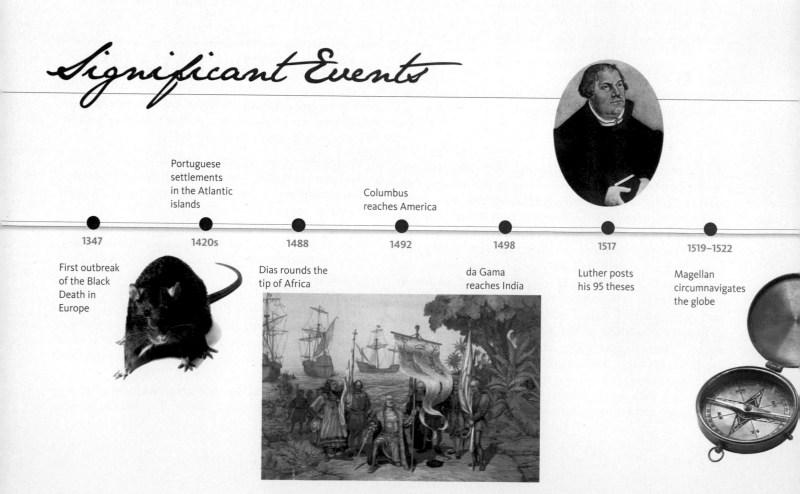

| 1347 | 1420s | 1488 | 1492 | 1498 | 1517 | 1519–1522 |

Portuguese settlements in the Atlantic islands

Columbus reaches America

First outbreak of the Black Death in Europe

Dias rounds the tip of Africa

da Gama reaches India

Luther posts his 95 theses

Magellan circumnavigates the globe

For a magisterial narrative of Spain's activities in North America, see David J. Weber, *The Spanish Frontier in North America* (1992). Rolena Adorno and Patrick Charles Pautz's translation of *The Narrative of Cabeza de Vaca* (2003) is unsurpassed, the castaways' ordeal is splendidly retold by Andrés Reséndez in *A Land So Strange* (2007). Coronado's sojourn is the subject of the exacting work by Richard Flint and Shirley Cushing Flint, *Documents of the Coronado Expedition, 1539–1542* (2005). For the Southeast, see Charles Hudson, *Knights of Spain, Warriors of the Sun: Hernando de Soto and the South's Ancient Chiefdoms* (1997).

For a good introduction to the Reformation in England, see Patrick Collinson, *The Birthpangs of Protestant England* (1988) and Christopher Haigh, *English Revolutions* (1993); Eamon Duffy's *The Voices of Morebath* (2001) offers a vivid depiction of how the Reformation transformed the lives of ordinary people. For early English attempts at colonization, in both Ireland and the Americas, consult Nicholas Canny, *Making Ireland British* (2001), Karen Kupperman, *The Jamestown Project* (2007), and Michael Leroy Oberg, *The Head in Edward Nugent's Hand* (2007).

Narváez leads
expedition
to Florida

Coronado
begins exploration of
present-day Southwest

Discovery of silver
in Mexico and Peru

| 1521 | 1528 | 1539 | 1540 | 1583 | 1584–1590 |

Tenochtitlán
surrenders to
Cortés

Gilbert's quest
for a North
American colony

Roanoke
voyages

Colonization

This Native American drawing on a canyon wall in present-day Arizona represents the progress of the Spanish into the Southwest. The horses, prominently featured, gave the invaders an initial advantage. "The most essential thing in new lands is horses," one of Coronado's men emphasized. "They instill the greatest fear in the enemy and make the Indians respect the leaders of the army." Many Indian peoples soon put the horse to their own uses, however, and even outshone the Spanish in their riding skills.

& Conflict in the South

1600–1750

3

>> **AN AMERICAN STORY**

OUTLANDISH STRANGERS

In the year 1617, as Europeans counted time, on a bay they called the Chesapeake, in a land they named Virginia, the mighty weroance Powhatan surveyed his domain. It had all worked according to plan, and Powhatan, leader of the Pamunkeys, had laid his plans carefully. While in his prime, the tall, robust man had drawn some 30 villages along the Virginia coast into a powerful confederacy numbering nearly 9,000 souls. The natives of the Chesapeake, like the peoples who inhabited the length of eastern >>

North America, lived for most of the year in small agricultural villages. As tribute for his protection and leadership Powhatan collected food, furs, and skins from the villagers. He forged alliances with communities too distant or too powerful for him to dominate. He married the daughters of prominent men, dozens in all, to solidify his network of patronage and power.

After 1607 Powhatan was forced to take into account yet another group. The English, as this new people called themselves, came by sea, crammed into three ships. They were 100 men and 4 boys, all clad in heavy, outlandish clothing, many dressed in gaudy colors. The ships followed a river deep into Powhatan's territory and built a fort on a swampy, mosquito-infested site that they called Jamestown.

Powhatan was not frightened. He knew of these strangers from across the waters. Even amid the bounty of the Chesapeake they failed to feed themselves. With bows and arrows, spears and nets, Indian men brought in an abundance of meat and fish. Fields tended by Indian women yielded generous crops of corn, beans, squash, and melon, and edible nuts and fruits grew wild. Still the English starved, and not just during the first few months of their settlement but for several years afterward. Powhatan could understand why the English refused to grow food. Cultivating crops was women's work—like building houses; or making clothing, pottery, and baskets; or caring for children. And the English settlement included no women until two arrived in the fall of 1608. Yet even after more women came, the English still starved, and they expected—no, they demanded—that Powhatan's people feed them.

And yet these hapless folk put on such airs. They boasted about the power of their god—they had only one—and denounced the Indians' "devil-worship" of "false gods." They crowed endlessly about the power of their king, James I, who expected Powhatan to become his vassal. Inconceivable—that Powhatan should willingly bow before this King James, the ruler of so small and savage a race! When the Indians made war, they killed the male warriors of rival communities but adopted their women and children. But when Powhatan's people withheld food or defended their land from these invaders, the English retaliated by murdering Indian women and children. Worse, the English could not even keep order among themselves. Too many of them wanted to lead, and they squabbled constantly.

The temptation to wipe out the helpless, troublesome, arrogant tribe of English—or simply to let them starve to death—had been almost overwhelming. But Powhatan allowed the English to survive. Like Wingina before him, he decided that even these barbaric people had their uses. English labor, English trading goods, and, most important, English guns would help quell resistance within his confederacy and subdue his Indian rivals to the west. In 1614 Powhatan cemented his claim on the English and their weapons with the marriage between his favorite child, Pocahontas, and an ambitious Englishman, John Rolfe.

By 1617 events had vindicated Powhatan's strategy of tolerating the English. His chiefdom flourished, ready to be passed on to his brother. Powhatan's people still outnumbered the English, who seldom starved out right now but continued to fight among themselves and sicken and die. Only one thing had changed in the Chesapeake by 1617: the English were clearing woodland along the rivers and planting tobacco.

That was the doing of Powhatan's son-in-law, Rolfe, a man as strange as the rest of the newcomers, all of them eager to store up wealth and worldly goods. Rolfe had been obsessed with finding a crop that could be grown in Virginia and then sold for gain across the sea. When he succeeded by growing tobacco, other English followed his lead. Odder still, not women but men tended the tobacco fields. Here was more evidence of English inferiority. Men wasted long hours laboring when they might supply their needs with far less effort.

In 1617 Powhatan, ruler of the Pamunkeys, surveyed his domain, and sometime in that year, he died. He had lived long enough to see the tobacco fields lining the riverbanks, straddling the charred stumps of felled trees. But perhaps he went to his grave believing that he had done what Wingina had failed to do: bend the English to his purposes. He died before those stinking tobacco weeds spread over the length of his land and sent his hard-won dominion up in smoke. ◀◀

SEEING WHAT WE WANT TO SEE

Pocahontas, daughter of the mighty weroance Powhatan and wife of English colonist John Rolfe, has long fascinated non-natives. In the first image from 1616 she is represented as a high-status English lady, stripped of all markings of her native culture save her name, Matoaka (Pocahontas was a nickname). The second image, from the 1995 Disney film, portrays her as a pretty and innocent child of nature. Now as then, we see in her what we want to.

Wingina and Powhatan were not the only native leaders that dreamed of turning Europeans to their advantage. Across North America, the fleeting if destructive encounters of the sixteenth century gave way to sustained colonialism in the seventeenth. As Europeans began to colonize the edges of North America in earnest, Indian peoples struggled not only to survive and adapt to new realities but also, when possible, to profit from the rapid changes swirling around them.

Those often dramatic changes reflected upheavals underway all across the globe. The tobacco John Rolfe had begun to cultivate was only one of several plantation **monocultures** that Europeans began to establish in their far-flung colonies. Sugar, already flourishing in the Atlantic islands off the coast of West Africa, was gaining a foothold in the islands of the Caribbean. Rice, long a staple in Asia and grown also in Africa, made its way into South Carolina toward the end of the seventeenth century. Because these crops were grown most efficiently on plantations and required intensive labor, African slavery spread during these years, fueled by an expanding international slave trade. Europeans, Africans, and Indians were all, in different ways, caught up in the wrenching transformations.

> **monoculture** growth of a single crop to the virtual exclusion of all others, either on a farm or more generally within a region.

SPAIN'S NORTH AMERICAN COLONIES

Just as Spain had been the first European power to explore North America's interior, so too it led the way in establishing lasting colonies north of Mexico. But while France and especially England eventually established large colonial populations on territory suited to European-style agriculture, Spain confined its northern ventures to the ecologically challenging regions of the upper Rio Grande and coastal Florida. Because economic opportunities and good farmland were abundant elsewhere in Spanish America, few Spaniards migrated to distant and difficult northern outposts. Even so, Spain's colonial endeavors had tremendous implications for North America's native peoples and for the geopolitics of the continent as a whole.

The Founding of a "New" Mexico >> By the 1590s Coronado's dismal expedition a half-century earlier had been all but forgotten. Again, rumors spread in Mexico about great riches in the North. New Spain's viceroy began casting about for a leader to establish a "new" Mexico as magnificent and profitable as its namesake. He chose Juan de Oñate, son of one of New Spain's richest miners and husband to Isabel de Tolosa Cortés Moctezuma, granddaughter of Hernán Cortés and great-granddaughter of Moctezuma. Ignorant of northern geography and overestimating New Mexico's riches, Oñate proposed to sail ships up the Pacific to Pueblo country, so that twice a year he could resupply his would-be colony and export its expected treasures.

The magnitude of his misconceptions came into focus in 1598, when he led 500 colonists, soldiers, and slaves to the Upper Rio Grande. Oñate found modest villages, no ocean, and no significant mineral wealth. Even so, he had come with women and children, with livestock and tools, with artisans and tradesmen, with seeds and books and bibles. He had come to stay. Eager to avoid the violence of earlier encounters, Tewa-speaking Pueblos evacuated a village for the newcomers to use. Many native leaders pledged Oñate their allegiance, Pueblo artisans labored on irrigation systems and other public works for the Spaniards, and Indian women (traditionally the builders in Pueblo society) constructed the region's first Catholic Church.

The colonizers mistook this cautious courtesy for subservience. Oñate's oldest nephew, Juan de Zaldívar,

↑ Like many other Pueblo peoples, the founders of Acoma built their village atop a sandstone mesa to gain protection from enemies. Constructed in the twelfth century C.E., Acoma may be the oldest continuously occupied settlement in the present-day United States.

was bolder and cruder than most. At Acoma Pueblo, known today as "Sky City" because of its position high atop a majestic mesa, he brazenly seized several sacred turkeys to kill and eat, answering Indian protests with insults. Outraged, Acoma's men fell upon Zaldívar, killing him and several companions. Fueled by grief and rage, Zaldívar's younger brother Vicente laid siege to Acoma Pueblo, killed perhaps 800 of its residents, and made slaves of several hundred more. The savagery of the Acoma siege and similar repressive measures educated all of the region's native communities about the risks of resistance.

But it was easier to instill terror than grow rich. Desperate to salvage their enterprise, Oñate and key followers toiled on long, fruitless expeditions in search of gold, silver, and cities. Vicente de Zaldívar, the headstrong conqueror of Acoma, tried to domesticate bison as had been done with cattle, rather than search for them on the plains. But the bison— "stubborn animals, brave beyond praise"— quickly broke free of the cottonwood coral his men constructed. Most Spaniards turned to the less hazardous pursuit of farming and husbandry to support their families. Others despaired of securing a living in arid New Mexico and fled back into New Spain.

In 1606 royal authorities recalled Oñate and brought him up on charges of mismanagement and abusing Indians. Meanwhile Spain nearly abandoned "worthless" New Mexico, except that the Franciscans insisted it would be a crime to forsake the thousands of Indians they claimed to have baptized since 1598. Spain's New Mexican outpost continued to struggle along.

The Growth of Spanish Florida >> Franciscans became key actors in Spanish North America. Members of a medieval religious order founded by St. Francis of Assisi, Franciscan monks owned no personal property, remained **celibate,** and survived by begging for alms or accepting donations from wealthy patrons. Franciscans accompanied Columbus on his second voyage, and they began ministering to the Indians of central Mexico soon after Tenochtitlán fell. By the 1570s Spanish authorities started secularizing central Mexico's missions, transforming them into self-supporting parishes. Franciscans went on to become powerful figures in colonial New Mexico, while Jesuits established several missions in present-day Arizona.

celibate abstaining from sexual intercourse; also unmarried.

For strategic reasons the Crown needed the Franciscans even more in Florida than in New Mexico's distant outposts. As long as pirates or rival colonies on the Atlantic seaboard threatened Spanish shipping, the king had to control Florida. Pedro Menéndez de Avilés did much to secure the peninsula in the 1560s when he destroyed France's Fort Caroline and established several posts on the coast (see Chapter 2). By

<< Artist Jacques Le Moyne recorded this scene of Florida Indians holding council in the 1560s. Observers from Jean Ribaut's French expedition can be seen in the foreground.

1600, however, Menéndez was dead and only St. Augustine endured, with a population of perhaps 500. Spanish Florida needed something more to survive.

To extend his influence the king first offered the peninsula's many native peoples trade privileges and regular diplomatic presents. In return, native leaders promised to support the Spanish in war, and tax their people on behalf of the king. Once these alliances were in place, Indian communities were made to accept Franciscan missions and a few resident soldiers, a policy critical to molding and monitoring native villages. By 1675, 40 missions were ministering to as many as 26,000 baptized Indians. The bishop of Cuba toured Florida and spoke enthusiastically of converts who embraced "with devotion the mysteries of our holy faith." Florida's mission system and network of Indian alliances convinced Spanish authorities that they could maintain their grip on this crucial peninsula.

Popé and the Pueblo Revolt >> As the
seventeenth century progressed, New Mexico also seemed to stabilize. Enough Spanish colonists remained to establish a separate town, La Villa Real de la Santa Fe, in 1610. Santa Fe (the second-oldest European town in the United States after St. Augustine) became the hub of Spanish life in New Mexico. Many families settled elsewhere on the Rio Grande, on well-watered lands near Pueblo villages. Economic and political life revolved around a dozen prominent families.

By 1675 New Mexico had a diverse colonial population of perhaps 2,500, including Spaniards, Africans, Mexican Indians, mestizos (persons of mixed Spanish-Indian heritage), and mulattos (of Spanish-African heritage).

This population also included large numbers of Indian captives. Occasionally captives came to Spanish households through war, as after the siege of Acoma. In addition, Spaniards purchased enslaved women and children from other Indians and regularly launched slave raids against so-called enemy Indians such as Utes, Apaches, and Navajos. By 1680 half of all New Mexican households included at least one Indian captive. Depending on age, gender, and the master's disposition, such captives could be treated affectionately as low-status family members or terrorized and abused as disposable human property.

The colonists also extracted labor from Pueblo Indians. Officially Pueblo households had to surrender three bushels of corn and one processed hide or large cotton blanket each year. Pueblos also sometimes labored on public works, and elite Spaniards often exploited their privileges by insisting on more tribute and labor than legally allowed. Still, the populous Pueblos could have satisfied Spanish demands with little difficulty except for other changes in their world. First and most importantly, colonialism meant epidemics. Beginning in the 1620s smallpox killed 70 percent of the population within a generation. Whereas New Mexico boasted about 100 native villages at contact, by 1680 only 30 remained inhabited.

SPANISH MISSIONS IN NORTH AMERICA, CA. 1675

From St. Augustine, Spanish missionaries spread into Guale Indian villages in present-day Georgia and westward among the Indians of Timucua, Apalachee, and Apalachicola. In New Mexico, missions radiated outward from the Rio Grande, as distant as Hopi villages in the west.

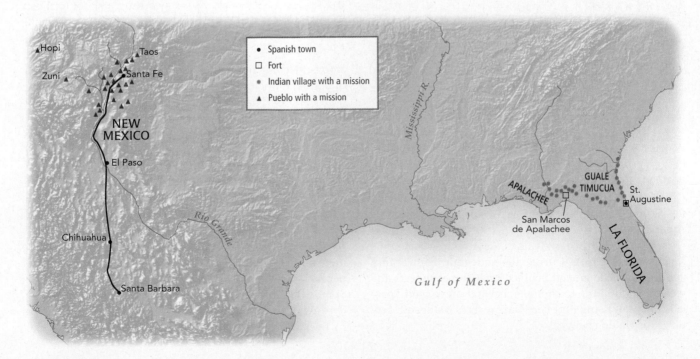

Infestations of locusts, severe droughts, and crop failures compounded the crisis. A distraught Franciscan reported starving native men, women, and children "lying dead along the roads, in the ravines, and in their hovels." Mounted Utes, Apaches, and Navajos, embittered by New Mexican slaving and barred from their customary trade in the pueblos, launched punishing raids against the most vulnerable Pueblo villages.

In their deepening misery Pueblos turned to religion—their own. Since 1598 the Franciscans had worked tirelessly to suppress the dances, idols, and ceremonies that long mediated Pueblo relationships with the divine. By the 1670s Pueblo elders were arguing that the calamities of the past decades could be reversed only by rejecting Christianity and returning to the old faith. Franciscans and civil authorities scrambled to extinguish the revival movement, arresting Pueblo leaders, executing two and whipping 43 others in front of large crowds.

One of the 43, a prominent Tewa man known to history as Popé, nursed his wounds in Taos and called for a war against the Spaniards to purify the land. Many individuals and some entire villages refused to participate. But on August 10, 1680, Indians from across New Mexico rose up and began killing Spaniards, pursuing astonished survivors all the way to Santa Fe. Within weeks the desperate Spanish governor, wounded by an arrow in the face and a gunshot to the chest, gathered the remainder of the colonial population and fled south out of New Mexico. The most successful pan-Indian uprising in North American history, the Pueblo Revolt sent shock waves throughout Spanish America and left the Catholic devout agonizing over what they had done to provoke God's wrath.

 REVIEW

Where and why did Spain establish colonies in North America, and how did native peoples resist colonization?

ENGLISH SOCIETY ON THE CHESAPEAKE

By 1700, then, Spain viewed its situation in the Americas very differently than it had 100 years earlier. The Pueblo Revolt had checked its power at the northern reach of its American possessions. Equally disturbing was the progress of Spain's European rivals in the Americas during the seventeenth century. During the sixteenth, both France and England had envied Spain's American conquests and wealth but did little to compete, beyond preying on Spanish ships and fishing for cod. During the seventeenth century, this would change.

In fact, even by 1600 other European kingdoms were beginning to view overseas colonies as essential to a nation's power and prosperity. They did so in part because of an economic model known as **mercantilism,** which guided Europe's commercial expansion for 200 years. The primary objective of mercantilism was to enrich the nation by fostering a favorable balance of trade. Once the value of exports exceeded the cost of imports, its advocates argued, gold and silver would flow into home ports.

mercantilism European economic doctrine calling for strict regulation of the economy in order to ensure a balance of exports over imports and increase the amount of gold and silver in a nation's treasury.

If a nation could make do without any imports from other countries, so much the better. It was here that the idea of colonies entered the mercantilist scheme. Colonial producers would supply raw materials that the mother country could not produce, while colonial consumers swelled demand for the finished goods and financial services that the mother country could provide. That logic led England's King James I to approve a private venture to colonize the Chesapeake Bay, a sprawling inlet of the Atlantic Ocean fed by over 100 rivers and streams.

The Virginia Company. >> In 1606 the king granted a charter to a number of English merchants, gentlemen, and aristocrats, incorporating them as the Virginia Company of London. The members of the new **joint stock company** sold stock in their venture to English investors, as well as awarding a share to those willing to settle in Virginia at their own expense. With the proceeds from the sale of stock, the company planned to send to Virginia hundreds of poor and unemployed people as well as scores of skilled craftworkers. These laborers were to serve the company for seven years in return for their passage, pooling their efforts to produce any commodities that would return a profit to stockholders. If gold and silver could not be found, perhaps North America would yield other valuable commodities—furs, pitch, tar, or lumber. In the spring of 1607—nearly a decade after Oñate had launched Spain's colonies in New Mexico—the first expedition dispatched by the Virginia Company founded Jamestown.

joint stock company business in which capital is held in transferable shares of stock by joint owners. The joint stock company was an innovation that allowed investors to share and spread the risks of overseas investments.

Making the first of many mistakes, Jamestown's 104 men and boys pitched their fort on a swampy inland peninsula in order to prevent a surprise attack from the Spanish. Weakened by bouts of the disease and beset by dysentery, typhoid, and yellow fever, however, they died by the scores.

the colony. It met for the first time in 1619, beginning what would become a strong tradition of representative government in the English colonies.

The new measures met with immediate success. The free and unfree laborers who poured into Virginia during the 1620s made up the first wave of an English migration to the Chesapeake that numbered between 130,000 and 150,000 over the seventeenth century. Drawn from the ranks of ordinary English working people, the immigrants were largely men, outnumbering women by six to one. Most were young, ranging in age from 15 to 24. Because of their youth, most lacked skills or wealth. Some of those who came to the Chesapeake as free immigrants prospered as Virginia's tobacco economy took off. When in the 1620s demand soared and prices peaked in European markets, colonists with an eye for profit planted every inch of their farms in tobacco and reaped windfalls.

Indentured servants accounted for three-quarters of all immigrants to Virginia. For most, the crossing was simply the last of many moves made in the hope of finding work. Although England's population had been rising since the middle of the fifteenth century, the demand for farm laborers was falling because many landowners were converting croplands into pastures for sheep. The search for work pushed young men and women out of their villages, sending them through the countryside and then into the cities. Down and out in London, Bristol, or Liverpool, some decided to make their next move across the Atlantic and signed indentures. Pamphlets promoting immigration promised land and quick riches once servants had finished their terms of four to seven years.

> **indentures** contract signed between two parties, binding one to serve the other for a specified period of time.

Even the most skeptical immigrants were shocked at what they found. The death rate in Virginia during the 1620s was higher than that of England during times of epidemic disease. The life expectancy for Chesapeake men who reached the age of 20 was a mere 48 years; for women

Even before sickness took its toll, many of Jamestown's colonists had little taste for labor. The gentlemen of the expedition expected to lead rather than to work, while most of the other early settlers were gentlemen's servants and craftworkers who knew nothing about growing crops. Many colonists suffered from malnutrition, which heightened their susceptibility to disease. Only 60 of Jamestown's 500 inhabitants lived through the winter of 1609–1610, known as the "starving time." Desperate colonists unearthed and ate corpses; one settler even butchered his wife. Others imitated their predecessors on Roanoke, bullying Indians for food. Martial law failed to turn the situation around, and skirmishes with native peoples became more brutal and frequent as rows of tobacco plants steadily invaded tribal lands.

Reform and a Boom in Tobacco >>

Determined to salvage their investment, Virginia Company managers in 1618 set in place sweeping reforms. To attract more capital and colonists, the company established a "headright" system for granting land to individuals. Those already settled in the colony received 100 acres apiece. New settlers each received 50 acres, and anyone who paid the passage of other immigrants to Virginia—either family members or servants—received 50 acres per "head." The company also abolished martial law, allowing the planters to elect a representative assembly. Along with a governor and an advisory council appointed by the company, the House of Burgesses had the authority to make laws for it was lower still. Servants fared worst of all, because malnutrition, overwork, and abuse made them vulnerable to disease. As masters scrambled to make quick profits, they extracted the maximum amount of work before death carried off their laborers. An estimated 40 percent of servants did not survive to the end of their indentured terms.

War with the Confederacy >>

The expanding cultivation of tobacco also claimed many lives by putting unbearable pressure on Indian land. After Powhatan's death in 1617 leadership of the confederacy passed to Opechancanough, who watched, year after year, as the tobacco mania grew. In March 1622 he coordinated a sweeping attack on white settlements that killed about a quarter of Virginia's colonial population. English retaliation over the next decade cut down an entire generation of young Indian men, drove the remaining Powhatans to the west, and won the colonists hundreds of thousands more acres for tobacco.

WITNESS

The Indian War of 1622

"They came unarmed into our houses . . . yea in some places sat down at Breakfast with our people at their tables, [and] immediately with [our people's] own tools and weapons, either laid down, or standing in their houses, they basely and barbarously murdered, not sparing either age or sex, man, woman, or child . . ."

—Edward Waterhouse, *A Declaration of the State of the Colonie and Affaires in Virginia* (1622)

News of the ongoing Indian war jolted English investors into determining the true state of their Virginia venture. It came to light that, despite the tobacco boom, the Virginia Company was plunging toward bankruptcy. Nor was that the worst news. Stockholders discovered that more than 3,000 immigrants had not survived the brutal conditions of Chesapeake life. An investigation by James I revealed the grisly truth, causing the king to dissolve the Virginia Company and take control of the colony himself in 1624. Henceforth Virginia would be governed as a royal colony.

As the tobacco boom broke in the 1630s and 1640s Virginians began producing more corn and cattle. Nutrition and overall health improved as a result. More and more poor colonists began surviving their indenture and

establishing modest farms of their own. For women who survived servitude, prospects were even better. With wives at a premium, single women stood a good chance of improving their status by marriage. Even so, high mortality rates still fractured families: one out of every four children born in the Chesapeake did not survive to maturity, and among those children who reached their 18th birthday, one-third had lost both parents to death.

By 1650 Virginia could boast about 15,000 colonists, with more arriving every year. But Virginians looking to expand into more northerly bays of the Chesapeake found their way blocked by a newer English colony.

The Founding of Maryland and the Renewal of Indian Wars >>

Unlike Virginia, established by a private corporation and later converted into a royal colony, Maryland was founded in 1632 by a single aristocratic family, the Calverts. They held absolute authority to dispose of 10 million acres of land, administer justice, and establish a civil government. All these powers they exercised, granting estates, or "manors," to their friends and dividing other holdings into smaller farms for ordinary immigrants. From all these "tenants"—that is, every settler in the colony—the family collected "quitrents" every year, fees for use of the land. The Calverts appointed a governor and a council to oversee their own interests while allowing the largest landowners to dispense local justice in manorial courts and make laws for the entire colony in a representative assembly.

Virginians liked nothing about Maryland. To begin with, the Calvert family was Catholic and had extended complete religious freedom to all Christians, making Maryland a haven for Catholics. Worse still, the Marylanders were a source of economic competition. Two thousand inhabitants had settled on Calvert holdings by 1640, virtually all of them planting tobacco on land coveted by the Virginians.

Another obstacle to Virginia's expansion was the remnant of the Powhatan confederacy. Hounded for corn and supplies (most colonial fields grew tobacco rather than food), and constantly pressured by the expanding plantation economy, Virginia's native peoples became desperate and angry enough to risk yet another war. Aged Opechancanough sent a new generation of Indians into battle in 1644 against the encroaching Virginia planters. Though his warriors killed several hundred English and brought the frontier to a standstill, Opechancanough was eventually captured and summarily shot through the head. The Powhatan confederacy died with him. Virginia's Indians would never again be in a position to go on the offense against the colony. Over the next decades and centuries, many Indians fled the region altogether. But whole communities remained, quietly determined to continue their lives and traditions in their homeland.

Earliest English settlements
Settlements by 1700
Direction of expansion by 1750
Boundary of physical regions

SUSQUEHANNOCK

MARYLAND

NEW JERSEY

Philadelphia

LENNI LANAPE

Susquehanna River

APPALACHIANS

SHENANDOAH VALLEY

BLUE RIDGE

Shenandoah River

TUSCARORA

FALL LINE

Potomac River

Annapolis

DELAWARE

Delaware Bay

VIRGINIA

PIEDMONT

James River

Richmond

Rappahannock River

St. Mary's

POWHATAN
CONFEDERACY

York River

Williamsburg
Jamestown
Yorktown

TIDEWATER

Chesapeake Bay

ATLANTIC
OCEAN

COLONIES OF THE CHESAPEAKE

Settlements in Virginia and Maryland spread out along the many bays of the Chesapeake, where tobacco could easily be loaded from plantation wharves. The "fall line" on rivers, dividing Tidewater and Piedmont regions, determined the extent of commercial agriculture, since ships could not pick up exports beyond that point.

NORTH CAROLINA

Edenton
Albemarle Sound

CHEROKEE

Roanoke River

Changes in English Policy in the Chesapeake >> Throughout the 1630s and 1640s colonial affairs drew little concern from royal officials. England itself had become engulfed first by a political crisis and then by a civil war.

Outraged at the contempt that King Charles I had shown toward Parliament, disaffected elites and radical Puritans overthrew the king and executed him in 1649. When the "republic" of Oliver Cromwell turned out to be something closer to a military dictatorship, most English were happy to see their throne restored in 1660 to Charles II, the son of the beheaded king. The new monarch was determined that not only his subjects at home but also his American colonies abroad would contribute to England's prosperity. His colonial policy was reflected in a series of regulations passed in the 1660s and 1670s known as the Navigation Acts.

The acts severely restricted colonial trade with Britain's imperial rivals. In this sense they were mercantilistic, designed to ensure that England alone would profit from colonial production and trade. Chesapeake planters chafed under the Navigation Acts. They were used to conducting their affairs as they pleased—and they were often pleased to trade with the Dutch. And, adding to the unhappiness, the new restrictions came just as tobacco prices were dropping. In the effort to consolidate its empire England had unintentionally worsened the economic and social difficulties of Chesapeake society.

 REVIEW

How did the Chesapeake colonies support the aims of British mercantilism?

CHESAPEAKE SOCIETY IN CRISIS

By the 1660s overproduction was depressing tobacco prices, and wealthy planters reacted by putting even more prime coastal land into production. Newly freed servants had either to become tenants or try to establish farms to the west in Indian country. Meanwhile, export duties on tobacco paid under the Navigation Acts helped plunge many small planters into crushing debt, and some were forced back into servitude. By 1676 one-quarter of Virginia's free white men remained landless and frustrated.

As the discontent of the poor mounted, so did the worries of big planters. The assembly of the colony lengthened terms of servitude, hoping to limit the number of servants entering the free population. It curbed the political rights of landless men, hoping to stifle opposition by depriving them of the vote. But these measures only set off a spate of mutinies among servants and protests over rising taxes among small planters.

Bacon's Rebellion and Coode's Rebellion >>

Tensions came to a head in 1676. The immediate spark to rebellion was renewed fighting between desperate Indians and the expanding colonial population. Virginia's royal governor, William Berkeley, favored building forts to guard against Indians, but frontier farmers opposed his plan as expensive and an ineffective way to defend their scattered plantations. When they clamored for an expedition to punish the Indians, Nathaniel Bacon stepped forward to lead it.

Wealthy and well connected, Bacon had arrived recently from England, expecting to receive every favor from the governor—including permission to trade with the Indians from his frontier plantation. But Berkeley and a few select friends already held a monopoly on the Indian trade. When they declined to include Bacon, he took up the cause of his poorer frontier neighbors. Other recent, well-to-do immigrants who resented being excluded from Berkeley's circle of power and patronage also joined the cause.

In the summer of 1676 Bacon marched into Jamestown with a body of armed men and bullied the assembly into approving his expedition to kill Indians. While Bacon carried out that grisly business, slaughtering friendly as well as hostile natives, Berkeley rallied his supporters and declared Bacon a rebel. Bacon retaliated by turning his forces against those led by the governor.

Both sides sought allies by offering freedom to servants and slaves willing to join their ranks. Many were willing: for months the followers of Bacon and Berkeley plundered one another's plantations. In September 1676 Bacon reduced Jamestown to a mound of ashes. Only his death from dysentery snuffed out the rebellion.

Political upheaval also shook Maryland, where colonists had long resented the sway of the Calvert family. As proprietors the Calverts and their favorites monopolized political offices, just as Berkeley's circle had in Virginia. Well-to-do planters wanted a share of the Calverts' power. Smaller farmers, like those in Virginia, wanted a less expensive and more representative government. Compounding the tensions were religious differences: the Calverts and their friends were Catholic, but other colonists, including Maryland's most successful planters, were Protestant.

The unrest peaked in July 1689. A former member of the assembly, John Coode, gathered an army, captured the proprietary governor, and then took grievances to authorities in England. There Coode received a sympathetic hearing. The Calverts' charter was revoked and not restored until 1715, by which time the family had become Protestant.

After the rebellions rich planters in both Chesapeake colonies fought among themselves less and cooperated more. In Virginia older leaders and newer arrivals divided the spoils of political office. In Maryland Protestants and Catholics shared power and privilege. Those arrangements ensured that no future Bacon or Coode would mobilize restless gentlemen against the government. By acting together in legislative assemblies, the planter elite managed to curb the power of royal and proprietary governors for decades.

But the greater unity among the Chesapeake's leading families did little to ease that region's most fundamental problem—the sharp inequality of white society. The gulf between rich and poor planters, which had been etched ever more deeply by the troubled tobacco economy, persisted long after the rebellions of Bacon and Coode. All that saved white society in the Chesapeake from renewed crisis and conflict was the growth of African slavery.

> By 1676 one-quarter of Virginia's free white men remained landless and frustrated.

From Servitude to Slavery >>

Like the tobacco plants that spread across Powhatan's land, a labor system based on African slavery was an on-the-ground innovation. Both early promoters and planters preferred paying for English servants to importing alien African slaves. Black slaves, because they served for life, were more expensive than white workers, who served only for several years. Because neither white nor black immigrants lived long, cheaper servant labor was the logical choice.

The black population of the Chesapeake remained small for most of the seventeenth century, constituting just 5 percent of all inhabitants in 1675.

Africans had arrived in Virginia by 1619, most likely via the Dutch, who dominated the slave trade until the middle of the eighteenth century. The lives of those newcomers resembled the lot of white servants, with whom they shared harsh work routines and living conditions. White and black bound laborers socialized with one another and formed sexual liaisons. They conspired to steal from their masters and ran away together; if caught, they endured similar punishments. There was more common ground: many of the first black settlers did not arrive directly from Africa but came from the Caribbean, where some had learned English and had adopted Christian beliefs. And not all were slaves: some were indentured servants. A handful were free.

A number of changes after 1680 caused planters to invest more heavily in slaves than in servants. First, as death rates in the Chesapeake began to drop, slaves became a more profitable investment. Although they were more expensive to buy than servants, planters could now expect to get many years of work from their bondspeople. Equally important, masters would have title to the children that slaves were now living long enough to have. At the same time, the influx of white servants was falling off just as the pool of available black labor was expanding. When the Royal African Company lost its monopoly on the English slave trade in 1698, other merchants entered the market. The number of Africans sold by British dealers swelled to 20,000 annually.

Africa and the Atlantic Slave Trade >>

From 1492 to 1820, enslaved African migrants outnumbered European migrants to the new world by nearly five to one. Put differently, before the twentieth-century, African workers did most of the heavy lifting in the economies of the Americas.

Would you have opposed slavery if you had lived in the seventeenth century?

For a century after Columbus's arrival, the traffic in slaves to the Americas had numbered a few thousand annually. But as sugar cultivation steadily prospered after 1600, slave imports rose to 19,000 a year during the seventeenth century and mushroomed to 60,000 a year in the eighteenth century. All told, as many as 21 million people were captured in West and Central Africa between 1700 and 1850: some 9 million among them entered the Americas as slaves, but millions died before or during the Atlantic crossing, and as many as 7 million remained slaves in Africa. Although slavery became indispensible to its economy, British North America played a relatively small role in the Atlantic slave trade. Nine-tenths of all Africans brought to the New World landed in Brazil or the Caribbean islands.

The rapid growth of the trade transformed not only the Americas but also Africa. Slavery became more widespread within African society, and slave trading more central to its domestic and international commerce. Most important, the African merchants and political leaders most deeply invested in the slave trade used their profits for political advantage—to build new chiefdoms and states such as Dahomey, Asante, and the Lunda Empire. Their ambitions and the greed of European slave dealers drew an increasingly large number of Africans, particularly people living in the interior, into slavery's web. By the late seventeenth century, Africans being sold into slavery were no longer only those who had put themselves at risk by committing crimes, running into debt, or voicing unpopular political and religious views. The larger number were instead captives taken by soldiers or kidnappers in raids launched specifically to acquire prisoners for the slave trade, or else desperate refugees captured while fleeing war, famine, and disease. During the decades after 1680, captives coming directly from Africa made up more than 80 percent of all new slaves entering the Chesapeake and the rest of mainland North America. Many were shipped from the coast of Africa that Portuguese explorers had first probed, between the Senegal and Niger rivers. Most of the rest came from Angola, farther south.

Seized by other Africans, captives were yoked together at the neck and marched hundreds of miles through the interior to coastal forts or other outposts along the Atlantic. There, they were penned in hundreds of prisons, in lots of anywhere from 20 or 30 to more than 1,000. They might be forced to wait for slaving vessels in French *captiveries* below the fine houses of traders on the island of Goree, or herded into "outfactories" on the Banana Islands upstream on the Sierra Leone River, or perhaps marched into the dank underground slaveholds at the English fort at Cape Coast. Farther south, captives were held in marshy, fever-ridden lowlands along

AFRICAN TRANSATLANTIC SLAVE TRADE, 1450–1760

Toward the end of the seventeenth century, Chesapeake and Carolina planters began importing increasing numbers of slaves. In Africa, the center of that trade lay along a mountainous region known as the Gold Coast, where more than a hundred European trading posts and forts funneled the trade. Unlike most of the rest of West Africa's shoreline, the Gold Coast had very little dense rain forest. Despite the heavy trade, only about 4 percent of the total transatlantic slave trade went to North America.

⋏ Katharina, sketched in 1521, was a servant living in the Netherlands. She was probably one of the increasing number of Africans being brought to Europe owing to the growing slave trade.

>> Slaves captured in the African interior were marched out in slave "coffles," a forced march in which captives were linked either by chains or by wooden yoke restraints linking two slaves together as they walked.

>> Africans found themselves in a variety of conditions in the Americas. Most toiled on plantations. Some, however, like these "watermen" along the James River in Virginia (*far right*), claimed more independence. Still others ran away to Maroon communities in the interior. This armed Maroon (*a runaway slave; near right*) is from Dutch Guiana, where conditions on the plantations were particularly harsh.

<< Slaves were often bought and sold on the decks of the ship they traveled on, as in this painting from the 1770s (*left*). Note that the ship has put up a barricade (*left side of the illustration*) to keep slaves separate from the rest of the ship while the selling is proceeding.

ENGLAND

EUROPE

3%

ATLANTIC OCEAN

NORTH AMERICA

BRITISH COLONIES

ARAB

BERBER

ARAB

ASIA

SAHARA DESERT

KAARTA

WEST INDIES

4%

French 17%

SEGU

KANEM-BORNU

ARAB

British 24%

HAUSA

CENTRAL AMERICA

Spanish 13%

DAHOMEY

ASHANTE

BENIN

OYO

AFRICA

The Middle Passage

Dutch 7%

GUIANAS

Portuguese 32%

62%

Equator

TEKE

NSUNDI

KONGO

MBUNDU

SWAHILI CITY-STATES

BRAZIL

36%

SOUTH AMERICA

ANGOLA

MOZAMBIQUE

MADAGASCAR

2%

| | Main slave sources 1450 to 1760 |
| **SUSU** | Ethnic groups |

Hip Mask from Benin

These images of mudfish alternate with those of Portuguese merchants. What might the mudfish be meant to symbolize? (Use a few key terms to find answers on the web.)

These pieces of inlaid iron represent medicine-filled incisions that were said to have given Idia metaphysical powers.

Object is hollow at the back; may have been used as receptacle for medicines, as well as a pendant for a hip belt.

This exquisite sixteenth-century ivory mask, now in New York's Metropolitan Museum of Art, graced the neck of Benin's king during ceremonial occasions. Its subtlety and precision suggest that it was produced by Benin's famed guild of royal ivory carvers, specifically for royalty. The object communicates a tremendous amount of visual information. The face itself is a portrait of Idia, mother of Benin's great early sixteenth-century leader Esigie. A powerful political figure in her own right, Idia helped secure the throne for her son and remained an influential advisor throughout his reign. On her head and around her neck are miniature faces of Portuguese merchants who brought great wealth to Benin and enriched and empowered its leaders through the slave trade.

THINKING CRITICALLY

Why pair the mudfish and the Portuguese? Do you think that the artist conceived of the Portuguese merchants as equals? Would you expect Benin's artistic sophistication to shape how the Portuguese regarded the kingdom?

Source: Metropolitan Museum of Art, www.metmuseum .org/toah/ho/o8/sfg/ho_1978.412.323.htm.

---

the Bight of Benin, waiting for a slaver to drop anchor. One African, Ottobah Cugoano, recalled finally being taken aboard ship:

> There was nothing to be heard but the rattling of chains, smacking of whips, and the groans and cries of our fellow-men. Some would not stir from the ground, when they were lashed and beat in the most horrible manner. . . . And when we found ourselves at last taken away, death was more preferable than life, and a plan was concerted amongst us that we might burn and blow

up the ship and to perish altogether in the flames.

Worse than the imprisonment was the voyage itself: the so-called Middle Passage, a nightmarish journey across the Atlantic that could take anywhere between three weeks and three months, depending on currents, weather, and where ships disembarked and landed. Often several hundred black men, women, and children were packed below decks, squeezed onto platforms built in tiers spaced so close that sitting upright was impossible. It was difficult to know whether the days or the nights were more hellish. Slaves were taken out and forced to exercise for their health for a few hours each day; the rest of the day, the sun beat down and the heat below the decks was "so excessive," one voyager recalled, that the doctors who went below to examine slaves "would faint away, and the candles would not burn." At night, the slaves "were often heard making a howling melancholy kind of noise," noted a doctor aboard another ship. It was because the slaves, in sleeping, had dreamed "they were back in their own country again, amongst their families and friends" and "when they woke up to find themselves in reality on a slave ship they began to bay and shriek." Historians estimate that for every 85 enslaved Africans that set foot in the Americas, 15 died during the middle passage.

After the numb, exhausted survivors reached American ports, they faced more challenges to staying alive. The first year in the colonies was the most deadly for new, "unseasoned" slaves. The sickle cell genetic trait gave them a greater immunity to malaria than Europeans, but slaves were highly susceptible to respiratory infections. One-quarter of all Africans died during their first year in the Chesapeake, and among Carolina and Caribbean slaves, mortality rates were far higher. In addition to the new disease environment, Africans had to adapt to lives without freedom in a wholly unfamiliar country and culture.

A Changing Chesapeake Society ≫

Exchanging a labor system based on servitude for one based on slavery transformed Chesapeake society. Most obviously, the number of Afro-Virginians rose sharply. By 1740, 40 percent of all Virginians were black, and most of those were African-born. Unlike many African men and women who had arrived earlier from the Caribbean, these new inhabitants had little familiarity with English language and culture. This larger, more distinctively African community was also locked into a slave system that was becoming ever more rigid and demeaning. By the late decades of the seventeenth century, new laws made it more difficult for masters to free slaves. Other legislation systematically separated the races by prohibiting free black settlers from having white servants and outlawing interracial marriages and sexual relationships. The legal code fostered racism and white contempt for black Virginians in a variety of other ways. While masters were prohibited from whipping their white servants on the bare back, slaves had no such protection. And "any Negro that shall presume to strike any white" was to receive 30 lashes for that rash act.

> **racism** discrimination based on inherited physical differences, which according to racist thought separated humans into a few distinct and unequal groups or "races."

The new laws both reflected and encouraged racism among white colonists of all classes. Deepening racial hatred, in turn, made it unlikely that poor white planters, tenants, and servants would ever join with poor black slaves to challenge the privilege of great planters. Instead of identifying with the plight of the slaves, the Chesapeake's poorer white residents considered black Virginians their natural inferiors. They could pride themselves on sharing with wealthy white gentlemen the same skin color and on being their equals in the eyes of the law.

The leaders of the Chesapeake colonies cultivated unity among white inhabitants by improving economic prospects for freed servants and lesser planters. The Virginia assembly made provisions for freed servants to get a better start as independent farmers. It lowered taxes, allowing small planters to keep more of their earnings. New laws also gave most white male Virginians a vote in elections, allowing them an outlet to express their grievances. Economic trends toward the end of the seventeenth century contributed to the greater prosperity of small planters, because tobacco prices rose slightly and then stabilized. As a result of Bacon's savage campaign against the Virginia Indians, new land on the frontier became available. Even the domestic lives of ordinary people became more secure as mortality rates declined and the numbers of men and women in the white population evened out. As a result, virtually all men were now able to marry, and families were fragmented less often by the premature deaths of spouses and parents.

After 1700 the Chesapeake evolved into a more stable society. Gone were the bands of wild, landless, young bachelors one step ahead of the law, the small body of struggling lesser planters one step ahead of ruin, and the great mass of exploited servants one step away from rebellion. Virginia and Maryland became colonies of farming families, most of them small planters who owned between 50 and 200 acres. These families held no slaves, or at most two or three. And they accepted, usually without question, the social and political leadership of their acknowledged "superiors," great planters who styled themselves the "gentry."

 REVIEW

Why did slavery replace servitude as the dominant labor system in Virginia and Maryland?

FROM THE CARIBBEAN TO THE CAROLINAS

During the same decade that the English invaded Powhatan's land, they began to colonize the Caribbean, whose islands extended north and west, like beads on a string, from the Lesser Antilles toward the more substantial lands of Puerto Rico, Hispaniola, Jamaica, and Cuba (see the map, page 55). At their long journey's end English sailors found what seemed a paradise: shores rimmed with white sand beaches that rose sharply to coral terraces, then to broad plateaus or mountain peaks shrouded in rain forests. The earliest arrivals came intending not to colonize but to steal from the Spanish. Even after 1604 when some English settled on the islands, few intended to stay.

Yet the English did establish permanent plantation colonies in the West Indies. Beyond that, their Caribbean settlements became the jumping-off points for a new colony on the North American mainland—South Carolina. Because of the strong West Indian influence, South Carolina developed a social order in some ways distinct from that of the Chesapeake colonies. In other ways, however, the development paralleled Virginia and Maryland's path. In both regions, extreme violence, high mortality, and uncertainty gave way to relative stability only over the course of many decades.

Paradise Lost >>
The English had traded and battled with the Spanish in the Caribbean since the 1560s. From those island bases English buccaneers conducted an illegal trade with Spanish settlements, sacked the coastal towns, and plundered silver ships bound for Seville. Weakened by decades of warfare, Spain could not hold the West Indies. The Dutch drove a wedge into Caribbean trade routes, and the French and the English began to colonize the islands.

In the 40 years after 1604 some 30,000 immigrants from the British Isles planted crude frontier outposts on St. Kitts, Barbados, Nevis, Montserrat, and Antigua. The settlers—some free, many others indentured servants, and almost all young men—devoted themselves to working as little as possible, drinking as much as possible, and returning to England as soon as possible. They cultivated for export a poor quality tobacco, which returned just enough profit to maintain straggling settlements of small farms.

Then, nearly overnight, sugar cultivation transformed the Caribbean. In the 1640s Barbados planters learned from the Dutch how to process sugarcane. The Dutch also supplied African slaves to work the cane fields and marketed the sugar for high prices in the Netherlands. Sugar plantations and slave labor rapidly spread to other English and French islands as Europeans developed an insatiable sweet tooth for the once scarce commodity. Caribbean sugar made more money for England than the total volume of commodities exported by all the mainland American colonies.

Even though its great planters became the richest people in English America, they could not have confused the West Indies with paradise. Throughout the seventeenth century disease took a fearful toll, and island populations grew only because of immigration. In the scramble for land, small farmers were pushed onto tiny plots that barely allowed them to survive.

The desperation of bound laborers posed another threat to British planters. After the Caribbean's conversion to cultivating sugar, African slaves gradually replaced indentured servants in the cane fields. By the beginning of the eighteenth century, resident Africans outnumbered English by four to one. Fear of servant mutinies and slave rebellions frayed the nerves of island masters. They tried to contain the danger by imposing harsh slave codes and inflicting brutal punishments on all laborers. But planters lived under a constant state of siege. One visitor to Barbados observed that whites fortified their homes with parapets from which they could pour scalding water on attacking servants and slaves. During the first century of settlement, seven major slave uprisings shook the English islands.

As more people squeezed onto the islands, some settlers looked for a way out. With all the land in use, the Caribbean no longer offered opportunity to freed servants or even planters' sons. It was then that the West Indies started to shape the history of the American South.

The Founding of the Carolinas >>
The colonization of the Carolinas began with the schemes of Virginia's royal governor, William Berkeley, and Sir John Colleton, a supporter of Charles I who had been exiled to the Caribbean at the end of England's civil war. Colleton saw that the Caribbean had a surplus of white settlers, and Berkeley knew that Virginians needed room to expand as well. Together the two men set their sights on the area south of Virginia. Along with a number of other aristocrats, they convinced Charles II to make them joint proprietors in 1663 of a place they called the Carolinas, in honor of the king.

A few hardy souls from Virginia had already squatted around Albemarle Sound in the northern part of the Carolina grant. The proprietors provided them with a governor and a representative assembly. About 40 years later, in 1701, they set off North Carolina as a separate colony. The desolate region proved a disappointment. Lacking good harbors and navigable rivers, the colony had no convenient way of marketing its produce. North Carolina remained a poor colony, its sparse population engaged in general farming and the production of masts, pitch, tar, and turpentine.

The southern portion of the Carolina grant held far more promise, especially in the eyes of one of its proprietors, Sir Anthony Ashley Cooper, Earl of Shaftesbury. In 1669 Cooper sponsored an expedition of a few hundred English and Barbadian immigrants, who planted the first permanent settlement in South Carolina. By 1680 the colonists had established the center of economic, social, and political life at the confluence of the Ashley and the Cooper rivers, naming the site Charles Town (later Charleston) after the king. Like others before him Cooper hoped to create an ideal society in America. His utopia was a place where a few landed aristocrats and gentlemen would rule with the consent of many smaller property holders. With his personal secretary, the renowned philosopher John Locke, Cooper drew up an intricate scheme of government, the Fundamental Constitutions. The design provided Carolina with a proprietary governor and a hereditary nobility who, as a Council of Lords, would recommend all laws to a Parliament elected by lesser landowners.

THE CAROLINAS AND THE CARIBBEAN

The map underscores the geographic link between West Indian and Carolina settlements. Emigrants from Barbados dominated politics in early South Carolina, while Carolinians provided foodstuffs, grain, and cattle to the West Indies. As South Carolinians began growing rice, Caribbean slave ships found it an easy sail north and west to unload their cargoes in Charleston.

The Fundamental Constitutions met the same fate as other lordly dreams for America. Instead of peacefully observing its provisions, most of the Carolinians, immigrants from Barbados, plunged into economic and political wrangling. They challenged proprietary rule, protested or ignored laws and regulations imposed on them, and rejected the proprietors' relatively benevolent vision of Indian relations. Instead the colonists fomented a series of Indian slave wars that nearly destroyed the colony altogether.

Carolina, Florida, and the Southeastern Slave Wars >>

Taking wealthy Barbados as the model, the colonists intended to grow Carolina's economy around cash crops tended by African slaves. But before they could afford to establish such a regime, the newcomers needed to raise capital through trade with Indians. Colonists gave textiles, metal goods, guns, and alcohol in exchange for hundreds of thousands of deer skins, which they then exported.

But the trade soon came to revolve around a commodity dearer still. As did most peoples throughout history, southeastern Indians sometimes made slaves of their enemies. Carolina's traders vastly expanded this existing slave culture by turning captives into prized commodities. Convinced that local Indians were physically weaker than Africans and more likely to rebel or flee, colonial traders bought slaves from Indian allies and then exported them to other mainland colonies or to the Caribbean. They found eager native partners in this business. Contact with Europe had unleashed phenomenal changes in interior North America. Epidemics ruined one people and gave advantage to another, new commercial opportunities sparked fierce wars over hunting and trading territories, and many thousands of Indian families became displaced and had to rebuild their lives somewhere new. The chaos, conflict, and movement gave enterprising Indians ample opportunity to enslave weak neighbors and stock Carolina's slave pens.

To ensure a steady supply of slaves, Carolinian merchants courted a variety of Indian allies during the late seventeenth and early eighteenth centuries and encouraged them to raid mission Indians in Spanish Florida. By 1700 Florida's Indian peoples were in sharp decline, and Charles Town's slave traders turned to the large and powerful Creek, Choctaw, Chickasaw, and Cherokee confederacies of the interior, encouraging them to raid one another. Before long the slave wars had a momentum all their own, extending as far west as the Mississippi River. Even native peoples who deplored the violence and despised the English felt compelled to participate, lest they too become victims.

The trade became central to Carolina's economy, and colonists high and low sought to profit from it. In 1702 Governor James Moore, one of the colony's chief slave traders, launched an audacious raid against Spanish St. Augustine and Florida's missions, returning with hundreds of Indian captives. His campaign inspired still more raids, and over the next few years Creeks, Yamasees, and Englishmen laid waste to 29 Spanish missions, shattering thousands of lives and destroying Spain's precarious system of Indian alliances. By 1706 Spanish authority was once again confined to St. Augustine and its immediate vicinity. Within another 10 years most of Florida had been depopulated of Indians.

It seemed a double victory from Charles Town's perspective. The English had bested a European rival for the Crown, and had reaped enormous profits besides. The fragmentary evidence suggests that Carolinians had purchased or captured between 30,000 and 50,000 Indian slaves before 1715. Indeed, before that date South Carolina exported more slaves than it imported from Africa or the Caribbean. But in 1715 Carolina's merchants finally paid a price for the wars that they had cynically fomented for over 40 years.

With Florida virtually exhausted of slaves, the Yamasees grew nervous. Convinced that Carolina would soon turn on them as it had on other one-time allies, the Yamasees struck first. They attacked traders, posts, and plantations on the outskirts of Charles Town, killing hundreds of colonists and dragging scores more to Florida to sell as slaves in St. Augustine. Panicked authorities turned to other Indian peoples in the region but found most had either joined the Yamasee or were too hostile and suspicious to help. Though it lasted only

<< Mulberry Plantation in South Carolina was first carved from coastal swamps in 1714. This painting, done half a century later, shows the Great House visible in the distance, flanked by slave quarters. African slaves skilled in rice cultivation oversaw the arduous task of properly planting and irrigating the crop.

a few months, the Yamasee War finally put an end to the destructive regional slave trade. Animal skins again dominated regional commerce. The powerful southern confederacies grew wary of aligning too closely with any single European power and henceforth sought to play colonies and empires off each other. It was a strategy that would bring them relative peace and prosperity for generations.

White, Red, and Black: The Search for Order >>

As for South Carolina, the Yamasee War set the colony back 20 years. In its aftermath, settlers invested more and more of their resources in African slaves and in the cultivation of rice, a crop that eventually made South Carolina's planters the richest cohort in mainland North America. Unfortunately, South Carolina's swampy coast, so perfectly suited to growing rice, was less suited for human habitation. Weakened by chronic malaria, settlers died in epic numbers from yellow fever, smallpox, and respiratory infections. The European population grew slowly, through immigration rather than natural increase, and numbered only 10,000 by 1730.

Early South Carolinians had little in common but the harsh conditions of frontier existence. Most colonists lived on isolated plantations; early deaths fragmented families and neighborhoods. Immigration after 1700 further intensified the colony's ethnic and religious diversity, adding Swiss and German Lutherans, Scots-Irish Presbyterians, Welsh Baptists, and Spanish Jews. The colony's only courts were in Charles Town; churches and clergy of any denomination were scarce. On those rare occasions when early Carolinians came together, they gathered at Charles Town to escape the pestilential air of their plantations, to sue one another for debt and haggle over prices, or to fight over religious differences and proprietary politics.

Finally, in 1729, the Crown formally established royal government; by 1730 economic recovery had done much to ease the strife. Even more important in bringing greater political stability, the European colonists of South Carolina came to realize that they must unite if they were to counter the Spanish in Florida and the French and their Indian allies on the Gulf Coast.

The growing African population gave European Carolinians another reason to maintain a united front. During the first decades of settlement, frontier conditions and the scarcity of labor had forced masters to allow enslaved Africans greater freedom within bondage. European and African laborers shared chores on small farms. On stock-raising plantations, called "cowpens," African cowboys ranged freely over the countryside. African contributions to the defense of the colony also reinforced racial interdependence and muted European domination. Whenever threats arose—during the Yamasee War, for example—Africans were enlisted in the militia.

European Carolinians depended on African labor even more after turning to rice as their cash crop. In fact, planters began to import slaves in larger numbers partly because of West African skill in rice cultivation. But Europeans harbored deepening fears of the African workers whose labor built planter fortunes. As early as 1708 African men and women had become a majority in the colony, and by 1730 they outnumbered European settlers by two to one. As their colony began to prosper, European Carolinians put into effect strict slave codes like those in the Caribbean that converted their colony into an armed camp and snuffed out the marginal freedoms that African settlers once enjoyed.

The Founding of Georgia >>

After 1730 Carolinians could take comfort not only in newfound prosperity and new political harmony but also in the founding of a new colony on their southern border. South Carolinians liked Georgia a great deal more than the Virginians had liked Maryland, because the colony formed a buffer between British North America and Spanish Florida in much the same way that Yamasees and Shawnees had, before the war.

Enhancing the military security of South Carolina was only one reason for the founding of Georgia. More important to General James Oglethorpe and other idealistic English gentlemen was the aim of aiding the "worthy poor" by providing them with land, employment, and a new start. They envisioned a colony of hardworking small farmers who would produce silk and wine, sparing England the need to import those commodities. That dream seemed within reach when George II made Oglethorpe and his friends the trustees of the new colony in 1732, granting them a charter for 21 years. At the end of that time Georgia would revert to royal control.

The trustees did not, as legend has it, empty England's debtors' prisons to populate Georgia. They freed few debtors but recruited from every country in Europe paupers who seemed willing to work hard—and who professed Protestantism. Trustees paid the paupers' passage and provided each with 50 acres of land, tools, and a year's worth of supplies. Settlers who could pay their own way were encouraged to come by being granted larger tracts of land. Much to the trustees' dismay, that generous offer was taken up not only by many hoped-for

> **Trustees paid the paupers' passage and provided each with 50 acres of land, tools, and a year's worth of supplies.**

Protestants but also by several hundred Ashkenazim (German Jews) and Sephardim (Spanish and Portuguese Jews), who established a thriving community in early Savannah.

The trustees were determined to ensure that Georgia became a small farmers' utopia. Rather than selling land, the trustees gave it away, but none of the colony's settlers could own more than 500 acres. The trustees also outlawed slavery and hard liquor in order to cultivate habits of industry and sustain equality among whites. This design for a virtuous and egalitarian utopia was greeted with little enthusiasm by Georgians. They pressed for a free market in land and argued that the colony could never prosper until the trustees revoked their ban on slavery. Because the trustees had provided for no elective assembly, settlers could express their discontent only by moving to South Carolina—which many did during the early decades. As mounting opposition threatened to depopulate the colony, the trustees caved in. They revoked their restrictions on land, slavery, and liquor a few years before the king assumed control of the colony in 1752. Under royal control Georgia continued to develop an ethnically and religiously diverse society, akin to that of South Carolina. Similarly, its economy was based on rice cultivation and the Indian trade.

 REVIEW

How was the colonization of Carolina both distinct from and parallel to that of the Chesapeake?

Empire . . . utopia . . . independence. . . . For more than a century after the founding of Oñate's colony on the upper Rio Grande in 1598, those dreams inspired residents of New Mexico, Florida, the Chesapeake, the English Caribbean, the Carolinas, and Georgia. Each of these regions served as staging grounds where kings and commoners, free and unfree, men and women, Native American, European, and African played out their hopes. Their acts were as often filled with desperation as with hope, for conditions were often harsh as the plantation monocultures of sugar and rice spread across the globe.

The dream of an expanding empire faltered for the Spanish, who found few riches in the Southwest and eventually found rebellion. The dream of empire failed, too, when James I and Charles I, England's early Stuart kings, found their power checked by Parliament. And the dream foundered fatally for Indians—for Powhatan's successors, who were unable to resist old-world diseases and land-hungry tobacco planters, and for Westos, Shawnees, and the many Indian peoples of Florida who sought to survive, accommodate, or exploit colonialism, but fell to ruin in the end.

English lords had dreamed of establishing feudal utopias in America. But proprietors such as the Calvert family in Maryland and Cooper in the Carolinas found themselves hounded by frontier planters and farmers who sought economic and political power. Georgia's trustees struggled in vain to nurture their dream of a utopia for the poor. The dream of a Spanish Catholic utopia brought by missionaries to the American Southwest dimmed with native resistance and rebellion.

The dream of independence proved the most deceptive of all, especially for the inhabitants of England's colonies. Just a bare majority of the European servant immigrants to the Chesapeake survived to enjoy freedom. The rest were struck down by disease or worn down at the hands of tobacco barons eager for profit. Not only in the Chesapeake but also in the Caribbean and the Carolinas, real independence eluded the English planters. Poorer folk—dependent on richer settlers for land and leadership—deferred to them at church and on election

Significant Events

LATE 1500s	1598	1607	1610	1620s	1632	1660
Formation of Powhatan's paramount chiefdom	Oñate colonizes New Mexico	English establish Jamestown	Founding of Santa Fe in New Mexico	Tobacco boom in Virginia; epidemics in New Mexico reduce Pueblo population by nearly 70 percent	Calvert founds Maryland	Parliament passes the first of the Navigation Acts

days and depended on them to buy crops or to extend credit. Even the richest planters were dependent on the English and Scottish merchants who supplied them with credit and marketed their crops, as well as on the English officials who made colonial policy.

And everywhere in the American Southeast and Southwest, the lingering dreams of Europeans were realized only through the labor of the least free members of colonial America. That stubborn reality would haunt all Americans who continued to dream of freedom and independence.

CHAPTER SUMMARY

During the seventeenth century, Spain and England moved to colonize critical regions of southern North America.

- Native peoples everywhere in the American South resisted colonization, despite losses from warfare, disease, and enslavement.
- Spanish colonies in New Mexico and Florida grew slowly and faced a variety of threats. By the late seventeenth century Spanish New Mexico had been lost to the Pueblo Revolt, and Florida's delicate mission system was under siege from English Carolina and its Indian allies.
- Thriving monocultures were established in all of England's southern colonies—tobacco in the Chesapeake, rice in the Carolinas, and sugar in the Caribbean.
- Despite a period of intense enslavement of native peoples, African slavery emerged as the dominant labor system throughout these regions.
- Instability and conflict characterized both Spanish and English colonies in the South for most of the first century of their existence.

Additional Reading

David J. Weber's *Spanish Frontier in North America* (1992) remains by far the best overview of Spain's colonies north of Mexico. For the Southwest more specifically, see also Ramón Gutiérrez, *When Jesus Came, The Corn Mothers Went Away* (1991), John L. Kessell's *Spain in the Southwest* (2002), and James F. Brooks' pathbreaking monograph *Captives and Cousins* (2002). For Spain in the Southeast, see Paul E. Hoffman's *Florida's Frontiers* (2002).

For enduring treatments of early Virginia, see Edmund S. Morgan, *American Slavery, American Freedom* (1975), and Rhys Isaac, *The Transformation of Virginia* (1982). For a more recent account, pivoting on ideas about gender, see Kathleen Brown, *Good Wives, Nasty Wenches, and Anxious Patriarchs* (1996). For native Virginia, see Helen C. Rountree, *Pocahontas's People* (1990), and Gregory A. Waselkov, Peter Wood, and Tom Hatley, eds., *Powhatan's Mantle* (2006).

In recent years there has been a surge in scholarship on African slavery in the New World. For a new and magisterial overview, see David Brion Davis, *Inhuman Bondage* (2006). For British North America, see Ira Berlin, *Many Thousands Gone* (1998), and Philip D. Morgan, *Slave Counterpoint* (1998). The classic account of the British Caribbean remains Richard Dunn's *Sugar and Slaves* (1972).

The Chesapeake has always drawn more notice from early American historians than South Carolina has, but in recent years some important studies have redressed that neglect. The best overview of that colony's development remains Robert Weir, *Colonial South Carolina* (1982). The complexities of Carolina's slave wars are explored in Alan Gallay, *The Indian Slave Trade* (2002). For fine explorations of more specialized topics, see Timothy Silver, *A New Face on the Countryside* (1990), and Christina Snyder, *Slavery in Indian Country,* (2010).

| 1675 | 1676 | 1680 | CA. 1700 | EARLY 1700s | 1700s | 1732 |

Bacon's Rebellion in Virginia

Pueblo Revolt in New Mexico

Rice boom begins in South Carolina

Average of 60,000 enslaved Africans cross the Atlantic annually

Height of Spanish mission system in Florida

Indian slave wars devastate much of the Southeast, especially Florida

Chartering of Georgia

of history and to discover in their performances some signs of personal salvation.

The divine plan, as the Puritans understood it, called for reforming both church and society along the lines laid down by John Calvin. It seemed to the Puritans that England's government hampered rather than promoted religious purity and social order. It tolerated drunkenness, theatergoing, gambling, extravagance, public swearing, and Sabbath-breaking. It permitted popular recreations rooted in pagan custom and superstition—sports such as bear baiting and maypole dancing and festivals such as the celebration of Christmas and saints' days.

Even worse, the state had not done enough to purify the English church of the "corruptions" of Roman Catholicism. The Church of England counted as its members everyone in the nation, saint and sinner alike. To the Puritans, belonging to a church was no birthright. They wished to limit membership and the privileges of baptism and communion to godly men and women. The Puritans also deplored the hierarchy of bishops and archbishops in the Church of England, as well as its elaborate ceremonies in which priests wore ornate vestments. Too many Anglican clergy were "dumb dogges" in Puritan eyes, too poorly educated to instruct churchgoers in the truths of Scripture or to deliver a decent sermon.

Because English monarchs refused to take stronger measures to reform church and society, the Puritans became their outspoken critics. Elizabeth I had tolerated this opposition, but James I would not endure it and intended to rid England of these radicals. With some of the Puritans, known as the Separatists, he seemed to succeed.

The Pilgrim Settlement at Plymouth Colony >> The Separatists were devout Congregationalists who concluded that the Church of England was too corrupt to be reformed. They abandoned Anglican worship and met secretly in small congregations. From their first appearance in England during the 1570s, the Separatists suffered persecution from the government—fines, imprisonment, and, in a few cases, execution. Always a tiny minority within the Puritan movement, the Separatists were people from humble backgrounds: craftworkers and farmers without influence to challenge the state. By 1608 some had become so discouraged that they migrated to Holland, where the Dutch government permitted complete freedom of religion. But when their children began to adopt

> They had arrived too late to plant crops and had failed to bring an adequate supply of food. By the spring of 1621, half the immigrants had died.

Dutch customs and other religions, some Separatists decided to move again, this time to Virginia.

It can only be imagined what fate would have befallen the unworldly Separatists had they actually settled in the Chesapeake during the tobacco boom. But a series of mistakes—including an error in charting the course of their ship, the *Mayflower*—brought the little band far to the North, to a region Captain John Smith had earlier dubbed "New England." In November 1620 some 88 Separatist "Pilgrims" set anchor at a place they called Plymouth on the coast of present-day southeastern Massachusetts. They were sick with scurvy, weak from malnutrition, and shaken by a shipboard mutiny, and neither the site nor the season invited settlement. As one of their leaders, William Bradford, later remembered:

> For summer being done, all things stand upon them with a weatherbeaten face, and the whole country, full of woods and thickets represented a savage hue. If they looked behind them, there was the mighty ocean which they had passed and was now as a main bar and gulf to separate them from all the civil parts of the world.

For some, the shock was too great. Dorothy Bradford, William's wife, is said to have fallen overboard from the *Mayflower* as it lay anchored off Plymouth. It is more likely that she jumped to her death.

Few Pilgrims could have foreseen founding the first permanent European settlement in New England, and many did not live long enough to enjoy the distinction. They had arrived too late to plant crops and had failed to bring an adequate supply of food. By the spring of 1621

Opinion

Did the Puritans really come to America for religious freedom?

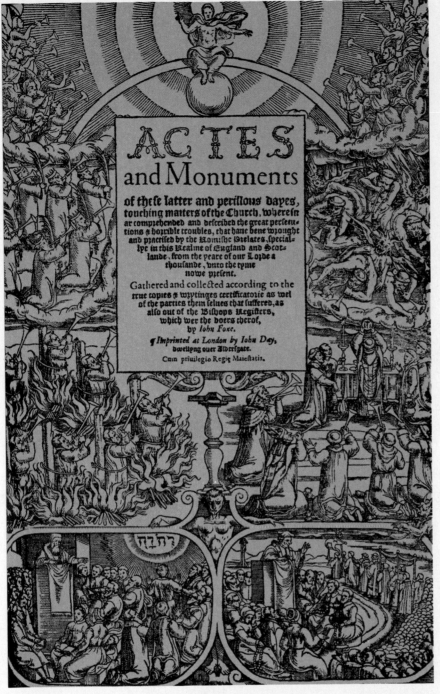

« John Foxe's *Actes and Monuments* (1563), a book revered by the Puritan founders of New England, arrayed the forces of righteousness (*left side of the illustration*) against a host of devil-worshiping priests and their sheeplike followers, who superstitiously hold rosary beads, lower right. Under the Catholic Queen Mary, Protestants were regarded as heretics, and some were burned at the stake (*middle left*).

reduced by as much as 90 percent. Abandoned villages lay in ruins up and down the coast, including the village of Patuxet, where the Pilgrims established Plymouth. Years later visitors would still marvel at heaps of unburied human remains dating from the epidemic.

The Wampanoags dominated the lands around Plymouth. Still reeling from loss in 1620 and eager to obtain trade goods and assistance against native enemies, Masasoit, their chief, agreed to help the starving colonists. At first, the peoples communicated through a remarkable Wampanoag named Squanto, who had been kidnapped by English sailors before the epidemic. Taken to Europe, Squanto learned English and returned to America in time to act as a mediator between Masasoit and the newcomers. The Pilgrims accepted Wampanoag hospitality and instruction, and invited native leaders to a feast in honor of their first successful harvest in 1621 (the genesis of the "First Thanksgiving" story).

The Pilgrims set up a government for their colony, the framework of which was the Mayflower Compact, drawn up on board ship before landing. That agreement provided for a governor and several assistants to advise him, all to be elected annually by Plymouth's adult males. In the eyes of English law the Plymouth settlers had no clear basis for their land claims or their government, for they had neither a royal charter nor approval from the Crown. But English authorities, distracted by problems closer to home, left the tiny colony of farmers alone.

half the immigrants had died. English merchants who had financed the *Mayflower* voyage failed to send supplies to the struggling settlement. Plymouth might have become another doomed colony except that the Pilgrims received better treatment from native inhabitants than they did from their English backers.

Though they understood it only dimly, the Pilgrims were, in one historian's memorable phrase, the "beneficiaries of catastrophe." Only four years before their arrival coastal New England had been devastated by a massive epidemic, possibly the plague. Losses varied locally, but overall the native coastal population may have been

The Puritan Settlement at Massachusetts Bay >>
Among the Crown's distractions were two groups of Puritans more numerous and influential than the Pilgrims. They included both the Presbyterians and the majority of Congregationalists who, unlike the Pilgrim Separatists, still considered the Church of England capable of being reformed. But the 1620s brought these Puritans only fresh discouragements. In 1625 Charles I inherited his father's throne and all his enemies. When Parliament attempted to

limit the king's power, Charles simply dissolved it, in 1629, and proceeded to rule without it. When Puritans pressed for reform, the king began to move against them.

This persecution swelled a second wave of Puritan migration that also drew from the ranks of Congregationalists. Unlike the humble Separatists, these emigrants included merchants, landed gentlemen, and lawyers who organized the Massachusetts Bay Company in 1629. Those able Puritan leaders aimed to build a better society in America, an example to the rest of the world. Unlike the Separatists, they had a strong sense of mission and destiny. They were not abandoning the English church, they insisted, but merely regrouping across the Atlantic for another assault on corruption.

 John Winthrop, first governor of the Massachusetts Bay Company.

Despite the company's Puritan leanings, it somehow obtained a royal charter confirming its title to most of present-day Massachusetts and New Hampshire. Advance parties in 1629 established the town of Salem on the coast well north of Plymouth. In 1630 the company's first governor, a tough-minded and visionary lawyer named John Winthrop, sailed from England with a dozen other company stockholders and a fleet of men and women to establish the town of Boston. The newcomers intended to build a godly "city on a hill" that would serve as an example to the world.

Once established in the Bay Colony, Winthrop and the other stockholders transformed the charter for their trading company into the framework of government for a colony. The company's governor became the colony's chief executive, and the company's other officers became the governor's assistants. The charter provided for annual elections of the governor and his assistants by company stockholders, known as the freemen. But to create a broad base of support for the new government, Winthrop and his assistants expanded the freemanship in 1631 to include every adult male church member.

The governor, his assistants, and the freemen together made up the General Court of the colony, which passed all laws, levied taxes, established courts, and made war and peace. In 1634 the whole body of the freemen stopped meeting and instead each town elected representatives or deputies to the General Court. Ten years later, the deputies formed themselves into the lower house of the Bay Colony legislature, and the assistants formed the upper house. By

refashioning a company charter into a civil constitution, Massachusetts Bay Puritans were well on the way to shaping society, church, and state to their liking.

Contrary to expectations, New England proved more hospitable to the English than did the Chesapeake. The character of the migration itself gave New England settlers an advantage, for most arrived in family groups—not as young, single, indentured servants of the sort whose discontents unsettled Virginia society. The heads of New England's first households were typically free men—farmers, artisans, and merchants. Most were skilled and literate. Since husbands usually migrated with their wives and children, the ratio of men to women within the population was fairly evenly balanced.

Most of the immigrants, some 21,000, came in a cluster between 1630 and 1642. Thereafter new arrivals tapered off because of the outbreak of the English Civil War. This relatively rapid colonization fostered solidarity, because immigrants shared a common past of persecution and a strong desire to create an ordered society modeled on Scripture.

✓ **REVIEW**

Who settled the earliest New England colonies, and why?

STABILITY AND ORDER IN EARLY NEW ENGLAND

Puritan emigrants and their descendants thrived in New England's bracing but healthy climate. The first generation of colonists lived to an average age of 70, nearly twice as long as Virginians and 10 years longer than men and women living in England. With 90 percent of all offspring reaching adulthood, the typical family consisted of seven or eight children who came to maturity. Because of low death rates and high birthrates, the number of New Englanders doubled about every 27 years—while the populations of

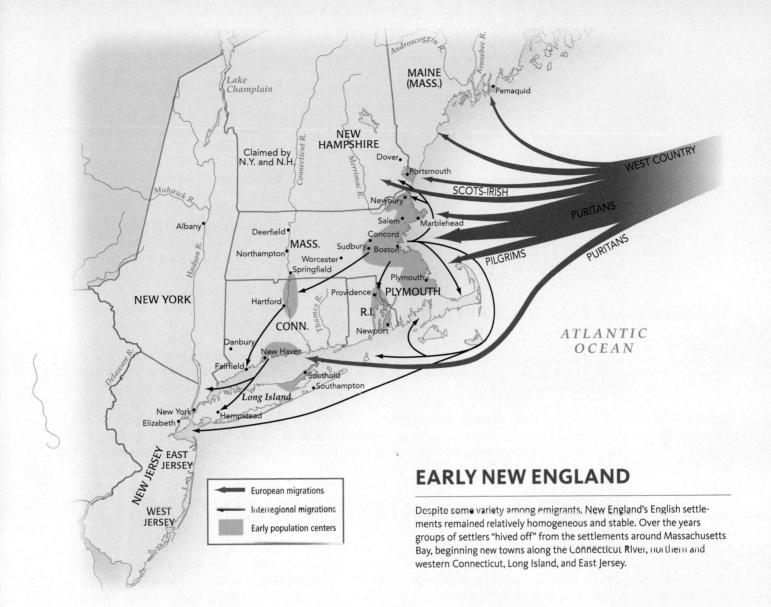

EARLY NEW ENGLAND

Despite some variety among emigrants, New England's English settlements remained relatively homogeneous and stable. Over the years groups of settlers "hived off" from the settlements around Massachusetts Bay, beginning new towns along the Connecticut River, northern and western Connecticut, Long Island, and East Jersey.

Europe and the Chesapeake barely reproduced themselves. By 1700 New England and the Chesapeake both had populations of approximately 100,000. But, whereas the southern population grew because of continuing immigration and the importation of slaves, New England's expanded primarily through natural increase.

Early immigrants to the Bay Colony carved out an arc of villages around Massachusetts Bay. Within a decade settlers pressed into Connecticut, Rhode Island, and New Hampshire. Connecticut and Rhode Island received separate charters from Charles II in the 1660s, guaranteeing their residents the rights to land and government. New Hampshire, at first part of Massachusetts, became a separate colony in 1679, whereas the handful of hardy souls living along the coast of present-day Maine still accepted the Massachusetts Bay Colony's authority.

Early New Englanders established most of their settlements with an eye to stability and order. Unlike

the Virginians, who scattered across the Chesapeake to isolated plantations, most New Englanders established tightly knit communities like those they had left behind in England. Each family received a lot for a house along with about 150 acres of land in nearby fields. Farmers left many of their acres uncultivated as a legacy for future generations, for most had only the labor of their own families to work their land. While the Chesapeake abounded with servants, tenant farmers, and slaves, almost every adult male in rural New England owned property. With little hope of prospering through commercial agriculture, New England farmers also had no incentive to import large numbers of servants and slaves or to create large plantations.

Strong family institutions contributed to New England's order and stability. While the early deaths of parents regularly splintered Chesapeake families, two adult generations were often on hand to encourage order within New England households. Husbands and fathers exacted

SUDBURY, MASSACHUSETTS

Everyday life in New England centered in small towns such as Sudbury, west of Boston. Families lived in houses clustered around the meeting house, in contrast to the decentralized plantations of the south. The privately held farm lots were mixed together as well, so that neighbors worked and lived in close contact with one another.

submission from wives and strict obedience from children. Land gave New England's long-lived fathers great authority over even their grown children; sons and daughters relied on paternal legacies of farms in order to marry and establish their own families.

Whereas churches were few and far between in seventeenth-century Virginia, they constituted the center of community life in colonial New England. Individual congregations ran their own affairs and regulated their own membership. Those wishing to join had to convince ministers and church members that they had experienced a genuine spiritual rebirth or "conversion." Most New Englanders sought and won membership. As majority institutions supported by public taxes, churches had the reach and the resources to oversee public morality, often censuring or expelling wayward neighbors. Still, ministers enjoyed less public power in New England than in the old country. New England's ministers did not serve as officers in the civil government, and the Congregational churches owned no property. In contrast, Catholic and Anglican church officials wielded real temporal power in European states, and the churches held extensive tracts of land.

Finally, New Englanders governed themselves more democratically than did their counterparts in England. Communities throughout the region held regular town meetings of all resident white men. The town fathers generally set the meeting's agenda and offered advice, but the unanimous consent of townsmen determined all decisions. Colony governments in early New England also evolved into representative and responsive institutions. Typically the central government of each colony, such as the General Court of Massachusetts Bay, consisted of a

governor and a bicameral legislature, including an upper house, or council, and a lower house, or assembly. All officials were elected annually by the freemen—white adult men entitled to vote in colony elections. Voting qualifications varied, but the number of men enfranchised made up a much broader segment of society than that in seventeenth-century England.

Communities in Conflict >>

Although most New Englanders called themselves Puritans and Congregationalists, the very fervency of their convictions often led them to disagree about how to carry out the teachings of the Bible and the ideas of John Calvin. During the first decades of colonization, such disagreements led to the founding of breakaway colonies. In 1636 Thomas Hooker, the minister of Cambridge, Massachusetts, led part of his congregation to establish the first English settlement in Connecticut. Somewhat more liberal than other Bay Puritans, Hooker favored more lenient standards for church membership. He also opposed the Bay's policy of limiting voting in colony elections to church members. In contrast, New Haven (a separate colony until it became part of Connecticut in 1662) was begun in 1638 by strict Congregationalists who found Massachusetts too liberal.

While Connecticut and New Haven emerged from voluntary migration, enforced exile filled Rhode Island with men and women whose radical ideas unsettled the rest of Massachusetts. Roger Williams, Rhode Island's founder, had come to New England in 1631, serving as a respected minister of Salem. But soon Williams announced that he was a Separatist, like the Pilgrims of Plymouth. He encouraged the Bay Colony to break all ties to the corrupt Church of England. He also urged a more complete **separation of Church and State** than most New Englanders were prepared to accept, and later in his career he endorsed full religious toleration. Finally, Williams denounced the Bay's charter—the legal document that justified Massachusetts's existence—on the grounds that the king had no right to grant land that he had not purchased from the Indians. When Williams boldly suggested that Massachusetts actually inform the king of his mistake, angry authorities prepared to deport him. Instead Williams fled the colony in the dead of winter to live with the Indians. In 1636 he

separation of Church and State principle that religious institutions and their representatives should exercise no civil or judicial powers and that civil governments should give no official sanction, privileges, or financial support to any religious denomination or organization.

became the founder and first citizen of Providence, later to be part of Rhode Island.

Another charismatic heretic from Massachusetts arrived soon after. Anne Hutchinson, a skilled midwife and the spouse of a wealthy merchant, came to Boston in 1634. Enthusiasm for her minister, John Cotton, started her on a course of explaining his sermons to gatherings of her neighbors—and then to elaborating ideas of her own. The fact that a woman would do such things made the authorities uneasy; they became positively alarmed when they learned that Hutchinson embraced controversial positions on doctrine. Soon a majority of the Bay's ministers accused the popular Hutchinson of holding heretical views. She in turn denounced her detractors, and the controversy escalated. In 1638 the Bay Colony government expelled Hutchinson and her followers for sedition. She settled briefly in Rhode Island before moving on to Long Island, where she died in an Indian attack.

Goodwives and Witches >>

If Anne Hutchinson had been a man, her ideas would still have been deemed heretical. However, if she had been a man, she might have found other ways to express her intelligence and magnetism. But life in colonial New England offered women, especially married women, little scope for their talents.

Most adult women were hardworking farm wives who cared for large households of children. Between marriage and middle age, most New England wives were pregnant except when breast-feeding. When they were not nursing or minding children, mothers were producing and preparing much of what was consumed and worn by their families. They planted vegetable gardens and pruned fruit trees, salted beef and pork and pressed cider, milked cows and churned butter, kept bees and tended poultry, cooked and baked, washed and ironed, spun, wove, and sewed. While husbands and sons engaged in farm work that changed with the seasons, took trips to taverns and mills, and went off to hunt or fish, housebound wives and daughters were locked into a humdrum routine with little time for themselves.

Women suffered legal disadvantages as well. In contrast to New Mexico and Florida with their Spanish civil law traditions, English common law and colonial legal codes accorded married women virtually no control over property. Wives could not sue or be sued, they could not

> Like most early modern Europeans, New Englanders believed in wizards and witches, men and women who were said to acquire supernatural powers by signing a compact with Satan.

make contracts, and they surrendered to their husbands any property that they had possessed before marriage. Divorce was almost impossible to obtain until the late eighteenth century. Only widows and a few single women had the same property rights as men, but they could not vote in colony elections.

The one arena in which women could attain something approaching equal standing with men was the churches. Puritan women could not become ministers, but after the 1660s they made up the majority of church members. In some churches membership enabled them to vote for ministerial candidates and to voice opinions about admitting and disciplining members. Puritan doctrine itself rejected the medieval Catholic suspicion of women as "a necessary evil," seeing them instead as "a necessary good." Even so, the Puritan ideal of the virtuous woman was a chaste, submissive "helpmeet," a wife and mother who served God by serving men.

Communities sometimes responded to assertive women with accusations of witchcraft. Like most early modern Europeans, New Englanders believed in wizards and witches, men and women who were said to acquire supernatural powers by signing a compact with Satan. A total of 344 New Englanders were charged with witchcraft during the first colonial century, with the notorious Salem Village episode of 1692 producing the largest outpouring of accusations and 20 executions. More than three-quarters of all accused witches were women, usually middle-aged and older, and most of those accused were regarded as unduly independent. Before they were charged with witchcraft, many had been suspected of heretical religious beliefs, others of sexual impropriety. Still others had inherited or stood to inherit property.

The People in the Way >>

Whatever their political battles, doctrinal disputes, and inequalities, New Englanders were all participants in a colonial project that depended on taking land from other people. At the time of first contact, perhaps 100,000 Algonquian men and women lived in the area reaching from the Kennebec River in Maine to Cape Cod. Like the Puritans, they relied on fishing in spring and summer, hunting year round, and cultivating and harvesting corn and other crops in spring and fall. To an even greater degree than among the colonists, Indian political authority was local. Within each village, a single leader known as the "sachem" or "sagamore" directed economic life, administered justice, and negotiated with other tribes and English settlers. As with New England's town fathers, a sachem's power depended on keeping the trust and consent of his people.

Thus, the newcomers had more in common with their hosts than they cared to admit. But English expansion in the region had to come at someone's expense, and colonists obtained Indian lands in one of three ways. Sometimes they purchased it. Sales varied—they might be free and fair, fraudulent, subtly coerced, or forced through intimidation and violence. Second, colonists eagerly expanded into lands emptied by epidemics. The English often saw God's hand in such events. "Without this remarkable and terrible stroke of God upon the natives," wrote one New Englander after a smallpox epidemic, "[we] would with much more difficulty have found room" to settle.

Third and finally, colonists commonly encouraged and participated in regional wars to obtain native lands. This proved easy enough to do, because, like Europeans, the Indians of New England quarreled frequently with neighboring nations. The antagonism among the English, Spanish, Dutch, and French was matched by the hostilities among the Abenakis, Pawtuckets, Massachusetts, Narragansetts, and Wampanoags of the north Atlantic coast. Epidemics only intensified existing rivalries, because they opened up new opportunities for stronger neighbors to press their advantage.

The English began by aligning with Masasoit and his Wampanoags against other coastal peoples in New England. In 1637 colonial forces joined the Narragansetts in a campaign against the formidable Pequots, who controlled coveted territory in Connecticut. The colonists shocked even their Indian allies when they set fire to the main Pequot village, killing hundreds of men, women, and children. Plymouth's William Bradford recalled that "it was a fearful sight to see them thus frying in the fire, and the streams of blood quenching the same, and horrible was the stink and scent thereof; but the victory seemed a sweet sacrifice, and they gave the praise thereof to God, who had wrought so wonderfully for them." Several years later the colonists turned against their former allies, joining forces with the Mohegans to intimidate the Narragansetts into ceding much of their territory. Only a few colonists objected to those ruthless policies, among them Roger Williams. "God Land," he warned one Connecticut leader, "will be . . . as great a God with us English as God Gold was with the Spaniards."

Metacom's War >>

Throughout these wars, the colonists more or less nurtured their original alliance with Masasoit and his Wampanoags. Indeed, certain colonists tried to bring the two societies closer together. While the impulse to convert was not nearly as strong in New England as in New Spain or New France, a few Englishmen worked tirelessly to bring the word of their God to Indians.

Puritan minister John Eliot began preaching in Algonquian in the 1640s. Over the next two decades he oversaw a project to publish the scriptures in Algonquian using the Latin alphabet. He also trained scores of native ministers (many of whom became literate), and established seven villages or "praying towns" for Christian Indians. Eliot was not alone. Harvard College defined its mission as "the education of English & Indian youth of this Country" and in 1655 established an Indian college and dormitory on campus. None of these efforts embodied respect for Indian culture or religion. But some New Englanders, at least, wanted to assimilate Indians rather than drive them away.

And yet the colony always grasped for more land. Over time the Puritan-Wampanoag partnership had become a relationship of subordination and suspicion. Rumors of potential native rebellion led colonial authorities to conduct humiliating interrogations and put in place

Point of View

Squanto's Advice

"Contrary to what American myth has long held, it is quite unlikely that alewives or other fish were used as fertilizer in Indian fields, notwithstanding the legendary role of the Pilgrims' friend Squanto in teaching colonists this practice. Squanto probably learned the technique while being held captive in Europe . . ."

WILLIAM CRONON, *Changes in the Land: Indians, Colonists, and the Ecology of New England*

severe rules and restrictions. The colonists' cows and pigs invaded and destroyed Indian fields, provoking innumerable conflicts. When Indians tried to adapt by raising their own cows and pigs, colonial authorities barred them from using common pasture or selling meat in Boston. At the same time, as many as half the dwindling Wampanoags had followed Eliot into the praying towns, threatening tribal unity in a time of mounting crisis.

By 1675 such pressures convinced Masasoit's son and heir, Metacom, whom the English called King Philip, that his nation could be preserved only by chancing war. Complaining that the English were plotting to kill him and other sachems and replace them with Christian Indians more willing to sell land, Metacom rallied most of southern New England's native peoples and laid waste to more than two dozen towns in Plymouth Colony. By the spring of 1676, Metacom's warriors were raiding settlements within 20 miles of Boston. The offensive threatened New England's very existence.

But its momentum could not be sustained. Faced with shortages of food and ammunition, Metacom asked assistance from the Abenakis of Maine and the Mahicans of New York. Both refused. In the summer of 1676 Metacom died in battle; colonial forces brought his severed head to Boston and his hands to Plymouth as trophies. His desperate gamble exhausted native military power in southern New England and virtually destroyed the Wampanoags as a coherent people.

In proportion to population, "King Philip's War" inflicted twice the casualties on New England that the United States as a whole would suffer in the American Civil War. But in the end the region's surviving Indians, Christian or not, found themselves consigned to quiet and often desperate lives on the margins of colonial life.

⌃ Though no images of Metacom survive from his time, in later years artists frequently portrayed him. This image is based on an engraving by Paul Revere.

 REVIEW

What were the sources of stability and conflict in early New England?

THE MID-ATLANTIC COLONIES

The inhabitants of the mid-Atlantic colonies—New York, New Jersey, Pennsylvania, and Delaware—enjoyed more secure lives than did most southern colonials. But they lacked the common bonds that lent stability to early New England. Instead, throughout the mid-Atlantic region a variety of ethnic and religious groups vied for wealth from farming and the fur trade and contended bitterly against governments that commanded little popular support.

English Rule in New York >> By the 1660s the Dutch experiment on the mid-Atlantic coast was faltering. While Fort Orange continued to secure furs for the Dutch West India Company, the colonial population remained small and fractious. The company made matters worse by appointing corrupt, dictatorial governors who ruled without an elective assembly. It also provided little protection for outlying Dutch settlements; when it did attack neighboring Indian nations, it did so savagely, triggering terrible retaliations. By the time the company went bankrupt in 1654, it had virtually abandoned its American colony.

Taking advantage of the disarray in New Netherlands, Charles II ignored Dutch claims in North America and granted his brother, James, the Duke of York, a proprietary charter there. The charter granted James all of New Netherlands to Delaware Bay as well as Maine, Martha's Vineyard, and Nantucket Island. In 1664 James sent an invading fleet, whose mere arrival caused the Dutch to surrender.

New York's dizzying diversity would make it difficult to govern. The Duke inherited 9,000 or so colonists: Dutch, Belgians, French, English, Portuguese, Swedes, Finns, and Africans—some enslaved, others free. The colony's ethnic diversity ensured a variety of religions. Although the Dutch Reformed church predominated, other early New Netherlanders included Lutherans, **Quakers**, and Catholics. There were Jews as well, refugees from Portuguese Brazil, who were required by law to live in a ghetto in New Amsterdam. The Dutch resented English rule, and only after a generation of intermarriage and acculturation did that resentment fade. James also failed to win friends among New Englanders who had come to Long Island seeking autonomy and cheap land during the 1640s. He grudgingly gave in to their demand for an elective assembly in 1683 but rejected its first act, the Charter of Liberties, which would have guaranteed basic political

Quakers Protestant sect, also known as the Society of Friends, founded in mid-seventeenth century England. The Quakers believed that the Holy Spirit dwelt within each human being and that religious conviction was the source of their egalitarian social practices, which included allowing women to speak in churches and to preach in public gatherings.

rights. The chronic political strife discouraged prospective settlers. By 1698 the colony numbered only 18,000 inhabitants, and New York City, the former New Amsterdam, was an overgrown village of a few thousand.

The Founding of New Jersey >> Confusion attended New Jersey's beginnings. The lands lying west of the Hudson and east of the Delaware River had been part of the Duke of York's proprietary grant. But in 1664 he gave about 5 million of these acres to Lord Berkeley and Sir George Carteret, two of his favorites who were already involved in the proprietary colonies of the Carolinas. New Jersey's new owners guaranteed settlers land, religious freedom, and a representative assembly in exchange for a small quitrent, an annual fee for the use of the land. The proprietors' terms promptly drew Puritan settlers from New Haven, Connecticut. At the same time, unaware that James had already given New Jersey to Berkeley and Carteret, New York's Governor Richard Nicolls granted Long Island Puritans land there.

More complications ensued when Berkeley and Carteret decided to divide New Jersey into east and west and sell both halves to Quaker investors—a prospect that outraged New Jersey's Puritans. Although some English Quakers migrated to West Jersey, the investors quickly decided that two Jerseys were less desirable than one Pennsylvania and resold both East and West Jersey to speculators. In the end the Jerseys became a patchwork of religious and ethnic groups. Settlers who shared a common religion or national origin formed communities and established small family farms. When the Crown finally reunited east and west as a single royal colony in 1702, New Jersey was overshadowed by settlements not only to the north but now, also, to the south and west.

Quaker Odysseys >> Religious and political idealism similar to that of the Puritans inspired the colonization of Pennsylvania, making it an oddity among the mid-Atlantic colonies. The oddity began with an improbable founder, William Penn. Young Penn devoted his early years to disappointing his distinguished father, Sir William Penn, an admiral in the Royal Navy. Several years after being expelled from college, young Penn finally chose a career that may have made the admiral yearn for mere disappointment: he undertook a lifelong commitment

to put into practice Quaker teachings. By the 1670s he had emerged as an acknowledged leader of the Society of Friends, as the Quakers formally called themselves.

The Quakers behaved in ways and believed in ideas that most people regarded as odd. They dressed in a deliberately plain and severe manner. They withheld from their social superiors the customary marks of respect, such as bowing, kneeling, and removing their hats. They refused to swear oaths or to make war. They allowed women public roles of religious leadership. That pattern of behavior reflected their egalitarian ideals, the belief that all men and women shared equally in the "Light Within." Some 40,000 English merchants, artisans, and farmers embraced Quakerism by 1660, and many suffered fines, imprisonment, and corporal punishment.

Since the English upper class has always prized eccentricity among its members, it is not surprising that Penn, despite his Quakerism, remained a favorite of Charles II. More surprising is that the king's favor took the extravagant form of presenting Penn in 1681 with all the land between New Jersey and Maryland. Perhaps the king was repaying Penn for the large sum that his father had lent the Stuarts. Or perhaps the king was hoping to export England's Quakers to an American colony governed by his trusted personal friend.

Penn envisioned that his proprietary colony would provide a refuge for Quakers while producing quitrents for himself. To publicize his colony, he distributed pamphlets praising its attractions throughout the British Isles and Europe. The response was overwhelming: by 1700 its population stood at 21,000. The only early migration of equal magnitude was the Puritan colonization of New England.

> The Quakers behaved in ways and believed in ideas that most people regarded as odd. They dressed in a deliberately plain and severe manner. They refused to swear oaths or to make war. They allowed women public roles of religious leadership.

Patterns of Growth >> Perhaps half of Pennsylvania's settlers arrived as indentured servants, while the families of free farmers and artisans made up the rest. The majority were Quakers from Britain, Holland, and Germany, but the colonists also included Catholics, Lutherans, Baptists, Anglicans, and Presbyterians. In 1682 when Penn purchased and annexed the Three Lower Counties (later the colony of Delaware), his colony included the 1,000 or so Dutch, Swedes, and Finns living there.

Quakers from other colonies—West Jersey, Maryland, and New England—also flocked to the new homeland. Those experienced settlers brought skills and connections

⌃ The tidy, productive farmsteads of the Pennsylvania countryside were the basis of that colony's prosperity during the eighteenth century. Their produce fueled the growth of Philadelphia and sustained the expansion of sugar plantations on England's Caribbean islands.

that contributed to Pennsylvania's rapid economic growth. Farmers sowed their rich lands into a sea of wheat, which merchants exported to the Caribbean. The center of the colony's trade was Philadelphia, a superb natural harbor situated at the confluence of the Delaware and Schuylkill rivers.

In contrast to New England's landscape of villages, the Pennsylvania countryside beyond Philadelphia was dotted with dispersed farmsteads. Commercial agriculture required larger farms, which kept settlers at greater distances from one another. As a result, the county rather than the town became the basic unit of local government in Pennsylvania.

Another reason that farmers did not need to cluster their homes within a central village was that they were at peace with the coastal Indians, the Lenni Lenapes (also called Delawares by the English). Thanks to two

Quaker beliefs—a commitment to pacifism and the conviction that the Indians rightfully owned their land—peace prevailed between native inhabitants and newcomers. Before Penn sold any land to colonists, he purchased it from the Indians. He also prohibited the sale of alcohol to the tribe, strictly regulated the fur trade, and learned the language of the Lenni Lenapes. "Not a language spoken in Europe," he remarked, "hath words of more sweetness in Accent and Emphasis than theirs."

"Our Wilderness flourishes as a Garden," Penn declared late in 1683, and in fact, his colony lived up to its promises. New arrivals readily acquired good land on liberal terms, while Penn's Frame of Government instituted a representative assembly and guaranteed all inhabitants the basic English civil liberties and complete freedom of worship.

Quakers and Politics >>

Even so, Penn's colony suffered constant political strife. Rich investors whom he had rewarded with large tracts of land and trade monopolies dominated the council, which held the sole power to initiate legislation. That power and Penn's own claims as proprietor set the stage for controversy. Members of the representative assembly battled for the right to initiate legislation. Farmers opposed Penn's efforts to collect quitrents. The Three Lower Counties agitated for separation, their inhabitants feeling no loyalty to Penn or Quakerism.

Penn finally bought peace at the price of approving a complete revision of his original Frame of Government. In 1701 the Charter of Privileges, Pennsylvania's new constitution, stripped the council of its legislative power, leaving it only the role of advising the governor. The charter also limited Penn's privileges as proprietor to the ownership of ungranted land and the power to veto legislation. Thereafter an elective unicameral assembly, the only single-house legislature in the colonies, dominated Pennsylvania's government.

As Pennsylvania prospered, Philadelphia became the commercial and cultural center of England's North American empire. Gradually the interior of Pennsylvania filled with immigrants—mainly Germans and Scots-Irish—who harbored no "odd" ideas about Indian rights, and the Lenni Lenapes and other native peoples were bullied into moving farther west. As for William Penn, he returned to England and spent time in a debtors' prison after being defrauded by his unscrupulous colonial agents. He died in 1718, an ocean away from his American utopia.

 REVIEW

In what ways were the Mid-Atlantic colonies more diverse than the other colonies of the period?

ADJUSTMENT TO EMPIRE

Whatever Penn's personal disappointments, his colony had enjoyed spectacular growth—as had British North America more generally. And yet by the 1680s England's king had reason to complain. Although North America now abounded in places named in honor of English monarchs, the colonies themselves lacked any strong ties to the English state. Until Parliament passed the first Navigation Acts in 1660, England had not even set in place a coherent policy for regulating colonial trade. And the acts had not produced the desired sense of patriotism in the colonies. While Chesapeake planters grumbled over the customs duties levied on tobacco, New Englanders, the worst of the lot, ignored the Navigation Acts altogether and traded openly with the Dutch. Royally appointed proprietors increasingly met defiance in New York, New Jersey, the Carolinas, and Pennsylvania. If England were to prosper from colonies as Spain's monarchs had, the crown needed to take matters in hand.

The Dominion of New England >>

The crown did so in 1686. At the urging of the new King James II (formerly the Duke of York), the Lords of Trade consolidated the colonies of Connecticut, Plymouth, Massachusetts Bay, Rhode Island, and New Hampshire into a single entity to be ruled by a royal governor and a royally appointed council. By 1688 James had added New York and New Jersey to that domain, called the Dominion of New England. Showing the typical Stuart distaste for representative government, James also abolished all northern colonial assemblies. The king's aim to centralize authority over such a large territory made the Dominion not only a royal dream but also a radical experiment in English colonial administration.

The experiment failed spectacularly. In England James II revealed himself to be yet another Stuart who tried to dispense with Parliament and who had embraced Catholicism besides. In a quick, bloodless coup d'état known as the Glorious Revolution, Parliament forced James into exile in 1688. In his place it elevated to the throne his daughter, Mary, and her Dutch husband, William of Orange. Mary was a distinctly better sort of Stuart—a staunch Protestant—and she agreed to rule with Parliament.

William and Mary officially dismembered the Dominion of New England and reinstated representative assemblies everywhere in the northern colonies. Connecticut and Rhode Island were restored their old charters, but Massachusetts received a new charter in 1691. Under its terms Massachusetts, Plymouth, and present-day Maine were combined into a single royal colony headed by a governor appointed by the Crown rather than elected by the people. The charter also imposed religious toleration and made property ownership rather than church membership the basis of voting rights.

Royal Authority in America in 1700 >>

William and Mary were more politic than James II, but no less interested in revenue. In 1696 Parliament enlarged the number of customs officials stationed in each colony to enforce the Navigation Acts. To prosecute smugglers, Parliament established colonial vice-admiralty courts, tribunals without juries presided over by royally appointed justices. To keep current on colonial matters, the king appointed a new Board of Trade to replace the old Lords of Trade. The new enforcement procedures generally succeeded in discouraging smuggling and channeling colonial trade through England.

These changes strengthened royal control enough to satisfy England's monarchs for the next half century. By 1700 Virginia, New York, Massachusetts, and New Hampshire all had royal governments. New Jersey, the Carolinas, and Georgia would soon join that list. Royal rule meant that the monarch appointed governors and (everywhere except Massachusetts) also appointed their councils. Royally appointed councils could veto any law passed by a colony's representative assembly, royally appointed governors could veto any law passed by both houses, and the Crown could veto any law passed by both houses and approved by the governor.

Even so, the sway of royal power remained more apparent than real after 1700. The Glorious Revolution asserted once and for all that Parliament's authority—rule by the legislative branch of government—would be supreme in the governing of England. In the colonies, members of representative assemblies grew more skilled at dealing with royal governors and more protective of their rights. They guarded most jealously their strongest lever of power—the right of the lower houses to levy taxes.

The political reality of the assemblies' power reflected a social reality as well. No longer mere outposts along the Atlantic, the colonies of 1700 were becoming more firmly rooted societies. Their laws and traditions were based not only on what they had brought from England but also on the conditions of life in America. That social reality had already blocked Stuart ambitions to shape the future of North America, just as it had thwarted the designs of lordly proprietors and the dreams of religious reformers.

 REVIEW

How did William and Mary try to increase colonial revenue?

Still, the dream of empire would revive among England's rulers in the middle of the eighteenth century—in part

⌃ England, in an effort to regulate colonial trade, required all ships bound from America to pass through British ports and pay customs duties. Places such as Plymouth, Liverpool, and Bristol (*shown here*) thrived as a result.

because French kings had never abandoned their own imperial visions. France had long been Europe's largest and most populous kingdom. By the 1660s bureaucratic, financial, and political reforms made it the mightiest military power as well. Eager to expand on the continent, France's ambitious king, Louis XIV, unleashed his titanic war machine against his neighbors four times between 1667–1714.

Even after 1714 France, England and, to a lesser extent, Spain waged a kind of cold war for a quarter of a century, jockeying for position and influence. Western European monarchs had come to realize that confrontations in North America's vast and distant interior could affect their wars closer to home. In this global chess game, the British had the advantage of numbers: nearly 400,000 subjects in the colonies in 1720, compared with only about 25,000 French spread along a thin line of fishing stations and fur-trading posts, and a meager 5,000 or so Spaniards in New Mexico, Texas, and Florida. But by a considerable margin, native peoples still represented the majority population in North America. Moreover, they still controlled more than 90 percent of its territory. If events in North America could effect the balance of power in Europe, then French and Spanish administrators could still believe that their Indian alliances might yet help them prevail against each other, and, especially, against Britain's booming colonies.

CHAPTER SUMMARY

While the French colonized Canada, the Protestant Reformation in England spurred the colonization of New England and Pennsylvania.

- During the seventeenth century, the French slowly established a fur trade, agricultural communities, and religious institutions in Canada while building Indian alliances throughout the Mississippi drainage.
- Competition over the fur trade in New France and New Netherlands contributed to a devastating series of wars between Iroquois, Hurons, and dozens of other Indian groups.
- Over the same period, English Puritans planted more populous settlements between Maine and Long Island.
- The migration of family groups and a rough equality of wealth lent stability to early New England society, reinforced by the settlers' shared commitment to Puritanism and a strong tradition of self-government.
- The mid-Atlantic colonies also enjoyed a rapid growth of people and wealth, but political wrangling as well as ethnic and religious diversity made for a higher level of social conflict.

Significant Events

Formation of the Iroquois League

LATE 1500s

Cartier makes first voyage to the Gulf of St. Lawrence

1535

Champlain founds Québec

1608

Epidemic devastates native peoples of the coastal Northeast

1616–1618

Puritans settle at abandoned village of Patuxet and rename it Plymouth

1620

Dutch found New Netherlands

1624

Winthrop fleet arrives in Massachusetts Bay; Boston established

1630

- Whereas New Englanders attempted to subdue native peoples, colonists in the mid-Atlantic enjoyed more harmonious relations with the region's original inhabitants, thanks in part to William Penn's Quaker principles.
- The efforts of the later Stuart kings to centralize England's empire ended with the Glorious Revolution in 1688, which greatly reduced tensions between the colonies and the parent country.

Additional Reading

For introductions to French and Indian encounters, see Olive Patricia Dickason, *Canada's First Nations* (1992) and Bruce G. Trigger, *Natives and Newcomers* (1995). Colin G. Calloway's *One Vast Winter Count* (2003) masterfully synthesizes the history of natives and Europeans in early North America west of the Appalachians, and Daniel K. Richter does the same for Eastern North America in *Facing East from Indian Country* (2001). For a recent history of Dutch America, see Jaap Jacobs, *New Netherland* (2005). Daniel K. Richter's *Ordeal of the Longhouse* (1992) presents a powerful portrait of the Iroquois before, during, and after the Beaver Wars. For important recent work on Indians in Colonial New England, see Jenny Hale Pulsipher, *Subjects unto the Same King* (2008) and David Silverman's *Faith and Boundaries* (2005). To understand the appeal of Puritanism, the best book to read is Charles Cohen, *God's Caress* (1986). For Puritanism in New England, read Stephen Foster's masterly study, *The Long Argument* (1991). And to learn more about the diversity of religious and supernatural views in New England, consult Philip Gura, *A Glimpse of Sion's Glory* (1984), and David Hall, *Worlds of Wonder, Days of Judgment* (1989).

For the everyday lives of northern colonists in New England and New York, rely on Virginia Dejohn Anderson's *New England's Generation* (1991), and Joyce Goodfriend's *Before the Melting Pot* (1991). The best assessment of British imperial policy in the late seventeenth century is Richard R. Johnson, *Adjustment to Empire* (1981). For the complex interplay among English colonialism, environmental change, and Indian power in the Northeast, see William Cronon's classic *Changes in the Land* (1983). The event and memory of "King Philip's War" is the subject of Jill Lepore's *The Name of War* (1998).

1637	1664	1675–1676	1681	1682	1688	1692

New Netherlands becomes English New York; founding of New Jersey

Metacom's War

Founding of Pennsylvania

Pequot War

La Salle becomes first European to descend the Mississippi to its mouth

Glorious Revolution; William and Mary become monarchs of England

Witchcraft trials in Salem

Eighteenth-Century America 1689–1768

>> AN AMERICAN STORY

THE TALE OF A TATTOOED TRAVELER

August 13, 1720: Morning sunlight reaches across the junction of the Platte and Loup Rivers in what today is Nebraska. Jean L'Archevêque rises stiffly from where he slept and looks about camp. Spanish soldiers don their wide-brimmed hats, and Pueblo Indian warriors talk softly to one another in the early light. A friar in his habit makes his way around the tents. Don Pedro de Villasur, lieutenant governor of New Mexico and leader of the party, threads his arms through a bright red officer's coat and orders the soldiers to bring in their horses. >>

Born in 1672 in Bayonne, France, L'Archevêque had followed a tangled path to that spot in Nebraska. Fleeing family bankruptcy, he was only a boy when he boarded ship to the French Caribbean and joined a scheme to colonize coastal Louisiana. Led by the famous French explorer René Robert Cavelier, Sieur de La Salle (the first European to navigate the immense Mississippi), L'Archevêque and nearly 300 colonists enlisted in the venture had reason for optimism.

But things sometimes go badly for kings and their servants. La Salle and his followers wound up shipwrecked on the coast of present-day Texas and proceeded to starve, sicken, and die. Weakened survivors blamed their leader and in 1687 hatched a plan to be rid of him. Young L'Archevêque seems to have played a part, distracting the great explorer while an accomplice blew his head apart with a musket shot. Jean and the other murderers soon found themselves unhappy guests among Caddo Indians in east Texas. The Caddos tattooed the Frenchmen's faces, carefully inserting a dye made from walnuts into countless tiny cuts. In 1690 Spanish explorers stumbled across L'Archevêque and a companion, ransomed the grateful pair from the Caddos, and sent them off in chains for interrogation in Mexico City, Spain, and then back to Mexico.

L'Archevêque had become a pawn in a high-stakes game. News of La Salle's stillborn colony convinced Spanish officials that they needed to secure their claims on the North American West and stop France from using the region as a base for threatening New Spain and its all too famous silver mines. Crucially, Spain had to reconquer New Mexico. Popé's Pueblo Revolt of 1680 had expelled the Spanish (Chapter 3), but the determined unity of the diverse Pueblo villages collapsed within a dozen years. When Spanish colonists returned in 1692 under Diego de Vargas, they met only fragmented resistance.

In reconquered New Mexico L'Archevêque found his first real home since boyhood. Sent north perhaps because of his facility not only with French but also Indian languages, L'Archevêque prospered in Santa Fe, marrying well and gaining the trust of his neighbors. But eventually the Spanish began hearing complaints from the Plains Apaches about Pawnee raiders armed with French guns. Sensing a threat, in 1719 New Mexico's governor ordered his lieutenant Villasur to take L'Archevêque and a mixed group of Indian and Spanish fighters to confront the French—hence the long trek to the Platte River the following summer, where the men awoke at daybreak on August 13 to do the king's business.

But things sometimes go badly for kings and their servants. Moments after ordering his men to bring in their horses, Villasur heard wild screams as dozens of painted Pawnee warriors rushed his camp. The lieutenant governor was one of the first to die, mouth agape just outside his tent; the well-traveled L'Archevêque fell soon after. Only 13 Spaniards and 40 Pueblo warriors escaped to bring the doleful news to Santa Fe, where for generations residents remembered the ambush as one of the great calamities of their history.

That a merchant's boy from Bayonne, France, could be shipwrecked, recruited to murder, tattooed in Texas, imprisoned in Mexico and Spain, married and made respectable on the Upper Rio Grande, and finally shot dead and buried somewhere in Nebraska, testifies in a very personal way to the unpredictable changes roiling eighteenth-century North America. As Europeans established colonies and began competing with one another across the continent, native peoples found life changing at astonishing speed. Europeans, with their animals, plants, technologies, diseases, and designs, sparked a fever pitch of transformation. But Europeans could not predict and did not control the process. Despite their grand ambitions, colonial newcomers often found their own plans upended and their lives reordered by the same forces reworking native life. **«**

CRISIS AND TRANSFORMATION IN NORTHERN NEW SPAIN

As European rivals laid claim to more and more of North America, nervous Spanish officials stared at their maps. Around the former Aztec empire, Spain controlled enormous cities, booming towns, and agricultural villages—a region still home to millions despite waves of epidemics. Though drier and less populated, the lands hundreds of miles north boasted remarkable silver mines. To protect these places from French designs, Spain had to start paying more attention to the blank spaces still farther north on their maps—spaces entirely controlled by Indians.

Defensive Expansion into Texas »

Nowhere did the French seem more menacing than in Texas, one of the many blank spots on Spanish maps. La

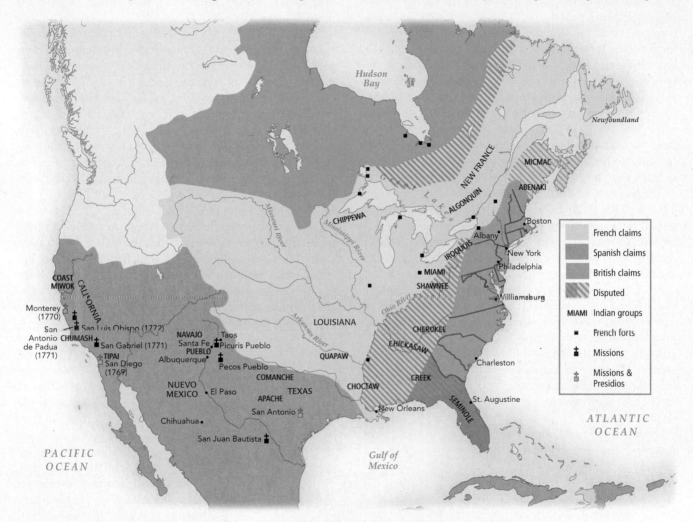

EUROPEAN TERRITORIAL CLAIMS IN THE EIGHTEENTH CENTURY

The French, English, and Indian nations all jockeyed for power and position across North America during the eighteenth century. The French expanded their fur trade through the interior, while the English at midcentury began to press the barrier of the Appalachians. But native peoples still controlled the vast majority of the continent and often held the balance of power in inter-imperial struggles.

Salle's adventure could have turned out differently: before his grisly death, the Frenchman pledged to invade northern New Spain with an army of thousands of Indians who, he believed, had "a deadly hatred of the Spaniards." Fearful that another French expedition might actually acquire such an army, in 1690 Spain began establishing missions among the native peoples of Texas. By the early 1720s the Spanish had fortified their claim on Texas with ten Franciscan missions, four presidios (military garrisons), and the beginnings of a civilian settlement on the San Antonio River.

Still, missions disappointed Franciscans and natives alike. Missionaries baptized Indians by the thousands and hoped to create orderly, regimented communities where converts could be shielded from outside influence and taught to be industrious and devout. But Indians insisted on coming and going when they pleased. Many sought the food and sanctuary missions offered, only to leave periodically to rendezvous with kin, hunt, and harvest wild plant foods. Their comings and goings confounded the missionaries. Matters were even worse for Franciscans in east Texas, where sedentary and relatively prosperous Caddos had no need of Spanish crops or protection and preferred to trade with the more liberal French in Louisiana.

However successful they were at retaining autonomy, Indians throughout Texas paid a steep price for any benefits they wrung from missions. Those compelled inside by hunger and insecurity often endured harsh discipline and corporal punishment for disobeying orders. Worse, missions proved ideal vectors for epidemic disease. In the 1730s alone smallpox killed more than 1,000 mission Indians near San Antonio. Other illnesses became commonplace in what were often filthy, cramped buildings. Children found missions especially dangerous. In eighteenth-century Mission San Antonio, for example, only one in three newborns survived to their third birthday.

Meanwhile, royal administrators encouraged Spanish emigration to Texas—but with little success. In 1731 the province's nonnative population barely amounted to 500 men, women, and children; by 1760 that figure had slightly more than doubled. In 1778 a Franciscan inspector described San Antonio, Texas's major civilian settlement, as "a town so miserable that it resembles a most wretched village." He counted "59 houses of stone and mud, and 79 of wood, but all poorly built." After many decades

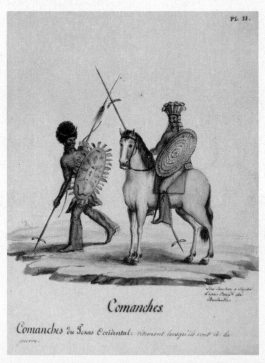

PL. 11.

Comanches

Comanches du Texas Occidental tellement lorsqu'ils vont à la guerre.

⌃ Comanche warriors painted by Lino Sanchez y Tapia.

Spain's push into Texas had created only a slender archipelago of missions, presidios, and a few towns.

Crisis and Rebirth in New Mexico ≫

Elsewhere the region remained in the hands of unconquered Indians whose regional power only seemed to be expanding. At first Apaches did most to threaten Spain's ambitions in Texas. Their raids thinned Spanish herds, prevented ranching and farming communities from expanding, and threatened missions with destruction. Spaniards responded with merciless slave raids on Apache camps, and the violence escalated.

By the 1730s, however, a new force appeared to eclipse even Apaches. They called themselves Nʉmʉnʉʉ, "the People." Their enemies came to call them Comanches. Emerging from the foothills of the Rockies in the late sixteenth century, Comanches acquired horses, moved permanently onto the Plains, and quickly became some of the most formidable equestrian warriors in history. They allied with Indians who could provide them French guns and ammunition from Louisiana and embarked on a program of territorial expansion. By the mid-eighteenth century Comanches drove most Apaches from the plains and took over their rich bison-hunting territories on the southern Plains. Without bison Apaches turned more and more to stealing Spanish animals to survive. Spaniards from Santa Fe to San Antonio soon found themselves at war with Apaches and Comanches both; New Mexico often came into conflict with Navajos and Utes as well. Much of northern New Spain became a theater of desolation, abandoned villages up and down the Rio Grande testifying to the limits of Spanish power.

Spaniards accused the "barbarians" of animalistic savagery, but all sides inflicted horrors. Outside the besieged town of Tucson, for example, Lt. Col. Pedro de Allende boasted that he had decapitated a fallen Apache in front of the dead man's comrades and "charged the Apache line single-handed, with the head stuck on his lance." Away from the din of battle a prominent Spaniard noted that his people accuse the Indians of cruelty but added dryly, "I do not know what opinion they would have of us."

By the 1780s nearly everyone had had enough of war. A farsighted Comanche leader named Ecueracapa helped broker peace with Spanish authorities in 1786, after which the new allies cooperated to entice or threaten Utes, Navajos, and even Apaches into peace as well. Northern New Spain gradually entered a period of relative peace, expansion, and economic growth.

Changes were most dramatic in New Mexico, where Spanish subjects opened up new farms and ranches, enlarged their flocks and herds, and devoted new energy to local manufacturing. As New Mexico's non-Indian population grew (20,000 by the close of the eighteenth century), new roads funded by the crown eased the province's isolation. Increased trade allowed caravans to set out from Santa Fe for Chihuahua City once or even twice a year.

Some of the New Mexicans who profited from the newfound opportunities patronized artists and skilled craftsmen. By the late eighteenth century a distinctive New Mexican culture emerged, marked by new traditions in such crafts as woodworking and weaving, as well as in religious art and practice. A master craftsman known only as the Laguna Santero helped define this movement by training local apprentices in his workshop and making pieces for wealthy patrons. The Laguna Santero, his apprentices, and others he inspired began making exquisite portraits of saints on pine boards (*retablos*), hide paintings, elaborate altar screens for churches, and wooden statues of saints (*bultos*)—all art forms still associated with New Mexican folk culture today.

Spanish California >>

Spanish California became the empire's last major colonial project in North America. Like the colonies in Texas and Florida, settlement was sparked by anxiety over foreign competition, this time from Russians moving south from Alaska. Though Spaniards first explored the California coast in 1542, not until 1768 did the crown authorize permanent colonization. A joint expedition of military men and Franciscans, led by the pragmatic Gaspar de Portolá and the physically frail but iron-willed Friar Junípero Serra, braved shipwrecks, scurvy, and earthquakes to establish ramshackle presidios (military garrisons) and missions at San Diego and Monterey.

Recruiting colonists was difficult. In desperation, officials even scoured the orphanages and prisons of New Spain. Those who journeyed north found the sea voyage difficult and sometimes deadly. The back-breaking overland route from

northwestern New Spain had to be abandoned after 1781, when an uprising of Yuma Indians shut down the crossing at the Colorado River. Still, the colony enjoyed modest growth. By 1800 California had two more presidios (at San Francisco and Santa Barbara), three Spanish towns (San José, Los Angeles, and Branciforte, near present-day Santa Cruz), and eighteen Franciscan missions, ministering to 13,000 Indian converts.

Like their colleagues in Texas and Florida, Franciscans in California tried to entice Indians into missions with promises of food, shelter, instruction, and protection. All the while Indians saw the world changing around them. In Monterey, for example, imported pigs, sheep, mules, horses, and cows multiplied at astonishing speed. These animals radiated out from the mission and presidio, overgrazing and annihilating native plants. Soon weeds and plants that Spaniards had unwittingly brought with them spread throughout the region. Pollen analysis of the vegetable matter in adobe from the early nineteenth century indicates that by the time the bricks were made, alien weeds had all but displaced native plants. With their lands transformed by overgrazing and invasive plant species, and their populations diminished by epidemics and hampered by falling birthrates, native families around Monterey abandoned their villages and either fled to the interior or surrendered to the discipline and danger of mission life. Indians provided labor and food for California's missions, presidios, and three colonial towns.

> # Recruiting colonists for California was difficult. In desperation, officials even scoured the orphanages and prisons of New Spain.

>> This *retablo*, or altarpiece, of San Jose (Saint Joseph) is typical of the art produced by the Laguna Santero and his workshop.

By 1800 California was home to only 1,800 Hispanic residents. Despite their relative poverty and isolation, they nurtured distinctive traditions ranging from the profound to the comical. In 1835, for example, an American guest recorded something curious at a wedding in Santa Barbara. Amid the singing, dancing, and celebrating, he watched young women knocking off men's sombreros and breaking cologne-filled eggs on their heads. The men were "bound in gallantry to find out the lady and return the compliment, though it must not be done if the person sees you."

English and American visitors to California wrote frequently about the women they encountered there but usually kept their observations to the superficial. But the most important differences separating women in California from counterparts in Boston and London had nothing to do with dress, hair, dancing, or wedding customs.

Women and the Law in New Spain and British North America >>
Women in California and throughout the Spanish world enjoyed a host of legal rights denied to women in English-speaking realms. When parents died, Spanish law insured that daughters inherited property equally with sons. English law, in contrast, allowed fathers to craft wills however they wished. If an Englishman died without a will ("intestate"), his eldest son inherited all the land and any buildings on it. Daughters and younger brothers received only a share of the remaining personal property.

In marriage Spanish women retained control over their personal property, and ownership of any dowry (sum of money) they brought into the union. They also maintained the right to buy and sell land and to legally represent themselves in court. Married English women had virtually no control over any kind of property, could not write a will, and could initiate no legal action without

a husband's consent. These differences in law persisted into widowhood. Spanish widows were legally entitled not only to their original dowries but also to at least one half of all property they and their deceased husbands had accumulated in marriage. Their English counterparts had no right to their dowries in widowhood—only to control over a third of their dead husband's property. Even this proved temporary; in contrast to Spanish law, English law maintained that this third share would revert to the deceased *husband's* family upon the widow's death.

For the poorest women such legal differences meant little. But for those who did have some property or wealth, it mattered a great deal whether they lived in New Spain or British North America.

 REVIEW

Why did Spain establish colonies in Texas and California, and what role did missions play in anchoring the Spanish presence?

EIGHTEENTH-CENTURY NEW FRANCE

Like Spain's vast and sprawling territorial claims in North America, France's imperial ambitions were nothing if not grand. French colonial maps laid claim to the heart of the continent, a massive imperial wedge stretching from Newfoundland southwest to the Mississippi Delta, then northwest across the Great Plains and into the cold north woods, and east again through Upper Canada to the North Atlantic.

Colonial Compromises >>
Despite these grand claims, most eighteenth-century French-Americans continued to live along the St. Lawrence River. They dwelt in farming communities up and down the river valley between the towns of Montreal and Quebec, capital of New France. Jesuit missions also lined the river, ministering to native converts. After a brief boost from colonization in the 1660s and 1670s, the French population grew almost totally through natural increase. Fortunately for France the colonists excelled at natural increase—nurturing large, thriving families and doubling their population every generation.

Those determined enough to endure darkness, isolation, and numbing cold in winter, then heat, humidity, and swarming mosquitoes in summer, found life in Canada considerably easier than life in France. Colonists lived longer, more often owned land, and enjoyed greater freedoms than peasants at home. By 1760 the valley contained 75,000 French colonists, soldiers, and priests. Many Canadian households also included Indian slaves: mostly

WITNESS
Dancing Californians

"[The Fandango] is performed by two persons of different sex who dance either to the Guittar alone or accompanied with the voice; they traverse the room with such nimble evolution, wheeling about, changing sides and smacking with their fingers at every motion; sometimes they dance close to each other, then retire, then approach again, with such wanton attitudes and motions, such leering looks, sparkling eyes & trembling limbs, as would decompose the gravity of a Stoic."

—Archibald Menzies, "California Journal" (1792)

women and children who were captured by other Indians in places as far away as Texas and the Arkansas Valley and eventually brought to New France.

To the west and north of New France, in the country known as the *pays d'en haut,* the French venture looked quite different. Here forts and missions rather than farms or towns anchored French ambition. More exactly, the goodwill of Indian peoples provided the anchor. Though certainly willing to use violence, the French in North America recognized that they were too few to secure their interests through force alone. France gained an edge over its rivals in the interior by being useful to Indians, primarily the Algonquian-speaking nations who spread across eastern Canada and the Upper Mississippi. French merchants brought coveted European presents and trade goods, while military men, administrators, and Jesuits often mediated in conflicts between native groups. Vastly outnumbered by Indians throughout most of the territory that it claimed in North America, France remained deeply dependent on native peoples.

Dependence meant compromise. The two peoples had radically divergent expectations about warfare, trade, marriage, child rearing, religion, food, beauty, and many other areas of life. Few cultural differences seemed as difficult to bridge as those concerning law. In 1706, for example, men associated with a prominent Ottawa leader known as Le Pesant killed a priest and a French soldier outside Fort Detroit. Enraged French authorities demanded that Le Pesant be surrendered so that he could be tried and, once found guilty, executed for murder. Ottawa leaders countered by offering to replace the dead Frenchmen with Indian slaves. "Raising" the dead this way was a common Ottawa remedy in cases of murder between allies, because it helped avoid a potentially disastrous cycle of blood revenge.

Neither side gave in to the other. Instead they crafted a novel solution that exemplified the pattern of creative, mutual compromises typical of what one scholar has called the "middle ground" characterizing French-Indian relations in the *pays d'en haut.* Ottawa leaders turned over Le Pesant to French authorities, whereupon this elderly, obese prisoner miraculously "escaped" just before his execution. Clearly the French and their Ottawa allies came to an understanding. Le Pesant would be surrendered and, once condemned, quietly released. The compromise satisfied both sides more or less and became a model solution to later French-Indian murder cases.

Necessary and inevitable, such compromises nonetheless rankled authorities in Paris. In 1731 one such official bemoaned the fact that after more than a century, colonial administrators in New France had failed to make the "savages" obedient to the crown. The colony's governor general dashed off a terse reply: "if this has not been done, it is because we have found the task to be an impossible one. Kindly apprise me of any means you should conceive of for securing such obedience."

France on the Gulf Coast >>

Forced into uncomfortable compromises in the north, authorities in Paris hoped to establish a colony on the Gulf Coast that could be more profitable, and more French. After La Salle's failure in Texas, it fell to Pierre Le Moyne d'Iberville to establish French Louisiana. A veteran sailor and soldier, d'Iberville spent much of the 1690s attacking British settlements in Newfoundland and the North Atlantic. Sent to the Gulf in 1698, he inaugurated the new colony of Louisiana with a post at Biloxi Bay. D'Iberville's successors established settlements at Mobile Bay and, in 1718, the town of New Orleans. Crown officers and entrepreneurs envisioned an agricultural bonanza, expecting Louisiana to have far more in common with the Caribbean's profitable sugar islands than the with maddening *pays d'en haut.*

Nothing went according to plan. Here, too, Indians forced the French into painful concessions. Louisiana came into conflict with the mighty Chickasaws, and in 1729 the Natchez Indians pushed back, killing or capturing some 500 colonists. Underfunded and usually neglected by the crown, Louisiana's officials became notoriously corrupt and arbitrary. The colony was, according to one observer, a place "without religion, without justice, without discipline, without order, and without police."

More to the point, the Gulf Coast was without many colonists, having acquired a reputation among would-be French migrants as unattractive and unhealthy. When colonists were not fighting Indians, they contended with heat, humidity, hurricanes, droughts, and crop failures, with never-ending battles to turn swamps and forests

⌄ Louisiana's socially mixed society is evident from this market scene: the buyers and sellers include Indians as well as colonials of French, Spanish, and African descent.

into farmland, and with the scourges of malaria and yellow fever. By 1731 two-thirds of the French who had journeyed to Louisiana had died or fled. Still, like New Mexico, Canada, California, and Texas, colonial Louisiana persevered and slowly become more populous and more prosperous. Nearly four thousand French men, women, and children called the colony home by 1746. Their fortunes had in large part come to depend on another, even larger group of newcomers: French Louisiana's African slaves.

Slavery and Colonial Society in French Louisiana >>
Within a year of its founding, New Orleans imported nearly 6,000 slaves—most men, brought directly from Africa. But Louisiana tobacco and, later, indigo proved inferior to the varieties exported from Britain's colonies, and the sudden influx of Africans challenged French control. In 1729 some newly arrived slaves joined forces with the Natchez Indians in their rebellion. The alliance sent waves of panic through the colony, whose population by then had more slaves than free French. The colonists retaliated in a devastating counterattack, enlisting both the Choctaw Indians, rivals of the Natchez, and other enslaved blacks, who were promised freedom in return for their support.

The planters' costly victory persuaded French authorities to stop importing slaves. Nonetheless blacks continued to make up a majority of all Louisianans, and by the middle of the eighteenth century nearly all were native-born. The vast majority remained enslaved, but their work routines—tending cattle, cutting timber, producing naval stores, manning boats—allowed them relative autonomy of movement. But the greatest prize—freedom—was awarded those black men who served in the French militia, defending the colony from the English and Indians as well as capturing slave runaways. The descendants of these black militiamen would become the core of Louisiana's free black community.

Imperial Rivalries >>
Male subjects throughout French America stood ready to perform militia duty, formally or informally. They had to. Disputes with Indians proved depressingly common. More to the point, European wars frequently spilled over into North America. In 1689 England joined the Netherlands and the League of Augsburg (several German-speaking states) in a war against France. While the main struggle raged in Europe, French and English colonials, joined by their Indian allies, skirmished in what was known as King William's War. Peace returned in 1697, but only until the Anglo-French struggle resumed with Queen Anne's War, from 1702 to 1713.

For a quarter of a century thereafter the two nations waged a kind of cold war, competing for advantage. At stake was not so much control over people or even territory as control over trade. In North America, France and England vied for access to the sugar islands of the Caribbean, a monopoly on supplying manufactured goods to Spanish America, and dominance of the fur trade. The British had the advantage of numbers: nearly 400,000 subjects in the colonies in 1720, the year of Jean L'Archevêque's death, compared with only about 25,000 French. But this is precisely where France's many compromises paid off. So long as the French maintained their network of alliances with powerful native peoples, British colonies had little chance of expanding west of the Appalachian Mountains.

 REVIEW

How did Louisiana differ from French Canada?

FORCES OF DIVISION IN BRITISH NORTH AMERICA

British colonials from Maine to the Carolinas distrusted the French and resented their empire of fish and furs. But the English were preoccupied with their own affairs and, by and large, uninterested in uniting against New France. Indeed a traveler during the first half of the eighteenth century would have been struck by how hopelessly divided and disunited England's mainland colonies were, split by ethnicity, race, region, wealth, and religion. The British colonies were a diverse and fragmented lot.

> The British had the advantage of numbers: Nearly 400,000 colonists in 1720, compared with 25,000 French.

Immigration and Natural Increase >>
One of the largest immigrant groups—250,000 black men, women, and children—had come to the colonies from Africa in chains. White arrivals included many English immigrants but also a quarter of a million Scots-Irish, the descendants of seventeenth-century Scots who had regretted settling in northern Ireland; perhaps 135,000 Germans; and a sprinkling of Swiss, Swedes, Highland Scots, and Spanish Jews. Most non-English white immigrants were fleeing lives torn by famine, warfare, and religious persecution. All the voyagers, English and non-English, risked the hazardous Atlantic crossing. Many had paid

for passage by signing indentures to work as servants in America.

The immigrants and slaves who arrived in the colonies between 1700 and 1775 swelled a colonial American population that was already growing dramatically from natural increase. The birthrate in eighteenth-century America was triple what it is today. Most women bore between five and eight children, and most children survived to maturity.

This astonishing population explosion exemplified a more general global acceleration of population in the second half of the eighteenth century. China's 150 million inhabitants in 1700 had doubled to more than 313 million by century's end. Europe's total rose from about 118 million to 187 million over the same period. The unprecedented global population explosion had several causes. Europe's climate, for one, had become warmer and drier, allowing for generally better harvests. Health and nutrition improved globally with the worldwide spread of Native American crops. Irish farmers discovered that a single acre planted with the American potato could support an entire family. The tomato added crucial vitamins to the Mediterranean diet, and in China the American sweet potato thrived in hilly regions where rice would not grow.

Dramatic population increase in the British colonies, fed by the importation of slaves, immigration, and natural increase, made it hard for colonials to share any common identity. Far from fostering political unity, almost every aspect of social development set Americans at odds with one another. And that process of division and disunity was reflected in the outpouring of new settlers into the backcountry.

Moving into the Backcountry >>
To immigrants from Europe weary of war or worn by want, the seaboard's established communities must have seemed havens of order and stability. But by the beginning of the eighteenth century land scarcity pushed both native-born and newly arrived families to look westward. While descendants of old Yankee families created new communities in frontier New England, immigrants from Europe had more luck obtaining land south of New York. By the 1720s German and Scots-Irish immigrants as well as native-born colonists were pouring into western Pennsylvania. Some settled permanently, but others streamed southward into the backcountry of

Virginia and the Carolinas, where they encountered native-born southerners pressing westward.

Living in the west could be profoundly isolating. From many farmsteads it was a day's ride to the nearest courthouse, tavern, or church. This forced self-sufficiency made the frontier, more than anywhere else in America, a society of equals. Most families crowded into one-room shacks walled with mud, turf, or crude logs. And everyone worked hard.

NON-ENGLISH SETTLEMENTS IN EIGHTEENTH-CENTURY BRITISH NORTH AMERICA

Many non-English settlers spilled into the backcountry: the Scots-Irish and the Germans followed the Great Wagon Road through the western parts of the middle colonies and southern colonies, while the Dutch and other Germans moved up the Hudson River valley.

Social Conflict and the Frontier >> Ethnic

differences heightened sectional tensions between the seaboard's established communities and the frontier. People of English descent predominated along the Atlantic coast, whereas Germans, Scots-Irish, and other white minorities were concentrated in the interior. Many English colonials regarded these new immigrants as culturally inferior and politically subversive. Charles Woodmason, an Anglican missionary in the Carolina backcountry, lamented the arrival of "5 or 6,000 Ignorant, mean, worthless, beggarly Irish Presbyterians, the Scum of the Earth, the Refuse of Mankind," who "delighted in a low, lazy, sluttish, heathenish, hellish life."

German immigrants were generally credited with steadier work habits, as well as higher standards of sexual morality and personal hygiene. But like the clannish Scots-Irish, the Germans preferred to live, trade, and worship among themselves. By 1751 Benjamin Franklin was warning that the Germans would retain their separate language and customs: the Pennsylvania English would be overrun by "the Palatine Boors."

ESTIMATED POPULATION OF COLONIAL CITIES, 1720–1770

Although Boston's population remained stable after 1740, it was surpassed owing to the sharp growth of New York and, especially, Philadelphia.

Eighteenth-Century Seaports >> While

most Americans on the move flocked to the frontier, others swelled the populations of colonial cities. By present-day standards such cities were small, harboring from 8,000 to 22,000 citizens by 1750. The scale of seaports remained intimate, too: all of New York City was clustered at the southern tip of Manhattan island, and the length of Boston or Charleston could be walked in less than half an hour.

All major colonial cities were seaports, their waterfronts fringed with wharves and shipyards. By the 1750s the grandest and most populous was Philadelphia, which boasted straight, neatly paved streets, flagstone sidewalks, and three-story brick buildings. Older cities such as Boston and New York had a more medieval aspect: most of their dwellings and shops were wooden structures with tiny windows and low ceilings, rising no higher than two

stories to steeply pitched roofs. The narrow cobblestone streets of Boston and New York also challenged pedestrians, who competed for space with livestock being driven to the butcher, roaming herds of swine and packs of dogs, clattering carts, carriages, and horses.

Commerce, the lifeblood of seaport economies, was managed by merchants who tapped the wealth of surrounding regions. Traders in New York and Philadelphia shipped the Hudson and Delaware Valleys' surplus of grain and livestock to the West Indies. Boston's merchants sent fish to the Caribbean and Catholic Europe, masts to England, and rum to West Africa. Charlestonians exported indigo to English dyemakers and rice to southern Europe.

No large-scale domestic industry produced goods for a mass market: instead craft shops filled orders for specific

⋀ In the mid-eighteenth century, Philadelphia became the largest city in the colonies and the second largest in all the British empire. Its busy harbor served not only as a commercial hub but also as the disembarkation point for thousands of immigrants.

A Woman's Cupboard

Using a technique known as polarized light microscopy, researchers determined that the paint on the columns combined white lead with a shade of blue first synthesized in Berlin in 1704.

Eighteenth-century Americans spelled names, even their own, inconsistently. Beneath the first 'A' in 'Barnard' curators found a faint 'E' for "Bernard."

What sorts of possessions do you think Hannah might have kept in these drawers?

Objects can help historians appreciate complex connections. For example, the owner of this exuberantly designed cupboard lived in western Massachusetts In the late seventeenth and early eighteenth centuries, a time of chronic warfare between the English and the French and their Indian allies. Hannah's husband John had been captured in a well-known Indian raid on Deerfield, Massachusetts, in 1704. Perhaps the cupboard can be seen as a defiant assertion of normality in a violent and insecure world. The imagery on the cupboard echoes patterns found on European manufactures from the time, illustrating transatlantic cultural connections even as the piece itself represents a distinct local craft tradition. Finally, the cupboard and the textiles it probably contained open a window into the sorts of property Anglo-American women retained in marriage and passed down to their descendants. According to historian Laurel Thatcher Ulrich, the cupboard's history "teaches us that material objects were not only markers of wealth but devices for building relationships and lineages over time, and it helps us to understand the cultural framework within which ordinary women became creators as well as custodians of household goods."

THINKING CRITICALLY

Why did the owner have her name emblazoned on the cupboard? Might it have something to do with restrictive English laws about what women could own in marriage? Do you think women in New Spain or New France would have done the same? What might objects such as these tell us about how women viewed property and identity in British North America?

Source: Henry Ford Museum, www.thehenryford.org/exhibits/pic/1997/hannah.asp.

---

items placed by individual purchasers. Some **artisans** specialized in the maritime trades as shipbuilders, blacksmiths, and sailmakers. Others, such as butchers, millers, and distillers, processed and packed raw materials for export or served the basic needs of their cities.

On the lowest rung of a seaport's social hierarchy were free and bound workers. Free laborers were mainly young white men and women—journeyman artisans, sailors,

> **artisan** skilled craftworker, such as a blacksmith, a cooper, a miller, or a tailor.

fishermen, domestic workers, seamstresses, and prostitutes. The ranks of unfree workers included apprentices and indentured servants doing menial labor in shops and on the docks.

Black men and women made up a substantial part of the bound labor force in colonial seaports, but the character of slavery there changed decisively during the mid-eighteenth century. As wars raging in Europe reduced the supply of white indentured servants, colonial cities imported a larger number of Africans. In the two decades after 1730 one-third of all immigrants arriving in New York harbor were black; by 1760 blacks constituted more than three-quarters of all bound laborers in Philadelphia.

Working women found a number of opportunities in port cities. Young single women from poor families worked in wealthier households as maids, cooks, laundresses, seamstresses, or nurses. The highest-paying occupations for women were midwifery and dressmaking, and both required long apprenticeships and expert skills. But less than 10 percent of women in seaports worked outside their own homes. Most women spent their workday caring for households: seeing to the needs of husbands and children, tending to gardens and domestic animals, and engaged in spinning and weaving—activities crucial to both household and local economies.

While city dwellers—perhaps 1 out of every 20 Americans—endured more ethnic division, poverty, and crime than countryfolk, they had more to do. Plays, balls, and concerts for the wealthiest; taverns, clubs, celebrations, and church services for everyone. Men of every class found diversion in drink and cockfighting. Crowds swarmed to tavern exhibitions of trained dogs or the spectacular waxworks of one John Dyer, featuring "a lively Representation of Margaret, Countess of Herrinburg, who had 365 Children at one Birth."

 REVIEW

What kinds of divisions led to social tensions and conflicts in British North America?

SLAVE SOCIETIES IN THE EIGHTEENTH-CENTURY SOUTH

Inequalities and divisions between slave and free in the south dwarfed those among seaport dwellers. By 1775 one out of every five Americans was of African ancestry, and more than 90 percent of all black Americans lived in the South, most along the seaboard.

The character of a slave's life depended to a great extent on whether he or she lived in the Chesapeake or the Lower South. Slaves in the low country of South Carolina and Georgia lived on large plantations with as many as 50 other black workers, about half African-born. They had infrequent contact with whites. "They are as 'twere, a Nation within a Nation," observed Francis LeJau, an Anglican priest in the low country. And their work was arduous, for rice required constant cultivation. Black laborers tended young plants and hoed fields in the sweltering summer heat of the mosquito-infested lowlands. During the winter and early spring, they built dams and canals to regulate the flow of water into the rice fields. But the use of the **task system** rather than gang labor widened the window of freedom within slavery. When a slave had completed his assigned task for the day, one planter explained, "his master feels no right to call upon him."

> **task system** way of organizing slave labor. Masters and overseers of rice and indigo plantations generally assigned individual slaves a daily task, and after its completion, slaves could spend the rest of the day engaged in pursuits of their own choosing.

Most Africans and African-Americans in the Chesapeake lived on plantations with fewer than 20 fellow slaves. Less densely concentrated than in the low country, Chesapeake slaves also had more contact with whites. Unlike Carolina's absentee owners, who left white overseers and black drivers to run their plantations, Chesapeake masters actively managed their estates and subjected their slaves to closer scrutiny.

The Slave Family and Community >>

The four decades following 1700 marked the heaviest years of slave importation into the Chesapeake and Carolina regions. The newcomers from Africa had to cope not only with the lingering traumas of capture and the middle passage but also with alien landscapes, new languages, and new threats. They also had to adjust to their fellow slaves. The "new Negroes" hailed from a number of diverse West African peoples, each with a separate language or dialect and distinctive cultures and kinship systems. Often they had little in common with one another and even less in common with the American-born black minority. Native-born African Americans enjoyed better health, command of English, and experience in dealing with whites. They were also more likely to enjoy a family life, because their advantages probably made them the preferred partners of black women, who were outnumbered two to one by black men. And, since immigrant women waited two or three years before marrying, some immigrant men died before they could find a wife.

Opinion

Was the most critical sectional division in eighteenth-century British North America between North and South or between East and West?

After the middle of the eighteenth century, a number of changes fostered the growth of black families and the vitality of slave communities. As slave importations began to taper off, the rate of natural reproduction among blacks started to climb. Gender ratios became more equal. These changes, along with the rise of larger plantations throughout the South, made it easier for black men and women to find partners and start families. Elaborate kinship networks gradually developed, often extending over several plantations in a single neighborhood. And, as the immigrant generations were replaced by native-born offspring, earlier sources of tension and division within the slave community disappeared.

Even so, black families remained vulnerable. If a planter fell on hard times, members of black families might be sold off to different buyers to meet his debts. When an owner died, black spouses, parents, and children might be divided among surviving heirs. Even under the best circumstances, fathers might be hired out to other planters for long periods or sent to work in distant quarters. Then as more slaveholders moved from the coast to the interior, black family life suffered. Between 1755 and 1782, masters on the move resettled fully one-third of all adult African Americans living in tidewater Virginia. Most slaves forced to journey west were men and women in their teens and early 20s, who had to begin again the long process of establishing families and neighborhood networks far from kin and friends.

Black families struggling with terrible uncertainties were sustained by the distinctive African American culture evolving in the slave community. The high percentage of native Africans among the eighteenth-century American black population made it easier for slaves to retain homeland traditions. Christianity won few converts, in part because masters feared that baptizing slaves might make them more rebellious but also because African Americans preferred their traditional religions. Slaves also brought agricultural skills and practices from Africa, as well as folktales, music, and dances.

⌃ *The Old Plantation* affords a rare glimpse of life in the slave quarters. At this festive gathering, both men and women dance to the music of a molo (a stringed instrument similar to a banjo) and drums.

Slave Resistance in Eighteenth-Century British North America >> British

North America had no shortage of African Americans who both resisted captivity and developed strategies for survival. Collective attempts at escape were most common among recently arrived Africans. Groups of slaves, often made up of newcomers from the same tribe, fled inland and formed **Maroon communities**

> **"Maroon" communities**
> groups of escaped slaves, often newly arrived Africans, who fled to the frontiers of colonial settlements in the American South, the Caribbean, and South America.

of runaways. These efforts rarely succeeded, because the Maroon settlements were too large to go undetected for long.

More acculturated blacks turned to subtler subversions, employing what one scholar has called "weapons of the weak." Domestics and field hands alike faked illness, feigned stupidity and laziness, broke tools, pilfered from storehouses, hid in the woods for weeks at a time, or simply took off to visit other plantations. Other slaves, usually escaping bondage as solitary individuals, found a new life as craftworkers, dock laborers, or sailors in the relative anonymity of colonial seaports.

Sometimes slaves rebelled openly. Whites in communities with large numbers of blacks lived in gnawing dread of arson, poisoning, and insurrection. Four slave conspiracies were reported in Virginia during the first half of the eighteenth century. In South Carolina more than two decades of abortive uprisings and insurrection scares culminated in the Stono Rebellion of 1739, the largest slave revolt of the colonial period. Nearly 100 African Americans, led by a slave named Jemmy, seized arms from a store in the coastal district of Stono and killed several white neighbors before they were caught and killed by the colonial militia. But throughout the eighteenth century slave rebellions occurred far less frequently on the mainland of North America than in the Caribbean or Brazil. Whites outnumbered blacks in all of Britain's mainland colonies except South Carolina, and only in Georgia did rebels have a haven for a quick escape—Spanish Florida. Faced with those odds, most slaves reasoned that the risks of rebellion outweighed the prospects for success—and most sought families and opportunities for greater personal freedom within the slave system itself.

 REVIEW

How did African American culture evolve in the slave community, and what forms did resistance to captivity take?

ENLIGHTENMENT AND AWAKENING IN AMERICA

Where colonists lived, how well they lived, whether they were male or female, native-born or immigrant, slave or free—all these variables fostered distinctive worldviews, differing attitudes and assumptions about the individual's relationship to nature, society, and God. The diversity of colonials' inner lives became even more pronounced during the eighteenth century because of the Enlightenment, an intellectual movement that started in Europe during the seventeenth century.

The Enlightenment in America >> The leading figures of the Enlightenment, the *philosophes,* stressed the power of human reason to promote progress by revealing the laws that governed both nature and society. Isaac Newton in England charted the orbits of the planets and devised a theory of gravity, and John Locke applied reason to the construction of political systems. In France, Voltaire wrote essays, novels, and plays criticizing religion, oppressive governments, and censorship.

Enlightenment intellectual movement that flourished in Europe from the mid-1600s through the eighteenth century and stressed the power of human reason to promote social progress by discovering the laws that governed both nature and society.

Like many devotees of the **Enlightenment**, Benjamin Franklin of Philadelphia was most impressed by its emphasis on useful knowledge and experimentation. He pondered air currents and then invented a stove that heated houses more efficiently. He toyed with electricity and then invented lightning rods to protect buildings in thunderstorms. Other amateur colonial scientists constructed simple telescopes, classified animal species native to North America, or sought to explain epidemics in terms of natural causes.

American colleges helped promote Enlightenment thinking. Although institutions such as Harvard (founded 1636) and Yale (1701) initially focused on training ministers, by the eighteenth century their graduates included lawyers, merchants, doctors, and scientists. Most offered courses in mathematics and the natural sciences, which taught students algebra and such advanced theories as Copernican astronomy and Newtonian physics.

By the middle of the eighteenth century Enlightenment ideals had given rise to "rational Christianity," which commanded a small but influential following among Anglicans and liberal Congregationalists in the colonies. Their God was not the Calvinists' awesome deity but a benevolent creator who offered salvation to everyone. They believed that God's greatest gift to humankind was reason, which enabled all human beings to follow the moral teachings of Jesus. Some even embraced deism, which rejected the divinity of Jesus and looked to nature rather than the bible for proof of God's existence.

Enlightenment philosophy and rational Christianity did little to change the lives of most colonials. Few colonial readers had the interest or the background necessary to tackle the learned writings of Enlightenment *philosophes.* The great majority still explained the workings of the world in terms of divine providence rather than natural law. Church attendance ran highest in the northern colonies, where some 80 percent of the population turned out for public worship on the Sabbath. In the South, because of the greater distances involved and the shortage of clergy, about half of all colonials regularly attended Sunday services.

Still, many ministers grew alarmed over the influence of rational Christianity. They also worried about isolated frontier families abandoning Christianity altogether. Exaggerated as these fears may have been, they gave rise to a major religious revival that swept the colonies during the middle decades of the eighteenth century.

The First Great Awakening >> The **Great Awakening**, as the revival came to be called, first appeared in the 1730s among Presbyterians and Congregationalists in the Middle Colonies and New England. Many ministers in these churches preached an "evangelical" message, emphasizing the

Great Awakening term used to describe periods of intense religious piety and commitment among Americans that fueled the expansion of Protestant churches.

need for individuals to experience "a new birth" through religious conversion. Among them was Jonathan Edwards, the pastor of a Congregational church in Northampton, Massachusetts. Edwards's Calvinist preaching combined moving descriptions of God's grace with terrifying portrayals of eternal damnation. "The God that holds you over the pit of hell, much as one holds a spider or some loathsome insect over the fire, abhors you and is dreadfully provoked," he declaimed to one congregation. "There is no other reason to be given, why you have not dropped into hell since you arise in the morning, but that God's hand has held you up."

These local revivals of the 1730s were mere tremors compared to the earthquake of religious enthusiasm that shook the colonies with the arrival in the fall of 1739 of George Whitefield. This handsome (though cross-eyed) "boy preacher" from England electrified crowds from Georgia to New Hampshire during his two-year tour of the colonies. He and his many imitators among colonial ministers turned the church into a theater, enlivening sermons with dramatic gestures, flowing tears, and gruesome depictions of hell. The drama of such performances appealed to people of all classes, ethnic groups, and races. By the time Whitefield sailed back to England in 1741, thousands of awakened souls were joining older churches or forming new ones.

hangovers. Like Franklin many colonials regarded the idle among England's rich and poor alike as ominous signs of a degenerate nation.

Politics in England and America >>

Colonials were also of two minds about England's government. Although they praised the English constitution as the basis of all liberties, they were alarmed by the actual workings of English politics. In theory, England's **balanced constitution** gave every order of society a voice in government. Whereas the Crown represented the monarchy and the House of Lords the aristocracy, the House of Commons represented the democracy, the people of England.

> **balanced constitution** view that England's constitution gave every part of English society some voice in the workings of its government.

Americans liked to think that their colonial governments mirrored the ideal English constitution. Most colonies had a royal governor who represented the monarch in America and a bicameral (two-house) legislature made up of a lower house (the assembly) and an upper house (or council). The democratically elected assemblies, like the House of Commons, stood for popular interests, whereas the councils, some of which were elected and others appointed, more roughly approximated the House of Lords.

But these formal similarities masked real differences between English and colonial governments. In any showdown with their assemblies most royal governors had to give way, because they lacked the government offices and contracts that bought loyalty. The colonial legislatures possessed additional leverage, since all of them retained the sole authority to levy taxes.

At the same time widespread ownership of land meant that more than half the colonies' white adult male population could vote. The larger electorate made it more difficult to buy votes. The colonial electorate was also more watchful. Representatives had to reside in the districts that they served, and a few even received binding instructions from their constituents about how to vote.

Most Americans were as pleased with their inexpensive and representative colonial governments as they were horrified by the conduct of politics in England, where webs of patronage and corruption compromised the entire system. John Dickinson, a young Pennsylvanian training as a lawyer in London, was scandalized by a parliamentary election he witnessed in 1754. The king and his ministers had spent over 100,000 pounds sterling to buy support for their candidates, he wrote his father, and "if a man cannot be brought to vote as he is desired, he is made dead drunk and kept in that state, never heard of by his family and friends, till all is over and he can do no harm."

The Imperial System before 1760 >>

Few Britons gave the colonists as much thought as the colonists gave them. Those few who thought about America at all believed that colonials resembled the "savage" Indians more than the "civilized" English. As a London acquaintance remarked to Thomas Hancock, it was a pity Mrs. Hancock had to remain in Boston when he could "take her to England and make her happy with Christians."

The same ignorant indifference contributed to England's haphazard administration of its colonies. Aside from passing an occasional law to regulate trade, restrict manufacturing, or direct monetary policy, Parliament made no effort to assert its authority in America. For the colonies this chaotic and inefficient system of colonial administration left them a great deal of freedom. Even England's regulation of trade rested lightly on the shoulders of most Americans. Southern planters were obliged to send their rice, indigo, and tobacco to Britain only, but they enjoyed favorable credit terms and knowledgeable marketing from English merchants. Colonials were prohibited from finishing iron products and exporting hats and textiles, but they had scant interest in developing domestic industries. Americans were required to import all manufactured goods through England, but by doing so, they acquired high-quality goods at low prices. At little sacrifice, most Americans obeyed imperial regulations.

Following this policy of **benign neglect** the British Empire rumbled along to the satisfaction of most people on both sides of the Atlantic. Economic growth and political **autonomy** kept most white Americans happy being English, despite their misgivings about the motherland.

> **benign neglect** policy also known as "salutary neglect," pursued by the British empire in governing its American colonies until the end of the Seven Years' War.
>
> **autonomy** condition of being independent or, in the case of a political structure, the right to self-government.

If imperial arrangements had remained as they were in 1754, the empire might have muddled on indefinitely.

But something important seemed to be changing, both within the British world and in the international order as well. For decades, Europe's imperial wars found their way to America almost as an afterthought. Colonial officials, traders, land speculators, and would-be pioneers regularly seized on news of the latest European conflict as an excuse to attack their Spanish or French or British counterparts in the North American borderlands. The interests of kings and queens had to be served, of course. But by and large it was easier to exploit war for local or personal purposes out on the far margins of Europe's empires. Eastern North America's native peoples likewise sought advantage in these interimperial flare-ups. But for them the stakes were higher. When Indian leaders joined in a fight for profit or revenge, or to please one or another colonial ally, they also put their own people at risk.

As all North Americans learned, however, the outcome of their struggles could be determined by men they would never see: well-heeled diplomats sipping drinks around mahogany tables in European capitals. Victories, defeats, territories won or lost—all this could be and often was undone

The Aftermath of the Great Awakening >>

Whitefield also left behind a raging storm of controversy. Many "awakened" church members now openly criticized their ministers as cold, unconverted, and uninspiring. To supply the missing fire some laymen—"and even Women and Common Negroes"—took to "exhorting" any audience willing to listen. The most popular ministers became "itinerants," traveling like Whitefield from one town to another.

Northern churches splintered and bickered over the Great Awakening, but the fires of revivalism spread rapidly to the South and its backcountry. From the mid-1740s until the 1770s, scores of new Presbyterian and Baptist churches formed, sparking controversy. Ardent Presbyterians disrupted Anglican worship by loosing packs of dogs in local chapels. County officials, prodded by resentful Anglican parsons, harassed, fined, and imprisoned Baptist ministers.

And so a diverse lot of Americans found themselves continually at odds with one another: arguing over religion and the Enlightenment, conflicted over racial and ethnic tensions, and divided between coastal and backcountry cultures. Benjamin Franklin, a man who made it his business to know, understood the depth of those divisions better than most. Yet even he harbored hopes for political unity among the fractious colonists. After all, most were English. That much they had in common.

↑ Benjamin Franklin and George Whitefield portrayed the contrasting facets of Enlightenment and Awakening. Franklin in his 30s appears worldly, sophisticated, and urbane—a look that was just the opposite of the modest, homespun appearance he adopted 30 years later while ambassador to France. The wig, the fancy white sleeves, the dignified tuck of hand in jacket all signify a man of wealth and culture. Whitefield's garb looks not so different, but whereas Franklin was playful, curious, and often disinterested in temperament, Whitefield was so fervent when preaching that many ministers refused to have him in their churches. Instead, he often took to the fields to preach outdoors. He cared little about denominations, only salvation. "Father Abraham, whom have you in heaven?" he called out in one sermon. "Any Episcopalians? No! Any Presbyterians? No! Any Independents or Methodists? No, no, no! Whom have you there? We don't know those names here. All who are here are Christians . . ."

✓ **REVIEW**

Describe the different outlooks of Enlightenment and evangelical Christians.

ANGLO-AMERICAN WORLDS OF THE EIGHTEENTH CENTURY

Although most Americans prided themselves on being English, some differences made colonials feel inferior, ashamed of their simplicity when compared with London's sophistication. But they also came to appreciate the greater equality of their society and the more representative character of their governments. If it was good to be English, it was, on balance, better still to be English in America.

English Economic and Social Development >>

The differences between England and America began with their economies. England's huge financial institutions and corporations, its growing factories and profitable mines, and its tenant-based commercial agriculture stood in sharp contrast to the mostly humble economic activity in British North America. England's more developed economy fostered the growth of cities, especially London, a teeming colossus of 675,000 in 1750. In contrast, 90 percent of all eighteenth-century colonials lived in towns of fewer than 2,000. But in another respect, England's more advanced economy drew the colonies and the parent country together. Americans were so eager to acquire British-made commodities that their per capita consumption of imported manufactures rose 120 percent between 1750 and 1773. People of all classes demanded and indulged in such small luxuries as a tin of tea, a pair of gloves, and a bar of Irish soap.

Inequality in England and America >>

Then there were people of no means. In England they were legion. London seethed with filth, crime, and desperate poverty. The poor and the unemployed as well as pickpockets and prostitutes crowded into its gin-soaked slums, taverns, and brothels. The contrast between the luxuries enjoyed by a wealthy few Londoners and the misery of the many disquieted colonial observers. Ebenezer Hazard, an American Quaker visiting London, knew for certain he was in "a Sink of Sin."

New wealth and the inherited privileges of England's landed aristocracy made for deepening class divisions. Two percent of England's population owned 70 percent of its land. By right of birth English aristocrats claimed membership in the House of Lords; by custom, certain powerful gentry families dominated the other branch of Parliament, the House of Commons.

The colonies had their own prominent families but no titled ruling class holding political privilege by hereditary right. And if England's upper classes lived more splendidly, its lower classes were larger and worse off than those in the colonies. Less than a third of England's inhabitants belonged to the "middling sort" of traders, professionals,

artisans, and tenant farmers. More than two-thirds struggled for survival at the bottom of society. In contrast, the colonial middle class counted for nearly three-quarters of the white population. With land cheap, labor scarce, and wages for both urban and rural workers 100 percent higher in America than in England, it was much easier for colonials to accumulate savings and farms of their own.

Colonials were both fascinated and repelled by English society. Benjamin Rush, a Philadelphia physician, felt in the House of Lords as if he "walked on sacred ground." He begged his guide for permission to sit on the throne therein and then sat "for a considerable time." Other colonials gushed over the grandeur of aristocratic estates and imported suits of livery for their servants, tea services for their wives, and wallpaper for their drawing rooms.

But colonials recognized that England's ruling classes purchased their luxury and leisure at the cost of the rest of the nation. In his autobiography Benjamin Franklin painted a devastating portrait of the degraded lives of his fellow workers in a London printshop, who drowned their disappointments by drinking throughout the workday, even more excessively on the Sabbath, and then faithfully observing the holiday of "St. Monday's" to nurse their

∧ Coffeehouses such as this establishment in London were favorite gathering places for eighteenth-century Americans visiting Britain. Here merchants and mariners, ministers and students, lobbyists and tourists warmed themselves, read newspapers, and exchanged gossip about commerce, politics, and social life.

---

five days later both Wolfe and Montcalm lay dead, along with 1,400 French soldiers and 600 British and American troops. Québec had fallen to the British. A year later the French surrender of Montreal finally ended the imperial war in North America, although it continued elsewhere around the world for another two years.

The Treaty of Paris, signed in February 1763, put an end to all French claims in North America and confirmed British title to all French territory east of the Mississippi. Spain had foolishly entered the war on France's side in 1762 and quickly lost Havana to British warships. The treaty restored Cuba to Spain, but at a high price: the Spanish ceded Florida to Britain. It reluctantly took nominal control of France's vast and ill-defined territory of Louisiana, west of the Mississippi, but only to prevent Britain from having it. That territory included the port of New Orleans. In addition to its North America spoils, Britain won several Caribbean islands in the war, as well as Senegal in West Africa.

After generations of inconclusive imperial wars, British North Americans found the victory almost impossibly grand. Towns up and down the Atlantic coast lit up the night with celebratory bonfires and rang with the sounds of clanking tankards and boisterous song. How good it was to be British!

Postwar Expectations >>

Grand expectations crowded on the heels of these joyful celebrations. The end of the war, Americans assumed, meant the end of high taxes and access to the fertile lands of the Ohio. Just as important, Americans expected to be given more consideration within the British Empire. Now, as one anonymous pamphleteer put it, Americans would "not be thought presumptuous, if they consider[ed] themselves upon an equal footing" with English in the parent country.

Point of View

The Seven Years' War

"The most important event to occur in eighteenth-century North America, the Seven Years War figures in most Americans' consciousness of the past as a kind of hazy backdrop to the Revolution."

FRED ANDERSON, *Crucible of War*

Few in England seemed to agree. British statesmen grumbled that colonial assemblies had been tightfisted when it came to supplying the army. British commanders charged that colonial troops had been lily-livered when it came to combat. Differing perspectives on the war and

differing expectations of the colonies' place in the empire primed the postwar generation for crisis.

 REVIEW

What started the Seven Years' War, and how did Britain emerge victorious?

THE IMPERIAL CRISIS

It was common sense. Great Britain had waged a costly war to secure its empire in America; now it needed to consolidate those gains. The empire's North American territory had to be protected, its administration tightened, and its colonies made more profitable for the parent nation. Thus Britain would have to leave a standing army of several thousand troops in America after the Seven Years' War. And, of course, armies needed to be paid for; taxes would be unavoidable. That the colonists, who benefited most from the great victory, ought to be the ones to pull out their purses for king and country—well, London thought that, too, was common sense.

Pontiac's Rebellion >>

British authorities justified the army's continued presence in part by pointing to the various alien peoples that the crown now had to administer. The army would have to police French colonists in Canada, Spaniards in Florida, and, most especially, dozens of formidable native peoples west of the Appalachians. General Jeffery Amherst, the top British officer in North America, believed Indian troubles could be avoided if military and civil authorities simply projected strength. With the French no longer on the continent, Amherst believed, Britain need not purchase Indian friendship with presents, subsidized trade, and tiresome diplomatic ceremonies. When knowledgeable colonists insisted that Indian relations hinged on such practices, Amherst scoffed. "When men of what race soever behave ill," the general scolded, "they must be punished but not bribed."

Still reeling from the war, Indian peoples reacted to Britain's triumphal attitude and the new westward surge of speculators and colonists with a religious revival that cut across tribal lines. The Delaware holy man Neolin told followers that God, or the Master of Life, believed his native children should "drive [the British] out, make war on them . . . they know me not, and are my enemies. Send them back to the lands I have created for them. . . ."

Pontiac, a charismatic Ottawa chief, embraced Neolin's message of Indian unity and organized attacks against British forts in the summer of 1763. Shawnees, Mingos, Potawatomis, Wyandots, and other Indian peoples in the Ohio Country, working with Pontiac or independently, captured every British fort west of Detroit by early July. Backcountry settlements from Pennsylvania to Virginia came under attack, leaving hundreds of colonials dead and hundreds more fleeing east. Determined to assert British rule, an enraged Amherst sent troops west to attack Indian forces and native villages. He also authorized the commander at Fort Pitt to give Indians blankets from the forts' infirmary, where several men had been stricken with smallpox.

THE APPALACHIAN FRONTIER, 1750–1775

Increasingly, land-hungry colonials spilled into the West through the Cumberland Gap, a notch in the chain of mountains stretching the length of the North American interior. A route through the gap was scouted in 1750 by Dr. Thomas Walker and a party of Virginians on behalf of a company of land speculators. In 1763, Indians led by Pontiac seized eight British forts before troops under Colonel Henry Bouquet stopped the offensive. In 1775 Daniel Boone led the first large party of pioneers through the gap to Boonesborough, in present-day Kentucky.

Hatreds mounted on all sides. In western Pennsylvania, where Indian raids had taken an especially grim toll, a number of Scots-Irishmen calling themselves the "Paxton Boys" set out to purge the colony of Indians altogether. In December of 1763 they burst into a small village of Christian Indians, killed six people, and burned the settlement to the ground. Fourteen other inhabitants fled to the town of Lancaster, which gave them protective custody. Leading a mob the Paxton Boys forced their way into the safe house and massacred all 14 men, women, and children with broadswords. Colonists and natives alike were increasingly willing to simplify difference and see all "Indians" or all "whites" as despicable enemies.

Officials in London blamed Pontiac's Rebellion on bad leadership and replaced General Amherst. More important, the crown issued the Proclamation of 1763, which significantly transformed colonial policy. Presents and respectful diplomacy were to resume, and the crown appointed two Indian superintendents (one in South Carolina and the other in New York) to oversee good relations. Most critically, colonial settlement was to cease west of the Appalachians. A so-called proclamation line reserved all western lands as Indian Territory. (Québec and Florida were exceptions, divided into eastern and western halves, for colonials and Indians.) Restricting westward movement might ease Indian fears, the British hoped, and so stave off future conflicts.

However sensible and just the Proclamation Line might have seemed from the perspective of the Ohio Country or London, most British colonists viewed it as a betrayal by their own government. Many wondered why they had fought and sacrificed in the war against France, if all the territory they helped win was set aside for Indians.

George Grenville's New Measures »

If Pontiac's Rebellion and the Proclamation of 1763 had been the only postwar disappointments colonists faced, that would have been trouble enough. But George Grenville, the first lord of the treasury, also confronted the dismal financial consequences of the Seven Years' War.

Britain's national debt had doubled in the decade after 1754. Adding to that burden was the drain of supporting troops in the colonies. As matters stood, heavy taxes were already triggering protests among hard-pressed Britons. Americans, in contrast, paid comparatively low taxes to their colonial governments and little in trade duties to the empire. Indeed, Grenville discovered that the colonial customs service paid out four times more in salaries to its collectors than it gathered in duties. Rampant bribery and tax evasion allowed merchants to avoid existing duties on foreign molasses, for example, which New England merchants imported to make rum.

George Grenville reasoned that if Americans could pay out a little under the table to protect an illegal trade, they would willingly pay a little more to go legitimate. Parliament agreed. In April 1764 it passed the Revenue Act, commonly called the Sugar Act. This **tariff** actually lowered the duty on foreign molasses from six to three pence a gallon. This time, however, the tax would be scrupulously collected, ships would be tightly monitored to make sure they complied, and violators would be tried in admiralty courts, far harsher than typical colonial courts.

tariff duty on trade, the purpose of which is primarily to regulate the flow of commerce rather than to raise a revenue.

Parliament approved other proposals by Grenville, all designed to improve British finances. The Currency Act of 1764 prohibited the colonies from making their paper money legal tender. That prevented Americans from paying their debts to British traders in currency that had fallen to less than its face value. The Quartering Act of 1765 obliged any colony in which troops were stationed to provide suitable accommodations. That contributed to the cost of keeping British forces in America. Finally, in March of 1765 Parliament passed the Stamp Act.

taxes duty on trade (known as external taxation) or a duty on items circulating within a nation or a colony (known as internal taxation) intended primarily to raise a revenue rather than to regulate the flow of commerce.

The Stamp Act placed **taxes** on legal documents, customs papers, newspapers, almanacs, college diplomas, playing cards, and dice. After November 1, 1765, all these items had to bear a stamp signifying that their possessor had paid the tax. Violators of the Stamp Act, like those disobeying the Sugar Act, were to be tried without juries in admiralty courts. The English had been paying a similar tax for nearly a century, so Grenville expected few objections. Little did he understand the colonial viewpoint.

⌃ One Pennsylvania newspaper showed what it thought of the Stamp Act.

The Beginning of Colonial Resistance

>> Like other Britons, colonials in America accepted a maxim laid down by the English philosopher John Locke: property guaranteed liberty. Property, in this view, was not merely real estate, or wealth, or material possessions. It was the source of strength for every individual, providing the freedom to think and act independently. It followed from this close connection between property, power, and liberty that no people should be taxed without consenting—either personally or through elected representatives. The power to tax was the power to destroy, by depriving a person of property. Yet both the Sugar Act and the Stamp Act were taxes passed by members of Parliament, none of whom had been elected by colonials.

Like the English, colonials also prized the right of trial by jury as one of their basic constitutional liberties. Yet both the Sugar Act and the Stamp Act would prosecute offenders in the admiralty courts, not in local courts, thus depriving colonials of the freedom claimed by all other English men and women.

The concern for protecting individual liberties was only one of the convictions shaping the colonies' response to Britain's new policies. Equally important was their deep suspicion of power itself, a preoccupation that colonials shared with a minority of radical English thinkers. These radicals were known by a variety of names: the Country Party, the Commonwealthmen, and **the Opposition.** They drew their inspiration from the ancient tradition of **classical republicanism,** which held that representative government safeguarded liberty more reliably than either monarchy or oligarchy did. Underlying that judgment was the belief that human beings were driven by passion and insatiable ambition. One person (a monarch), or even a few people (an oligarchy), could not be entrusted with governing, because they would inevitably become corrupted by power and turn into despots. Even in representative governments, the people were obliged to watch those in power at all times. The price of liberty was eternal vigilance.

The Opposition believed that the people of England were not watching their rulers closely enough. During the first half of the eighteenth century, they argued, the entire executive branch of England's government—monarchs and their ministers—had been corrupted by their appetite for power. Proof of their ambition could be found in the bloated state bureaucracy, the massive standing army, and the rising taxes. The Opposition warned that a sinister conspiracy originating in the executive branch of government threatened English liberty.

Opposition writers were more or less ignored in England, but colonial leaders revered them. The Opposition's view of politics confirmed colonial anxieties about England, doubts that ran deeper after 1763. Parliament's attempt to tax the colonies and the quartering of a standing army on the frontier smacked of a corrupt plot to enslave the colonies.

Britain's attempt to raise revenue after 1763 was a disaster of timing, not just psychologically but also economically. By then the colonies were in the throes of a recession. The boom produced in America by government spending during the war had collapsed once British subsidies were withdrawn. Colonial response to the Sugar Act reflected these painful postwar trends. New England merchants led the opposition, objecting to the Sugar Act principally on economic grounds.

But with the passage of the Stamp Act, the terms of the imperial debate widened. The new act took money from the pockets of anyone who made a will, filed a deed, traded out of a colonial port, bought a newspaper, consulted an almanac, graduated from college, took a chance at dice, or played cards. More important, the Stamp Act served notice that Parliament claimed the authority to tax the colonies directly.

> Britain's attempt to raise revenue was a disaster of timing, not just psychologically but economically.

the Opposition diverse group of political thinkers and writers in Great Britain, also known as the Country Party and the Commonwealthmen, who elaborated the tradition of classical republicanism from the late seventeenth century through the eighteenth century.

classical republicanism emphasized that all rulers needed to be watched because of a tendency for power to corrupt human nature.

Riots and Resolves

>> That unprecedented assertion provoked an unprecedented development: the first display of colonial unity. During the spring and summer of 1765 American assemblies passed resolves denying Parliament's authority to tax the colonies. That right belonged to colonial assemblies alone, they argued, by the law of nature and by the liberties guaranteed in colonial charters and in the British constitution.

Virginia's assembly, the House of Burgesses, took the lead in protesting the Stamp Act, prodded by Patrick Henry. Just 29 years old in 1765, Henry had tried his hand at planting in western Virginia before recognizing his real talent—demagoguery. Blessed with the eloquence of an evangelical preacher, the dashing charm of a southern gentleman, and a mind uncluttered by much learning, Henry parlayed his popularity as a smooth-talking lawyer into a place among the Burgesses. He took his seat just 10 days before introducing the Virginia Resolves against the Stamp Act.

The Burgesses passed Henry's resolutions upholding their exclusive right to tax Virginians. Other assemblies followed suit, affirming that the sole right to tax Americans resided in their elected representatives. In October 1765 delegates from nine colonies convened in New York, where they prepared a joint statement of the American position and petitioned the king and Parliament to repeal both the Sugar Act and the Stamp Act.

Meanwhile, colonial leaders turned to the press to arouse popular opposition to the Stamp Act. Disposed by the writings of the English Opposition to think of politics in conspiratorial terms, they warned that Grenville and the king's other ministers schemed to deprive the colonies of their liberties by unlawfully taxing their property. The Stamp Act was only the first step in a sinister plan to enslave Americans. In response the merchants of Boston, New York, and Philadelphia agreed to stop importing English goods in order to pressure British traders to lobby for repeal. In every colony organizations emerged to ensure that the Stamp Act, if not repealed, would never be enforced.

The new resistance groups, which styled themselves the "Sons of Liberty," consisted of traders, lawyers, and prosperous artisans. With great success, they organized the lower classes of the seaports in opposition to the Stamp Act. The sailors, dockworkers, poor artisans, apprentices, and servants who poured into the streets resembled mobs that had been organized from time to time earlier in the century. Previous riots against houses of prostitution, merchants who hoarded goods, or supporters of smallpox inoculation had not been spontaneous, uncontrolled outbursts. Crowds chose their targets and their tactics carefully and usually carried out the communal will with little personal violence.

In every colonial city the mobs of 1765 burnt the stamp distributors in effigy, insulted them on the streets, demolished their offices, and attacked their homes. One hot night in August 1765 a mob went further than the Sons of Liberty had planned. They all but leveled the stately mansion of Thomas Hutchinson, the unpopular lieutenant governor of Massachusetts and the brother-in-law of the colony's stamp distributor. The destruction stunned Bostonians, especially the Sons of Liberty, who resisted Britain in the name of protecting private property. Thereafter they took care to keep crowds under tighter control.

By the first of November, the day that the Stamp Act took effect, most of the stamp distributors had resigned.

Repeal of the Stamp Act

>> Meanwhile repeal of the Stamp Act was already underway back in England. The man who came—unintentionally—to America's relief was George III. The young king was a good man, industrious and devoted to the empire, but he was also immature and not particularly bright. Insecurity made him an irksome master, and he ran through ministers rapidly. By the end of 1765 George had replaced Grenville with a new first minister, the Marquis of Rockingham. Opposed to the Stamp Act from the outset, Rockingham secured its repeal in March of 1766.

⌃ The Stamp Act riots had their roots in raucous demonstrations by "people out of doors," as such crowds were known during the eighteenth century. One annual celebration, the anti-Catholic "Pope's Day," was held every year in Boston. In this engraving boys dressed as devil's imps accompany a cart bearing an effigy of the pope. In the 1760s effigies of tax collectors and royal officials appeared instead.

The Stamp Act controversy demonstrated to colonials how similar in political outlook they were to one another and how different they were from the British. Most fundamentally, Americans agreed about the meaning of representation. To counter colonial objections to the Stamp Act, Grenville and his supporters had claimed that Americans were virtually represented, because each member of Parliament stood for the interests of the whole empire. But colonials put little stock in the theory of **virtual representation.** After all, living an ocean away, their interests differed significantly from those of Britons. They insisted on **actual representation,** emphasizing that elected officials were directly accountable to their constituents.

Americans also agreed that Parliament had no legitimate right to tax the colonies. Colonials conceded Parliament's right to legislate and to regulate trade for the good of the whole empire. But taxation, in their view, was the free gift of the people through their representatives—who were not sitting in Parliament.

Members of Parliament brushed aside colonial petitions and resolves, all but ignoring these constitutional arguments. To make its own authority clear, Parliament accompanied the repeal of the Stamp Act with a Declaratory Act, asserting that it had the power to make laws for the colonies "in all cases whatsoever." In fact, the Declaratory Act clarified nothing. Did Parliament understand the power of legislation to include the power of taxation?

The Townshend Acts >> In the summer of

1766 George III—again unintentionally—gave the colonies what should have been an advantage by changing ministers yet again. The king replaced Rockingham with William Pitt, who enjoyed great favor among colonials for his leadership during the Seven Years' War and for his opposition to the Stamp Act. Almost alone among British politicians, Pitt had grasped and approved the colonists' constitutional objections to taxation. During Parliament's debate over repeal of the Stamp Act, Grenville asked sarcastically, "Tell me when the colonies were emancipated?" Pitt immediately shot back, "I desire to know when they were made slaves!"

If the man who believed that Americans were "the sons not the bastards of England" had been well enough to govern, matters between Great Britain and the colonies might have turned out differently. But almost immediately after Pitt took office his health collapsed, and power passed into the hands of Charles Townshend, the chancellor of the exchequer, who wished only to raise more

> **virtual representation** view that representation is not linked to election but rather to common interests. During the imperial crisis, the British argued that Americans were virtually represented in Parliament, even though colonials elected none of its members.
>
> **actual representation** view that the people can be represented only by a person whom they have actually elected to office.

revenue. In 1767 Townshend persuaded Parliament to tax the lead, paint, paper, glass, and tea that Americans imported from Britain. Then he used revenue from these new tariffs to pay the salaries of many royal officials serving in the colonies.

This was a change—and an important one. Previously, governors and other officers such as customs collectors and judges had received their salaries from colonial legislatures. The assemblies lost that crucial leverage when Townshend used the revenues to pay those bureaucrats directly. Royal officials depended less, now, on coming to terms with American legislators. Finally, in order to ensure more effective enforcement of all the duties on imports, Townshend created an American Board of Customs Commissioners, who appointed a small army of new customs collectors. He also established three new vice-admiralty courts in Boston, New York, and Charleston to bring smugglers to justice.

The Resistance Organizes >> In Townshend's efforts to centralize the administration of the empire, Americans saw new evidence that they were not being treated like the English. A host of newspapers and pamphlets took up the cry against taxation. The most widely read publication, "A Letter from a Farmer in Pennsylvania," was the work of John Dickinson—who was, in fact, a Philadelphia lawyer. He urged Americans to protest the Townshend duties by consuming fewer imported English luxuries. The virtues of hard work, thrift, and home manufacturing, Dickinson argued, would bring about repeal.

As Dickinson's star rose over Philadelphia, the Townshend Acts also shaped the destiny of another man farther north. Samuel Adams was a leader in the Massachusetts assembly, one whose rise had been unlikely. Adams's earlier ventures as a merchant ended in bankruptcy; his stint as a tax collector left all of Boston in the red. But he proved a consummate political organizer and agitator. First his enemies and later his friends claimed that Adams had decided on independence for America as early as 1768. In that

>> This 1766 porcelain of Lord Chatham and America attests to the popularity of William Pitt, Earl of Chatham, among Americans who resisted the Stamp Act. The artist's representation of "America" as a black woman kneeling in gratitude echoes the colonists' association of taxation with slavery.

year he persuaded the assembly to send to other colonial legislatures a circular letter condemning the Townshend Acts and calling for a united American resistance.

As John Dickinson and Samuel Adams whipped up public outrage, the Sons of Liberty again organized the opposition in the streets. Customs officials, like the stamp distributors before them, became targets of popular hatred. But the customs collectors gave as good as they got. Using the flimsiest excuses, they seized American vessels for violating royal regulations. With cold insolence they shook down American merchants for what amounted to protection money. The racketeering in the customs service brought tensions in Boston to a flash point in June 1768 after officials seized and condemned the *Liberty,* a sloop belonging to one of the city's biggest merchants, John Hancock. Several thousand Bostonians vented their anger in a night of rioting, searching out and roughing up customs officials.

The new secretary of state for the colonies, Lord Hillsborough, responded to the *Liberty* riot by sending two regiments of troops to Boston. In the fall of 1768 the redcoats, like a conquering army, paraded into town under the cover of warships lying off the harbor. In the months that followed, citizens bristled when challenged on the streets by armed soldiers. Even more disturbing to Bostonians was the execution of British military justice on the Common. British soldiers were whipped savagely for breaking military discipline, and desertion was punished by execution.

The *Liberty* riot and the arrival of British troops in Boston pushed colonial assemblies to coordinate their resistance more closely. Most legislatures endorsed the Massachusetts circular letter of protest sent to them by Samuel Adams. They promptly adopted agreements not to import or to consume British goods. The reluctance among some merchants to revive nonimportation in 1767 gave way to greater enthusiasm by 1768, and by early 1769 such agreements were in effect throughout the colonies.

The Stamp Act crisis had also called forth intercolonial cooperation and tactics such as nonimportation. But the protests against the Townshend Acts raised the stakes by creating new institutions to carry forward the resistance. Subscribers to the nonimportation agreements established "committees of inspection" to enforce the ban on trade with Britain. The committees publicly denounced merchants who continued to import, vandalized their warehouses, forced them to stand under the gallows, and sometimes resorted to tar and feathers.

After 1768 the resistance also brought a broader range of colonials into the politics of protest. Artisans, who recognized that nonimportation would spur domestic manufacturing, began to organize as independent political groups. In many towns women took an active part in opposing the Townshend duties. The "Daughters of Liberty" took to heart John Dickinson's advice: they wore homespun clothing instead of English finery, served coffee instead of tea, and boycotted shops selling British goods.

The International Sons of Liberty »

The resistance after 1768 grew broader in another sense. Many of its supporters in the colonies felt a new sense of kinship with freedom fighters throughout Europe. Eagerly they read about the doings of men such as Charles Lucas, an Irish newspaper editor and member of the Irish Parliament, and John Wilkes, a London journalist and a leading politician of the Opposition. Both men charged the king's ministers with corrupting the political life of the British Isles. The doings of political rebels even in distant Poland and Turkey engaged colonial sympathies, too. But perhaps the international cause dearest to American lovers of liberty was the fate of Corsica.

For years this tiny island off the coast of Italy had fought for its independence, first from the Italian state of Genoa and then from France, which bought the island in 1768. The leader of the Corsican rebellion, Pascal Paoli, hoped that England would rally to defend Corsica's freedom, if only to keep France from seizing this strategic Mediterranean outpost. But British statesmen had no intention of going to war with France over mere Corsica, and when French troops routed his rebel army, Paoli fled to exile in England in 1769. Adding insult to injury this "greatest man of earth," as he was lionized, began to hobnob with British nobles. He even accepted a pension of 1,000 pounds a year from George III. The moral of the sad story, according to more than one colonial newspaper, was that British corruption pervaded not only the empire but all of Europe. Within a few years Europeans sympathizing with these notions would cross the Atlantic to fight in the American Revolution.

The Boston Massacre »

Meanwhile the situation in Boston deteriorated steadily. British troops found themselves regularly cursed by citizens and occasionally pelted with stones, dirt, and human excrement. The British regulars were particularly unpopular among Boston's laboring classes, because they competed with them for jobs. Off-duty soldiers moonlighted as maritime laborers, and they sold their services at rates cheaper than the wages paid to locals. By 1769 brawls between British regulars and waterfront workers broke out frequently.

> By 1769 brawls between British regulars and Boston's waterfront workers broke out frequently.

>> Like a swarm of angry bees British troops disembark on one of Boston's long wharves in 1768. American colonials who had cheered the triumphs of British soldiers only a few years earlier now complained bitterly about the presence of a standing army designed to intimidate them.

With some 4,000 redcoats enduring daily contact with some 15,000 Bostonians under the sway of Samuel Adams, what happened on the night of March 5, 1770, was nearly inevitable. A crowd gathered around the customs-house for the sport of heckling the 10 soldiers who guarded it. The redcoats panicked and fended off insults and snowballs with live fire, hitting 11 rioters and killing 5. Adams and other propagandists seized on the incident. Labeling the bloodshed "the Boston Massacre," they publicized that "atrocity" throughout the colonies. The radical Boston *Gazette* framed its account in an eye-catching black-bordered edition headed with a drawing of five coffins.

While Townshend's policies spurred the resistance in America, the obvious finally dawned on Parliament. They recognized that Townshend's duties on imported English goods only discouraged sales to colonials and encouraged them to manufacture at home. The argument for repeal was overwhelming, and the way had been cleared by the unexpected death of Townshend. In 1770 his successor, Lord North, convinced Parliament to repeal all the Townshend duties except the one on tea, allowing that tax to stand as a source of revenue and as a symbol of Parliament's authority.

Resistance Revived >> Repeal of the Townshend duties took the wind from the sails of American resistance for more than two years. But the controversy between England and the colonies had not been resolved. Colonials still paid taxes on molasses and tea, taxes to which they had not consented. They were still subject to trial in admiralty courts, which operated without juries. They still lived with a standing army in their midst. Beneath the banked fires of protest smoldered the live embers of Americans' political inequality. Any shift in the wind could fan those embers into flames.

The wind did shift, quite literally, on Narragansett Bay in 1772, running aground the *Gaspee,* a British naval schooner in hot pursuit of Rhode Island smugglers. Residents of nearby Providence quickly celebrated the *Gaspee*'s misfortune by burning it down to the water line. Outraged British officials sent a special commission to look into the matter, intending once again to bypass the established colonial court system. The arrival of the Gaspee Commission reignited the imperial crisis, and in America, once again, resistance flared.

Opinion

Were the Whigs right to worry about the dangers of a standing army? If so, does our standing army pose a danger today?

It did so through an ingenious mechanism, the **committees of correspondence.** Established in all the colonies by their assemblies, the committees drew up statements of American rights and grievances, distributed those documents within and among the colonies, and solicited responses from towns and counties. The brainchild of Samuel Adams, the committee structure formed a new communications network, one that fostered an intercolonial agreement on resistance to British measures. The strategy succeeded, and not only among colonies. The committees spread the scope of the resistance from colonial seaports into rural areas, engaging farmers and other country folk in the opposition to Britain.

The committees had much to talk about when Parliament passed the Tea Act in 1773. The law was an effort to bail out the bankrupt East India Company by granting that corporation a monopoly on the tea trade to Americans. Because the company could use agents to sell its product directly, cutting out the middlemen, it could offer a lower price than that charged by colonial merchants. Thus, although the Tea Act would hurt American merchants, it promised to make tea cheaper for ordinary Americans. Still, many colonials saw the act as Parliament's attempt to trick them into accepting its authority to tax the colonies. They set out to deny that power once and for all.

In the early winter of 1773 popular leaders in Boston called for the tea cargoes to be returned immediately to England. On the evening of December 16, thousands of Bostonians, as well as farmers from the surrounding countryside, packed into the Old South Meetinghouse. Some members of the audience knew what Samuel Adams planned for the evening's agenda, and they awaited their cue. It came when Adams told the meeting that they could do nothing more to save their country. War whoops rang through the meetinghouse, the crowd spilled onto the streets and out to the waterfront, and the Boston Tea Party commenced. From the throng emerged 50 men dressed as Indians to disguise their identities. The party boarded three vessels docked off Griffin's Wharf, broke open casks containing 90,000 pounds of tea, and brewed a beverage worth 10,000 pounds sterling in Boston harbor.

The Empire Strikes Back >> The Boston Tea Party proved to British satisfaction that the colonies aimed at independence. Lord North's assessment was grim: "We are now to dispute whether we have, or have not, any authority in that country." To reassert its authority, Parliament passed the Coercive Acts, dubbed in the colonies the "Intolerable Acts." The first of these came in March 1774, after hearing of the Tea Party, when Parliament passed the Boston Port Bill, closing that harbor to all oceangoing traffic until such time as the king saw fit to reopen it. And George, Parliament announced, would not see fit until colonials paid the East India Company for their losses.

During the next three months Parliament approved three other "intolerable" laws designed to punish Massachusetts. The Massachusetts Government Act handed over the colony's government to royal officials. Even convening town meetings would require royal permission. The Impartial Administration of Justice Act permitted any royal official accused of a crime in Massachusetts to be tried in England or in another colony. The Quartering Act allowed the housing of British troops in uninhabited private homes, outlying buildings, and barns—not only in Massachusetts but in all the colonies.

Many colonials saw the Coercive Acts as proof of a plot to enslave the colonies. In truth, the taxes and duties, laws and regulations of the past decade *were* part of a deliberate design—a plan to centralize the administration of the British empire that seemed only common sense to British officials. But those efforts by the king's ministers and Parliament to run the colonies more efficiently and profitably were viewed by more and more Americans as a sinister conspiracy against their liberties.

⋀ While the new political activism of some American women merely amused male leaders of the resistance, it inspired the scorn of some defenders of British authority. When the women of Edenton, North Carolina, renounced imported tea, this British cartoon mocked them. Can you find at least five details in the drawing used by the artist to insult the Americans?

For colonials the study of history confirmed that interpretation, especially their reading of the histories written by the English Opposition. The Opposition's favorite historical subject was the downfall of republics, whether those of ancient Greece and Rome or more recent republican governments in Venice and Denmark. The lesson of their histories was always the same: power overwhelmed liberty, unless the people remained vigilant. The pattern, argued radicals, had been repeated in America over the previous dozen years: costly wars waged; oppressive taxes levied to pay for them; standing armies sent to overawe citizens; corrupt governors, customs collectors, and judges appointed to enrich themselves by enforcing the measures. Everything seemed to fit.

Week after week in the spring of 1774, reports of legislative outrages came across the waters. Shortly after approving the Coercive Acts, Parliament passed the Québec Act, which established a permanent government in what had been French Canada. Ominously, it included no representative assembly. Equally ominous to Protestant colonials, the Québec Act officially recognized the Roman Catholic Church and extended the bounds of the province to include all land between the Mississippi and Ohio rivers. Suddenly New York, Pennsylvania, and Virginia found themselves bordering a British colony whose subjects had no voice in their own government.

With the passage of the Coercive Acts, many more colonials came to believe not only that ambitious men plotted to enslave the colonies but also that those conspirators included almost all British political leaders. At the time of the Stamp Act and again during the agitation against the Townshend Acts, most colonials had confined their suspicions to the king's ministers. By 1774 members of Parliament were also implicated in that conspiracy—and a few radicals were wondering aloud about George III.

As alarm deepened in the wake of the Coercive Acts, one colony after another called for an intercolonial congress—like the one that had met during the Stamp Act crisis—to determine the best way to defend their freedom. But many also remained unsettled about where the logic of their actions seemed to be taking them: toward a denial that they were any longer English.

 REVIEW

How did British colonial policy change after the Seven Years' War, and in what ways did colonial Americans resist it?

TOWARD THE REVOLUTION

By the beginning of September 1774, when 55 delegates to the First Continental Congress gathered in Philadelphia, the news from Massachusetts was grim. The colony verged on anarchy, it was reported, as its inhabitants resisted the enforcement of the Massachusetts Government Act.

In the midst of this atmosphere of crisis, the members of Congress also had to take one another's measure. Many of the delegates had not traveled outside their own colonies. (All but Georgia sent representatives.) Although the delegates encountered a great deal of diversity, they quickly discovered that they esteemed the same traits of character, attributes that they called "civic virtue." These traits included simplicity and self-reliance, industry and thrift, and above all, an unselfish commitment to the public good. Most members of the Congress also shared a common mistrust of England, associating the mother country with vice, extravagance, and corruption. Still, the delegates had some misgivings about those from other colonies. Massachusetts in particular brought with it a reputation—well deserved, considering that Samuel Adams was along—for radical action and a willingness to use force to accomplish its ends.

The First Continental Congress >> As the delegates settled down to business, their aim was to reach agreement on three key points. How were they to justify the rights they claimed as American colonials? What were the limits of Parliament's power? And what were the proper tactics for resisting the Coercive Acts? Congress quickly agreed on the first point. The delegates affirmed that the law of nature, the colonial charters, and the British constitution provided the foundations of American liberties. This position was what most colonials had argued since 1765.

On the two other issues, Congress charted a middle course between the demands of radicals and the reservations of conservatives. Since the time of the Stamp Act, most colonials had insisted that Parliament had no authority to tax the colonies. But later events had demonstrated that Parliament could undermine colonial liberties by legislation as well as by taxation. The suspension of the New York legislature, the Gaspee Commission, and the Coercive Acts all fell into this category. Given those experiences, the delegates adopted a Declaration of Rights and Grievances on October 14, 1774, asserting the right of the colonies to tax and legislate for themselves. The Declaration of Rights thus limited Parliament's power over Americans more strictly than colonials had a decade earlier.

By denying Parliament's power to make laws for the colonies, the Continental Congress blocked efforts of the most conservative delegates to reach an accommodation with England. Their leading advocate, Joseph Galloway of Pennsylvania, proposed a plan of union with Britain similar to the one set forth by the Albany Congress in 1754. Under it, a grand council of the colonies would handle all common concerns, with any laws it passed subject to review and veto by Parliament. For its part, Parliament would have to submit for the grand council's approval any acts it passed affecting America. A majority of delegates judged that Galloway left Parliament too much leeway in legislating for colonials, and they rejected his plan.

Although the Congress denied Parliament the right to impose taxes or to make laws, delegates stopped short of declaring that it had no authority at all in the colonies. They approved Parliament's regulation of trade, but only because of the interdependent economy of the empire. And although some radical pamphleteers were attacking the king for plotting against American liberties, Congress acknowledged the continuing allegiance of the colonies to George III. In other words, the delegates called for a return to the situation that had existed in the empire before 1763, with Parliament regulating trade and the colonies exercising all powers of taxation and legislation.

On the question of resistance, the Congress satisfied the desires of its most radical delegates by drawing up the Continental Association, an agreement to cease all trade with Britain until the Coercive Acts were repealed. They agreed that their fellow citizens would immediately stop drinking East India Company tea and that by December 1, 1774, merchants would no longer import goods of any sort from Britain. A ban on the export of American produce to Britain and the West Indies would go into effect a year later, during September 1775—the lag being a concession to southern rice and tobacco planters, who wanted to market crops already planted.

The Association provided for the total cessation of trade, but Samuel Adams and other radicals wanted bolder action. They received help from Paul Revere, a Boston silversmith who had long provided newspapers with lurid engravings showing British abuses. On September 16 Revere galloped into Philadelphia bearing a copy of resolves drawn up by Bostonians and other residents of Suffolk county. The Suffolk Resolves, as they were called, branded the Coercive Acts as unconstitutional and called for civil disobedience to protest them. Congress endorsed the resolves, as Adams had hoped. But it would not approve another part of the radicals' agenda—preparing for war by authorizing proposals to strengthen and arm colonial militias.

Thus the First Continental Congress steered a middle course. Although determined to bring about repeal of the Coercive Acts, it held firm in resisting any revolutionary course of action. If British officials had responded to its recommendations and restored the status quo of 1763, the war for independence might have been postponed—perhaps indefinitely. However, even though the Congress did not go to the extremes urged by the radicals, its decisions drew colonials farther down the road to independence.

The Last Days of the British Empire in America >> Most colonials applauded the achievements of the First Continental Congress. They expected that the Association would bring about a speedy repeal of the Coercive Acts. But fear that the colonies were moving toward a break with Britain led others to denounce the doings of the Congress. Conservatives were convinced that if independence were declared, chaos would ensue. Colonials, they argued, would quarrel over land claims and sectional tensions and religious differences, as they had so often in the recent past. Without Britain to referee such disputes, they feared, the result would be civil war, followed by anarchy.

The man in America with the least liking for the Continental Congress sat in the hottest seat in the colonies, that of the governor of Massachusetts. General Thomas Gage watched as royal authority crumbled in Massachusetts and the rebellion spread to other colonies. In June 1774 a desperate Gage dissolved the Massachusetts legislature, only to see it re-form, on its own, into a Provincial Congress. That new body assumed the government of the colony in October and began arming the militia. Gage then started to fortify Boston and pleaded for more troops—only to find his fortifications damaged by saboteurs and his requests for reinforcements ignored by Britain.

Outside Boston royal authority fared no better. Farmers in western Massachusetts forcibly closed the county courts, turning out royally appointed justices and establishing their own tribunals. Popularly elected committees of inspection charged with enforcing the Association took over towns everywhere in Massachusetts, not only restricting trade but also regulating every aspect of local life. The committees called on townspeople to display civic virtue by renouncing "effeminate" English luxuries such as tea and fine clothing and "corrupt" leisure activities such as dancing, gambling, and racing. The committees also assigned spies to report on any citizen unfriendly to the resistance. "Enemies of American liberty" risked being roundly condemned in public or beaten and pelted with mud and dung by hooting, raucous mobs.

Throughout the other colonies a similar process was under way. During the winter and early spring of 1775 provincial congresses, county conventions, and local committees of inspection were emerging as revolutionary governments, replacing royal authority at every level. As the spectacle unfolded before General Gage, he concluded that only force could subdue the colonies. It would take more than he had at his command, but reinforcements might be on the way. In February of 1775 Parliament had approved an address to the king declaring that the colonies were in rebellion.

The Fighting Begins >> As spring came to Boston the city waited. A band of artisans, organized as spies and express riders by Paul Revere, watched General Gage and waited for him to act. On April 14 word from Lord North finally arrived: Gage was to seize the leaders of the Provincial Congress, an action that would behead the rebellion, North said. Gage knew better than to believe North—but he also knew that he had to do something.

On the night of April 18 the sexton of Boston's Christ Church hung two lamps from its steeple. It was a signal that British troops had moved out of Boston and were marching toward the arms and ammunition stored by the

↗ Amos Doolittle engraved this scene of retreating British troops after the skirmishes at Lexington and Concord. As the engraving makes clear, American militia took advantage of the stone fences to provide cover as sharpshooters picked off the retreating redcoats.

Provincial Congress in Concord. As the lamps flashed the signal, Revere and a comrade, William Dawes, rode out to arouse the countryside.

When the news of a British march reached Lexington, its Minuteman militia of about 70 farmers, chilled and sleepy, mustered on the Green at the center of the small rural town. Lexington Green lay directly on the road to Concord. About four in the morning 700 British troops massed on the Green, and their commander, Major John Pitcairn, ordered the Lexington militia to disperse. The townsmen, outnumbered and overawed, began to obey. Then a shot rang out—whether the British or the Americans fired first is unknown—and then two volleys burst from the ranks of the redcoats. With a cheer the British set off for Concord, five miles distant, leaving eight Americans dead on Lexington Green.

By dawn hundreds of Minutemen from nearby towns were surging into Concord. The British entered at about seven in the morning and moved, unopposed, toward their target, a house lying across the bridge that spanned the Concord River. While three companies of British soldiers searched for American guns and ammunition, three others, posted on the bridge, had the misfortune to find those American arms—borne by the rebels and being fired with deadly accuracy. By noon the British were retreating to Boston.

The narrow road from Concord to Boston's outskirts became a corridor of carnage. Pursuing Americans fired on the column of fleeing redcoats from the cover of fences and forests. By the end of April 19 the British had sustained 273 casualties; the Americans, 95. It was only the beginning. By evening of the next day some 20,000 New England militia had converged on Boston for a long siege.

Common Sense >>

The bloodshed at Lexington Green and Concord's North Bridge committed colonials to a course of rebellion—and independence. That was the conclusion drawn by Thomas Paine, who urged other Americans to join the rebels.

Paine himself was hardly an American. He was born in England, first apprenticed as a corsetmaker, appointed later a tax collector, and fated finally to become midwife to the age of republican revolutions. Paine came to Philadelphia late in 1774, set up as a journalist, and made the American cause his own. "Where liberty is, there is my country," he declared. In January 1776 he wrote a pamphlet to inform colonials of their identity as a distinct people and their destiny as a nation. *Common Sense* enjoyed tremendous popularity and wide circulation, selling 120,000 copies.

After Lexington and Concord Paine wrote, as the imperial crisis passed "from argument to arms, a new era for politics is struck—a new method of thinking has arisen." That new era of politics for Paine was the age of republicanism. He denounced monarchy as a foolish and dangerous form of government, one that violated the dictates of reason as well as the word of the Bible. By ridicule and remorseless argument, he severed the ties of colonial allegiance to the king. *Common Sense* scorned George III as "the Royal Brute of Britain," who had enslaved the chosen people of the new age—the Americans.

Nor did Paine stop there. He rejected the idea that colonials were or should want to be English. The colonies occupied a huge continent an ocean away from the tiny British Isles—clear proof that nature itself had fashioned America for independence. England lay locked in Europe, doomed to the corruption of an Old World. America had been discovered anew to become an "asylum of liberty."

 REVIEW

What course of events had occurred by the mid-1770s to transform non-importation and political protest into organized rebellion?

Many Americans had liked being English, but being English hadn't worked. Perhaps that is another way of saying that over the course of nearly two centuries colonial society and politics had evolved in such a way that for Americans an English identity no longer fit.

The radicals in America viewed this change in identity in terms of age-old conspiracies that repeated themselves throughout history. First, the people of a republic were impoverished by costly wars—as the colonists could appreciate after the Seven Year's War. Then the government burdened the people with taxes to pay for those wars—as in the case of the Sugar Act or the Stamp Act or the Townshend duties. Next those in power stationed a standing army in the country, pretending to protect the people but actually lending military force to their rulers. The rhetoric of the Opposition about ministerial conspiracies gave such talk a fervid quality that, to some modern ears, may seem an exaggeration.

Take away the rhetoric, however, and the argument makes uncomfortable sense. The British administration began its "backwoods" war with France, intending to limit it to the interior of North America. But the war aims of William Pitt—the leader Americans counted as their friend—grew with every victory, turning the conflict into a world war, driving France out of India and attacking Spain's colonies in the Philippines and Cuba. Peace came only once Britain and the major powers had bankrupted their treasuries. Conspiracy may not have been at the heart of the plan. But wars must be paid for. And so began the effort to regulate and bring order to Britain's "ungrateful" colonies.

In America, colonials were ungrateful precisely because their political institutions made the rights of "freeborn Britons" more available to ordinary citizens than they were in the nation that had created those liberties. Ironically, perhaps most Americans had succeeded *too* well at becoming English, regarding themselves as political equals entitled to basic constitutional freedoms. The imperial crisis made clear that despite all that the English and Americans shared, they stood fundamentally at odds over the distribution of political power. The call to arms at Lexington and Concord made retreat impossible.

On that point Paine was clear. It was the destiny of Americans to be republicans, not monarchists. It was the destiny of Americans to be independent, not subject to British dominion. It was the destiny of Americans to be American, not English. That, according to Thomas Paine, was common sense.

CHAPTER SUMMARY

Following its victory in the Seven Years' War Britain adopted policies designed to administer new territories and boost revenue. But these policies provoked a colonial backlash that led ultimately to the Revolutionary War.

Significant Events

Braddock defeated by French and Indians	Decisive English victory at Quebec			Stamp Act; Quartering Act		Repeal of the Stamp Act; Declaratory Act
1755	**1756**	**1759**	**1763**	**1764**	**1765**	**1766**
	England and France declare war		Treaty of Paris ends the Seven Years' War; Pontiac's Rebellion	Sugar Act; Currency Act		

THE PENNSYLVANIA JOURNAL; AND WEEKLY ADVERTISER.

- French and Indian forces did well at first during the Seven Years' War, as British policies alienated colonials and Indians alike.
- But William Pitt's reforms galvanized the colonies, won Britain Indian allies, and triumphed over France throughout the continent.
- Partly in response to Pontiac's Rebellion, Britain moderated its Indian policies and, with the Proclamation of 1763, forbade all colonial settlement west of the Appalachians.
- The new measures passed by Parliament in the early 1760s—the Proclamation of 1763, the Sugar Act, the Stamp Act, the Currency Act, and the Quartering Act—were all designed to generate revenue and bind the colonies more closely to the empire.
- These new measures deflated American expectations that they would be treated equally and violated what they held to be their right to consent to taxation, their right to trial by jury, and their right to freedom from standing armies.
- Although Parliament repealed the Stamp Act in the face of colonial protests, it reasserted its authority to tax Americans by passing the Townshend Acts in 1767.
- The Coercive Acts of 1774 led Americans to conclude that British actions in the past decade were part of a plot to enslave Americans by depriving them of property and liberty.
- At the First Continental Congress delegates resisted both radical demands to mobilize for war and conservative appeals to reach an accommodation. The Congress denied Parliament any authority in the colonies except the right to regulate trade; it also drew up the Continental Association, an agreement to cease all trade with Britain until the Coercive Acts were repealed.
- When General Thomas Gage sent troops from Boston in April 1775 to seize arms being stored at Concord, the first battle of the Revolution took place.

Additional Reading

Fred Anderson, *Crucible of War* (2000), offers a magisterial account of the Seven Years' War, and Gregory Evans Dowd, *War Under Heaven* (2002), explores the implications of that conflict for American Indians. *The Stamp Act Crisis* (1953) by Edmund S. Morgan and Helen M. Morgan remains the clearest and most vivid portrayal of that defining moment. For American resistance after the Stamp Act, see Pauline Maier, *From Resistance to Revolution* (1972), and to understand that struggle as lived and recalled by a Boston artisan, read Alfred F. Young's engaging book, *The Shoemaker and the Tea Party* (1999). Two key interpretations of the logic of revolutionary resistance in Massachusetts and Virginia are Robert Gross, *The Minutemen and Their World* (1976), and Timothy Breen, *Tobacco Culture* (1985). A more recent study by Breen, *The Marketplace Revolution* (2005), sheds light on the role of a transatlantic consumer culture in fueling tensions within the British Empire.

Bernard Bailyn, *The Ideological Origins of the American Revolution* (1967), remains the classic study of the English Opposition and republican political thought in America. For biographies of eighteenth-century Americans who led—or opposed—the resistance to Britain see Pauline Maier, *The Old Revolutionaries* (1980); Bailyn's *The Ordeal of Thomas Hutchinson* (1974); and two recent biographies of Thomas Paine (both published in 2006) by Harvey Kaye and Craig Nelson.

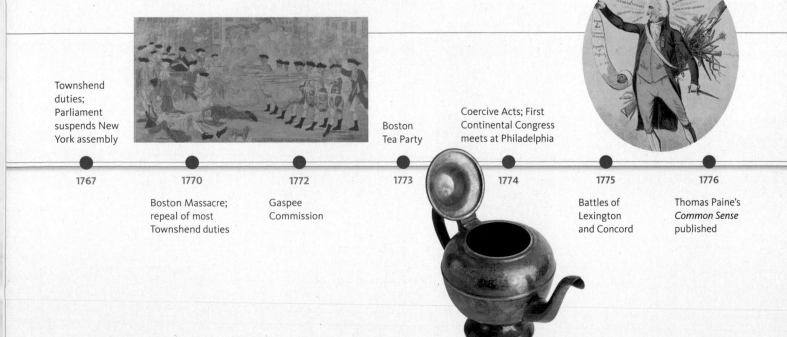

Townshend duties; Parliament suspends New York assembly

Boston Tea Party

Coercive Acts; First Continental Congress meets at Philadelphia

1767

1770

Boston Massacre; repeal of most Townshend duties

1772

Gaspee Commission

1773

1774

1775

Battles of Lexington and Concord

1776

Thomas Paine's *Common Sense* published

Only 18 miles outside Philadelphia, at Valley Forge, Washington and his Continentals were assessing their own situation. Some 11,000 rebel soldiers had passed a harrowing winter in that isolated spot, starving for want of food, freezing for lack of clothing, huddling in miserable huts, and hating the British who lay 18 miles away in Philadelphia. The army also cursed their fellow citizens, for its misery resulted from congressional disorganization and civilian indifference. Congress lacked both money to pay and maintain the army and an efficient system for dispensing provisions to the troops. Most farmers and merchants preferred to supply the British, who could pay handsomely, than to do business with financially strapped Congress. What little did reach the army often was food too rancid to eat or clothing too rotten to wear. Perhaps 2,500 perished at Valley Forge, the victims of cold, hunger, and disease.

Why did civilians who supported the rebel cause allow the army to suffer? Probably because by the winter of 1777 the Continentals came mainly from social classes that received little consideration at any time. The respectable, propertied farmers and artisans who had laid siege to Boston in 1775 had stopped enlisting. Serving in their stead were single men in their teens and early twenties, some who joined the army out of desperation, others who were drafted, still others who were hired as substitutes for the more affluent. The landless sons of farmers, unemployed laborers, drifters, petty criminals, vagrants, indentured servants, slaves, even captured British and Hessian soldiers—all men with no other means and no other choice—were swept into the Continental Army. The social composition of the rebel rank and file had come to resemble that of the British army. It is the great irony of the Revolution: a war to protect liberty and property was waged by those Americans who were poorest and least free.

The beginning of spring in 1778 brought a reprieve. Supplies arrived at Valley Forge, and so did a fellow calling himself Baron von Steuben, a penniless Prussian soldier of fortune. Although Washington's men had shown spirit and resilience ever since Trenton, they still lacked discipline and training. Those defects and more von Steuben began to remedy. Barking orders and spewing curses in German and French, the baron (and his translators) drilled the rebel regiments to march in formation and to handle their bayonets like proper Prussian soldiers. By the summer of 1778 morale had rebounded.

Spoiling for action after their long winter, Washington's army, now numbering nearly 13,500, harassed Clinton's army as it marched overland from Philadelphia

Perhaps 2,500 perished at Valley Forge, the victims of cold, hunger, and disease.

to New York. On June 28 at Monmouth Courthouse, a long, confused battle ended in a draw. After both armies retired for the night Clinton's forces slipped away to safety in New York City. Washington pursued, but he lacked the numbers to launch an all-out assault on New York City.

During the two hard winters that followed, resentments mounted among the rank and file over spoiled food, inadequate clothing, and arrears in pay. The army retaliated with **mutinies**. Between 1779 and 1780 officers managed to quell uprisings in three New England regiments. But in January 1781 both the Pennsylvania and the New Jersey lines mutinied outright and marched on Philadelphia, where Congress had reconvened. Order returned only after Congress promised back pay and provisions and Washington put two ringleaders in front of a firing squad.

mutiny refusal of rank-and-file soldiers to follow the commands of their superior officers.

War in the West >>
The battles between Washington's Continentals and the British made the war in the West seem, by comparison, a sideshow of attacks and counterattacks that settled little. American fighters, such as George Rogers Clark, captured outposts such as Kaskaskia and Vincennes without materially affecting the outcome of the war. Yet the conflict sparked a tremendous upheaval in the West, both from the dislocations of war and from the disease that spread in war's wake.

The disruptions were so widespread because the "War for Independence" had also become a war involving the imperial powers of Britain, France, and Spain. Those European powers and the United States pressed Indian tribes to become allies and attacked them when they did not. Caught in the crossfire, some Indian nations were pushed to the brink of their own civil war, splitting into pro-American or British factions.

Indians understood that the pressures of war always threatened to deprive them of their homelands. "You are drawing so close to us that we can almost hear the noise of your axes felling our Trees," one Shawnee told the Americans. Thousands fled the raids and counter-raids, while whole villages relocated. Hundreds made their way even beyond the Mississippi, to seek shelter in territory claimed by Spain.

The political instability was vastly compounded by a smallpox epidemic that broke out first among American troops besieging Québec in 1775. The disease soon spread to Washington's troops in New England

THE SMALLPOX PANDEMIC, 1775–1782

Smallpox spread across North America beginning late in 1775 as American forces attacked the city of Québec in Canada. The routes of transmission give only a rough idea of the disease's impact, as it moved down the eastern seaboard and around the Gulf of Mexico, and then penetrated the interior, where the scattered surviving data make the pandemic harder to track. But the ravages of smallpox, combined with the disruptions sparked by the western raids of the Revolutionary War, placed severe stress on Indian peoples all across the continent.

The seasons of intense fighting drew men off into military service just when their labor was most needed on family farms. Wives and daughters were left to assume the work of husbands and sons while coping with loneliness, anxiety, and grief. Often enough the disruptions, flight, and loss of family members left lasting scars. Two years after she fled before Burgoyne's advance into upstate New York, Ann Eliza Bleecker confessed to a friend, "I muse so long on the dead until I am unfit for the company of the living."

Despite these hardships, many women vigorously supported the revolutionary cause in a variety of ways. The Daughters of Liberty joined in harassing those who opposed the rebel cause. One outspoken loyalist found himself surrounded by angry women who stripped off his shirt, covered him with molasses, and plastered him with flower petals. In more genteel fashion, groups of well-to-do women collected not only money but medicines, food, and pewter to melt for bullets.

and then south along the coast; it eventually reached New Orleans and leapt to Mexico City by the autumn of 1779. From New Orleans it spread via fur traders up the Mississippi River and across the central plains, and from New Spain northward as well. By the time the pandemic burned out in 1782, it had felled over 130,000. By contrast, the Revolutionary War caused the deaths of some 8,000 soldiers while fighting in battle and another 13,000 from disease, including the mortality from smallpox.

The Home Front in the North >> By 1779
most northern civilians along the eastern seaboard gained a respite from the war. But disease and military demands disrupted family economies throughout the countryside.

 REVIEW

How did the Revolution become a global war, and what were conditions like for both soldiers and civilians?

THE STRUGGLE IN THE SOUTH

By the autumn of 1778 the British had come to believe that their most vital aim was to regain their colonies in the mainland South. The Chesapeake and the Carolinas were more profitable to the empire and more strategically important, being so much closer to rich British sugar islands in the West Indies. Inspired by this new "southern strategy," Clinton dispatched forces to the Caribbean and Florida. In addition, the British laid plans for a new offensive drive into the Carolinas and Virginia.

English politicians and generals believed that the war could be won in the South. Loyalists were numerous, they believed, especially in the backcountry, where resentment of the seaboard, a rebel stronghold, would breed readiness among frontier folk to take up arms for the king at the first show of British force. And southern rebels—especially the vulnerable planters along the coast—could not afford to turn their guns away from their slaves. So, at least, the British theorized. All that was needed, they concluded, was for the British army to establish a beachhead in the South and then, in league with loyalists, drive northward, pacifying the population while pressing up the coast.

The Siege of Charleston >> The southern strategy worked well for a short time in a small place. In November 1778 Clinton sent 3,500 troops to Savannah, Georgia. The resistance in the tiny colony quickly collapsed, and a large number of loyalists turned out to help the British. Encouraged by that success, the British moved on to South Carolina.

During the last days of 1779 an expedition under Clinton himself set sail from New York City. Landing off the Georgia coast, his troops mucked through the swamps to the peninsula lying between the Ashley and the Cooper rivers. At the tip of that neck of land stood Charleston, and the British began to lay siege. By then an unseasonably warm spring had set in, making the area a heaven for mosquitoes and a hell for human beings. Sweltering and swatting, redcoats weighted down in their woolen uniforms inched their siegeworks toward the city. By early May Clinton's army had closed in, and British shelling was setting

WITNESS

Partisan War in the Backcountry

"I was invited by some of my comrades to go and see some of the prisoners. We went to where six were standing together. Some discussion was taking place, I heard some of our men cry out, 'Remember Buford,' [a rebel soldier killed by loyalists] and the prisoners were immediately hewed to pieces with broadswords. At first I bore the scene without any emotion, but upon a moment's reflection, I felt such horror as I never felt before nor have since . . ."

—Moses Hall, *Description of a Battle's Aftermath in North Carolina*, **February 1781**

fire to houses within the city. On May 12 Charleston surrendered.

Clinton sailed back to New York at the end of June 1780, leaving behind 8,300 redcoats to carry the British offensive northward to Virginia. The man charged with leading that campaign was his ambitious and able subordinate Charles, Lord Cornwallis.

The Partisan Struggle in the South >>

Cornwallis's task in the Carolinas was complicated by the bitter animosity between rebels and loyalists there. Many Carolinians had taken sides years before Clinton's conquest of Charleston. In the summer and fall of 1775 the supporters of Congress and the new South Carolina revolutionary government mobbed, tortured, and imprisoned supporters of the king in the backcountry. These attacks only hardened loyalist resolve: roving bands seized ammunition, broke their leaders out of jail, and besieged rebel outposts. But within a matter of months, a combined force of rebel militias from the coast and the frontier managed to defeat loyalist forces in the backcountry.

With the fall of Charleston in 1780 the loyalist movement on the frontier returned to life. Out of loyalist vengefulness and rebel desperation issued the brutal civil war that seared the southern backcountry after 1780. Neighbors and even family members fought and killed one another as members of roaming rebel and tory militias. The intensity of **partisan warfare** in the backcountry produced unprecedented destruction. All of society, observed one minister, "seems to be at an end. Every person keeps close on his own plantation. Robberies and murders are often committed on the public roads. . . . Poverty, want, and hardship appear in almost every countenance."

partisan warfare armed clashes among political rivals, typically involving guerilla fighting and the violent intimidation of civilians by militias.

Cornwallis, when confronted with the chaos, erred fatally. He did nothing to stop his loyalist allies or his own troops from mistreating civilians. A Carolina loyalist admitted that "the lower sort of People, who were in many parts originally attached to the British Government, have suffered so severely . . . that Great Britain has now a hundred enemies, where it had one before."

A growing number of civilians outraged by the king's men cast their lot with the rebels. That upsurge of popular support enabled Francis Marion, the "Swamp Fox," and his band of white and black raiders to cut British lines of communication between Charleston and the interior. It mobilized the "over-the-mountain men," a rebel militia in western Carolina, who claimed victory at the Battle of King's Mountain in October 1780. By the end of 1780 these successes had persuaded most civilians that only the rebels could restore order.

If rebel fortunes prospered in the partisan struggle, they faltered in the conventional warfare being waged at the same time in the South. In August 1780 the Continentals commanded by Horatio Gates lost a major engagement to the British force at Camden, South Carolina. In the fall of 1780 Congress replaced Gates with Washington's candidate for the southern command, Nathanael Greene, an energetic, 38-year-old Rhode Islander and a veteran of the northern campaigns.

Greene Takes Command »

Greene bore out Washington's confidence by grasping the military situation in the South. He understood the needs of his 1,400 hungry, ragged, and demoralized troops and instructed von Steuben to lobby Virginia for food and clothing. He understood the importance of the rebel militias and sent Lieutenant Colonel Henry "Lighthorse Harry" Lee to assist Marion's raids. He understood the weariness of southern civilians and prevented his men from plundering the countryside.

Above all Greene understood that his forces could never hold the field against the whole British army. That led him to break the first rule of conventional warfare: he divided his army. In December 1780 he dispatched to western South Carolina a detachment of 600 men under the command of Brigadier General Daniel Morgan of Virginia.

Back at the British camp Cornwallis worried that Morgan and his rebels, if left unchecked, might rally the entire backcountry against the British. However, Cornwallis reckoned that he could not commit his entire army to the pursuit of Morgan's men, for then Greene and his troops might retake Charleston. The only solution, unconventional to be sure, was for Cornwallis to divide his army. That he did, sending Lieutenant Colonel Banastre Tarleton and 1,100 men west after Morgan. Cornwallis had played right into Greene's hands: the rebel troops might be able to defeat a British army split into two pieces. For two weeks Morgan led Tarleton's troops on a breakneck chase across the Carolina countryside. In January 1781 at an open meadow called Cowpens, Morgan routed Tarleton's force.

Now Cornwallis took up the chase. Morgan and Greene joined forces and agreed to keep going north until the British army wore out. Cornwallis finally stopped at Hillsboro, North Carolina, but few local loyalists responded to his call for reinforcements. To ensure that loyalist ranks remained thin, Greene decided to make a show of force near the tiny village of Guilford Courthouse. On a brisk March day the

THE FIGHTING IN THE SOUTH, 1780–1781

In December 1780 Nathanael Greene made the crucial decision to split his army, sending Daniel Morgan west, where he defeated the pursuing Banastre Tarleton at Cowpens. Meanwhile Greene regrouped and replenished at Cheraw, keeping Cornwallis off balance with a raid (dotted line) toward Charleston and the coast. Then, with Cornwallis in hot pursuit, Greene and Morgan rejoined at Salisbury, retreating into Virginia. Cornwallis was worn down in this vain pursuit and lost three-quarters of the troops he began with before finally abandoning the Carolina campaign.

two sides joined battle, each sustaining severe casualties before Greene was forced to retreat. But the high cost of victory convinced Cornwallis that he could not put down the rebellion in the Carolinas.

Although Nathanael Greene's command provided the Continentals with effective leadership in the South, it was the resilience of rebel militias that thwarted the British offensive in the Carolinas. Many Continental Army officers complained about the militia's lack of discipline, its habit of melting away when homesickness set in or harvest approached, and its record of cowardice under fire in conventional engagements. But when set the task of ambushing supply trains and dispatch riders, harrying bands of local loyalists, or making forays against isolated British outposts, the militia came through. Many southern civilians refused to join the British or to provide the redcoats with food and information because they knew that once the British army left their neighborhoods, the rebel militia would always be back. The Continental Army in the South lost many conventional battles, but the militia kept the British from restoring political control over the backcountry.

manpower, policy changed. Northern states actively encouraged black enlistments, and in the Upper South, some states allowed free men of color to join the army or permitted slaves to substitute for their masters.

Slaves themselves sought freedom from whichever side seemed most likely to grant it. Perhaps 10,000 slaves took up Dunmore's offer in 1775 and deserted their masters, and thousands more flocked to Clinton's forces after the fall of Charleston.

For many runaways the hope of liberation proved an illusion. Although some served the British army as laborers, spies, and soldiers, many died of disease in army camps (upward of 27,000 by one estimate) or were sold back into slavery in the West Indies. About 5,000 black soldiers served in the revolutionary army in the hope of gaining freedom. In addition, the number of runaways to the North soared during the Revolution. In total perhaps 100,000 men and women—nearly a fifth of the total slave population—attempted to escape bondage. Their odysseys to freedom took some to far-flung destinations: loyalist communities in Nova Scotia, a settlement established by the British in Sierra Leone on the West African coast, even the Botany Bay penal colony in Australia.

African Americans in the Age of Revolution >>

The British also lost in the Carolinas because they did not seek greater support from those southerners who would have fought for liberty with the British: African American slaves.

Black Americans, virtually all in bondage, made up one-third of the population between Delaware and Georgia. Since the beginning of the resistance to Britain, white southerners had worried that the watchwords of liberty and equality would spread to the slave quarters. Gripped by the fear of slave rebellion, southern revolutionaries began to take precautions. Marylanders disarmed black inhabitants and issued extra guns to the white militia. Charlestonians hanged and then burned the body of Thomas Jeremiah, a free black who was convicted of spreading the word to others that the British "were coming to help the poor Negroes."

Southern whites fully expected the British to turn slave rebelliousness to their strategic advantage. As early as 1775 Virginia's royal governor, Lord Dunmore, confirmed white fears by offering to free any slave who joined the British. When Clinton invaded the South in 1779 he renewed that offer. According to Janet Schaw, an Englishwoman visiting her brother's North Carolina plantation, the neighbors had heard that loyalists were "promising every Negro that would murder his master and family he should have his Master's plantation" and that "the Negroes have got it amongst them and believe it to be true."

But in Britain there was overwhelming opposition to organizing support among African Americans. British leaders dismissed Dunmore's ambitious scheme to raise a black army of 10,000 and another plan to create a sanctuary for black loyalists on the southeastern coast. Turning slaves against masters, they recognized, was not the way to conciliate southern whites.

Even so, southern fears of insurrection made the rebels reluctant to enlist black Americans as soldiers. At first, Congress barred African Americans from the Continental Army. But as the rebels became more desperate for

 REVIEW

Why did the British fail to achieve their military and political goals in the South?

THE WORLD TURNED UPSIDE DOWN

Despite his losses in the Carolinas, Cornwallis still believed that he could score a decisive victory against the Continental Army. The theater he chose for that showdown was the Chesapeake. During the spring of 1781 he and his army joined forces along the Virginia coast with the hero of Saratoga and newly turned loyalist, Benedict Arnold. Embarrassed by debt and disgusted by Congress's shabby treatment of the Continental Army, Arnold had started exchanging rebel secrets for British money in 1779 before defecting outright in 1780. By June of 1781 Arnold and Cornwallis were fortifying a site on the tip of the peninsula formed by the York and the James rivers, a place called Yorktown.

Meanwhile, Washington and his French ally, the comte de Rochambeau, met in Connecticut to plan a major attack. Rochambeau urged a coordinated land-sea assault on the Virginia coast. Washington insisted instead on a full-scale offensive against New York City. Just when the rebel commander was about to have his way, word arrived that a French fleet under the comte de Grasse was sailing for the Chesapeake to blockade Cornwallis by sea. Washington's Continentals headed south.

Surrender at Yorktown >> By the end of
September, 7,800 Frenchmen, 5,700 Continentals, and 3,200 militia had sandwiched Yorktown between the devil of an allied army and the deep blue sea of French warships. "If you cannot relieve me very soon," Cornwallis wrote to Clinton, "you must expect to hear the worst." The British navy did arrive—but seven days after Cornwallis surrendered to the rebels on October 19, 1781.

It need not have ended at Yorktown, but timing made all the difference. At the end of 1781 and early in 1782 the British army received setbacks in the other theaters of the war: India, the West Indies, and Florida. The French and the Spanish were everywhere in Europe as well, gathering in the English Channel, planning a major offensive against Gibraltar. The cost of the fighting was already enormous. British leaders recognized that the rest of the empire was at stake and set about cutting their losses in America.

The Treaty of Paris, signed on September 3, 1783, was a diplomatic triumph for the American negotiators: Benjamin Franklin, John Adams, and John Jay. They dangled before Britain the possibility that a generous settlement might weaken American ties to France. The British jumped at the bait. They recognized the independence of the United States and agreed to ample boundaries for the new nation: the Mississippi River on the west, the 31st parallel on the south, and the present border of Canada on the north. American negotiators then persuaded a skeptical France to approve the treaty by arguing that, as allies, they were bound to present a united front to the British. When the French finally persuaded Spain, the third member of the alliance, to reduce its demands on Britain for territorial concessions, the treaty became an accomplished fact. The Spanish settled for Florida and Minorca, an island in the Mediterranean.

Those present at Yorktown on that clear autumn afternoon in 1781 watched as the British second-in-command to Cornwallis (who had sent word that he was "indisposed") surrendered his superior's sword. He offered the sword first, in a face-saving gesture, to the French commander Rochambeau, who politely refused and pointed to Washington. But the American commander in chief, out of a mixture of military protocol, nationalistic pride, and perhaps even wit, pointed to his second-in-command, Benjamin Lincoln.

✅ REVIEW

How did the United States manage to prevail in the war and in the treaty negotiations?

Some witnesses recalled that British musicians arrayed on the Yorktown green played "The World Turned Upside Down." Their recollections may have been faulty, but the story has persisted as part of the folklore of the American Revolution. The world had, it seemed, turned upside down with the coming of American independence. The colonial rebels shocked the British with their answer to the question: would they fight?

⌄ On September 30, 1780, a wagon bearing this two-faced effigy was drawn through the streets of Philadelphia. The effigy represents Benedict Arnold, who sits between a gallows and the devil. Note the similarities between this piece of street theater and the demonstrations mounted on Pope's Day several decades earlier, shown on page 110.

The answer had been yes—but on their own terms. By 1777 most propertied Americans avoided fighting in the Continental Army. Yet whenever the war reached their homes, farms, and businesses, many Americans gave their allegiance to the new nation by turning out with rifles or supplying homespun clothing, food, or ammunition. They rallied around Washington in New Jersey, Gates in upstate New York, Greene in the Carolinas. Middle-class American men fought, some from idealism, others out of self-interest, but always on their own terms, as members of the militia. These citizen-soldiers turned the world upside down by defeating professional armies.

Of course, the militia did not bear the brunt of the fighting. That responsibility fell to the Continental Army, which by 1777 drew its strength from the poorest ranks of American society. Yet even the Continentals, for all their desperation, managed to fight on their own terms. Some asserted their rights by raising mutinies, until Congress redressed their grievances. All of them, as the Baron von Steuben observed, behaved differently than European soldiers did. Americans followed orders only if the logic of commands was explained to them. The Continentals, held in contempt by most Americans, turned the world upside down by sensing their power and asserting their measure of personal independence.

Americans of African descent dared as much and more in their quests for liberty. Whether they chose to escape slavery by fighting for the British or the Continentals or by striking out on their own as runaways, their defiance, too, turned the world upside down. Among the tens of thousands of slaves who would not be mastered was one Henry Washington, a native of Africa who became the slave of George Washington in 1763. But Henry Washington made his own declaration of independence in 1776, slipping behind British lines and serving as a corporal in a black unit. Thereafter, like thousands of former slaves, he sought to build a new life elsewhere in the Atlantic world, settling first in Nova Scotia and finally in Sierra Leone. By 1800 he headed a community of former slaves who were exiled to the outskirts of that colony for their determined efforts to win republican self-government from Sierra Leone's white British rulers. Like Thomas Paine, Henry Washington believed that freedom was his only country.

In all those ways a revolutionary generation turned the world upside down. They were a diverse lot—descended from Indians, Europeans, and Africans, driven by desperation or idealism or greed—but joined, even if they did not recognize it, by their common struggle to break free from the rule of monarchs or masters. What now awaited them in the world of the new United States?

CHAPTER SUMMARY

The American Revolution brought independence to Britain's former colonies after an armed struggle that began in 1775 and concluded with the Treaty of Paris in 1783.

- When the Second Continental Congress convened in the spring of 1775, many of the delegates still hoped for

Significant Events

Second Continental Congress convenes at Philadelphia; Congress creates the Continental Army; Battle of Bunker Hill

British summer drive to occupy Philadelphia; battles of Brandywine Creek, Germantown; Burgoyne surrenders at Saratoga; Continental Army encamps for winter at Valley Forge

1775

1776

1777

Publication of *Common Sense;* British troops evacuate Boston; Declaration of Independence; British occupy New York City, forcing Washington to retreat through New Jersey into Pennsylvania; Washington counterattacks at Battle of Trenton reconciliation—even as they approved the creation of the Continental Army.

- The Second Continental Congress adopted the Declaration of Independence on July 4, 1776, hoping that they could count on a majority of Americans to support the Revolution.
- The British scored a string of victories in the North throughout 1776 and 1777, capturing both New York and Philadelphia.
- The British suffered a disastrous defeat at the Battle of Saratoga in October of 1777, which prompted France to openly ally with the American rebels soon thereafter.
- By 1780 Britain aimed to win the war by claiming the South and captured both Savannah, Georgia, and Charleston, South Carolina.
- The Continental Army in the South, led by Nathanael Greene, foiled the British strategy, and Cornwallis surrendered after the Battle of Yorktown in 1781.
- Except for the first year of fighting, the rank and file of the Continental Army was drawn from the poorest Americans, whose needs for food, clothing, and shelter were neglected by the Continental Congress.

Additional Reading

The outstanding military histories of the American Revolution are Don Higginbotham, *The War for American Independence* (1971), and Robert Middlekauff, *The Glorious Cause, 1763 to 1789* (1982). Both provide a wealth of detail about battles, contending armies, and the role of militias and civilian populations in the fighting. For a compelling treatment of the lives of soldiers in the Continental Army, read Caroline Cox, *A Proper Sense of Honor* (2004), and to become better acquainted with their commander-in-chief, turn to *His Excellency: George Washington* (2004) by Joseph Ellis. Colin Calloway, *The American Revolution in Indian Country* (1995), offers a fine summary of the role of American Indians in that conflict. Benjamin Franklin's efforts to secure an alliance with France come in for lively chronicling by Stacy Schiff in *A Great Improvisation* (2005). Impressive interpretations of the war's impact on American society include Charles Royster, *A Revolutionary People at War* (1979), and John Shy, *A People Numerous and Armed* (1976). Sylvia Frey offers a thoughtful history of African Americans during this era in *Water from the Rock* (1991), and Cassandra Pybus, *Epic Journeys of Freedom* (2006), recounts the experiences of runaway slaves who seized on the wartime crisis to gain liberty. The role of women in revolutionary America receives excellent coverage in Carol Berkin, *Revolutionary Mothers* (2005), and in Mary Beth Norton's classic study, *Liberty's Daughters* (1980).

British occupy Charleston; partisan warfare of Marion, Sumter; rebel victory at King's Mountain, South Carolina; Nathanael Greene takes southern command

LORD CORNWALLIS

Treaty of Paris

1778

1780

1781

1783

France allies with rebel Americans; France and Britain declare war; British shift focus to the South; Savannah falls

NATHANAEL GREENE

Engagements at Cowpens, Guilford Courthouse; Cornwallis surrenders at Yorktown

It followed that allegiance to the states, not the Union, determined the shape of the first republican political experiments.

For a decade after independence the revolutionaries were less committed to creating an American nation than to organizing 13 separate state republics. The Declaration of Independence referred explicitly not to the United States but to these United States. It envisioned not one republic so much as a federation of 13.

Only when peace was restored during the decade of the 1780s were Americans forced to face some unanswered questions raised by their revolution. The Declaration proclaimed that these "free and independent states" had "full power to levy war, conclude peace, contract alliances, establish commerce." Did that mean that New Jersey could sign a trade agreement with France, excluding the other states?

If the United States were to be more than a loose federation, how could it assert power on a national scale? Similarly, American borderlands to the west presented problems. If these territories were settled by Americans would they eventually join the United States? Go their own ways as independent nations? Become new colonies of Spain or England?

Such problems were more than political; they were rooted in social realities. For a political union to succeed the inhabitants of 13 separate states had to start thinking of themselves as Americans. When it came right down to it, what united a Vermont farmer working his rocky fields and a South Carolina gentleman presiding over a vast rice plantation? What bonds existed between a Kentuckian rafting the Ohio River and a Salem merchant sailing to China for porcelain?

And in a society in which all citizens were said to be "created equal," social inequalities had to be confronted. How could women participate in the Revolution's bid for freedom if they were not free to vote or to hold property? How would free or enslaved African Americans live in a republic based on equality? How could black Americans feel a bond with white Americans when so often the only existing bonds had been forged with chains?

To such questions there were no final answers in 1781. There was ferment, excitement, and experimentation as 13 states each sought to create their governments anew; as Americans—or rather, Virginians and New Yorkers and Georgians and citizens of other countries—began to imagine how the revolutionary virtue of equality might transform their societies. But as the decade progressed, the sense of crisis deepened. **<<**

REPUBLICAN EXPERIMENTS

After independence was declared in July 1776, many of America's best political minds turned to draw up **constitutions** for their individual states. In truth, the

constitution framework of government establishing the contract between rulers and ruled.

state constitutions were crucial republican experiments, the first efforts at establishing a government of and by the people. All the revolutionaries agreed that the people—not a king or a few privileged aristocrats—should rule. Yet they were equally certain that republican governments were best suited to small territories. They believed that the new United States was too sprawling and its people too diverse to be safely consolidated into a single national republic. They feared, too, that the government of a large republic would inevitably grow indifferent to popular concerns, being distant from many of its citizens. Without being under the watchful eye of the people, representatives would become less accountable to the electorate and turn tyrannical. A federation of small state republics, they reasoned, would stand a far better chance of enduring.

The State Constitutions >> The new state constitutions retained the basic form of their old colonial governments, most providing for a governor and a bicameral legislature. But most states dramatically changed the balance of power among the different branches of government.

From the republican perspective in 1776 the greatest problem of any government lay in curbing executive power. What had driven Americans into rebellion was the abuse of authority by the king and his appointed government appeared to exceed the limits of its authority, Americans wanted to have at hand the written contract between rulers and ruled. When eighteenth-century Englishmen used the word constitution, they meant the existing arrangement of government—not an actual document but a collection of parliamentary laws, customs, and precedents. But Americans believed that a constitution should be a written code that stood apart from and above government, a yardstick against which the people measured the performance of their rulers. After all, they reasoned, if Britain's constitution had been written down, available for all to consult, would American rights have been violated?

^ Americans responded to independence with rituals of "killing the king," as did this New York crowd in 1776, which is pulling down a statue of George III. Americans also expressed their mistrust of monarchs by establishing state governments with weak executive branches.

officials. To ensure that the executive could never again threaten popular liberty, the new states either accorded almost no power to their governors or abolished that office entirely. The governors had no authority to convene or dissolve the legislature. They could not veto the legislatures' laws, grant land, or erect courts. Most important, governors had few powers to appoint other state officials. All these limits were designed to deprive the executive of any patronage or other form of influence over the legislature.

What the state governors lost, the legislatures gained. To ensure that those powerful legislatures truly represented the will of the people, the new state constitutions called for annual elections and required candidates for the legislature to live in the district they represented. Many states even asserted the right of voters to instruct the men elected to office how to vote on specific issues. Although no state granted universal manhood suffrage, most reduced the amount of property required of qualified voters. Finally, state supreme courts were also either elected by the legislatures or appointed by an elected governor.

With all power vested in popular assemblies, a majority of voters within a state could do whatever they wanted, unchecked by governors or courts—which opened the door for legislatures to turn as tyrannical as governors. But the revolutionaries brushed that prospect aside: republican theory assured them that the people possessed a generous share of civic virtue, the capacity for selfless pursuit of the general welfare.

In an equally momentous change, the revolutionaries insisted on written state constitutions. Whenever

From Congress to Confederation ≫

While Americans lavished attention on their state constitutions, the national government nearly languished during the decade after 1776. With the coming of independence the Second Continental Congress conducted the common business of the federated states. It created and maintained the Continental Army, issued currency, and negotiated with foreign powers.

But although Congress acted as a central government by common consent, it lacked any legal basis for its authority. To redress that need, in July 1776 Congress appointed a committee to draft a constitution for a national government. The urgent business of waging the war made for delay, but Congress approved the first national constitution in November 1777. It took four more years—until February 1781—for all of the states to ratify these Articles of Confederation.

The Articles of Confederation provided for a government by a national legislature—essentially a continuation of the Second Continental Congress. That body had the authority to declare war and make peace, conduct diplomacy, regulate Indian affairs, appoint military and naval officers, and requisition men from the states. In affairs of finance it could coin money and issue paper currency. Extensive as these responsibilities were, Congress could not levy taxes or even regulate trade. The crucial power of the purse rested entirely with the states, as did the final power to make and execute laws. Even worse, the national government had no distinct executive branch. Congressional committees, constantly changing in their membership, not only had to make laws but had to administer and enforce them as well.

Those weaknesses appear more evident in hindsight. For Congress in 1777 it was no easy task to frame a new government in the midst of a war. And most American leaders in the 1770s had given little thought to federalism, the means by which political power could be divided

>> As the stumps dotting the landscape indicate, western farmers first sought to "improve" their acreage by felling trees. But their dwellings were far less substantial than those depicted in this idealized sketch of an "American New Cleared Farm." And although some Indians guided parties of whites into the West, as shown in the foreground, more often they resisted white encroachment. For that reason dogs, here perched placidly in canoes, were trained to alert their white masters to the approach of Indians.

among the states and the national government. In any case, creating a strong national government would have antagonized many Americans, who after all had just rebelled against the distant, centralized authority of Britain's king and Parliament.

Guided by republican political theory and by their colonial experience, American revolutionaries created a loose confederation of 13 independent state republics under a nearly powerless national government. They succeeded so well that the United States almost failed to survive its first decade of independence. The problem was that lessons from the colonial past were not always useful guides to postwar realities. Only when events forced Americans to think nationally did they begin to consider the possibility of reinventing "these United States"—this time under the yoke of a truly federal republic.

 REVIEW

What political concerns shaped the first constitutions?

THE TEMPTATIONS OF PEACE

The surrender of Cornwallis at Yorktown in 1781 marked the end of military crisis in America. But as the threat from Britain receded, so did the source of American unity. The many differences among Americans, most of which lay submerged during the struggle for independence, surfaced in full force. Those domestic divisions, combined with challenges to the new nation from Britain and Spain, created conflicts that neither the states nor the national government proved equal to handling.

The Temptations of the West >> The greatest opportunities and the greatest problems for postwar Americans awaited in the rapidly expanding West. With the boundary of the new United States now set at the Mississippi River, more settlers spilled across the Appalachians, planting farmsteads and towns throughout Ohio,

Kentucky, and Tennessee. By 1790 places that had been almost uninhabited by whites in 1760 held more than 2.25 million people, one-third of the nation's population.

After the Revolution, as before, western settlement fostered intense conflict. American claims that its territory stretched all the way to the Mississippi were by no means taken for granted by European and Indian powers. The West also confronted Americans with questions about their own national identity. Would the newly settled territories enter the nation as states on an equal footing with the original 13 states? Would they be ruled as dependent colonies? The fate of the West, in other words, constituted a crucial test of whether "these" United States could grow and still remain united.

Foreign Intrigues >> Both the British from their base in Canada and the Spanish in Florida and Louisiana hoped to chisel away at American borders. Their considerable success in the 1780s exposed the weakness of Confederation diplomacy.

Before the ink was dry on the Treaty of Paris, Britain's ministers were secretly instructing Canadians to maintain their forts and trading posts inside the United States' northwestern frontier. They reckoned—correctly—that with the Continental Army disbanded, the Confederation could not force the British to withdraw.

The British also made mischief along the Confederation's northern borders, mainly with Vermont. For decades Ethan Allen and his Green Mountain Boys had waged a war of nerves with neighboring New York, which claimed Vermont as part of its territory. After the Revolution the British tried to woo Vermont into their empire as a province of Canada, a flirtation that pressured Congress into granting Vermont statehood in 1791.

The loyalty of the southwestern frontier was even less certain. By 1790 more than 100,000 settlers had poured through the Cumberland Gap to reach Kentucky and

Tennessee. But the commercial possibilities of the region depended entirely on access to the Mississippi and the port of New Orleans, since it was far too costly to ship southwestern produce over the rough trails east across the Appalachians. And the Mississippi route was still dominated by the Spanish, who controlled Louisiana as well as forts along western Mississippi shores as far north as St. Louis. The Spanish, seeing their opportunity, closed the Mississippi to American navigation in 1784. That action prompted serious talk among southwesterners about seceding from the United States and joining Spain's empire.

The Spanish also tried to strengthen their hold on North America by making common cause with the Indians. Of particular concern to both groups was protecting Spanish Florida from the encroachment of American settlers filtering south from Georgia. Florida's governor complained that those backwoods folk were "distinguished from savages only in their color, language, and the superiority of their depraved cunning and untrustworthiness."

So Spanish colonial officials responded eagerly to the overtures of Alexander McGillivray, a young Indian leader whose mother was of French-Creek descent and whose father was a Scots trader. His efforts brought about a treaty of alliance between the Creeks and the Spanish in 1784, quickly followed by similar alliances with the Choctaws and the Chickasaws.

Disputes among the States >>

As if foreign intrigues were not divisive enough, the states continued to argue among themselves over western land claims. The old royal charters for some colonies had extended their boundaries all the way to the Mississippi and beyond. (See the map, below.) But the charters were often vague, granting both Massachusetts and

> **landed states and landless states** some of the 13 colonies that became the United States had originally been granted land whose western boundaries were vague or overlapped the land granted to other colonies. During the Confederation period, the so-called "landless" states had boundaries that were firmly drawn on all sides, such as Maryland, New Jersey, and Massachusetts. "Landed" states possessed grants whose western boundaries were not fixed.

Virginia, for example, undisputed possession of present-day Wisconsin. In contrast, other charters limited state boundaries to within a few hundred miles of the Atlantic coast. "Landed" states such as Virginia wanted to secure control over the large territory granted by their charters. "Landless" states (which included Maryland, Delaware, Pennsylvania, Rhode Island, and New Jersey) called on Congress to restrict the boundaries of landed states and to convert western lands into a domain administered by the Confederation.

The landless states lost the opening round of the contest over ownership of the West. The Articles of Confederation acknowledged the old charter claims of the landed states. Then Maryland, one of the smallest landless states, retaliated by refusing to ratify the Articles. Since every

WESTERN LAND CLAIMS, 1782–1802

The Confederation's settlement of conflicting western land claims was an achievement essential to the consolidation of political union. Some states asserted that their original charters extended their western borders to the Mississippi River. A few states, such as Virginia, claimed western borders on the Pacific Ocean.

BUT HOW MANY DOTS PER INCH?

This polygraph machine represented the state-of-the-art in duplicating technology when it was patented in 1803. It could produce four copies of a handwritten page, its pens exactly following the motion of the penman's hand. Among the satisfied owners of this predecessor to the purring photocopier was Thomas Jefferson.

state had to approve the Articles before they were formally accepted, the fate of the United States hung in the balance. One by one the landed states relented. The last holdout, Virginia, in January 1781 ceded its charter rights to land north of the Ohio River.

The More Democratic West >>

An even greater source of contention concerned the sort of men westerners elected to political office. The state legislatures of the 1780s were both larger and more democratic in their membership than the old colonial assemblies were. Before the Revolution no more than a fifth of the men serving in the assemblies were middle-class farmers or artisans; government was almost exclusively the domain of the wealthiest merchants, lawyers, and planters. After the Revolution twice as many state legislators were men of moderate wealth. The shift was more marked in the North, where middle-class men predominated among representatives. But in every state some men of modest means, humble background, and little formal education attained political power.

State legislatures became more democratic in membership mainly because as backcountry districts grew, so did the number of their representatives. Since western districts tended to be less developed economically and culturally, their leading men were less rich and cultivated than the seaboard elite.

But many eastern republican gentlemen, while endorsing government by popular consent, doubted whether ordinary people were fit to rule. The problem, they contended, was that the new western legislators concerned themselves only with the narrow interests of their constituents, not with the good of the whole state. As Ezra Stiles, the president of Yale College, observed, the new breed of politicians were those with "the all-prevailing popular talent of coaxing and flattering," who "whenever a bill is read in the legislature . . . instantly thinks how it will affect his constituents." And if state legislatures could not rise above petty bickering and narrow self-interest, how long would it be before

civic virtue and a concern for the general welfare simply withered away?

The Northwest Territory >>

Such fears of "democratic excess" also influenced policy when Congress debated what to do with the **Northwest Territory.** Carved out of the land ceded by the states to the national government, the Northwest Territory comprised the present-day states of Ohio, Indiana, Illinois, Michigan, and Wisconsin. With so many white settlers moving into these lands, Congress dealt with the issue of expansion by adopting three ordinances.

Northwest Territory present-day states of Ohio, Indiana, Illinois, Michigan, and Wisconsin.

The first, drafted by Thomas Jefferson in 1784, divided the Northwest Territory into 10 states, each to be admitted to the Union on equal terms as soon as its population equaled that in any of the existing states. In the meantime, Jefferson provided for democratic self-government of the territory by all free adult males. A second ordinance of 1785 set up an efficient mechanism for dividing and selling public lands. The Northwest Territory was surveyed into townships of six miles square. Each township then was divided into 36 lots of one square mile, or 640 acres.

Congress waited in vain for buyers to flock to the land offices it established. The cost of even a single lot—$640—was too steep for most farmers. Disappointed by the shortage of buyers and desperate for money, Congress finally accepted a proposition submitted by a private company of land speculators that offered to buy some 6 million acres in present-day southeastern Ohio. That several members of Congress numbered among the company's stockholders no doubt added to enthusiasm for the deal.

The transaction concluded, Congress calmed the speculators' worries that incoming settlers might enjoy too much self-government by scrapping Jefferson's democratic design and substituting the Northwest Ordinance of 1787. That ordinance provided for a period in which Congress held sway in the territory through its appointees—a governor, a secretary, and three judges. When the population reached 5,000 free adult males a legislature was to be established, although its laws required the governor's approval. A representative could sit in Congress but had no vote. When the population reached 60,000 the inhabitants might apply for statehood, and the whole Northwest Territory was to be divided into not less than three or more than five states. The ordinance outlawed slavery throughout the region, but it provided for the return of fugitive slaves to the South. It also guaranteed basic rights— freedom of religion and trial by jury—and provided for the support of public education.

With the Northwest Ordinance in place, Congress had succeeded in extending republican government to the West and incorporating the frontier into the new nation. The Republic now had an orderly way to expand its federation of states in a way that minimized the tensions between the genteel East and the democratic West that had plagued the colonies and the Confederation throughout much of the eighteenth century. Yet ironically, the new ordinance served to heighten tensions in a different way. By limiting the spread of slavery in the northern states, Congress deepened the critical social and economic differences between the North and South, evident already in the 1780s.

The consequences of the new territorial system were also significant for hundreds of thousands of the continent's other inhabitants. In the short term the ordinance ignored completely the rights of the Shawnee, Chippewa, and other Indian peoples who lived in the region. In the long term the system "laid the blueprint," as one historian noted, for bringing new lands into the United States. The ordinance thus accelerated the pressures on Indian lands and aggravated the social and geographic dislocations already set in motion by disease and the western conflicts of the Revolutionary War.

Slavery and Sectionalism >> When white Americans declared their independence, they owned nearly

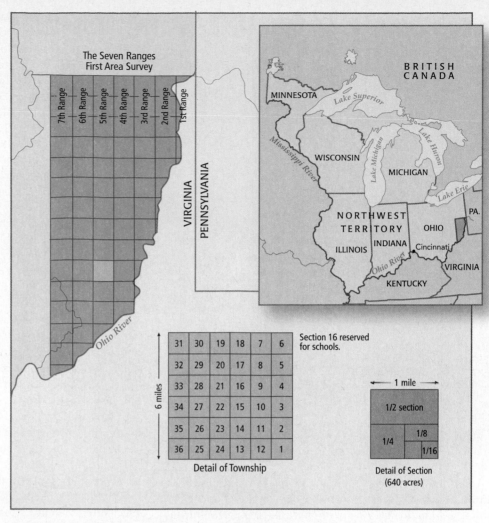

THE ORDINANCE OF 1785

Surveyors entered the Northwest Territory in September of 1785, imposing on the land regular grids of six square miles to define new townships, as shown on this range map of a portion of Ohio. Farmers purchased blocks of land within townships, each one mile square, from the federal government or from land speculators.

half a million black Americans. African Americans of the revolutionary generation, most of them enslaved, constituted 20 percent of the total population of the colonies in 1775, and nearly 90 percent of them lived in the South. Yet few political leaders directly confronted the issue of whether slavery should be permitted to exist in a truly republican society.

When political discussion did stray toward the subject of slavery, southerners—especially ardent republicans— bristled defensively. Theirs was a difficult position, riddled with contradictions. On the one hand, they had condemned parliamentary taxation as tantamount to political "slavery" and had rebelled, declaring that all men were "created equal." On the other hand, enslaved African Americans formed the basis of the South's plantation economy. To surrender slavery, southerners believed, would be to usher in economic ruin.

Some planters in the Upper South resolved the dilemma by freeing their slaves. Such decisions were

⌃ In 1787 in Philadelphia, the year delegates to the Constitutional Convention met, Richard Allen and Absalom Jones founded Bethel African Methodist Episcopal Church. The first church was a former black-smith's shop that the members hauled to a site they purchased on Sixth Street. By the time this illustration was created in 1829, a more spacious building had replaced the first church.

made easier by changing economic conditions in the Chesapeake. As planters shifted from tobacco toward wheat, a crop demanding a good deal less labor, Virginia and Maryland liberalized their manumission statutes, laws providing for freeing slaves. Between 1776 and 1789 most southern states also joined the North in prohibiting the importation of slaves, and a few antislavery societies appeared in the Upper South. But no southern state legally abolished slavery. Masters defended their right to hold human property in the name of republicanism.

Eighteenth-century republicans regarded property as crucial, because it provided a man and his family with security, status, and wealth. More important, it provided a measure of independence: to be able to act freely, without fear or favor of others. People without property were dangerous, republicans believed, because the poor could never be politically independent. Southern defenders of slavery thus argued that free, propertyless black people would pose a political threat to the liberty of propertied white citizens. Subordinating the human rights of blacks to the property rights of whites, southern republicans reached the paradoxical conclusion that their freedom depended on keeping African Americans in bondage.

The North followed a different course. Because its economy depended far less on slave labor, black emancipation did not run counter to powerful economic interests. Antislavery societies, the first founded by the Quakers in 1775, spread throughout the northern states during the next quarter century. Over the same period the

legislatures of most northern states provided for the immediate or gradual abolition of slavery. Freedom for most northern African Americans came slowly, but by 1830 there were fewer than 3,000 slaves out of a total northern black population of 125,000.

The Revolution, which had been fought for liberty and equality, did little to change the status of most black Americans. By 1800 more enslaved African Americans lived in the United States than had lived there in 1776. Slavery continued to grow in the Lower South as the rice culture of the Carolinas and Georgia expanded and as the new cotton culture spread westward.

Still, a larger number of slaves than ever before became free during the war and in the decades following, whether through military service, successful escape, manumission, or gradual emancipation. All these developments fostered the growth of free black communities, especially in the Upper South and in northern cities. By 1810 free African Americans made up 10 percent of the total population of Maryland and Virginia. The composition of the postwar free community changed as well. Before independence most free blacks had been either mulattoes—the offspring of interracial unions—or former slaves too sick or aged to have value as laborers. In contrast, the free population of the 1780s were darker skinned, younger, and healthier. This group injected new vitality into black communal life, organizing independent schools, churches, and mutual benefit societies for the growing number of "free people of color."

peculiar institution
euphemism for slavery, perhaps revealing in its use. Peculiar also suggests the contradiction with the ideals of the Declaration of Independence, that "all men are created equal."

After the Revolution slavery ceased to be a national institution. It became the "**peculiar institution**" of a single region, the American South.

Wartime Economic Disruption >>
With the outbreak of the Revolution Americans had suffered an immediate loss of the manufactured goods, markets, and credit that Britain had formerly supplied. Matters did not improve with the coming of peace. France and Britain flooded the new states with their manufactures, and postwar Americans, eager for luxuries, indulged in a most unrepublican spending spree. The flurry of buying left some American merchants and consumers as deeply in debt as their governments. When loans from private citizens and foreign creditors such as France had proved insufficient to finance the fighting, both Congress and the states had printed paper money—a whopping total of $400 million.

The paper currency was backed only by the government's promise to redeem the bills with money from future taxes, since legislatures balked at the unpopular alternative of levying taxes during the war. For the bills to be redeemed the United States had to survive, so by the end of 1776, when Continental forces sustained a series of defeats, paper money started to depreciate dramatically. By 1781 it was virtually without value, and Americans coined the expression "not worth a Continental."

The printing of paper money, combined with a wartime shortage of goods, triggered an inflationary spiral of scarcer and scarcer goods costing more and more worthless dollars. In this spiral, creditors were gouged by debtors, who paid them back with depreciated currency. At the same time, soaring prices for food and manufactured goods eroded the buying power of wage earners and small farmers. And the end of the war brought on demands for prompt repayment from the new nation's foreign creditors as well as from soldiers seeking backpay and pensions.

Congress could do nothing. With no power to regulate trade, it could neither dam the stream of imported goods rushing into the states nor stanch the flow of gold and silver to Europe to pay for these items. With no power to prohibit the states from issuing paper money, it could not halt depreciation. With no power to regulate wages or prices, it could not curb inflation. With no power to tax, it could not reduce the public debt. Efforts to grant Congress greater powers met with determined resistance from the states.

Within states, too, economic problems aroused discord. Some major merchants and large commercial farmers had profited handsomely during the war by selling supplies to the American, British, and French armies at high prices. Eager to protect their windfall, they lobbied state legislatures for an end to inflationary monetary policies. That meant passing high taxes to pay wartime debts, a paper currency that was backed by gold and silver, and an active policy to encourage foreign trade.

Less affluent men fought back, pressing legislatures for programs that met their needs. Western farmers, often in debt, urged the states to print more paper money and to pass laws lowering taxes and postponing the foreclosure of mortgages. Artisans opposed merchants by calling for protection from low-priced foreign imports that competed with the goods they produced. They set themselves against farmers as well by demanding price regulation of the farm products they consumed. In the continuing struggle the state legislatures became the battleground of competing economic factions.

As the 1780s wore on, conflicts mounted. As long as the individual states remained sovereign, the Confederation was crippled—unable to conduct foreign affairs effectively, unable to set coherent economic policy, unable to deal with discontent in the West. Equally dismaying was the discovery that many Americans, instead of being selflessly concerned for the public good, selfishly pursued their private interests.

 REVIEW

What challenges did the West pose for the new republic?

REPUBLICAN SOCIETY

The war for independence transformed not only America's government and economy but also its society and culture. Inspired by the Declaration's ideal of equality, some Americans rejected the subordinate position assigned to them under the old colonial order. Westerners, newly wealthy entrepreneurs, urban artisans, and women all claimed greater freedom, power, and recognition. The authority of the traditional leaders of government, society, and the family came under a new scrutiny; the impulse to defer to social superiors became less automatic. The new assertiveness demonstrated how deeply egalitarian assumptions were taking root in American culture.

The New Men of the Revolution >> The
Revolution gave rise to a new sense of social identity and a new set of ambitions among several groups of men who had once accepted a humbler status. The war also offered opportunities to aspiring entrepreneurs everywhere, and often they were not the same men who had prospered before the war. At a stroke, independence swept away the prominence of loyalists, whose ranks included an especially high number of government officials, large landowners, and major merchants. And while loyalists found their properties confiscated by revolutionary governments, other Americans grew rich. Many northern merchants gained newfound wealth from privateering or military contracts. Commercial farmers in the mid-Atlantic states prospered from the high food prices caused by wartime scarcity and army demand.

The Revolution effected no dramatic redistribution of wealth. Indeed, the gap between rich and poor increased during the 1780s. But the Revolution's republican ideals of equality and experience emboldened city artisans to demand a more prominent role in politics. Calls for men of their own kind to represent them in government came as a rude shock to such gentlemen as South Carolina's William Henry Drayton, who balked at sharing power with men "who were never in a way to study" anything except "how to cut up a beast in the market to best advantage, to cobble an old shoe in the neatest manner, or to build a necessary house." The journeymen who worked for master craftsmen also exhibited a new sense of independence, forming new organizations to secure higher wages.

But the greatest gains came to those men newly enriched by the war and by the opportunities of independence. Representative of this aspiring group was William Cooper, a Pennsylvania Quaker who did not support the

Revolution but in its aftermath strove to transform himself from a wheelwright into a gentleman. He hoped to effect that change through another: the transformation of thousands of acres of hilly, heavily forested land around Otsego Lake in upstate New York into wheat-producing farms clustered around a market village called Cooperstown. Yankee emigrants fleeing the shrinking farms of long-settled New England made Cooper's vision a reality and made him the leading land developer of the 1790s. But the influx of white settlement radically altered the environment of what had once been part of Iroquoia. Farmers killed off panthers, bears, and wolves to protect their livestock. Grain farming leeched nutrients from the thin topsoil, forcing farmers to clear more trees, and as the forest barrier fell, weeds and insects invaded. By the beginning of the nineteenth century the children of many small farmers were migrating to western New York and northern Ohio.

Similar scenarios played out on frontiers throughout the new United States. And everywhere, too, men like William Cooper demanded and received social recognition and political influence. Even though some, like Cooper, never lost the crude manners that betrayed humble origins, they styled themselves as the "aristocracy of merit" enshrined by republican ideals.

Point of View

The Impact of the American Revolution

"For some historians the Revolution seems to be little more than a colonial rebellion or a war for independence. Even when we have recognized the radicalism of the Revolution, we admit only a political, not a social radicalism. . . . But if we measure the radicalism by the amount of social change that actually took place—by the transformations in the relationships that bound people to each other—then the American Revolution was not conservative at all; on the contrary: it was as radical and revolutionary as any in history."

GORDON WOOD *The Radicalism of the American Revolution*

The New Women of the Revolution >>

Not long after the fighting with Britain had broken out, Margaret Livingston of New York wrote to her sister Catherine, "You know that our Sex are doomed to be obedient in every stage of life so that we shant be great gainers by this contest." By war's end, however, Eliza Wilkinson from rural South Carolina was complaining boldly to a woman friend: "The men say we have no business with political matters . . . it's not our sphere. . . . [But] I won't have it thought that because we are the weaker Sex (as to bodily strength my dear) we are Capable of nothing more, than minding the Dairy . . . surely we may have enough sense to give our Opinions."

What separated Margaret Livingston's resignation from Eliza Wilkinson's confidence was the Revolution. Wilkinson had managed her parents' plantation during the war and defended it from British marauders. Other women discovered similar reserves of skill and resourcefulness. When soldiers returned home, some were surprised to find their wives and daughters, who had been running family farms and businesses, less submissive and more self-confident.

But American men had not fought a revolution for the equality of American women. In fact, male revolutionaries gave no thought to the role of women in the new nation, assuming that those of the "weaker sex" were incapable of making informed and independent political decisions. Most women of the revolutionary generation agreed that the proper female domain was the home, not the public arena of politics. Still, the currents of the Revolution occasionally left gaps that allowed women to display their political interests. When a loosely worded provision in the New Jersey state constitution gave the vote to "all free inhabitants" owning a specified amount of property, white widows and single women went to the polls. Only in 1807 did the state legislature close the loophole.

Mary Wollstonecraft's Vindication >>

In the wake of the Revolution there also appeared in England a book that would become a classic text of modern feminism, Mary Wollstonecraft's *A Vindication of the Rights of Women* (1792). Attracting a wide, if not widely approving, readership in America as well, it called not only for laws to guarantee women civil and political equality but also for educational reforms to ensure their social and economic equality.

Wollstonecraft dashed off *Vindication* in six short months. She charged that men deliberately conspired to keep women in "a state of perpetual childhood" by giving them inferior, frivolous educations. That encouraged young girls to fixate on fashion and flirtation and made them "only anxious to inspire love, when they ought to cherish a nobler ambition, and by their abilities and virtues exact respect." Girls, she proposed, should receive the same education as boys, including training that would prepare them for careers in medicine, politics, and business. No woman should have to pin her hopes for financial security on making a good marriage, Wollstonecraft argued. On the contrary, well-educated and resourceful women capable of supporting themselves would make the best wives and mothers, assets to the family and the nation.

Vindication might have been written in gunpowder rather than ink, given the reaction it aroused on both sides

A Woman's Compass

A woman drinking spirits as her baby tumbles from her lap.

A woman crying, pointing to letters on a table. Was she jilted by a lover? Other possibilities?

A woman at hard labor in prison.

A woman being apprehended by the authorities. For prostitution? Drunkenness? Debt?

Could there be any more eloquent testimony to the anxieties aroused by the newly confident (and sometimes outspoken) women of postrevolutionary America? Much like jokes, idealized images (for example, the smiling woman within the compass) can point historians toward areas of tension and conflict in the past. In this illustration, the four scenes displayed outside the compass send even clearer signals. Published sometime between 1785 and 1805 and entitled "Keep Within Compass," the illustration celebrates domesticity and wifely devotion while also warning women tempted to stray from that straight and narrow path. It promises a contented and prosperous life—lovely home, thriving garden, swishy silk dress, killer hat, and even a pet squirrel—to the woman "whose bosom no passion knows." But woe betide her erring sisters who strayed from the path of virtue, disgracing themselves as well as the men in their lives! Those twin themes proved equally popular in American novels published during the decades after the American Revolution.

THINKING CRITICALLY

Is the kind of virtue promoted by the illustration similar to or different from the republican understanding of virtue? What accounts for the concern about the virtue of women in the decades after the American Revolution? Why did the virtue of women loom so large, since they had few legal or political rights?

"Keep Within Compass," illustration, ca. 1785–1805, Winterthur Museum.

of the Atlantic. Even so, Wollstonecraft won many defenders among both men and women, who sometimes publicly and more often privately expressed their agreement with her views. Among them was the Philadelphia Quaker Elizabeth Drinker, who confided to her diary that "in very many of her sentiments, she . . . speaks my mind."

Seduction Literature and the Virtues of Women >>

The decades around 1800 also witnessed a heightened concern for the chastity of women. Books, magazines, and newspapers on both sides of the Atlantic overflowed with cautionary tales of young white women who were seduced or coerced into surrendering their virginity by unscrupulous "rakes," only to be abandoned by these faithless lovers, disowned by their families for becoming pregnant out of wedlock, and finally reduced to beggary or prostitution.

"Seduction literature" sent the unmistakable message that young women must preserve their sexual purity. Women were equipped with greater self-control by nature, authors advised, and they were obliged to inspire the same restraint in their suitors, because men were naturally passionate and impulsive. Depicting women as the guardians of sexual virtue marked a major shift in cultural attitudes, because for centuries before, most male writers had insisted that women were the more dangerous sex, their insatiable lust and deceitful ways luring men into sin.

Republican Motherhood and Education for Women >>

In the new republic, the new image of women as the upholders of private virtue met with an enthusiastic reception, especially among those who believed that wives and mothers had an obligation to encourage republican virtue in their husbands and children. That view, known as "**republican motherhood**," inspired many educational reformers in the revolutionary generation. Philadelphian Benjamin Rush argued that only educated and independent-minded women could raise the informed and self-reliant citizens that a republican government required, while New Englander Judith Sargent Murray urged the cultivation of women's minds to encourage self-respect. Their efforts contributed to the most dramatic change in the lives of women after the war—the spread of female literacy.

republican motherhood redefinition of the role of women promoted by many American reformers in the 1780s and 1790s, who believed that the success of republican government depended on educated and independent-minded mothers who would raise children to become informed and self-reliant citizens.

Between 1780 and 1830 the number of American colleges and secondary academies rose dramatically, and some of these new institutions were devoted to educating women. Not only did the number of schools for women increase, but these schools also offered a solid academic curriculum. By 1850— for the first time in American history—there were as many literate women as there were men.

The Revolution also prompted some states to reform their marriage laws, making divorce somewhat easier, although it remained extremely rare. But although women won greater freedom to divorce, married women still could not sue or be sued, make wills or contracts, or buy and sell property. Any wages that they earned went to their husbands; so did all personal property that wives brought into a marriage; so did the rents and profits of any real estate they owned. Despite the high ideals of "republican motherhood," most women remained confined to the "domestic sphere" of the home and deprived of the most basic legal and political rights.

The Attack on Aristocracy >>

Why wasn't the American Revolution more revolutionary? Independence secured the full political equality of white men who owned property, but women were still deprived of political rights, African Americans of human rights. Why did the revolutionaries stop short of extending equality to the most unequal groups in American society—and with so little sense that they were being inconsistent?

In part, the lack of concern was rooted in republican ideas themselves. Republican ideology viewed property as the key to independence and power. Lacking property, women and black Americans were easily consigned to the custody of husbands and masters. Then, too, prejudice played its part: the perception of women and blacks as naturally inferior beings.

But revolutionary leaders also failed to press for greater equality because they conceived their crusade in terms of eliminating the evils of a European past dominated by kings and aristocrats. They believed that the great obstacle to equality was monarchy—kings and queens who bestowed hereditary honors and political office on favored individuals and granted legal privileges and monopolies to favored churches and businesses. These artificial inequalities posed the real threat to liberty, most republicans concluded. In other words, the men of the Revolution were intent on attaining equality by leveling off the top of society. It did not occur to most republicans that the cause of equality could also be served by raising up the bottom—by attacking the laws and prejudices that kept African Americans enslaved and women dependent.

The most significant reform of the republican campaign against artificial privilege was the dismantling of state-supported churches. Most states had a religious establishment. In New York and the South, it was the Anglican Church; in New England, the Congregational Church. Since the 1740s dissenters who did not worship at state churches had protested laws that taxed all citizens to support the clergy of established denominations. After the Revolution, as more dissenters became voters, state legislators gradually abolished state support for Anglican and Congregational churches.

Not only in religious life but in all aspects of their culture, Americans rejected inequalities associated with a monarchical past. In that spirit reformers attacked the Society of Cincinnati, a group organized by former officers of the Continental Army in 1783. The society, which was merely a social club for veterans, was forced to disband for its policy of passing on its membership rights to eldest sons. In this way, critics charged, the Society of Cincinnati was creating artificial distinctions and perpetuating a hereditary warrior nobility.

Today many of the republican efforts at reform seem misdirected. While only a handful of revolutionaries worked for the education of women and the emancipation of slaves, enormous zeal went into fighting threats from a monarchical past that had never existed in America. Yet the threat from kings and aristocrats was real to the revolutionaries—and indeed remained real in many parts of Europe. Their determination to sweep away every shred of formal privilege ensured that these forms of inequality never took root in America.

 REVIEW

How did the Revolution alter American society?

FROM CONFEDERATION TO CONSTITUTION

While Americans from many walks of life sought to realize the republican commitment to equality, Congress wrestled with the problem of preserving the nation itself. With the new republic slowly rending itself to pieces, some political leaders concluded that neither the Confederation nor the state legislatures were able to remedy the basic difficulties facing the nation. But how could the states be convinced to surrender their sovereign powers? The answer came in the wake of two events—one foreign, one domestic—that lent momentum to the cause of strengthening the central government.

The Jay-Gardoqui Treaty >> The international episode that threatened to leave the Confederation in shambles was a debate over a proposed treaty with Spain. In 1785 southwesterners still could not legally navigate the Mississippi and still were threatening to secede from the union and annex their territory to Spain's American empire. To shore up southwestern loyalties Congress instructed its secretary of foreign affairs, John Jay, to negotiate an agreement with Spain preserving American rights to navigate on the Mississippi River. But the Spanish emissary, Don Diego de Gardoqui, sweet-talked Jay into accepting a treaty by which the United States would give up all rights to the Mississippi for 25 years. In return Spain agreed to grant trading privileges to American merchants.

Jay, a New Yorker, knew more than a few northern merchants who were eager to open new markets. But when the proposed treaty became public knowledge, southwesterners denounced it as nothing short of betrayal. The treaty was never ratified, but the hostility stirred up during the debate revealed the strength of sectional feelings. Only a decade later, when the Senate ratified a treaty negotiated with Spain by Thomas Pinckney in 1796, did Americans gain full access to the Mississippi.

Shays's Rebellion >> On the heels of this humiliation by Spain came an internal conflict that challenged the notion that individual states could maintain order in their own territories. The trouble erupted in western Massachusetts, where many small farmers were close to ruin. Yet they still had to pay mortgages on their farms, still had other debts, and were perpetually short of money. In 1786 the lower house of the Massachusetts legislature obliged the farmers with a package of relief measures. But creditors in eastern Massachusetts, determined to safeguard their own investments, persuaded the upper house to defeat the measures.

In the summer of 1786 western farmers responded, demanding that the upper house of the legislature be abolished and that the relief measures go into effect. That autumn 2,000 farmers rose in armed rebellion, led by Captain Daniel Shays, a veteran of the Revolution. They closed the county courts to halt creditors from foreclosing on their farms and marched on the federal arsenal at Springfield. The state militia quelled the uprising by February 1787, but the insurrection left many in Massachusetts and the rest of the country thoroughly shaken.

Daniel Shays's rebels were no impoverished rabble. They were reputable members of western communities who wanted their property protected and believed that government existed to provide that protection. The Massachusetts state legislature had been unable to safeguard the property of farmers from the inroads of recession or to protect the property of creditors from the armed debtors who closed the courts. It had failed, in other words, to fulfill the most basic aim of republican government.

Other states with discontented debtors feared what the example of western Massachusetts might mean for the future of the Confederation itself. But by 1786 Shays's Rebellion supplied only the sharpest jolt to a movement for reform that was already under way. Even before the rebellion, a group of Virginians had proposed a meeting of the states to adopt a uniform system of commercial regulations. Once assembled at Annapolis in September 1786, the delegates from five states agreed to a more ambitious undertaking. They called for a second, broader meeting in Philadelphia, which Congress approved, for the "express purpose of revising the Articles of Confederation."

Framing a Federal Constitution >>

It was the wettest spring anyone could remember. The 55 men who traveled over muddy roads to Philadelphia in May 1787 arrived drenched and bespattered. Fortunately, most of the travelers were men in their 30s and 40s, young enough to survive a good soaking. Since most were gentlemen of some means—planters, merchants, and lawyers with powdered wigs and prosperous paunches—they could recover from the rigors of their journey in the best accommodations offered by America's largest city.

The delegates came from all the states except Rhode Island. The rest of New England supplied shrewd backroom politicians—Roger Sherman and Oliver Ellsworth from Connecticut and Rufus King and Elbridge Gerry, Massachusetts men who had learned a trick or two from Sam Adams. The middle states marshaled much of the intellectual might: two Philadelphia lawyers, John Dickinson and James Wilson; one Philadelphia financier, Robert Morris; and the aristocratic Gouverneur Morris. From New York there was Alexander Hamilton, the mercurial and ambitious young protégé of Washington. South Carolina provided fiery orators Charles Pinckney and John Rutledge.

It was "an assembly of the demigods," gushed Thomas Jefferson, who, along with John Adams, was serving as a diplomat in Europe when the convention met. In fact, the only delegate who looked even remotely divine was the convention's presiding deity. Towering a full half foot taller than most of his colleagues, George Washington displayed his usual self-possession from a chair elevated on the speaker's platform where the delegates met, in the Pennsylvania State House. At first glance, the delegate of least commanding presence was Washington's fellow Virginian, James Madison. Short and slightly built, the 36-year-old Madison had no profession except hypochondria. But he was an astute politician and a brilliant political thinker who, more than anyone else, shaped the framing of the federal Constitution.

The delegates from 12 different states had two things in common. They were all men of considerable political experience, and they all recognized the need for a stronger national union. So when the Virginia delegation introduced Madison's outline for a new central government, the convention was ready to listen.

⌃ James Madison, the scholar and statesman whose ideas and political skill shaped the Constitution.

The Virginia and New Jersey Plans >>

What Madison had in mind was a truly national republic, not a confederation of independent states. His "Virginia Plan" proposed a central government with three branches: legislative, executive, and judicial. Furthermore, the legislative branch, Congress, would possess the power to veto all state legislation. In place of the Confederation's single assembly, Madison substituted a bicameral legislature, with a lower house elected directly by the people and an upper house chosen by the lower from nominations made by state legislatures. Representatives to both houses would be apportioned according to population—a change from practice under the Articles, in which each state had a single vote in Congress. Madison also revised the structure of government that had existed under the Articles by adding an executive, who would be elected by Congress, and an independent federal judiciary.

After two weeks of debate over the Virginia Plan, William Paterson, a lawyer from New Jersey, presented a less radical counterproposal. While his "New Jersey Plan" increased Congress's power to tax and to regulate trade, it kept the national government as a unicameral assembly, with each state receiving one vote in Congress under the policy of equal representation. The delegates took just four days to reject Paterson's plan. Most endorsed Madison's design for a stronger central government.

Even so, the issue of apportioning representation continued to divide the delegates. While smaller states pressed for each state's having an equal vote in Congress, larger states backed Madison's provision for basing representation on population. Underlying the dispute over representation was an even deeper rivalry between southern and northern states. While northern and southern populations were nearly equal in the 1780s, and the South's population was growing more rapidly, the northern states were more numerous. Giving the states equal votes would put the South at a disadvantage. Southerners feared being outvoted in Congress by the northern states and felt that only proportional representation would protect the interests of their section.

That division turned into a deadlock as the wet spring burned off into a blazing summer. The stifling heat was made even worse because the windows remained shut, to keep any news of the proceedings from drifting out onto the Philadelphia streets.

The Deadlock Broken >>

Finally, as the heat wave broke, so did the political stalemate. On July 2 a committee headed by Benjamin Franklin suggested a compromise. States would be equally represented in the upper house of Congress, each state legislature appointing two senators to six-year terms. That satisfied the smaller states. In the lower house of Congress, which alone could initiate money bills, representation was to be apportioned according to population. Every 30,000 inhabitants would entitle a state to send one representative for a two-year term. A slave was to count as three-fifths of a free person in the calculation of population, and the slave trade was to continue until 1808. That satisfied the larger states and the South.

By the end of August the convention was prepared to approve the final draft of the Constitution. The delegates agreed that the executive, now called the president, would be chosen every four years. Direct election seemed out of the question—after all, how could citizens in South Carolina know anything about a presidential candidate who happened to live in distant Massachusetts, or vice versa? But if each state chose presidential electors, either by popular election or by having the state legislature name them, those eminent men would likely have been involved in national politics, have known the candidates personally, and be prepared to vote wisely. Thus the Electoral College was established, with each state's total number of senators and representatives determining its share of electoral votes.

An array of other powers ensured that the executive would remain independent and strong: the president would have command over the armed forces, authority to conduct diplomatic relations, responsibility to nominate judges and officials in the executive branch, and the power to veto congressional legislation. Just as the executive branch was made independent, so, too, the federal judiciary was separated from the other two branches of government. Madison believed that this clear **separation of powers** was essential to a balanced republican government.

Madison's only real defeat came when the convention refused to give Congress veto power over state legislation. Still, the new bicameral national legislature enjoyed much broader authority than Congress had under the Confederation, including the power to tax and to regulate commerce. The Constitution also limited the powers of state legislatures, prohibiting them from levying duties on trade, coining money or issuing paper currency, and conducting foreign relations. The Constitution and the acts passed by Congress were declared the supreme law of the land, taking precedence over any legislation passed by the states. And changing the Constitution would not be easy. Amendments could be proposed only by a two-thirds vote of both houses of Congress or in a convention requested by two-thirds of the state legislatures. Ratification of amendments required approval by three-quarters of the states.

On September 17, 1787, 39 of the 42 delegates remaining in Philadelphia signed the Constitution. Charged only with revising the Articles, the delegates had instead written a completely new frame of government. And to speed up ratification, the convention decided that the Constitution would go into effect after only nine states had approved it. They further declared that the people themselves—not the state legislatures—would pass judgment on the Constitution in special ratifying conventions. To serve final notice that the new central government was a republic of the people and not merely another confederation of states, Gouverneur Morris of Pennsylvania hit on a happy turn of phrase to introduce the Constitution. "We the People," the document begins, "in order to form a more perfect union . . ."

> **separation of powers**
> principle that each branch of government—the legislature (Congress), the executive (the President), and the judiciary (the Supreme Court)—should wield distinct powers independent from interference or infringement by other branches of government.

> Charged only with revising the Articles, the delegates had instead written a completely new frame of government.

Opinion

Does the electoral college ensure fair outcomes in presidential contests?

Ratification >>

With grave misgivings on the part of many, the states called for conventions to decide whether to ratify the new Constitution.

Those with the gravest misgivings—the Anti-Federalists, as they came to be called—voiced familiar republican fears. Older and less cosmopolitan than their **Federalist** opponents, the Anti-Federalists drew on their memories of the struggle with England to frame their criticisms of the Constitution. Expanding the power of the central government at the expense of the states, they warned, would lead to corrupt and arbitrary rule by new aristocrats. Extending a republic over a large territory, they cautioned, would separate national legislators from the interests and close oversight of their constituents.

federalism governing principle established by the Constitution in which the national government and the states divide power.

Madison responded to these objections in The Federalist Papers, a series of 85 essays written with Alexander Hamilton and John Jay during the winter of 1787–1788. He countered Anti-Federalist concerns over the centralization of power by pointing out that each separate branch of the national government would keep the others within the limits of their legal authority. That mechanism of **checks and balances** would prevent the executive from oppressing the people while preventing the people from oppressing themselves.

checks and balances mechanism by which each branch of government—executive, legislative, and judicial—keeps the others within the bounds of their constitutional authority.

To answer Anti-Federalist objections to a national republic Madison drew on the ideas of an English philosopher, David Hume. In his famous 10th essay in *The Federalist Papers,* Madison argued that in a great republic "the Society becomes broken into a greater variety of interests, of pursuits, of passions, which check each other." The larger the territory, the more likely it was to contain multiple political interests and parties, so that no single faction could dominate. Instead, each would cancel out the others.

The one Anti-Federalist criticism Madison could not get around was the absence of a national bill of rights. Opponents insisted on an explicit statement of rights to prevent the freedoms of individuals and minorities from being violated by the federal government. Madison finally promised to place a bill of rights before Congress immediately after the Constitution was ratified.

Throughout the early months of 1788 Anti-Federalists continued their opposition. But they lacked the articulate and influential leadership that rallied behind the Constitution and commanded greater access to the public press. In the end, too, Anti-Federalist fears of centralized power proved less compelling than Federalist prophecies of the chaos that would follow if the Constitution were not adopted.

By the end of July 1788 all but two states had voted in favor of ratification. The last holdout, Rhode Island, finally came aboard in May 1790, after Madison had carried through on his pledge to submit a bill of rights to the new Congress. Indeed, these 10 amendments—ratified by enough states to become part of the Constitution by the end of 1791—proved to be the Anti-Federalists' most impressive legacy. The bill of rights set the most basic terms for defining personal liberty in the United States. Among the rights guaranteed were freedom of religion, the press, and speech, as well as the right to assemble and petition and the right to bear arms. The amendments also established clear procedural safeguards, including the right to a trial by jury and protection against illegal searches and seizures. They prohibited excessive bail, cruel and unusual punishment, and the quartering of troops in private homes.

 REVIEW

What short-term crises precipitated the Constitutional Convention, and what were the main points of debate at that meeting?

Within the life span of a single generation, Americans had declared their independence twice. In many ways the political freedom claimed from Britain in 1776 was less remarkable than the intellectual freedom from the Old World that Americans achieved by agreeing to the Constitution. The Constitution represented a triumph of the imagination—a challenge to many beliefs long cherished by western Europe's republican thinkers.

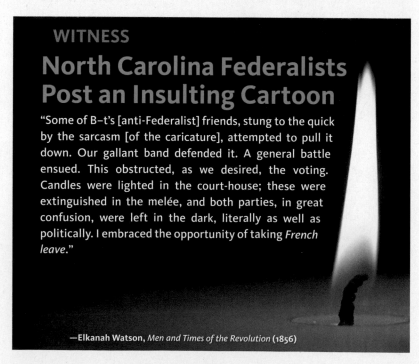

WITNESS

North Carolina Federalists Post an Insulting Cartoon

"Some of B–t's [anti-Federalist] friends, stung to the quick by the sarcasm [of the caricature], attempted to pull it down. Our gallant band defended it. A general battle ensued. This obstructed, as we desired, the voting. Candles were lighted in the court-house; these were extinguished in the melée, and both parties, in great confusion, were left in the dark, literally as well as politically. I embraced the opportunity of taking *French leave.*"

—Elkanah Watson, *Men and Times of the Revolution* (1856)

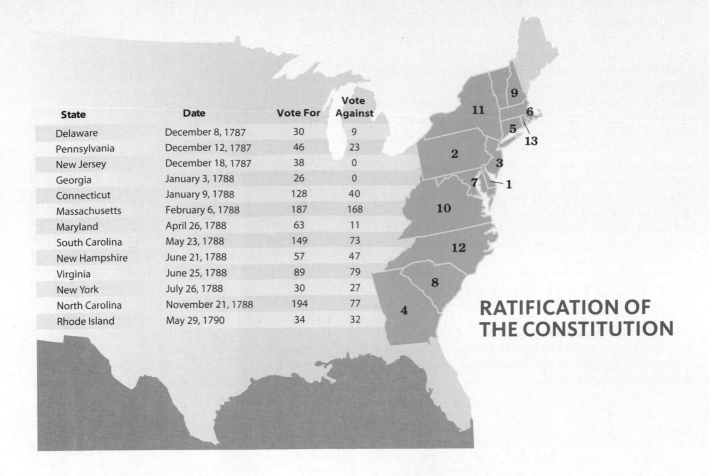

State	Date	Vote For	Vote Against
Delaware	December 8, 1787	30	9
Pennsylvania	December 12, 1787	46	23
New Jersey	December 18, 1787	38	0
Georgia	January 3, 1788	26	0
Connecticut	January 9, 1788	128	40
Massachusetts	February 6, 1788	187	168
Maryland	April 26, 1788	63	11
South Carolina	May 23, 1788	149	73
New Hampshire	June 21, 1788	57	47
Virginia	June 25, 1788	89	79
New York	July 26, 1788	30	27
North Carolina	November 21, 1788	194	77
Rhode Island	May 29, 1790	34	32

RATIFICATION OF THE CONSTITUTION

Revolutionary ideals had been deeply influenced by the conflicts of British politics, in particular the Opposition's warnings about the dangers of executive power. Those concerns at first committed the revolutionaries to making legislatures supreme. In the end, though, Americans ratified a constitution that provided for an independent executive and a balanced government. The Opposition's fears of distant, centralized power had at first prompted the revolutionaries to embrace state sovereignty. But in the Constitution Americans established a national government with authority independent of the states. Finally, the common sense among all of western Europe's republican theorists—that large national republics were an impossibility—was rejected by Americans, making the United States an impossibility that still endures.

What, then, became of the last tenet of the old republican creed—the belief that civic virtue would sustain popular liberty? The hard lessons of the war and the crises of the 1780s withered confidence in the capacity of Americans to sacrifice their private interests for the public welfare. Many came to share Washington's sober view that "the few . . . who act upon Principles of disinterestedness are, comparatively speaking, no more than a drop in the Ocean." The Constitution reflected the new recognition that interest rather than virtue shaped the

behavior of most people most of the time and that the clash of diverse interest groups would remain a constant of public life.

Yet Madison and many other Federalists did not believe that the competition between private interests would somehow result in policies fostering public welfare. That goal would be met instead by the new national government acting as "a disinterested and dispassionate umpire in disputes between different passions and interests in the State." The Federalists looked to the national government to fulfill that role, because they trusted that a large republic, with its millions of citizens, would yield more of that scarce resource—disinterested gentlemen dedicated to serving the public good. Such gentlemen, in Madison's words, "whose enlightened views and virtuous sentiments render them superior to local prejudices," would fill the small number of national offices.

Not all the old revolutionaries agreed. Anti-Federalists drawn from the ranks of ordinary Americans still believed that common people were more virtuous and gentlemen more interested than the Federalists allowed. "These lawyers and men of learning, and moneyed men, that talk so finely," complained one Anti-Federalist, would "get all the power and all of the money into their own hands, and then they will swallow up all us little folks." Instead of being dominated by enlightened gentlemen, the national government should be composed of representatives from every social class and occupational group.

The narrow majorities by which the Constitution was ratified reflected the continuing influence of such sentiments, as well as fear that the states were surrendering too much power. That fear made Patrick Henry so ardent an Anti-Federalist that he refused to attend the Constitutional Convention in 1787, saying that he "smelt a rat." "I am not a Virginian, but an American," Henry had once declared. Most likely he was lying. Or perhaps Patrick Henry, a southerner and a slaveholder, could see his way clear to being an "American" only as long as sovereignty remained firmly in the hands of the individual states. Henry's convictions, 70 years hence, would rise again to haunt the Union.

CHAPTER SUMMARY

Leading Americans would give more thought to federalism, the organization of a United States, as the events of the postrevolutionary period revealed the weaknesses of the state and national governments.

- For a decade after independence the revolutionaries were less committed to creating a single national republic than to organizing 13 separate state republics, each dominated by popularly elected legislatures.
- The Articles of Confederation provided for a government by a national legislature but left the crucial power of the purse, as well as all final power to make and execute laws, entirely to the states.
- Many conflicts in the new republic were occasioned by westward expansion, which created both international difficulties with Britain and Spain and internal tensions over the democratization of state legislatures.
- In the wake of the Revolution, ordinary Americans struggled to define republican society: workers began to organize; some women claimed a right to greater political, legal, and educational opportunities; and religious dissenters called for disestablishment.
- In the mid-1780s the political crisis of the Confederation came to a head, prompted by the controversy over the Jay-Gardoqui Treaty and Shays's Rebellion.
- The Constitutional Convention of 1787 produced an entirely new frame of government that established a truly national republic and provided for a separation

Significant Events

Continental Congress approves the Articles of Confederation

1777

Articles of Confederation ratified

1781

Jay-Gardoqui Treaty negotiated but not ratified

1785

Shays's Rebellion; Annapolis convention calls for revising the Articles

1786

of powers among a judiciary, a bicameral legislature, and a strong executive.

- The Anti-Federalists, opponents of the Constitution, softened their objections when promised a bill of rights after ratification, which was incorporated into the Constitution by 1791.

Additional Reading

The work of Gordon Wood is indispensable for understanding the transformation of American politics and culture during the 1780s and thereafter; see especially *The Creation of the American Republic* (1969) and *The Radicalism of the American Revolution* (1992). To understand the arguments in favor of the Constitution, consult Garry Wills, *Explaining America* (1981), and to appreciate the contributions of its opponents, read Saul Cornell, *The Other Founders* (1999) and the classic writings of Cecilia Kenyon collected in *Men of Little Faith* (2003).

To explore the meaning of republicanism for American women, see two fine studies by Linda Kerber, *Women of the Republic* (1980) and *No Constitutional Right to Be Ladies* (1998), as well as Rosemarie Zagarri's superb biography of Mercy Otis Warren, *A Woman's Dilemma* (1995). For a vivid sense of how the 1780s transformed local society and politics in one Massachusetts county, read John Brooke, *The Heart of the Commonwealth* (1991), and for a fascinating tale of how the Revolution made one ordinary man's life extraordinary, enjoy Alan Taylor, *William Cooper's Town* (1995). The best accounts of how the Revolution's legacy affected the lives of African Americans in the North include Shane White, *Somewhat More Independent* (1991), and Joan Pope Melish, *Disowning Slavery* (1998).

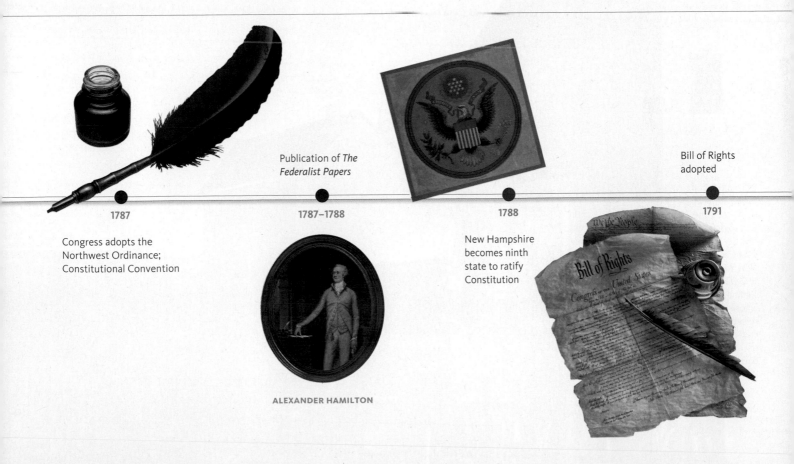

Publication of *The Federalist Papers*

Bill of Rights adopted

1787

1787–1788

1788

1791

Congress adopts the Northwest Ordinance; Constitutional Convention

ALEXANDER HAMILTON

New Hampshire becomes ninth state to ratify Constitution

"Yes," Neville replied, without turning around.

"Then I must give you a whipping!" cried the rider and leapt from his horse. He grabbed Neville by the hair and lunged at his throat. Breaking free, Neville finally managed to knock the man down: he recognized his attacker as Jacob Long, a local farmer. After Long fled Neville resumed his journey, badly shaken.

John Neville was not accustomed to such treatment. As one of the wealthiest men in the area, he expected respect from those of lower social rank. And he had received it—until becoming embroiled in a controversy over the new "whiskey tax" on distilled spirits. In a frontier district like western Pennsylvania, farmers regularly distilled their grain into whiskey for barter and sale. Not surprisingly, the **excise tax,** passed

excise tax internal tax placed on the production or sale of a commodity, usually a luxury item or nonessential.

by Congress in 1791, was notoriously unpopular. Still, Neville had accepted an appointment to be one of the tax's regional inspectors. For three years he had endured threats as he enforced the law, but this roadside assault showed that popular hostility was rising.

As spring turned to summer the grain ripened, and so did the people's anger. In mid-July a federal marshal arrived to serve summonses to a

▲ In this antigovernment cartoon, a devil's imp with horns and barbed tail offers to escort a tax collector—the Exciseman—to his master. Like the Stamp Act riots of the Revolutionary period, protesters in western Pennsylvania against the excise tax ritually hanged tax collectors in effigy (left).

number of farmer-distillers who had not paid taxes. One, William Miller, squinted at the paper and was amazed to find the government ordering him to appear in court—hundreds of miles away in Philadelphia—in little more than a month. Even worse, the papers claimed he owed $250.

And there, next to this unknown federal marshal, stood the unyielding John Neville.

"I felt myself mad with passion," recalled Miller. "I thought $250 would ruin me; and . . . I felt my blood boil at seeing General Neville along to pilot the sheriff to my very door." Word of the marshal's presence brought 30 or 40 laborers swarming from a nearby field. Armed with muskets and pitchforks, they forced Neville and the marshal to beat a hasty retreat.

Next morning the local militia company marched to Neville's estate. A battle ensued, and the general, aided by his slaves, beat back the attackers. A larger group, numbering 500 to 700, returned the following day to find Neville fled and his home garrisoned by a group of

soldiers from nearby Fort Pitt. The mob burned down most of the outbuildings and, after the soldiers surrendered, torched Neville's elegantly furnished home.

Throughout the region that summer, marauding bands roamed the countryside, burning homes and attacking tax collectors. While the greatest unrest flared in western Pennsylvania, farmers in the western districts of several other states also defied federal officials and refused to pay the tax, thus launching a full-scale "Whiskey Rebellion" in the summer of 1794.

Alexander Hamilton, a principal architect of the strong federal government established by the Constitution, knew a challenge to authority when he saw one: "Shall there be a government, or no government?" So did an alarmed George Washington, now president and commander-in-chief of the new republic, who led an army of 13,000 men—larger than that he had commanded at Yorktown against the British—into the Pennsylvania countryside.

That show of force cowed the Pennsylvania protesters, snuffing out the Whiskey Rebellion. But the riots and rebellion deepened fears for the future of the new republic. As Benjamin Franklin remarked in 1788, Americans were skilled at overthrowing governments, but only time would tell whether they were any good at sustaining them. By 1794 Franklin's warning seemed prophetic. «

Federalists such as Washington and Hamilton—supporters of a powerful national government—had high hopes for their newly created republic. Stretching over some 840,000 square miles in 1789, it was approximately four times the size of France, five times the size of Spain, ten times the size of Great Britain. Yet the founders of the republic knew how risky it was to unite such a vast territory. Yankee merchants living along Boston wharves had economic interests and cultural traditions distinct from those of backcountry farmers who raised hogs, tended a few acres of corn, and distilled whiskey. Even among farmers, there was a world of difference between a South Carolina planter who shipped tons of rice to European markets and a New Hampshire family whose stony fields yielded barely enough to survive. Could the new government established by the Constitution provide a framework strong enough to unite such a socially diverse nation? Within a decade national political leaders split into two sharply opposed political parties, drawing ordinary men and women into civic life.

Social and political divisions within the nation were sharpened by currents of global change, both across the Atlantic and westward across the continent. After 1789 an increasingly bloody revolution in France sharpened old rivalries, and as Europe plunged into war, Americans were torn in their loyalties. Britain also determined to make Americans fight for their independence once again, while in the west, Spain and later France pressured white settlers beyond the Appalachians. Indian nations, buffeted by disease and dislocation, sought to unite in a confederacy west of the Appalachian Mountains.

In short, the early republic was a fragile creation, buffeted by changes beyond its borders and struggling to create a stable government at home. During the nation's first three decades its survival depended on balancing the interests of a socially and economically diverse population.

1789: A SOCIAL PORTRAIT

When the Constitution went into effect, the United States stretched from the Atlantic Ocean to the Mississippi River. The first federal census, compiled in 1790, counted approximately 4 million people, divided about evenly between the northern and southern states. Only about 100,000 settlers lived beyond the Appalachians in the Tennessee and Kentucky territories, which were soon to become states.

> ## In short, the early republic was a fragile creation, buffeted by changes beyond its borders and struggling to create a stable government at home.

Within the Republic's boundaries were two major groups that lacked effective political influence: African Americans and Indians. In 1790 black Americans numbered 750,000, almost one-fifth the total population. More than 90 percent lived in the southern states from Maryland to Georgia; most were slaves who worked on tobacco and rice plantations, but there were free blacks as well. The census did not count the number of Indians living east of the Mississippi. North of the Ohio, the powerful Miami Confederacy discouraged settlement, while to the south, five strong, well-organized tribes—the Creeks, Cherokees, Chickasaws, Choctaws, and Seminoles—dominated the region from the Appalachians to the Mississippi River.

That composition would change as the white population continued to double about every 22 years. Immigration contributed only a small part to this astonishing growth. On average, fewer than 10,000 Europeans arrived annually between 1790 and 1820. The primary cause was natural increase, since, on average, American white women gave birth to nearly eight children each. As a result, the United States had an unusually youthful population: in 1790 almost half of all white Americans were under 16 years old. The age at first marriage was about 25 for men, 24 for women—and three or four years younger in newly settled areas—which contributed to the high birthrate.

This youthful, growing population remained overwhelmingly rural. Only 24 towns and cities boasted 2,500 or more residents, and 19 out of 20 Americans lived outside them. In fact, more than 80 percent of American families in 1800 were engaged in agriculture. In such a rural environment the movement of people, goods, and information was slow. Few individuals used the expensive postal system, and most roads were still little more than dirt paths hacked through the forest. In 1790 the country had 92 newspapers, but they were published mostly in towns and cities along major avenues of transportation.

Life in isolated regions contrasted markedly with that in bustling urban centers, such as New York and Philadelphia. But the most basic division in American society was not between the cities and the countryside, important as that was. What would divide Americans most broadly over the coming decades was the contrast between **semisubsistence** and commercial ways of life. Semisubsistence farmers lived on the produce of their own land and labor. Americans in the commercial economy were tied more closely to the larger markets of a far-flung world.

> **semisubsistence economy**
> economy in which individuals and families produce most of what they need to live on.

SEMISUBSISTENCE & COMMERCIAL AMERICA, 1790

To prosper, a commercial economy demanded relatively cheap transportation to move goods. Thus in 1790 American commerce was confined largely to settled areas along the coast and to navigable rivers below the fall line. Because commerce depended on an efficient flow of information and goods, newspapers flourished in these areas.

Semisubsistence and Commercial Economies >>
Most rural white Americans in the interior of the northern states and the backcountry of the South lived off the produce of their own land. Wealth in those areas, although not distributed equally, was spread fairly broadly. And subsistence remained the goal of most white families. "The great effort was for every farmer to produce anything he required within his own family," one European visitor noted. In such an economy women played a key role. Wives and daughters had to be skilled in making such articles as candles, soap, clothing, and hats, since the cost of buying them was steep.

With labor scarce and expensive, farmers also depended on their neighbors to help clear fields, build homes, and harvest crops. If a farm family produced a small surplus, it usually exchanged it locally rather than selling it for cash in a distant market. In this barter economy, money was seldom seen and was used primarily to pay taxes and purchase imported goods.

Indian economies were also based primarily on subsistence. In the division of labor women raised crops, while men fished or hunted—not only for meat but also for skins to make clothing. Because Indians followed game more seasonally than did white settlers, they moved their villages to several different locations over the course of a year. But both whites and Indians in a semisubsistence economy moved periodically to new fields after they had exhausted the old ones. Indians exhausted agricultural lands less quickly, because they planted beans, corn, and squash in the same field, a technique that better conserved soil nutrients.

Despite the image of both the independent "noble savage" and the self-reliant yeoman farmer, virtually no one in the backcountry operated within a truly self-sufficient economy. Although farmers tried to grow most of the food their families ate, they normally bought salt, sugar, and coffee, and they often traded with their neighbors for food and other items. In addition, necessities such as iron, glass, lead, and gunpowder had to be purchased, and many farmers hired artisans to make shoes and weave cloth. Similarly, Indians were enmeshed in the wider world of European commerce, exchanging furs for iron tools or clothing and ornamental materials.

Outside the backcountry, Americans were tied much more closely to a **commercial economy.** Here, merchants, artisans, and even farmers did not subsist on what they produced but instead sold goods or services in a wider market and lived on their earnings. Cities and towns, of course, played a key part in the commercial economy. But so did the agricultural regions near the seaboard and along navigable rivers.

> **commercial economy** economy in which individuals are involved in a network of markets and commercial transactions. Such economies are often urban, where goods and services are exchanged for money and credit; agricultural areas are also commercial when crops and livestock are sold in markets rather than consumed by those who grew or raised them.

For commerce to flourish, goods had to move from producers to market cheaply enough to reap profits. Water offered the only cost-effective transportation over any distance; indeed, it cost as much to ship goods a mere 30 miles over primitive roads as to ship by boat 3,000 miles across the Atlantic to London. Cost-effective transportation was available to the planters of the Tidewater South, and city merchants used their access to the sea to establish trading ties to the West Indies and Europe. But urban artisans and workers were also linked to this market economy, as were many farm families in the Hudson valley, southeastern Pennsylvania, and southern New England.

In commercial economies, wealth was less equally distributed. By 1790 the richest 10 percent of Americans living in cities and in the plantation districts of the Tidewater South owned about 50 percent of the wealth. In the backcountry the top 10 percent was likely to own 25 to 35 percent of the wealth.

The Constitution and Commerce >> In many ways the fight over ratification of the Constitution represented a struggle between the commercial and the subsistence-oriented elements of American society. Urban merchants and workers as well as commercial farmers and planters generally rallied behind the Constitution. They took a broader, more cosmopolitan view of the nation's future, and they had a more favorable view of government power.

Americans who remained a part of the semisubsistence **barter economy** tended to oppose the Constitution. More provincial in outlook, they feared concentrated power, were suspicious of cities and commercial institutions, opposed aristocracy and special privilege, and in general just wanted to be left alone.

> **barter economy** networks of trade based on the mutual exchange of goods and services with little or no use of coin or currency.

And so in 1789 the United States embarked on its new national course, with two rival visions of the direction that the fledgling Republic should take. Which vision would prevail—a question that was as much social as it was political—increasingly divided the generation of revolutionary leaders in the early republic.

 REVIEW

Describe the semisubsistence and commercial economies of the United States in 1789, and explain their differing visions of how the country should develop.

THE NEW GOVERNMENT

Whatever the Republic was to become, Americans agreed that George Washington personified it. When the first Electoral College cast its votes, Washington was unanimously elected, the only president in history so honored. John Adams became vice president. Loyalty to the new Republic, with its untried form of government and diversity of peoples and interests, rested to a great degree on the trust and respect Americans gave Washington.

⌃ Washington's trip from Virginia to New York City to assume the presidency was a triumphant procession, as Americans enthusiastically greeted him with cheers and even flowers strewn along his path.

Washington Organizes the Government >>

George Washington realized that as the first occupant of the executive office, everything he did was fraught with significance. "I walk on untrodden ground," he commented. "There is scarcely any part of my conduct which may not hereafter be drawn into precedent."

The Constitution made no mention of a cabinet. Yet the drafters of the Constitution, aware of the experience of the Continental Congress under the Articles of Confederation, clearly assumed that the president would have some system of advisers. Congress authorized the creation of four departments—War, Treasury, State, and Attorney General—whose heads were to be appointed with the consent of the Senate. Washington's most important choices were Alexander Hamilton as secretary of the treasury and Thomas Jefferson to head the State Department. Washington gradually excluded Adams from cabinet discussions, and any meaningful role for the vice president, whose duties were largely undefined by the Constitution, soon disappeared.

The Constitution created a federal Supreme Court but beyond that was silent about the court system. The Judiciary Act of 1789 set the size of the Supreme Court at 6 members; it also established 13 federal district courts and 3 circuit courts of appeal. Supreme Court justices spent much of their time serving on these circuit courts, a distasteful duty whose long hours "riding the circuit" caused one justice to grumble that Congress had made him a "traveling postboy." The Judiciary Act made it clear that federal courts had the right to review decisions of the state courts and specified cases over which the Supreme Court

would have original jurisdiction. Washington appointed John Jay of New York, a staunch Federalist, as the first chief justice.

Hamilton's Financial Program >> When

Congress called on Alexander Hamilton to prepare a report on the nation's finances, the new secretary of the treasury undertook the assignment eagerly. A brilliant thinker and an ambitious politician, he did not intend to be a minor figure in the new administration. Convinced that human nature was fundamentally selfish, Hamilton was determined to link the interests of the wealthy with those of the new government. He also intended to use federal power to encourage manufacturing and commerce in order to make the United States economically strong and independent of Europe.

Neither goal could be achieved until the federal government solved its two most pressing financial problems: revenue and credit. Without revenue it could not be effective. Without credit—the faith of merchants and other nations that the government would repay its debts—it would lack the ability to borrow. Hamilton proposed that all $52 million of the federal debt, much of it generated by the Revolutionary War, be paid in full (or funded). He also recommended that the federal government assume responsibility for the remaining $25 million in debts that individual states owed—a policy of "assumption." He intended with these twin policies to put the new federal government on a sound financial footing and enhance its power by increasing its need for revenue and making the wealthy look to the national government, not the states. Hamilton also proposed a series of excise taxes, including a controversial 25 percent levy on whiskey, to help meet government expenses.

After heated debate Congress deadlocked over funding and assumption. Finally, at a dinner with Hamilton, Jefferson and James Madison of Virginia agreed to support his proposal if, after 10 years in Philadelphia, the permanent seat of government would be located in the South, on the Potomac River between Virginia and Maryland. Aided by this understanding, funding and assumption passed Congress. In 1791 Congress also approved a 20-year charter for the first Bank of the United States. The bank would hold government deposits and issue banknotes that would be received in payment of all debts owed the federal government. Congress proved less receptive to the rest of Hamilton's program, although a limited tariff to encourage manufacturing and several excise taxes, including the one on whiskey, won approval.

The passage of Hamilton's program caused a permanent rupture among supporters of the Constitution. Madison, who had collaborated closely with Hamilton in the 1780s, broke with his former ally over funding and assumption. Jefferson finally went over to the opposition when Hamilton announced plans for a national bank. Eventually the two warring factions organized themselves into political parties: the Republicans, led by Jefferson and Madison, and the Federalists, led by Hamilton and Adams.[1] But the division emerged slowly over several years.

Hamilton's program promoted the commercial sector at the expense of semisubsistence farmers. Thus it rekindled many of the concerns that had surfaced during the struggle over ratification of the Constitution. The ideology of the Revolution had stressed that republics inevitably contained groups who sought power in order to destroy popular liberties and overthrow the republic. To some Americans, Hamilton's program seemed a clear threat to establish a privileged and powerful financial aristocracy—perhaps even a monarchy.

Who, after all, would benefit from the funding proposal? During and after the Revolution, the value of notes issued by the Continental Congress dropped sharply. Speculators had bought up most of these notes for a fraction of their face value from small farmers and workers. If the government finally paid back the debt, speculators would profit accordingly. Equally disturbing, members of Congress had been purchasing the notes before the adoption of Hamilton's program. Nearly half the members of the House owned U.S. securities, a dangerous mimicking of Britain, where the Bank of England's loans to many members of Parliament gave it great political influence.

Fears were heightened, because Americans had little experience with banks: only three existed in the country when the Bank of the United States was chartered. One member of Congress expressed a common attitude when he said that he would no more be caught entering a bank than a house of prostitution. Then, too, banks and commerce were a part of the urban environment that rural Americans so distrusted. Although Hamilton's opponents admitted that a certain amount of commerce was necessary, they believed that it should remain subordinate. Hamilton's program, in contrast, encouraged manufacturing and urbanization, developments

that history suggested were incompatible with liberty and equality.

After Congress approved the bank bill Washington hesitated to sign it. When he consulted his cabinet, Jefferson stressed that the Constitution did not specifically authorize Congress to charter a bank. Both he and Madison upheld the idea of strict construction—that the Constitution should be interpreted narrowly and the federal government restricted to powers expressly delegated to it. Otherwise, the federal government would be the judge of its own powers, and there would be no safeguard against the abuse of power.

Hamilton countered that the Constitution contained implied as well as enumerated powers. He particularly emphasized the clause that permitted Congress to make all laws "necessary and proper" to carry out its duties. A bank would be useful in carrying out the enumerated powers of regulating commerce and maintaining the public credit; Congress thus had a right to decide whether to establish one. In the end Washington accepted Hamilton's arguments and signed the bill.

Economically Hamilton's program was a success. The government's credit was restored, and the national bank ended the inflation of the previous two decades and created a sound currency. In addition, Hamilton's theory of implied powers and broad construction gave the nation the flexibility necessary to respond to unanticipated crises.

Foreign Debt
$11.7

State Debt
$21.5

Domestic Debt
$42.4

HAMILTON'S FINANCIAL SYSTEM

Under Hamilton's financial system, more than 80 percent of federal revenues went to pay the interest on the national debt. Note that most of the revenue came from tariff duties (customs).

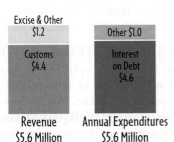

Excise & Other
$1.2

Customs
$4.4

Other $1.0

Interest
on Debt
$4.6

Debt
$75.6 Million

Revenue
$5.6 Million

Annual Expenditures
$5.6 Million

[1] The Republican party of the 1790s, sometimes referred to as the Jeffersonian Republicans, is not to be confused with the modern-day Republican party, which originated in the 1850s.

statement and then promptly forgot it. Only years later would it be referred to as the Monroe Doctrine.

 REVIEW

What were the causes of the War of 1812?

The three decades after 1789 demonstrated how profoundly events in the wider world could affect life within the United States, shaping its politics, its boundaries, its economy—its future.

The French Revolution contributed to splintering the once-united leaders of the American Revolution into two rival parties. The wars that followed, between France and England, deepened the divisions between Federalists and Republicans and prompted both parties to mobilize the political loyalties of ordinary white American men and women. Napoleon's ambitions to conquer Europe handed Jefferson the Louisiana Territory, while British efforts to reclaim its American empire tempted some New Englanders to secede from the Union and encouraged Tecumseh's hopes of mounting a pan-Indian resistance on the frontier. The Haitian Revolution in the Caribbean prompted free blacks in northern cities to protest racial inequalities and slavery within the United States.

But by the 1820s most white Americans paid less attention to events abroad than to expanding across the vast North American continent. Jefferson had dreamed of an "empire of liberty," delighting in expansion as the means to preserve a nation of small farmers. But younger, more nationalistic Republicans had a different vision of expansion. They spoke of internal improvements, protective tariffs to foster American industries, roads and canals to link farmers with towns, cities, and wider markets. These new Republicans were not aristocratic, like the Federalists of old. Still, their dream of a national, commercial republic resembled Franklin's and Hamilton's more than Jefferson's. They had seen how handsomely American merchants and commercial farmers profited when European wars swelled demand for American wheat and cotton. They looked to profit from speculation in land, the growth of commercial agriculture, and new methods of industrial manufacturing. If they represented the rising generation, what would be the fate of Crèvecoeur's semisubsistence farm communities? The answer was not yet clear.

CHAPTER SUMMARY

Basic social divisions between the commercial and semi-subsistence regions shaped the politics of the new United States. Between 1789 and the 1820s the first parties emerged and, along with them, a more popular and participatory political culture. Over the same decades Indian confederacies mounted a sustained resistance to westward expansion, while events in Europe deepened divisions among Federalists and Republicans and threatened the very existence of the fledgling American republic.

- The first party to organize in the 1790s was the Federalists, led by Alexander Hamilton and George Washington.
- Divisions over Hamilton's policies as secretary of the treasury led to the formation of the Republicans, led by James Madison and Thomas Jefferson.
- The commercially minded Federalists believed in order and hierarchy, supported loose construction of the Constitution, and wanted a powerful central government to promote economic growth.

Significant Events

1789	1793	1794	1796	1798	1801	1803
Washington inaugurated president; French Revolution begins		Battle of Fallen Timbers; Whiskey Rebellion			House elects Jefferson; Cane Ridge religious revival	*Marbury v. Madison*; Louisiana Purchase
	War breaks out between France and England; Washington proclaims American neutrality		First contested presidential election—Adams defeats Jefferson	XYZ Affair; Alien and Sedition Acts passed; Virginia and Kentucky resolutions		

- The Republican party, with its sympathy for agrarian ideals, endorsed strict construction of the Constitution, wanted a less active federal government, and harbored a strong fear of aristocracy.

- The French Revolution, the XYZ Affair, the naval war, and the Alien and Sedition Acts also deepened the partisan division between Federalists and Republicans during the 1790s. The Federalists' controversial domestic and foreign policies, internal divisions, and hostility to the masses eventually led to their downfall.

- Before becoming president, Jefferson advocated the principles of agrarianism, limited government, and strict construction of the Constitution. But once in power, he failed to dismantle Hamilton's economic program and promoted western expansion by acquiring Louisiana from France.

- Chief Justice John Marshall proclaimed that the courts were to interpret the meaning of the Constitution (judicial review), a move that helped the judiciary emerge as an equal branch of government.

- Lewis and Clark produced the first reliable information and maps of the Louisiana territory. The lands they passed through had been transformed over the previous 25 years by disease, dislocation, and the arrival of horses and guns.

- The Shawnee prophet Tenskwatawa and his brother Tecumseh organized the most important Indian resistance to the expansion of the new republic, but the movement collapsed with the death of Tecumseh during the War of 1812.

- France and Britain both interfered with neutral rights, and the United States went to war against Britain in 1812.

- After 1815 a surge in American nationalism was reinforced by Britain's recognition of American sovereignty and the Monroe Doctrine's prohibition of European intervention in the Western Hemisphere. But the Missouri crisis foreshadowed growing sectional rivalries.

Additional Reading

Two good overviews of early national politics are Stanley Elkins and Eric McKitrick's *The Age of Federalism* (1993) and James Roger Sharp, *American Politics in the Early Republic* (1993). Another approach to understanding the politics of this period is to read about the lives of leading political figures: among the best are Joseph Ellis's biographies of John Adams (*Passionate Sage,* 1993) and Thomas Jefferson (*American Sphinx,* rev. ed., 1998) and two biographies of Alexander Hamilton by Ron Chernow and Gerald Stourzh (all cited in the full bibliography). To become better acquainted with the popular political culture of the early republic, consult *Beyond the Founders* (2004), a superb collection of essays edited by Jeffrey Pasley, Andrew W. Robertson, and David Waldstreicher. For an engaging narrative about the political influence exerted by white women, see Catherine Allgor, *Parlor Politics* (2000), and for rich descriptions of the social and political interactions among whites, African Americans, and Indians in the new republic, see Joshua-Rothman, *Notorious in the Neighborhood* (2003), and John Wood Sweet, *Bodies Politic* (2003). To gain a fuller understanding of the lives of both Indians and western frontier settlers, rely on Gregory Evans Dowd, *A Spirited Resistance* (1993); John Mack Faragher's *Sugar Creek* (1986); Adam Rothman, *Slave Country* (2005); Alan Taylor, *William Cooper's Town* (1995); and R. David Edmunds, *The Shawnee Prophet* (1983).

A. DISH OF "BLACK TURTLE".

1804–1806	1807	1809	1812	1814	1815	1820	1823
Lewis and Clark expedition	Embargo Act passed	Tecumseh's confederacy organized	War declared against Great Britain	Washington burned; Hartford Convention; Treaty of Ghent signed	Battle of New Orleans	Missouri Compromise enacted	Monroe Doctrine proclaimed

status. Unlike most American social thinkers of the day they accepted the idea of conflict between different classes. They did not believe that the interests of workers and employers could be reconciled, and they blamed the plight of labor on monopolies, especially banking and paper money, and on machines and the factory system.

If the unions' rhetoric sounded radical, the solutions they proposed were moderate. Reformers agitated for public education, abolition of imprisonment for debt, political action by workers, and effective unions as the means to guarantee social equality and restore labor to its former honored position. Proclaiming the republican virtues of freedom and equality, they attacked special privilege, denounced the lack of equal opportunity, and decried workers' loss of independence.

⌃ Waterfalls at mill towns, like this one in Pawtucket, Rhode Island, were places to swim, fish, and relax, as the people do in the foreground. Jumpers like Sam Patch leaped off the Pawtucket bridge and also off the roof of a nearby building into the foamy froth.

The labor movement gathered some momentum in the decade before the Panic of 1837, but in the depression that followed, labor's strength collapsed. During hard times few workers were willing to strike or engage in collective action. Nor did skilled craftworkers, who spearheaded the union movement, feel a particularly strong bond with semiskilled factory workers and unskilled laborers. More than a decade of agitation did finally win the 10-hour day for some workers by the 1850s, and the courts also recognized workers' right to strike, but these gains had little immediate impact.

Workers were united in resenting the industrial system and their loss of status, but they were divided by ethnic and racial antagonisms, gender, conflicting religious perspectives, occupational differences, party loyalties, and disagreements over tactics. For them, the factory and industrialism were not agents of opportunity but reminders of their loss of independence and a measure of control over their lives.

Sam Patch and a Worker's "Art" >> Some

fought against the loss of independence in unusual ways. The waterfalls that served as a magnet for capitalists building mills also attracted their workers. Such cascades were places to visit during off-hours to picnic, swim, fish, or laze about. And for those with nerve, the falls provided a place to show off skills in a different way. Every mill town had its waterfall jumpers, with their own techniques to survive the plunge (knees bent, chest thrust forward). No jumper won more fame than Sam Patch, a young man who had begun working at the Pawtucket mills at the age of seven.

Patch gained wider attention when he jumped at Passaic Falls, New Jersey, where a mill owner was opening a private park that charged admission, in order to keep away "the lazy, idle, rascally" and lower-class riffraff. Workers who resented this undemocratic practice rejoiced when Patch spoiled the park's opening by leaping 70 feet into the foaming water. Thousands of ordinary folk cheered him from outside the park. Eventually Patch's daring led him to the biggest challenge of all: Niagara Falls. Twice he leapt more than 80 feet into the cascade's churning waters. But he drowned a month later when he dared Genesee Falls in another mill town along the Erie Canal—Rochester, New York. Still, his fame persisted for decades. Leaping waterfalls was "an art which I have knowledge of and courage to perform," he once declared defiantly. In a market economy where skilled "arts" were being replaced by machine labor, Sam Patch's acts were a defiant protest against the changing times.

 REVIEW

What factors contributed to the beginnings of industrialization in the United States?

- The Republican party, with its sympathy for agrarian ideals, endorsed strict construction of the Constitution, wanted a less active federal government, and harbored a strong fear of aristocracy.

- The French Revolution, the XYZ Affair, the naval war, and the Alien and Sedition Acts also deepened the partisan division between Federalists and Republicans during the 1790s. The Federalists' controversial domestic and foreign policies, internal divisions, and hostility to the masses eventually led to their downfall.

- Before becoming president, Jefferson advocated the principles of agrarianism, limited government, and strict construction of the Constitution. But once in power, he failed to dismantle Hamilton's economic program and promoted western expansion by acquiring Louisiana from France.

- Chief Justice John Marshall proclaimed that the courts were to interpret the meaning of the Constitution (judicial review), a move that helped the judiciary emerge as an equal branch of government.

- Lewis and Clark produced the first reliable information and maps of the Louisiana territory. The lands they passed through had been transformed over the previous 25 years by disease, dislocation, and the arrival of horses and guns.

- The Shawnee prophet Tenskwatawa and his brother Tecumseh organized the most important Indian resistance to the expansion of the new republic, but the movement collapsed with the death of Tecumseh during the War of 1812.

- France and Britain both interfered with neutral rights, and the United States went to war against Britain in 1812.

- After 1815 a surge in American nationalism was reinforced by Britain's recognition of American sovereignty and the Monroe Doctrine's prohibition of European intervention in the Western Hemisphere. But the Missouri crisis foreshadowed growing sectional rivalries.

Additional Reading

Two good overviews of early national politics are Stanley Elkins and Eric McKitrick's *The Age of Federalism* (1993) and James Roger Sharp, *American Politics in the Early Republic* (1993). Another approach to understanding the politics of this period is to read about the lives of leading political figures: among the best are Joseph Ellis's biographies of John Adams (*Passionate Sage,* 1993) and Thomas Jefferson (*American Sphinx,* rev. ed., 1998) and two biographies of Alexander Hamilton by Ron Chernow and Gerald Stourzh (all cited in the full bibliography). To become better acquainted with the popular political culture of the early republic, consult *Beyond the Founders* (2004), a superb collection of essays edited by Jeffrey Pasley, Andrew W. Robertson, and David Waldstreicher. For an engaging narrative about the political influence exerted by white women, see Catherine Allgor, *Parlor Politics* (2000), and for rich descriptions of the social and political interactions among whites, African Americans, and Indians in the new republic, see Joshua-Rothman, *Notorious in the Neighborhood* (2003), and John Wood Sweet, *Bodies Politic* (2003). To gain a fuller understanding of the lives of both Indians and western frontier settlers, rely on Gregory Evans Dowd, *A Spirited Resistance* (1993); John Mack Faragher's *Sugar Creek* (1986); Adam Rothman, *Slave Country* (2005); Alan Taylor, *William Cooper's Town* (1995); and R. David Edmunds, *The Shawnee Prophet* (1983).

1804–1806	1807	1809	1812	1814	1815	1820	1823
Lewis and Clark expedition	Embargo Act passed	Tecumseh's confederacy organized	War declared against Great Britain	Washington burned; Hartford Convention; Treaty of Ghent signed	Battle of New Orleans	Missouri Compromise enacted	Monroe Doctrine proclaimed

A. DISH OF "BLACK TURTLE".

10

The Erie Canal was pivotal in transforming many inland settlements from semisubsistence economies into commercial ones. Mary Keys painted this watercolor of Lockport, New York, along the canal. A team of three horses pulls the canal boat as the respectably clothed passengers enjoy the scenery.

THE Opening

>> AN AMERICAN STORY

FROM BOOM TO BUST WITH ONE-DAY CLOCKS

In the years before the Civil War, the name of Chauncey Jerome could be found traced in neat, sharp letters in a thousand different places across the globe: everywhere from the fireplace mantels of southern planters to the log cabins of Illinois farmers, and even in Chinese trading houses. For Chauncey Jerome was a New England clockmaker whose clever and inexpensive machines had conquered the markets of the world. >>

OF America 1815–1850

As a boy Jerome had apprenticed himself to a carpenter, but after serving in the War of 1812 he decided to try clock-making. For years he eked out a living peddling his products from farmhouse to farmhouse, until 1824, when his career took off thanks to a "very showy" bronze looking-glass clock. Between 1827 and 1837 Jerome's factory produced more clocks than any other in the country. But when the Panic of 1837 struck Jerome had to scramble to avoid financial ruin.

Looking for a new opportunity he set out to produce an inexpensive brass "one-day" clock—so called because its winding mechanism kept it running that long. Traditionally, the works of these clocks were made of wood, and the wheels and teeth had to be painstakingly cut by hand. Jerome's brass version proved more accurate and cheaper to boot. Costs came down further when he began to use interchangeable parts and combined his operations for making cases and movements within a single factory in New Haven, Connecticut. By systematically organizing the production process, Jerome brought the price of a good clock within the reach of ordinary people. So popular were the new models that desperate competitors began attaching Jerome labels to their own inferior imitations.

Disaster loomed again in 1855 when Jerome took on several unreliable

<< Peddlers like this one helped spread the market economy to every corner of the United States. Early in his career, Chauncey Jerome himself peddled his clocks from farmhouse to farmhouse.

partners. Within a few years his business faltered, then failed. At the age of 62 the once-prominent business leader found himself working again in a clock factory as an ordinary mechanic. He lived his last years in poverty.

Chauncey Jerome's life spanned the transition from the master-apprentice system of production to the beginnings of mechanization and the rise of the factory system. By 1850 the notion of independent American farmers living mainly on what they themselves produced had become a dream of the past. In its place stood a commercial republic in which a full-blown national market encompassed most settled areas of the country.

The concept of the market is crucial here. Americans tied themselves to one another eagerly, even aggressively, through the mechanism of the free market. They sold cotton or wheat and bought manufactured cloth or brass one-day clocks. They

borrowed money not merely to buy a house or farm but also to speculate and profit. They relied, even in many rural villages, on cash and paper money instead of bartering for goods and services. American life moved from less to more specialized forms of labor. It moved from subsistence-oriented to more commercially oriented outlooks and from face-to-face local dealings to impersonal, distant transactions. It shifted from the mechanically simple to the technologically complex and from less dense patterns of settlement on farms to more complex arrangements in cities and towns. Such were the changes Chauncey Jerome witnessed—indeed, changes he helped to bring about himself, with his clocks that divided the working days of Americans into more disciplined, orderly segments.

As these changes took place, Jerome sensed that society had taken on a different tone—that the marketplace and its ethos had become dominant. "It is all money and business, business and money which make the man now-a-days," he complained. "Success is every thing...." The United States, according to one foreign traveler, had become "one gigantic workshop, over the entrance of which there is the blazing inscription 'No admission here except on business.'" <<

THE NATIONAL MARKET ECONOMY

The national market economy began to develop following the War of 1812. As the United States entered a period of unprecedented economic expansion, the economy became varied enough to grow without relying on international trade. Before the war, if European nations suddenly stopped purchasing American commodities such as tobacco and timber, the domestic economy faltered. Since so many Americans remained rural and primarily self-sufficient, they could not absorb any increase in goods produced by American manufacturers.

But the War of 1812 marked an important turning point in the creation and expansion of a domestic market. First the embargo and then the war itself stimulated manufacturing, particularly in textiles. In addition, war had also bottled up capital in Europe. When peace was restored this capital flowed into the United States to take advantage of new investment opportunities. Finally, the war experience led the federal government to adopt policies designed to spur economic expansion.

The New Nationalism >>

After the war with Britain, leadership passed to a new generation of the Republic—younger men such as Henry Clay, John C. Calhoun, and John Quincy Adams. Each was an ardent nationalist eager to use federal power to promote development. Increasingly dominant within the Republican party, they advocated the "New Nationalism," a set of economic policies designed to help all regions prosper and bind the nation more tightly together.

Even James Madison saw the need for increased federal activity, given the problems the government experienced during the war. The national bank had closed its doors in 1811 when its charter expired, and the result had been financial chaos. With Madison's approval Congress in 1816 chartered the Second Bank of the United States for a period of 20 years. Madison also agreed to a mildly protective tariff to aid young American industries by raising the price of competing foreign goods. Finally, Madison supported federal aid for internal improvements such as roads, canals, and bridges, since the war had

Did the national market economy benefit most Americans?

demonstrated how cumbersome it was to move troops or supplies overland.

The Cotton Trade >>

The most important spur to American economic development after 1815 was the growing cotton trade. By the end of the eighteenth century southern planters had discovered that short-fiber cotton would grow in the lower part of the South. But the cotton contained sticky green seeds that could not be easily separated from the lint by hand, until a mechanical engine, or "cotton 'gin,'" patented by Eli Whitney, was developed to do the job. With a slave now able to clean 50 pounds of cotton a day (compared with only 1 pound by hand), and with prices high on the world market, cotton production in the Lower South soared. By 1840 the South produced more than 60 percent of the world supply, and cotton accounted for almost two-thirds of all American exports.

As for the North, its factories increasingly made money by turning raw cotton into cloth, while northern merchants reaped profits from shipping the cotton and then reshipping the textiles. Planters used the income they earned to purchase foodstuffs from the West and goods and services from the Northeast.

The Transportation Revolution >>

For a market economy to become truly national, a transportation network linking various parts of the nation was essential. The economy had not become self-sustaining earlier partly because the only way to transport goods cheaply was by water. Thus trade was limited largely to coastal and international markets, for even on rivers, bulky goods moved easily in only one direction: downstream.

After 1815 all that changed. From 1825 to 1855—the span of a single generation—the cost of transportation on land fell 95 percent, while its speed increased fivefold. As a result, new regions were drawn quickly into the market.

Canals attracted considerable investment capital, especially after the success of the Erie Canal. Built between 1818 and 1825 the canal stretched 364 miles from Albany on the Hudson River to Buffalo on Lake Erie. Its construction by the state was an act of faith, for in 1816 the United States had only 100 miles of canals, none longer than 28 miles. But within a few years of opening, the Erie Canal paid for itself. It reduced the cost of shipping a ton of goods from Buffalo to New York City from more than 19 cents a mile to less than 3 cents. Where the canal's busy traffic passed, settlers flocked, and towns such as Rochester and Lockport sprang up and thrived by moving goods and serving markets. The steady flow of goods eastward gave New York City the dominant position in the scramble for control of western trade.

New York's commercial rivals, like Philadelphia and Baltimore, were soon frantically trying to build their own canals

TRAVEL TIMES TO NEW YORK, 1800 AND 1830

1800 Travel Times

1830 Travel Times

to the West. Western states such as Ohio and Indiana, convinced that their prosperity depended on cheap transportation, constructed canals to link interior regions with the Great Lakes. By 1840 the nation had completed more than 3,300 miles of canals at a cost of about $125 million. Almost half of that amount came from state governments.

Because of its vast expanse, the United States depended particularly on river transportation. But shipping goods downstream from Pittsburgh to New Orleans took 6 weeks, and the return journey required 17 weeks or more. Steamboats reduced the time of an upstream trip from New Orleans to Louisville from 90 to 8 days while cutting costs by 90 percent.

Robert Fulton in 1807 demonstrated the commercial possibilities of propelling a boat with steam when his ship, the Clermont, traveled from New York City to Albany on the Hudson River. But steamboats had the greatest effect on transportation on western rivers, where the flat-bottomed boats could haul heavy loads even in low water.

The first significant railroads appeared in the 1830s, largely as feeder lines to canals. Soon enough, cities and towns saw that their future depended on having good rail links. The country had only 13 miles of track in 1830, but 10 years later railroad and canal mileage were almost exactly equal (3,325 miles). By 1850, the nation had a total of 8,879 miles. Railroad rates were usually higher, but railroads were twice as fast as steamboats, offered more direct routes, and could operate year-round. Although railroads increasingly dominated the transportation system after 1850, canals and steamboats were initially the key to creating a national market.

Revolution in Communications >> What rail and steam engines did for transportation, Samuel F. B. Morse's telegraph did for communications. Morse in 1837 patented a device that sent electrical pulses over a wire, and before long, telegraph lines fanned out in all directions, linking various parts of the country in instantaneous communication. The new form of communication sped business information, helped link the transportation network, and enabled newspapers to provide readers with up-to-date news.

Indeed, the invention of the telegraph and the perfection of a power press in 1847 by Robert Hoe and his son Richard revolutionized journalism. The mechanical press sharply increased the speed with which sheets could be printed over the old hand method and brought newspapers within economic reach of ordinary families. Hoe's press had a similar impact on book publishing, since thousands of copies could be printed at affordable prices.

The Postal System >> A national market economy depended on mass communications to transmit commercial information and bring into contact producers and sellers separated by great distances. Although postage was relatively expensive, the American postal system subsidized the distribution of newspapers and helped spread other forms of commercial information. Indeed, in the years before the Civil War, the postal system employed more laborers than did any other enterprise in the country. Although the system's primary purpose was to promote commerce, the system had a profound social impact by accustoming people to long-range and even impersonal communication.

Profile of Erie Canal

Buffalo Lockport Rochester Syracuse Utica Little Falls Canajoharie Schenectady Albany
Lake Erie 570 ft. Rome

Mohawk R. Hudson R.

THE TRANSPORTATION NETWORK OF A MARKET ECONOMY, 1840

Canals played their most important role in the Northeast, where they linked eastern cities to western rivers and the Great Lakes. Steamboats were most crucial in the extensive river systems of the South and the West.

When traveling in the United States in 1831 the French commentator Alexis de Tocqueville was amazed at the scope of the postal system. "There is an astonishing circulation of letters and newspapers among these savage woods," he reported from the Michigan frontier. Although the British and French post offices handled a greater volume of mail, the American system was much more extensive.

Agriculture in the Market Economy >>

The new forms of transportation had a remarkable effect on farm families: they became linked ever more tightly to a national market system. Given cheap transportation, farmers increased their output in order to sell the surplus at distant markets. In this shift toward commercial agriculture, farmers began cultivating more acres, working longer hours, and adopting scientific farming methods, including crop rotation and the use of manures as fertilizer. Instead of bartering goods with neighbors they more often paid cash or depended on banks to extend them credit. Instead of marketing crops themselves, they began to rely on regional merchants. Like southern planters, western wheat farmers increasingly sold in a world market.

As transportation and market networks connected more areas of the nation they encouraged regional specialization. The South increasingly concentrated on staple crops for export, and the West grew foodstuffs, particularly grain. Eastern farmers, unable to compete with the wheat yields of western farms, shifted to producing fruits, vegetables, and dairy products for rapidly growing urban areas. The cities of the East no longer looked primarily to the sea for their trade; they looked to southern and western markets. That, indeed, was a revolution in markets.

Point of View
The Market Revolution

"To be sure, markets expanded vastly in the years after the end of the War of 1812, but their expansion partook more of the nature of a continuing evolution than a sudden revolution. Furthermore, their expansion did not occur in the face of resistance from any substantial group of people preferring subsistence farming to market participation. Most American family farmers welcomed the chance to buy and sell in larger markets."

DANIEL WALKER HOWE *What Hath God Wrought*

John Marshall and the Promotion of Enterprise >>

A national market system also needed a climate favorable to investment. Under the leadership of Chief Justice John Marshall, the Supreme Court became the branch of the federal government most aggressive in protecting the new forms of business central to the growing market economy.

Marshall, who presided over the Court from 1801 to 1835, convinced his colleagues to uphold the sanctity of private property and the power of the federal government to promote economic growth. In the case of *McCulloch v. Maryland* (1819) the Court upheld the constitutionality of the Second Bank of the United States. Just as Alexander Hamilton had argued in the debate over the first national bank, Marshall emphasized that the Constitution gave Congress the power to make all "necessary and proper" laws to carry out its delegated powers. If Congress believed that a bank would help it meet its responsibilities, such as maintaining the public credit and regulating the currency, then the bank was constitutional. By upholding Hamilton's doctrine of implied powers, Marshall enlarged federal power to an extraordinary degree.

He also encouraged a more freewheeling commerce in *Gibbons v. Ogden* (1824), which gave Marshall a chance to define the greatest power of the federal government in peacetime, the right to regulate interstate commerce. In striking down a steamboat monopoly granted by the state of New York, the chief justice gave the term *commerce* the broadest possible definition, declaring that it covered all commercial dealings and that Congress's power over interstate commerce could be "exercised to its utmost extent." The result was increased business competition throughout society.

At the heart of most commercial agreements were private contracts, made between individuals or companies. Marshall took an active role in defining contract law, which was then in its infancy. The case of *Fletcher v. Peck* (1810) showed how far he was willing to go to protect private property. The justices unanimously struck down a Georgia law that struck down a land grant to a group of speculators that had bribed the legislature to get it. A grant was a contract, Marshall declared, and since the Constitution forbade states to impair "the obligation of contracts," the legislature could not interfere with the grant once it had been made. Although the framers of the Constitution probably meant contracts to refer only to agreements

between private parties, Marshall made no distinction between public and private agreements, thereby greatly expanding the meaning of the contract clause.

The most celebrated decision Marshall wrote on the contract clause was in *Dartmouth College v. Woodward,* decided in 1819. This case arose out of the attempt by New Hampshire to alter the college's charter of 1769. The Court overturned the state law on the grounds that state charters were also contracts and could not be altered by later legislatures. By this ruling Marshall intended to protect **corporations**, which conducted business under charters granted by individual states.

> **corporation** business entity that has been granted a charter granting it legal rights, privileges, and liabilities distinct from the individual members that are a part of it.

Thus the Marshall Court sought to encourage economic risk-taking by protecting property and contracts, by limiting state interference, and by creating a climate of business confidence.

 REVIEW

Describe the workings of the national market economy and the ways in which it was shaped by the revolutions in transportation and communications.

A RESTLESS TEMPER

Between 1815 and 1850 the nation reverberated with almost explosive energy. An emphasis on speed affected nearly every aspect of American life. Steamboat captains risked boiler explosions for the honor of having the fastest boat on the river, prompting the visiting English novelist Charles Dickens to comment that traveling under these conditions seemed like taking up "lodgings on the first floor of a powder mill." American technology emphasized

>> Europeans were shocked that Americans bolted their food or gorged themselves on anything within reach, as this English drawing indicates.

speed over longevity. Unlike European railroads American railroads were lightweight, were hastily constructed, and paid little heed to the safety or comfort of passengers. Americans ate so quickly that one disgruntled European insisted food was "pitch-forked down."

Population Growth >>
If the economic hallmark of this new order was the growth of a national market, there were social factors that also contributed to American restlessness. The American population continued to double about every 22 years—more than twice the rate of Great Britain. The census, which stood at fewer than 4 million in 1790, surpassed 23 million in 1850. Although the birthrate peaked in 1800, it declined only slowly before 1840.

From 1790 to 1820 natural increase accounted for virtually all of the country's population growth. But immigration, which had been disrupted by the Napoleonic Wars in Europe, revived after 1815. In the 1830s some 600,000 immigrants arrived, more than double the number in the quarter century after 1790.

The Restless Movement West >>
The vast areas of land opened for settlement absorbed much of the burgeoning population. As settlers streamed west, speculation in western lands reached frenzied proportions. Whereas only 68,000 acres of the public domain had been sold during the year 1800, sales peaked in 1818, at a staggering 3.5 million acres.

The Panic of 1819 sent sales and prices crashing, and in the depression that followed many farmers lost their farms. Congress reacted by abolishing credit sales of federal land and demanding payment in cash, but it tempered this policy by lowering the price of the cheapest lands to $1.25 an acre and reducing the minimum tract to 80 acres.

Even so, speculators purchased most of the public lands sold, since there was no limit on the amount of acreage an individual or a land company could buy. These land speculators played a leading role in settlement of the West. To hasten sales they usually sold land partially on credit— a vital aid to poorer farmers. They also provided loans to purchase needed tools and supplies. Many farmers became

⌃ This traffic jam in New York City conveys the rapid pace and impatient quality of American life in the first half of the nineteenth century. "In the streets all is hurry and bustle," one European visitor to the city reported. "Carts, instead of being drawn by horses at a walking pace, are often met at a gallop, and always in a brisk trot. . . . The whole population seen in the streets seem to enjoy this bustle and add to it by their own rapid pace, as if they were all going to some place of appointment, and were hurrying on under the apprehension of being too late."

speculators themselves, buying up property in the neighborhood and selling it to latecomers at a tidy profit.

Given such rapid settlement, geographic mobility became one of the most striking characteristics of the American people. The 1850 census revealed that nearly half of all native-born free Americans lived outside the state where they had been born. The typical American "has no root in the soil," visiting Frenchman Michel Chevalier observed, but "is always in the mood to move on, always ready to start in the first steamer that comes along from the place where he had just now landed."

It was the search for opportunity, more than anything else, that accounted for such restlessness. In 1851 a new railroad line bypassed the village of Auburn, Illinois. Despite the village's handsome location, residents quickly abandoned it in order to live in the new town that sprang up around the depot, even though that land was swampier. A neighboring farmer purchased the old village and plowed up the streets, and Auburn reverted to a cornfield.

Urbanization >> Even with the growth of a national market the United States remained a rural nation. Nevertheless, the four decades after 1820 witnessed the fastest rate of urbanization in American history. As a result the ratio of farmers to city dwellers steadily dropped, from 15 to 1 in 1800 to 5.5 to 1 in 1850. Improved transportation, the declining productivity of many eastern farms, the beginnings of industrialization, and the influx of immigrants all stimulated the growth of cities.

The most heavily urbanized area of the country was the Northeast, where in 1860 more than a third of the population lived in cities.[1] Important urban centers such as St. Louis and Cincinnati arose in the West. The South, with only 10 percent of its population living in cities, was the least urbanized region.

 REVIEW

What were the effects of population growth and movement in the United States during the first half of the nineteenth century?

THE RISE OF FACTORIES

It was an isolated life, growing up in rural, hilly Vermont. But stories of the textile factories that had sprung up in Lowell and other towns in Massachusetts reached even small villages, such as Barnard. Fifteen-year-old Mary Paul was working there as a domestic servant when, in 1845,

[1] The Northeast included New England and the mid-Atlantic states (New York, Pennsylvania, and New Jersey). The South comprised the slave states plus the District of Columbia.

⌃ St. Louis, a major urban center that developed in the West, depended on the steamboat to sustain its commerce, as this 1859 illustration makes clear.

two friends helped her find her first job at the Lowell mills. "I am in need of clothes which I cannot get about here," she explained to her farm-bound father. After four years she returned home, but now found "countryfied" life too confining, and before long she left her rural hometown—this time for good.

Mary Paul was one of thousands of rural Americans whose lives were fundamentally altered by the economic transformations of the young republic. The changes in her lifestyle and her working habits demonstrated that the new factories and industries needed more than technological innovation to run smoothly. Equally crucial, labor needed to be reorganized.

Technological Advances >> Before 1815 manufacturing had been done in homes or shops by skilled artisans. As master craftworkers they imparted the knowledge of their trades to apprentices and **journeymen.** In addition, women often worked in their homes part-time under the putting-out system, making finished articles from raw material supplied by merchant capitalists. After 1815 this older form of manufacturing began to give way to factories with machinery tended by unskilled or semiskilled laborers.

> **journeyman** person who has served an apprenticeship in a trade or craft and who is a qualified worker employed by another person.

From England came many of the earliest technological innovations. But Americans often improved on the British machines. "Everything new is quickly introduced here," one visitor commented in 1820. "There is no clinging to old ways; the moment an American hears the word 'invention' he pricks up his ears." From 1790 to 1860 the United States Patent Office granted more patents than England and France combined.

The first machines required highly skilled workers both to build and to repair them. Eli Whitney had a better idea. Having won a contract to produce 10,000 rifles for the government, he developed machinery that would mass-produce parts that were interchangeable from rifle to rifle. Such parts had to be manufactured to rigid specifications, but once the process was perfected, these parts allowed a worker to assemble a rifle quickly with only a few tools. Simeon North applied the same principle to the production of clocks, and Chauncey Jerome followed North's example and soon surpassed him.

Textile Factories >> The factory system originated in the Northeast, where capital, water power, and transportation facilities were available. As in England, the production of cloth was the first manufacturing process to use the new technology on a large scale. Eventually all the processes of manufacturing fabrics were brought together in a single location, and machines did virtually all the work.

In 1820 a group of wealthy Boston merchants known as the Boston Associates set up operations at Lowell, Massachusetts, which soon became the nation's most famous center of textile manufacturing. Its founders intended to avoid the misery that surrounded English factories by combining **paternalism** with high profits. Instead of relying primarily on child labor or a permanent working class, the Lowell mills employed daughters of New England farm families. Female workers lived in company boardinghouses under the watchful eye of a matron. To its many visitors, Lowell presented an impressive sight, with huge factories and well-kept houses. Female workers were encouraged to attend lectures and use the library; they even published their own magazine, *the Lowell Offering.*

> **paternalism** attitude or policy of treating individuals or groups in a fatherly manner, by providing for their needs without granting them rights of responsibilities.

The reality of factory life, however, involved strict work rules and long hours of tedious, repetitive work. At Lowell, for example, workers could be fined for lateness or misconduct, such as talking on the job, and the women's morals in the boardinghouses were strictly guarded. Work typically began at 7 A.M. (earlier in the summer) and continued until 7 at night, six days a week. With only 30 minutes for the noon meal, many workers had to run to the boardinghouse and back to avoid being late. Winter was the "lighting up" season, when work began before daylight and ended after dark. The only light after sunset came from whale oil lamps that filled the long rooms with smoke.

The reality of factory life involved strict work rules and long hours of tedious, repetitive work.

Although the labor was hard the female operators earned from $2.40 to $3.20 a week, wages considered good by the standards of the time. (Domestic servants and seamstresses were paid less than a dollar a week.) The average "mill girl" was between 16 and 30 years old. Most were not working to support their families back home on the farm; instead, they wanted to accumulate some money for perhaps the first time in their lives and sample some of life's pleasures. "I must . . . have something of my own before many more years have passed," Sally Rice wrote in rejecting her parents' request that she return home to Somerset, Vermont. "And where is that something coming from if I go home and earn nothing?"

Like Rice, few women in the mills intended to work permanently. The majority stayed no more than five

>> Mill workers, Lowell. "I am in need of clothes which I cannot get about here," Mary Paul had told her father in rural Vermont. Indeed, these workers wear the textiles they helped produce in factories like Lowell's, each pattern slightly different.

years before getting married. The sense of sisterhood that united women in the boardinghouses made it easier for farm daughters to adjust to the stress and regimen the factory imposed on them.

As competition in the textile industry intensified, factory managers tried to raise productivity. In the mid-1830s the mills began to increase the workloads and speed up the machinery. Even these changes failed to maintain previous profits, and on several occasions factories cut wages. The ever-quickening pace of work finally provoked resistance among the women in the mills. Several times in the 1830s wage cuts sparked strikes in which a minority of workers walked out. In the 1840s workers' protests focused on the demand for a 10-hour day.

WITNESS
Life in the Lowell Mills

"At first the hours seemed very long, but I was so interested in learning that I endured it very well; and when I went out at night the sound of the mill was in my ears, as of crickets, frogs, and jewsharps, all mingled together in strange discord ... but now I do not mind it at all. ... It makes my feet ache and swell to stand so much, but I suppose I shall get accustomed to that too. The girls generally wear old shoes about their work, and you know nothing is easier; but they almost all say that when they have worked here a year or two they have to procure shoes a size or two larger than before they came."

—Harriet Farley, "Letters from Susan," *Lowell Offering*, 1844

As the mills expanded a smaller proportion of the workers lived in company boardinghouses, and moral regulations were relaxed. But the greatest change was a shift in the work-force from native-born females to Irish immigrants, including men and children. The Irish, who made up only 8 percent of the Lowell work-force in 1845, amounted to almost half by 1860. Desperately poor and eager for any work, they did not view their situation as temporary. Wages continued to decline, and a permanent working class took shape.

Lowell and the Environment >> Lowell was a city built on water power. Early settlers had used the power of the Merrimack River to run mills, but never on the scale of the textile factories. As the market spread Americans came to link progress with the fullest use of the environment's natural resources.

By 1836 Lowell had seven canals, with a supporting network of locks and dams, to govern the Merrimack's flow and distribute water to the city's 26 mills. As more and more mills were built, both at Lowell and other sites, the Boston Associates erected dams at several points along the river to store water and divert it into power canals for factories. At Lawrence they constructed the largest dam in the world at the time, a 32-foot-high granite structure that spanned 1,600 feet across the river. But even dammed, the Merrimack's waters proved insufficient. So the Associates gained control of over 100 square miles of New Hampshire lakes that fed the river system. Damming these lakes provided a regular flow of water, especially in the drier summer months.

By regulating the river's waters the Associates made the Merrimack valley the nation's greatest industrial center in the first half of the nineteenth century. But not all who lived there benefited. By raising water levels the dams flooded farmlands, blocked the transportation of logs downstream, and damaged mills upstream by reducing the current. The dams also devastated the fish population by preventing upstream spawning, while factories routinely dumped their wastes into the river to be carried downstream, eventually contaminating water supplies. Epidemics of typhoid, cholera, and dysentery increased, so that by midcentury Lowell had a reputation as a particularly unhealthy city.

DEVELOPMENT OF THE LOWELL MILLS

As more mills were built at Lowell the demand increased for water to power them. By 1859 the mills drew water from lakes 80 to 100 miles upstream, including Winnipesauke, Squam, and Newfound. The map at left shows the affected watersheds. In the city of Lowell (*right*), a system of canals was enlarged over several decades. In the painting (done in 1845), the machine shop can be seen at left, with a row of mills alongside a canal. Rail links tied Lowell and Boston together.

Industrial Work >>

The creation of an industrial labor force that was accustomed to working in factories did not occur easily. Previously artisans had worked within the home. Apprentices were considered part of the family, and masters were responsible not only for teaching their apprentices a trade but also for providing them some education and for supervising their moral behavior. Journeymen knew that if they perfected their skill, they could become respected master artisans with their own shops. And skilled artisans worked not by the clock, at a steady pace, but rather in bursts of intense labor alternating with greater leisure.

The factory changed that. Factory goods were not so finished or elegant as those done by hand, and pride in artisanship gave way to rates of productivity. At the same time, workers were required to discard old habits, because industrialism demanded a worker who was sober, dependable, and self-disciplined. Absenteeism, lateness, and drunkenness hurt productivity and disrupted the regular factory routine. Thus industrialization not only produced a fundamental change in the way work was organized but also transformed the very nature of work.

With the loss of personal freedom also came the loss of standing in the community. The master-apprentice relationship gave way to factories' sharp separation of workers from management. Few workers rose through the ranks to supervisory positions, and even fewer could set up their own businesses, as many artisans dreamed. Even well-paid workers sensed their decline in status.

The Labor Movement >>

In this newly emerging economic order workers sometimes organized to protect their rights and traditional ways of life. Craftworkers such as carpenters, printers, and tailors formed unions, and in 1834 individual unions came together in the National Trades' Union.

Union leaders argued that labor was degraded in America: workers endured long hours, low pay, and low status. Unlike most American social thinkers of the day they accepted the idea of conflict between different classes. They did not believe that the interests of workers and employers could be reconciled, and they blamed the plight of labor on monopolies, especially banking and paper money, and on machines and the factory system.

If the unions' rhetoric sounded radical, the solutions they proposed were moderate. Reformers agitated for public education, abolition of imprisonment for debt, political action by workers, and effective unions as the means to guarantee social equality and restore labor to its former honored position. Proclaiming the republican virtues of freedom and equality, they attacked special privilege, denounced the lack of equal opportunity, and decried workers' loss of independence.

ethnic and racial antagonisms, gender, conflicting religious perspectives, occupational differences, party loyalties, and disagreements over tactics. For them, the factory and industrialism were not agents of opportunity but reminders of their loss of independence and a measure of control over their lives.

Sam Patch and a Worker's "Art" >> Some

fought against the loss of independence in unusual ways. The waterfalls that served as a magnet for capitalists building mills also attracted their workers. Such cascades were places to visit during off-hours to picnic, swim, fish, or laze about. And for those with nerve, the falls provided a place to show off skills in a different way. Every mill town had its waterfall jumpers, with their own techniques to survive the plunge (knees bent, chest thrust forward). No jumper won more fame than Sam Patch, a young man who had begun working at the Pawtucket mills at the age of seven.

Patch gained wider attention when he jumped at Passaic Falls, New Jersey, where a mill owner was opening a private park that charged admission, in order to keep away "the lazy, idle, rascally" and lower-class riff-raff. Workers who resented this undemocratic practice rejoiced when Patch spoiled the park's opening by leaping 70 feet into the foaming water. Thousands of ordinary folk cheered him from outside the park. Eventually Patch's daring led him to the biggest challenge of all: Niagara Falls. Twice he leapt more than 80 feet into the cascade's churning waters. But he drowned a month later when he dared Genesee Falls in another mill town along the Erie Canal—Rochester, New York. Still, his fame persisted for decades. Leaping waterfalls was "an art which I have knowledge of and courage to perform," he once declared defiantly. In a market economy where skilled "arts" were being replaced by machine labor, Sam Patch's acts were a defiant protest against the changing times.

Waterfalls at mill towns, like this one in Pawtucket, Rhode Island, were places to swim, fish, and relax, as the people do in the foreground. Jumpers like Sam Patch leaped off the Pawtucket bridge and also off the roof of a nearby building into the foamy froth.

The labor movement gathered some momentum in the decade before the Panic of 1837, but in the depression that followed, labor's strength collapsed. During hard times few workers were willing to strike or engage in collective action. Nor did skilled craftworkers, who spearheaded the union movement, feel a particularly strong bond with semiskilled factory workers and unskilled laborers. More than a decade of agitation did finally win the 10-hour day for some workers by the 1850s, and the courts also recognized workers' right to strike, but these gains had little immediate impact.

Workers were united in resenting the industrial system and their loss of status, but they were divided by

REVIEW

What factors contributed to the beginnings of industrialization in the United States?

SOCIAL STRUCTURES OF THE MARKET SOCIETY

Thousands of miles beyond Lowell's factory gates a different class of Americans roamed who at first appeared unconnected to the bustle of urban markets. These were the legendary mountain men, who flourished from the mid-1820s through the mid-1840s. Traveling across the Great Plains, along upland streams, and over the passes of the Rockies, outdoorsmen such as Jim Bridger, Jedediah Smith, and James Walker wore buckskin hunting shirts, let their hair grow to their shoulders, and stuck pistols and tomahawks in their belts. Wild and exotic, the mountain men became romantic symbols of the American quest for individual freedom.

Yet these wanderers, too, were tied to the emerging market society. The mountain men hunted beaver pelts and shipped them east, to be turned into fancy hats for gentlemen. The fur trade was not a sporting event but a business, dominated by organizations such as John Jacob Astor's American Fur Company, and the trapper was the agent of an economic structure that stretched from the mountains to eastern cities and even to Europe. Most of these men went into the wilderness not to flee civilization but to make money. Of those who survived the fur trade most returned and took up respectable new careers as shopkeepers, traders, ranchers, politicians, and even bankers. They, like farmers, were expectant capitalists for whom the West was a land of opportunity.

The revolution in markets, in other words, affected Americans from all walks of life: mountain men as well as merchants, laborers as well as farmers. Equally critical, it restructured American society as a whole.

Economic Specialization >>
To begin with, the spread of the market produced greater specialization. Transportation networks made it possible for farmers to concentrate on producing certain crops, while factories could focus on making a single item such as cloth or shoes. Within factories, the division of labor meant that the process of manufacturing an item became more specialized, broken down into less skilled tasks.

This process evolved at different rates. Textiles and milling were completely mechanized, while other sectors of the economy, such as shoes and men's clothing, depended little on machinery. Moreover, large factories were the exception rather than the rule. Still, the tendency was toward more technology, greater efficiency, and increasing specialization.

Specialization had consequences at home as well as in the workplace. The average eighteenth-century American woman produced items such as thread, cloth, clothing, and candles in the home for family use. As factories spread, however, household manufacturing all but disappeared, and women lost many of the economic functions they had previously performed in the family unit. Again, textiles are a striking example. Between 1815 and 1860 the price of cotton cloth fell from 18 to 2 cents a yard, and because it was also smoother and more brightly colored than homespun, most women purchased cloth rather than making it themselves. Similarly, the development of ready-made men's clothing reduced the amount of sewing women did, especially in urban centers.

Materialism >>
European visitors were struck during these years by how much Americans were preoccupied with material goods. The new generation did not invent materialism, but the spread of the market after 1815 made it much more evident. "I know of no country, indeed,"

˄ Thomas Hicks's painting, *Calculating*, captures the spirit of the United States as the market revolution unfolded. Americans, one foreign visitor reported, were a "guessing, reckoning, expecting and calculating people." During this period the phrase "I calculate" came to mean "I think." The man carefully going over his figures wears a beaver hat, the end product of the fur trade, and many mountain men ended up as calculating businessmen.

Tocqueville commented, "where the love of money has taken stronger hold on the affections of men."

In a nation that had no legally recognized aristocracy, no established church, and class lines that were only informally drawn, wealth became the most obvious symbol of status. Materialism reflected more than a desire for goods and physical comfort. It represented a quest for respect and recognition. The esteem of the founding generation for intellectual achievement was mostly lost in the scramble for wealth that seemed to consume the new generation.

Wealth and the Emerging Middle Class

>> In the years after 1815 a new middle class took shape in American society. A small class of shopkeepers, professionals, and master artisans had existed earlier, but the creation of a national market economy greatly expanded its size and influence. As specialization increased, office work and selling were more often physically separated from the production and handling of merchandise. Businesspeople, professionals, storekeepers, clerks, office workers, and supervisors began to think of themselves as a distinct social group. Members of the growing middle class had access to more education and enjoyed greater social mobility. They were paid not only more but differently. A manual worker might earn $300 a year, paid as wages computed on an hourly basis. Professionals received a yearly salary and might make $1,000 a year or more.

Middle-class neighborhoods, segregated along income and occupational lines, also began to develop in towns and cities. In larger cities improved transportation enabled middle-class residents to move to surrounding suburbs and commute to work. Leisure also became segregated, as separate working-class and middle-class social organizations and institutions emerged.

As middle-class Americans accumulated greater wealth they were able to consume more. Thus material goods became emblems of success and status—as clockmaker Chauncey Jerome sadly discovered when his business failed and his wealth vanished. Indeed, this materialistic ethos was most apparent in the middle class, as they strove to set themselves apart from other groups in society.

Furthermore, as American society became more specialized after 1815, greater extremes of wealth appeared. As the new markets created fortunes for the few, the factory system lowered the wages of workers by dividing labor into smaller, less skilled tasks. At the upper end of the social scale, wealth was most highly concentrated in large eastern cities and in the cotton kingdom of the South. Still, throughout the nation the tendency was for the rich to get richer and own a larger share of the community's total wealth. By 1860, 5 percent of American families owned more than 50 percent of the nation's wealth. In villages where the market revolution had not penetrated, wealth tended to be less concentrated.

In a market society, the rich were able to build up their assets, because those with capital were in a position to increase it dramatically by taking advantage of new investment opportunities. Although a few men, such as Cornelius Vanderbilt and John Jacob Astor, vaulted from the bottom ranks of society to the top, most of the nation's richest individuals came from wealthy families.

Social Mobility

>> The existence of great fortunes is not necessarily inconsistent with the idea of **social mobility** or property accumulation. Although the gap between the rich and the poor widened after 1820, even the incomes of most poor Americans rose, because the total amount of wealth produced in America had become much larger. From about 1825 to 1860 the average per capita income almost doubled, to $300. Voicing the popular belief, a New York judge proclaimed, "In this favored land of liberty, the road to advancement is open to all."

social mobility movement of individuals from one social class to another.

Social mobility existed in these years, but not as much as contemporaries boasted.

Social mobility existed in these years, but not as much as contemporaries boasted. Most laborers—or more often their sons—did manage to move up the social ladder, but only a rung or two. Few unskilled workers rose higher than to a semiskilled occupation. Even the children of skilled workers normally did not escape the laboring classes to enter the middle-class ranks of clerks, managers, or lawyers. For most workers improved status came in the form of a savings account or home ownership, which gave them some security during economic downswings and in old age.

A New Sensitivity to Time

>> It was no accident that Chauncey Jerome's clocks spread throughout the nation along with the market economy. The new methods of doing business involved a new and stricter sense of time. Factory life necessitated a more regimented schedule, where work began at the sound of a bell, workers kept machines going at a constant pace, and the day was divided into hours and even minutes.

Clocks began to invade private as well as public space. With mass production ordinary families could now afford clocks, and even farmers became more sensitive to time as they were integrated into the market.

 REVIEW

What was the effect of the new market economy on social structure and values in the antebellum United States?

PROSPERITY AND ANXIETY

As Americans watched their nation's frontiers expand and its market economy grow, many began to view history in terms of continuous improvement. The path of commerce, however, was not steadily upward. Rather, it advanced in a series of wrenching **boom-bust cycles:** accelerating growth, followed by a crash, and then depression.

boom-bust cycle periods of expansion and recession or depression that an economy goes through. Also referred to as *business cycle*.

The country remained extraordinarily prosperous from 1815 until 1819, only to sink into a depression that lasted from 1819 to 1823. During the next cycle the economy expanded slowly during the 1820s, followed by almost frenzied speculation in the 1830s. Then came the inevitable contraction in 1837, and the country suffered an even more severe depression from 1839 to 1843. The third cycle followed the same pattern: gradual economic growth during the 1840s, frantic expansion in the 1850s, and a third depression, which began in 1857 and lasted until the Civil War. In each of these "panics" thousands of workers were thrown out of work, overextended farmers lost their farms, and many businesses closed their doors.

In such an environment, prosperity and personal success seemed all too fleeting. Because Americans believed the good times would not last—that the bubble would burst and another "panic" set in—their optimism was often tinged by insecurity and anxiety. They knew too many individuals like Chauncey Jerome, who had been rich and then lost all their wealth in a downturn.

The Panic of 1819 >>

The initial shock of this boom-and-bust psychology came with the Panic of 1819, the first major depression in the nation's history. From 1815 to 1818 cotton had commanded truly fabulous prices on the Liverpool market. In this heady prosperity the federal government extended liberal credit for land purchases, and the new national bank encouraged merchants and farmers to borrow in order to catch the rising tide.

>> This mock banknote illustrates the anxieties often felt in times of "bust," when the value of currencies plummeted and it was difficult to tell whether the banks that issued paper money were solvent.

But in 1819 the price of cotton collapsed and took the rest of the economy with it. Once the inflationary bubble burst, land values, which had been driven to new heights by the speculative fever, plummeted 50 to 75 percent almost overnight. As the economy went slack, so did the demand for western foodstuffs and eastern manufactured goods and services, pushing the nation into a severe depression. Because the market economy had spread to new areas, the downturn affected not only city folk but rural Americans as well. New cotton planters in the Southwest, who were most vulnerable to the ups and downs of the world market, were especially hard hit.

✔ REVIEW

In what ways did the new market economy shape the hopes and fears of antebellum Americans?

As depression spread in the years following 1819, most Americans could not guess that the ups and downs of the boom-and-bust cycle would continue through the next three decades, their swings made sharper by the growing networks of the market economy both nationally and internationally. But the interconnections between buyers and sellers did feed both prosperity and panic. Farmers and factories specialized in order to sell goods to distant buyers. Canals and railroads widened the network, speeding products, information, and profits. And as markets tied distant lands more tightly together, international events contributed to the business cycles.

It was the Liverpool market in England, in fact, that bid the price of American cotton to its high at over 32 cents. Then in 1816 and 1817 English textile manufacturers, looking for cheaper cotton, began to import more cotton from India, plummeting the price of New Orleans cotton to 14 cents. Broader changes also hurt American markets. The French and the British had been at war with each other for decades—more than 100 years, if the imperial wars of the seventeenth and eighteenth centuries were counted.

In 1814 and 1815 the major powers of Europe hammered out a peace at the Congress of Vienna, one that lasted, with only minor interruptions, until the coming of World War I in 1914. When Europe had been at war American farmers had found a ready market abroad. With thousands of European soldiers returning to their usual work as farmers, demand for American goods dropped.

The stresses of the panic of 1819 shook the political system at home, too. As the depression deepened and hardship spread, Americans viewed government policies as at least partly to blame. The postwar nationalism, after all, had been based on the belief that government should stimulate economic development through a national bank and protective tariff, by improving transportation, and by opening up new lands. As Americans struggled to make sense of their new economic order, they looked to take more direct control of the government that was so actively shaping their lives. During the 1820s the popular response to the market and the Panic of 1819 produced a strikingly new kind of politics in the Republic.

CHAPTER SUMMARY

By uniting the country in a single market, the new market economy transformed the United States during the quarter century after 1815.

- The federal government promoted the creation of a market through a protective tariff, a national bank, and internal improvements.
- The development of new forms of transportation, including canals, steamboats, and eventually railroads, allowed goods to be transported cheaply on land.
- The Supreme Court adopted a pro-business stance that encouraged investment and risk-taking.
- Economic expansion generated greater national wealth, but it also brought social and intellectual change.
  - Americans pursued opportunity, embraced a new concept of progress, viewed change as normal, developed a strong materialist ethic, and considered wealth the primary means to determine status.
  - Entrepreneurs reorganized their operations to increase production and sell in a wider market.
- The earliest factories were built to serve the textile industry, and the first laborers in them were young women from rural families.
  - Factory work imposed on workers a new discipline based on time and strict routine.
  - Workers' declining status led them to form unions and resort to strikes, but the depression that began in 1837 destroyed these organizations.
- The new market economy distributed wealth much more unevenly and left Americans feeling alternatively buoyant and anxious about their social and economic status.

Significant Events

Eli Whitney patents the cotton gin

Cotton boom begins in the South

Panic and depression

| 1793 | 1810 | 1810–1820 | 1811 | 1816 | 1819 | 1819–1823 |

Fletcher v. Peck

First steamboat trip from Pittsburgh to New Orleans

Second Bank of the United States chartered; protective tariff enacted

Dartmouth College v. Woodward; McCulloch v. Maryland

JOHN MARSHALL

- Social mobility existed, but it was more limited than popular belief claimed.
- The economy lurched up and down in a boom-bust cycle.
- In hard times Americans looked to the government to relieve economic distress.

Additional Reading

The best study of early nineteenth century United States history is Daniel Walker Howe, *What Hath God Wrought* (2009). For a provocative overview of the economic changes during this period and their impact on society and culture, consult Charles Sellers, *The Market Revolution* (1991). Then dip into two fine anthologies of essays: Melvin Stokes and Stephen Conway, eds., *The Market Revolution in America* (1996), and Scott C. Martin, ed., *Cultural Change and the Market Revolution in America, 1789–1860* (2005). The best recent book on the transportation revolution is John Larson, *Internal Improvements* (2001), and for a fascinating study of the role played by the postal system in linking Americans, see Richard John, *Spreading the News* (1995). There are many fine studies of urban social classes during the first half of the nineteenth century, and among the best are Sean Wilentz, *Chants Democratic* (1984), which traces the formation of New York City's working class, and Stuart Blumin, *The Emergence of the Middle Class* (1989). To understand the market economy's affect on rural society, read John Mack Faragher's vivid account of the transformation of a farming community in frontier Illinois, *Sugar Creek* (1986), and Robert Shalhope, *A Tale of New England* (2003), which traces the fortunes of a Vermont farmer and his family.

There is also no shortage of excellent books exploring the relationship between the market revolution and antebellum American culture. Begin with Karen Halttunen's classic study of middle-class culture, *Confidence Men and Painted Women* (1982), and a more recent study, Thomas Augst, *The Clerk's Tale* (2003), and then turn to Paul Johnson's lively exploration of working-class culture, *Sam Patch, the Famous Jumper* (2003). To celebrate any occasion, treat yourself to Stephen Nissenbaum, *The Battle for Christmas* (1996). And to console yourself in between celebrations, turn to Scott Sandage, *Born Losers: A History of Failure in America* (2005).

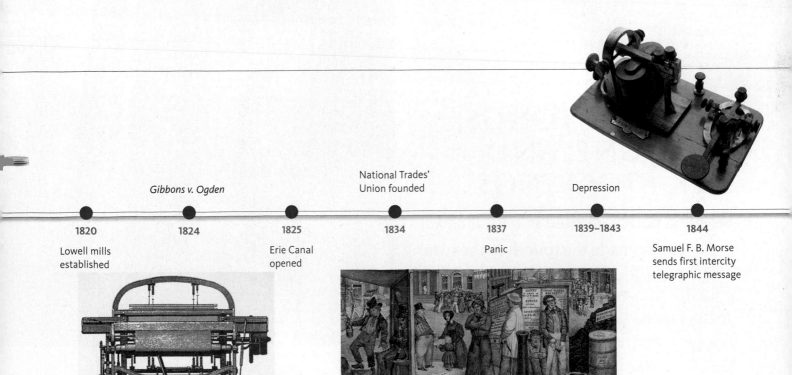

1820 — Lowell mills established

Gibbons v. Ogden — **1824**

1825 — Erie Canal opened

National Trades' Union founded — **1834**

1837 — Panic

Depression — **1839–1843**

1844 — Samuel F. B. Morse sends first intercity telegraphic message

11

>> AN AMERICAN STORY

"WANTED: CURLING TONGS, COLOGNE, AND SILK-STOCKINGS . . ."

The notice, printed in a local newspaper, made the rounds in the rural Pearl River district of Mississippi. A traveler, the advertisement announced, had lost a suitcase while fording the Tallahala River. The contents included "6 ruffled shirts, 6 cambric handkerchiefs, 1 hairbrush, 1 toothbrush, 1 nail-brush . . ." >>

THE Rise

OF Democracy

As citizens give their oath to an election judge at this county election, party workers dispense free drinks, offer party tickets (center, below the banner), and keep a tally of who has voted (the man sitting on the steps). Drinking is prominently featured: one groggy voter has to be held up as he stands in line.

As the list went on, the popular reaction would inevitably shift from amusement to disdain: "1 pair curling tongs . . . 1 bottle Cologne, 1 [bottle] rose-water, 4 pairs silk stockings, and 2 pairs kid gloves." The howls of derision that filled the air could only have increased on learning that anyone finding said trunk was requested to contact the owner—Mr. Powhatan Ellis of Natchez.

Powhatan Ellis was no ordinary backcountry traveler. Born into a genteel Virginia family, Ellis had moved in 1816 to the raw Southwest to enlarge his fortune. With his cultivated tastes and careful dress, he upheld the tradition of the gentleman politician. In Virginia he would have commanded respect: indeed, in Mississippi he had been appointed district judge and U.S. senator. But for the voters along the Pearl River the advertisement for his trunk of ruffled shirts, hair oils, and fancy "skunkwater" proved to be the political kiss of death. His opponents branded him an aristocrat and a dandy, and his support among the piney woods farmers evaporated faster than a morning mist along Old Muddy on a sweltering summer's day.

No one was more satisfied with this outcome than the resourceful Franklin E. Plummer, one of Ellis's political enemies. For in truth, although the unfortunate Powhatan Ellis had lost a trunk fording a stream, he had not placed the advertisement trying to locate it. That was the handiwork of Plummer, who well understood the new playing field of American politics in the 1820s. Born in New England Plummer had made his way as a young man to the new state of Mississippi, where he set himself up as an attorney, complete with a law library of three books, and was quickly elected to the legislature.

Plummer's ambition soon extended beyond the state capital, and in 1830 he announced his candidacy for Congress. In his campaign he portrayed himself as the champion of the people battling the aristocrats of Natchez. Contrasting his humble background with that of his wealthy opponent, Plummer proclaimed: "We are taught that the highway to office, distinction and honor, is as free to the meritorious poor man, as to the rich; to the man who has risen from obscurity by his own individual exertions, as to him who has inherited a high and elevated standing in society, founded on the patrimony of his ancestors." Taking as his slogan "Plummer for the People, and the People for Plummer," he was easily elected.

As long as Plummer maintained his image as one of the people he remained invincible. But when he was a candidate for the U.S. Senate, his touch deserted him. Borrowing money from a Natchez bank, he purchased a stylish coach, put his servant in a uniform, and campaigned across the state. Aghast at such aristocratic pretensions, his followers promptly abandoned him. He died in 1852 in obscurity and poverty. Ah, Plummer! Even the trustiest tribune of the People may succumb to the temptations of power and commerce. «

⌃ By 1840 the new style of democratic politics was in full swing. This rally in Knoxville, Tennessee, uses a camp meeting-style platform in the woods to rally supporters. The makeup of this audience underscores another feature of Jacksonian democracy; the vote went only to adult white males.

In fact, Franklin Plummer was being pulled two ways by the forces transforming American society. The growth of commerce opened up opportunities for more and more Americans during the quarter century after 1815. Through his connections with bankers and the well-to-do, Plummer saw the opportunity to accumulate wealth and to gain status and respect.

Yet at the same time that new markets were producing a more **stratified**, unequal society, the nation's politics were becoming more democratic. The new political system that developed after 1820 differed from that of the early Republic. Just as national markets linked the regions of America economically, the new system of national politics with its mass electioneering techniques involved more voters than ever before. Plummer's world reflected that more egalitarian **political culture.** But the relationship between the new equalities of politics and the new opportunities of the market was an uneasy one.

> **stratified** layered; in this case according to class or social station.
>
> **political culture** patterns, habits, institutions, and traits associated with a political system.

EQUALITY, OPPORTUNITY, AND THE NEW POLITICAL CULTURE OF DEMOCRACY

Middle- and upper-class Europeans who visited the United States during these decades were especially sensitive to the egalitarian quality of American life. To begin with, they discovered that only one class of seats was available on stagecoaches and railcars. These were filled according to the rough-and-ready rule of first come, first served. In steamboat dining rooms or at country taverns, everyone ate at a common table, sharing food from the same serving plates. As one upper-class gentleman complained: "The rich and the poor, the educated and the ignorant, the polite and the vulgar, all herd on the cabin floor, feed at the same table, sit in each others laps, as it were." Indeed, the democratic "manners" of Americans seemed positively shocking. In Europe social inferiors would speak only if spoken to. But Americans felt free to strike up a conversation or to shake hands with anyone, including total strangers.

Americans were proud of such democratic behavior, which they viewed as a valued heritage of the Revolution. The keelboaters who carried the future King

>> As this nattily dressed butcher suggests, clothes were not much help in sorting out social status in America. Although the clothing of the upper class was often made of finer material, by the 1820s less prosperous Americans wore similar styles. "The washerwoman's Sunday attire is now as nearly like that of the merchant's wife as it can be," commented one astonished observer.

Louis-Philippe of France on a trip down the Mississippi made their republican feelings plain when the keelboat ran aground. "You kings down there!" bellowed the captain. "Show yourselves and do a man's work, and help us three-spots pull off this bar!" The ideology of the Revolution made it clear that, in the American deck of cards at least, "three-spots" counted as much as jacks, kings, and queens. Kings were not allowed to forget that—and neither was Franklin Plummer.

By equality, Americans did not mean equality of wealth or property. "I know of no country where profounder contempt is expressed for the theory of permanent equality of property," Alexis de Tocqueville wrote. Nor did equality mean that all citizens had equal talent or capacity. In the end, what Americans upheld was equality of opportunity, not equality of condition. "True republicanism requires that every man shall have an equal chance— that every man shall be free to become as unequal as he can," one American commented. In an economy that could go bust as well as boom, Americans agreed that one primary objective of government was to safeguard opportunity. Thus the new politics of democracy walked hand in hand with the new opportunities of the market.

The stately James Monroe, with his powdered hair and buckled shoes and breeches, was not part of the new politics. But in 1824 as he neared the end of his second term, a host of new leaders in the Republican party looked to succeed him. The Republican congressional caucus finally settled on William H. Crawford of Georgia as the party's presidential nominee. Condemning "King Caucus" as undemocratic, three other Republicans, all ardent nationalists, refused to withdraw from the race: Secretary of State John Quincy Adams; John C. Calhoun, Monroe's secretary of war; and Henry Clay, the Speaker of the House.

None of these men bargained on the sudden emergence of another Republican candidate, Andrew Jackson, the hero of the Battle of New Orleans. Because of his limited experience, no one took Jackson's candidacy seriously at first, including Jackson himself. But soon the general's

Candidate (No parties)	Electoral Vote (%)	Popular Vote (%)
Andrew Jackson	99 (38)	153,544 (43)
John Quincy Adams	84 (32)	108,740 (31)
William Harris Crawford	41 (16)	46,618 (13)
Henry Clay	37 (14)	47,136 (13)
Nonvoting territories		
Not U.S. territory		

to distinguish it from Jefferson's old party. For the next decade the political system continued to evolve. By the mid-1830s the National Republicans gave way to the Whigs, a political party that also drew members from another party that flourished briefly, the Anti-Masons.[1] The Democrats as the other major party came together under the leadership of Andrew Jackson. Once established, this second party system dominated the nation's politics until the 1850s.

Social Sources of the New Politics >>

Why was it that a new style and new system of politics emerged in the 1820s? Part of the answer lay in the Panic of 1819. During the depression that followed, many Americans became convinced that government policy had aggravated, if not actually produced, hard times. Consequently, they decided that the government had a responsibility to relieve distress and promote prosperity.

The connection made between government policy and economic well-being stimulated rising popular interest in politics during the 1820s. Agitation mounted, especially at the state level, for government to enact debtor relief and provide other forms of assistance. Elections became the means through which the majority expressed its policy preferences, by voting for candidates pledged to specific programs. The older idea that representatives should be independent, voting their best judgment, gave way to the notion that representatives were to carry out the will of the people, as expressed in the results of elections.

With more citizens championing the "will of the people," pressure mounted to open up the political process. Most states eliminated property qualifications for voting in favor of white manhood suffrage, under which all adult white males were allowed to vote. Similarly, property requirements for office holders were reduced or dropped.

[1] The Anti-Masons had led a campaign against the Freemasons or Masons, a fraternal order whose members shared the Enlightenment belief in the power of reason but whose secret meetings and rituals seemed aristocratic and undemocratic to many Americans.

supporters and rivals began receiving reports of his popularity. Savvy politicians flocked to his standard, but it was the people who first made Jackson a serious candidate.

The Election of 1824 >> Calhoun eventually dropped out of the race, but none of the four remaining candidates received a majority of the popular vote. Still, Jackson led the field and also finished first in the Electoral College. Under the terms of the Twelfth Amendment, the House was to select a president from the top three candidates. Henry Clay, who finished fourth and was therefore eliminated, met privately with Adams and then rallied the votes in the House needed to put Adams over the top.

Two days later Adams announced that Clay would be his secretary of state, the usual stepping-stone to the presidency. Jackson and his supporters promptly charged that there had been a "corrupt bargain" between Adams and Clay. Before Adams had even assumed office, the 1828 race was under way.

More significant, the election of 1824 shattered the old party system. Henry Clay and John Quincy Adams began to organize a new party, known as the National Republicans

Did the period between the American Revolution and the 1830s bring about a significant democratization in American politics?

> Democratic reforms of the 1820s and 1830s brought a new sort of politician to prominence, one whose life was devoted to party service and whose living often depended on public office. This cartoon from 1834 shows the downside of the new situation. Andrew Jackson sports the wings, horns, and tail of a devil as he dangles the rewards of various political offices above a clamoring group of eager job-seekers.

Presidential elections became more democratic as well. By 1832 South Carolina was the only state where the legislature rather than the voters still chose presidential electors. Parties began to hold conventions as a more democratic method of nominating candidates and approving a platform. And because a presidential candidate had to carry a number of states in different sections of the country, the backing of a national party, with effective state and local organizations, became essential.

The democratic winds of change affected European societies and eventually other areas of the world as well. In no other major country, however, were these reforms achieved as early and with as little resistance as in the United States. Suffrage provides a good example. In Britain, in response to growing demonstrations and the cautionary example of the French monarchy's overthrow in 1830, Parliament approved the Reform Bill of 1832, which enfranchised a number of property holders and gave Britain the broadest electorate in Europe. Yet in fact, only about 15 percent of the adult males in Britain enjoyed the right of suffrage after the bill's passage. Even Britain's second Reform Act (1867) enfranchised only about one-third

of the adult males. Likewise, virtually all the Latin American republics established in the 1820s and 1830s imposed property requirements on voting or forbade certain occupational groups, such as servants and peasants, to vote.

As the new reforms went into effect in the United States, voter turnout soared. Whereas in the 1824 presidential election, only 27 percent of eligible voters had bothered to go to the polls, in 1840, 78 percent cast ballots, probably the highest turnout in American history.

All these developments favored the emergence of a new type of politician: one whose life was devoted to party service and whose living often depended on public office. As the number of state internal improvement projects increased during the 1820s, so did the number of government jobs that could support party workers. No longer was politics primarily the province of the wealthy, who spent only part of their time on public affairs. Instead, political leaders were more likely to come from the middle ranks of society, especially outside the South. As Franklin Plummer demonstrated, a successful politician now had to mingle with the masses and voice their feelings—requirements that put the wealthy elite at a disadvantage.

Politics became mass entertainment, with campaign hoopla frequently overshadowing issues. Parades, massive rallies, and barbecues were used to rouse voters, and treating to drinks became an almost universal campaign tactic. ("The way to men's hearts is down their throats," quipped one Kentucky vote-getter.) Although politicians talked often about principles, political parties were pragmatic organizations, intent on gaining and holding power.

The Jacksonian era has been called the Age of the Common Man, but such democratic tendencies had distinct limits. Women and slaves were not allowed to vote, nor could free African Americans (except in a few states) or Indians. Nor did the parties always deal effectively with (or even address) basic problems in society. Despite such limitations, however, popular political parties provided an essential mechanism for peacefully resolving differences among competing interest groups, regions, and social classes.

REVIEW

In what ways did the political culture of the 1820s and 1830s differ from that of the 1780s and 1790s?

JACKSON'S RISE TO POWER

When he assumed the presidency in 1825 John Quincy Adams might have worked to create a mass-based party. On the state level, the new democratic style of politics was already making headway. But Adams, a talented diplomat and a great secretary of state, had hardly a political bone in his body. Cold and tactless, he could build no popular support for the ambitious and often farsighted programs he proposed. His proposals that government promote not only manufacturing and agriculture but also the arts, literature, and science left his opponents aghast.

Nor would Adams take any steps to gain reelection. Henry Clay finally undertook to organize the National Republicans, but with a reluctant candidate he labored under serious handicaps. The new style of politics came into its own nationally only when Andrew Jackson swept to power at the head of a new party, the Democrats. During the campaign, he remained vague about his position on many issues, and the 1828 race descended into a series of personal attacks, splattering mud on all involved. But Jackson emerged victorious, with enormous majorities behind him in the South.

President of the People >> The election of 1828 marked the beginning of politics as Americans have practiced it ever since, with two disciplined national parties actively competing for votes, emphasizing personalities over issues, and resorting to mass electioneering techniques. Yet in terms of public policy, the meaning of the election was anything but clear. The people had voted for Jackson as a national hero without any real sense of what he would do with his newly won power.

The first president from west of the Appalachians, Jackson was a man of action, and though he had a quick mind, he had little use for learning. His troops had nicknamed him Old Hickory out of respect for his toughness, but that strength sometimes became arrogance, and he could be vindictive and a bully. Over the course of his turbulent career he had fought several duels, one of which left a bullet embedded for the rest of his life within inches of his heart. For all his flaws, however, Jackson was a shrewd politician. He knew how to manipulate men and could be affable or abusive as the occasion demanded. He also

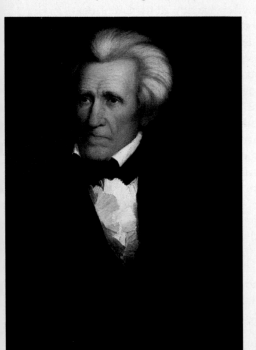

<< Jackson's stubborn determination shines through in this portrait painted in 1835. "His passions are terrible," Jefferson noted. "When I was President of the Senate, he was Senator, and he could never speak on account of the rashness of his feelings. I have seen him attempt it repeatedly, and as often choke with rage."

WITNESS

Jackson's Tumultuous Inauguration

"What a scene did we witness [at the White House]! The *Majesty of the People* had disappeared, and a rabble, a mob, of boys, negroes, women, children, scrambling, fighting, romping . . . the whole house had been inundated by the rabble mob. . . . The President, after having been *literally* nearly pressed to death and almost suffocated and torn to pieces by the people in their eagerness to shake hands with Old Hickory, had retreated through the back way. . . ."

—Margaret Bayard Smith, writing to a woman friend, March 11, 1829 displayed a keen sense of public opinion, reading the shifting national mood better than any of his contemporaries.

As the nation's chief executive Jackson defended the **spoils system,** under which government jobs were awarded to political supporters. Replacing officials regularly was a democratic reform, he insisted: the practice would guard against insensitive bureaucrats who presumed that they held their positions by right. The cabinet, he believed, existed more to carry out his will than to offer counsel. Throughout his term he insisted on his way—and usually got it.

> **spoils system** practice of rewarding loyal party members with jobs in government.

The Political Agenda in the Market Economy >>
Jackson took office at a time when the market economy was expanding throughout America and the nation's population was spreading geographically. The three major problems his administration faced were directly caused by the resulting growing pains.

First, the demand for new lands put continuing pressure on Indians, whose valuable cornfields and hunting grounds could produce marketable commodities such as cotton and wheat. Second, as the economies of the North, South, and West became more specialized, their rival interests forced a confrontation over the tariff. And finally, the booming economy focused attention on the role of credit and banking in society and on the new commercial attitudes that were a central part of the developing market economy. The president attacked all three issues in his characteristically combative style.

 REVIEW

What were the most pressing problems faced by President Andrew Jackson?

DEMOCRACY AND RACE

As a planter Jackson benefited from the international demand for cotton that was drawing new lands into the market. He had gone off to the Tennessee frontier in 1788, a rowdy, ambitious young man who could afford to purchase only one slave. Caught up in the speculative mania of the frontier, he became a prominent land speculator, established himself as a planter, and, by the time he became president, owned nearly 100 slaves. His popularity derived not only from defeating the British but also from opening extensive tracts of valuable Indian lands to white settlement.

Even so, in 1820 an estimated 125,000 Indians remained east of the Mississippi River. In the Southwest the Choctaws, Creeks, Cherokees, Chickasaws, and Seminoles retained millions of acres of prime agricultural land in the heart of the cotton kingdom. Led by Georgia, southern states demanded that the federal government clear these titles.

As white pressure for removal intensified, a shift in the attitude toward Indians and toward race in general occurred. In the past whites most often had attributed cultural differences among whites, blacks, and Indians to the environment. Increasingly after 1815 the dominant white culture stressed "innate" racial differences that could never be erased. A growing number of Americans began to argue that the Indian was a permanently inferior savage who blocked progress.

Accommodate or Resist? >>
The clamor among southern whites for removal placed the southwestern tribes in a difficult situation. Understandably, they rejected the idea of abandoning their lands. They diverged, however, over how to respond. Among the Cherokees, mixed-bloods led by John Ross argued that a program of accommodation—of adopting white ways—would best stave off removal. After a bitter struggle Ross prevailed, and in 1827 the Cherokees adopted a written constitution modeled after that of the United States. They also enacted the death penalty for any member who sold tribal lands to whites without consent of the governing general council. Developing their own alphabet, they published a bilingual newspaper, the *Cherokee Phoenix.*

The division between traditionalists and those favoring accommodation reflected the fact that Indians too had been drawn into a web of market relationships. As more Cherokee families began to sell their surplus crops, they ceased to share property communally as in the past. Cherokee society became more stratified and unequal, just as white society had, and economic elites dominated the tribal government. Nor were the Cherokees untouched by the cotton boom. Some tribal leaders, particularly half-bloods who could deal easily with white culture, became wealthy planters who owned many black slaves and thousands of acres of cotton land. Largely of mixed ancestry, slaveholders were the driving force behind acculturation.

As cotton cultivation expanded among the Cherokees, slavery became harsher and a primary means of determining status, just as in southern white society. The general council passed several laws forbidding intermarriage with blacks and excluding blacks and mulattoes from voting or holding office. Ironically, at the same time that white racial attitudes toward Indians were deteriorating, the Cherokees' view of African Americans drew closer to that of white society.

Trail of Tears >>
As western land fever increased and racial attitudes hardened, Jackson prodded Congress to provide funds for Indian removal. At the same time, the

INDIAN REMOVAL

During Jackson's presidency the federal government concluded nearly 70 treaties with Indian tribes in the Old Northwest as well as in the South. Under their terms, the United States acquired approximately 100 million acres of Indian land.

Creeks reluctantly agreed to move to tracts in present-day Oklahoma. In the process land-hungry schemers cheated tribal members out of as much as 90 percent of their land allotments.

The Cherokees held out longest, but to no avail. In order to deal with more pliant leaders of the tribe, Georgia authorities kidnapped Chief John Ross, who had led the resistance to relocation, and threw him into jail. Ross was finally released but not allowed to negotiate the treaty, which stipulated that the Cherokees leave their lands no later than 1838. When that time came, most refused to go. In response, President Martin Van Buren had the U.S. Army round up resistant members and force them, at bayonet point, to join the westward march. Of the 15,000 who traveled this Trail of Tears, approximately one-quarter died along the way of exposure, disease, and exhaustion.

Some Indians chose resistance. In the Old Northwest a group of the Sauk and Fox led by Black Hawk recrossed the Mississippi into Illinois in 1832 and were crushed by federal troops and the militia. More successful was the resistance of a minority of Seminoles led by Osceola. Despite Osceola's death the Seminoles held out until 1842 in the Florida Everglades before being subdued and removed. In the end, only a small number of southern tribe members were able to escape removal.

In his farewell address in 1837 Jackson defended his policy by piously asserting that the eastern tribes had been finally "placed beyond the reach of injury or oppression, and that [the] paternal care of the General Government will hereafter watch over them and protect them." Indians, however, knew the bitter truth of the matter. Without effective political power, they were at the mercy of the pressures of the marketplace and the hardening racial attitudes of white Americans.

Georgia legislature declared Cherokee laws null and void and decreed that tribal members would be tried in state courts. In 1830 Congress finally passed a removal bill.

But the Cherokees brought suit in federal court against Georgia's actions. In 1832 in the case of *Worcester v. Georgia,* the Supreme Court, in an opinion written by Chief Justice John Marshall, ruled that Georgia had no right to extend its laws over Cherokee territory. Pronouncing Marshall's decision "stillborn," Jackson ignored the Court's edict and went ahead with plans for removal.

Although Jackson assured Indians that they could be removed only voluntarily, he paid no heed when state governments harassed tribes into surrendering lands. Under the threat of coercion, the Choctaws, Chickasaws, and

Free Blacks in the North >>

Unlike with Indian removal, the rising discrimination against free African Americans did not depend directly on presidential action. Still, it was Jackson's Democratic party, which was in the vanguard of promoting white equality, that was also the most strongly proslavery and the most hostile to black rights. The intensifying racism that accompanied the emergence of democracy in American life bore down with particular force on free African Americans.

Before the Civil War, the free black population remained small: about 171,000 in 1840. Although those numbers amounted to less than 2 percent of the North's population, most states enacted laws to keep African Americans in an inferior position. (For a discussion of free African Americans in the South, see page 257.)

Most black northerners lacked meaningful political rights. Black men could vote on equal terms with whites in only five New England states. New York imposed a property requirement only on black voters, which disfranchised the vast majority. Moreover, in New Jersey, Pennsylvania, and Connecticut, African American men lost the right to vote after having previously enjoyed that privilege.

Blacks in the North were also denied basic civil rights that whites enjoyed. Five states forbade them to testify against whites, and either law or custom kept African Americans from juries everywhere except in Massachusetts. In addition, several western states passed black exclusion laws prohibiting free African Americans from immigrating into the state. These laws were seldom enforced, but they were available to harass the free black population.

Segregation, or the physical separation of the races, was widely practiced in the free states. African Americans

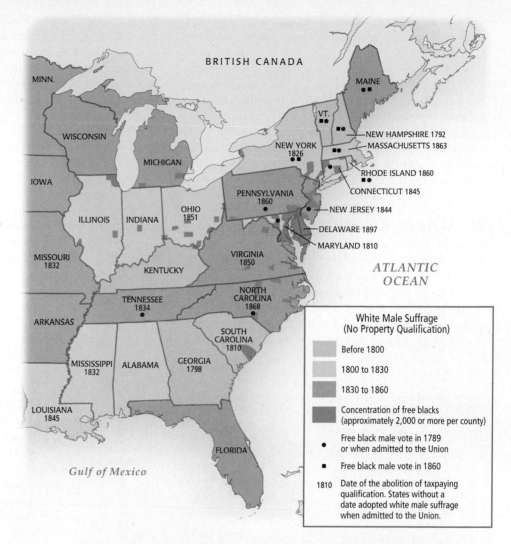

THE SPREAD OF WHITE MANHOOD SUFFRAGE

White manhood suffrage became the norm during the Jacksonian era, but in a number of states free black males who had been voting by law or by custom lost the right to vote. After 1821 a $250 property requirement disfranchised about 90 percent of adult black males in New York.

were excluded from public transportation or assigned to separate sections. Throughout the North they could not go into most hotels and restaurants, and if permitted to enter theaters and lecture halls, they sat in the corners and balconies. In white churches they sat in separate pews and took communion after white members. In virtually every community black children were excluded from the public schools or forced to attend overcrowded and poorly funded separate schools. Commented one English visitor: "We see, in effect, two nations—one white and another black—growing up together . . . but never mingling on a principle of equality."

Discrimination pushed African American males into the lowest-paying and most unskilled jobs: servants, sailors, waiters, and common laborers. African American women normally continued working after marriage, mostly as servants, cooks, laundresses, and seamstresses, since their wages were critical to the family's survival. Blacks were willing strikebreakers, because white workers, fearing economic competition and loss of status, were overtly hostile and excluded them from trade unions. A number of antiblack riots erupted in northern cities during these years. Driven into abject poverty, free blacks in the North suffered from inadequate diet, were more susceptible to disease, and in 1850 had a life expectancy 8 to 10 years less than that of whites.

The African American Community >>

Free blacks had long suffered from such oppression and injustice. Between the Revolution and the War of 1812 they had responded by founding schools, churches, and mutual aid societies to sustain their communities. Some, like Paul Cuffe, sought to escape white prejudice entirely by establishing settlements of free blacks in West Africa. The Quaker son of a West African father and a Wampanoag Indian

mother, Cuffe became a sea captain, and in 1816 his merchant ship brought 38 free black New Englanders to settle in West Africa. Cuffe's venture drew white sympathizers who formed the American Colonization Society (ACS) and founded Liberia in West Africa in 1821–1822. Several state legislatures in the North and the upper South as well as all the major Protestant churches endorsed ACS plans to encourage free black emigration, but its members were an unlikely and unstable coalition. Some opposed slavery and hoped that colonization would encourage manumissions and gradual emancipation, while others believed that ridding the nation of free blacks would secure the future of slavery.

Even as white support for colonization swelled during the 1820s, black enthusiasm for emigration diminished. Many African American leaders in the North were turning to more confrontational tactics: they advocated resistance to slavery and condemned racism and inequality. Among the most outspoken of this new, more militant generation was David Walker, whose *Appeal to the Colored Citizens of the World* (1829) denounced colonization and urged slaves to use violence to end bondage.

↑ The confident air of this African American, who had a daguerrotype taken around 1856, suggests the dignity free blacks maintained in the face of unrelenting hostility and discrimination.

Racism Strikes a Deeper Root

>> What prompted greater militancy among African Americans after the 1820s was also the growth of an increasingly virulent racism among whites. Ironically, the success of efforts to promote education, religious piety, and temperance within the free black community threatened many lower-class whites and intensified their resentment of African Americans. That animosity found vent in race riots, which erupted in Pittsburgh, Boston, Cincinnati, and New Haven.

The depth of racism in the culture could be seen in the rise of the minstrel show, the most popular form of entertainment in Jacksonian America. Originating in the 1830s and 1840s, these shows played to packed houses in cities and towns throughout the nation. They featured white actors performing in blackface, whose skits dealt in the broadest of racial stereotypes, ridiculing blacks as physically different and portraying them as buffoons.

Minstrelsy's greatest success came in northern cities. Its basic message was that African Americans could not cope with freedom and therefore did not belong in the North. Slaves were portrayed as happy and contented, whereas free blacks were caricatured either as strutting dandies or as helpless ignoramuses. Drawing its patrons from workers, Irish immigrants, and the poorer elements in society, minstrelsy assured these white champions of democracy that they remained superior.

The unsettling economic, social, and political changes of the Jacksonian era heightened white Americans' fear of failure, which stimulated racism. The popular yet unrealistic expectation was that any white man might become rich. Yet in fact, 20 percent or more of white adult males of this era never accumulated any property. Their lack of success prompted them to relieve personal tensions through increased hostility toward their black neighbors. The power of racism in Jacksonian America stemmed at least in part from the fact that equality remained part of the nation's creed while it steadily receded as a social reality.

 REVIEW

In what ways did Indians and free African Americans attempt to protect their communities in Jacksonian America?

THE NULLIFICATION CRISIS

Indian removal and antiblack discrimination provided one answer to the question of who would be given equality of opportunity in America's new democracy: Indians and African Americans would not. The issue of nullification raised a different, equally pressing question. As the North, South, and West increasingly specialized economically in response to the market revolution, how would a democratic system of government help various regions or interest groups to accommodate their differences?

> **Calhoun argued that the Union was a compact between sovereign states.**

The Growing Crisis in South Carolina »

South Carolina had been particularly hard-hit by the depression of 1819. When prosperity returned to the rest of the nation, many of the state's cotton planters still suffered. With lands exhausted from years of cultivation, they could not compete with the fabulous yields of frontier planters in Alabama and Mississippi.

Under these difficult conditions South Carolinians increasingly blamed federal tariffs for their miseries. When Congress raised the duty rates in 1824, they assailed the tariff as an unfair tax that raised the prices of goods

they imported while it benefited other regions of the nation. Other southern states opposed the 1824 tariff as well, though none so vehemently.

The one southern state in which black inhabitants outnumbered whites, South Carolina had also been growing more sensitive about the institution of slavery. In 1822 Denmark Vesey, a daring and resourceful free black carpenter in Charleston, secretly organized a plan to seize control of the city and raise the standard of black liberty. At the last moment white officials thwarted the conspiracy and executed Vesey and his chief lieutenants; nevertheless, white South Carolinians were convinced that other conspirators still lurked in their midst. As an additional measure of security, they began to push for stronger constitutional protection of slavery. After all, the constitutional doctrine of broad construction and implied powers had already been used to justify higher protective tariffs. What was to prevent it from being used to end slavery?

When Congress, over the protests of the state's representatives, raised the duty rates still higher in 1828 with the so-called Tariff of Abominations, South Carolina's legislature published the *South Carolina Exposition and Protest,* which outlined for the first time the theory of nullification. Only later was it revealed that its author was Jackson's own vice president, John C. Calhoun.

Calhoun was the most impressive intellect of his political generation. During the 1820s the South Carolina leader made a slow but steady journey away from nationalism toward an extreme states' rights position. When he was elected Jackson's vice president, South Carolinians assumed that tariff reform would be quickly forthcoming. But Jackson and Calhoun soon quarreled, and Calhoun lost all influence in the administration.

In his theory of nullification Calhoun argued that the Union was a compact between sovereign states. Thus the people of each state, acting in special conventions, had the right to nullify any federal law that exceeded the powers granted to Congress under the Constitution. In response, Congress could either repeal the law or propose a constitutional amendment expressly giving it the power in question. If the amendment was ratified, the nullifying state could either accept the decision or exercise its ultimate right as a sovereign state and secede from the Union.

In 1830 Senator Daniel Webster of Massachusetts responded that the Union was not a compact of sovereign states. The people, and not the states, he argued, had created the Constitution. "It is the people's constitution, the people's government, made for the people, made by the people, and answerable to the people." Webster also insisted that the federal government did not merely act as the agent of the states but had sovereign powers in those areas where it had been delegated responsibility.

The Nullifiers Nullified >> When Congress passed another tariff in 1832 that failed to give the state any relief, South Carolina's legislature called for the election of delegates to a popular convention, which overwhelmingly adopted an ordinance in November that declared the tariffs of 1828 and 1832 "null, void, and no law, nor binding upon this state, its officers or citizens" after February 1, 1833.

Jackson, who had spent much of his life defending the nation, was not about to tolerate any defiance of his authority or the federal government's. In his Proclamation on Nullification, issued in December 1832, he insisted that the Union was perpetual and that under the Constitution, no state had the right to secede. To reinforce his announced determination to enforce the tariff laws, Congress passed the Force Bill, reaffirming the president's military powers.

Yet Jackson was also a skillful politician. At the same time that he threatened South Carolina, he urged Congress to reduce the tariff rates. With no other state willing to follow South Carolina's lead, Calhoun reluctantly agreed to a compromise tariff in 1833. South Carolina's convention repealed the nullifying ordinance, and the crisis passed.

Calhoun's doctrine had proved too radical for the rest of the South. Even so, the controversy convinced many southerners that they were becoming a permanent minority. "We are divided into slave-holding and non-slave-holding states," concluded nullifier William Harper, "and this is the broad and marked distinction that must separate us at last." As that feeling of isolation grew, it was not nullification but the threat of secession that ultimately became the South's primary weapon.

> ### REVIEW
> What were the issues being contested in the debate over nullification?

THE BANK WAR

Jackson understood well the political ties that bound the nation. He grasped much less firmly the economic and financial connections that linked regions of the country through banks and national markets. His clash with the Second Bank of the United States led to the greatest crisis of his presidency.

The National Bank and the Panic of 1819 >> Chartered by Congress in 1816 for a 20-year period, the Second Bank of the United States suffered from woeful mismanagement. At first it helped fuel the speculative pressures in the economy. Then it turned about-face and sharply contracted credit by calling in loans when the depression hit in 1819. Critics viewed the Bank's policies not as a consequence but as the cause of the financial downswing. To many Americans, the Bank had already become a monster.

The psychological effects of the Panic of 1819 were almost as momentous as the economic. The shock of the depression made the 1820s a time of soul-searching, during which many uneasy farmers and workers came to view the hard times as punishment for having lost sight of the old virtues of simplicity, frugality, and hard work. For these Americans, banks were a symbol of the commercialization of American society and the rapid passing of a simpler way of life.

In 1823 Nicholas Biddle, a rich 37-year-old Philadelphia businessman, became president of the national bank. Biddle was intelligent and thoroughly familiar with the banking system, but he was also impossibly arrogant and politically dense. He set out to use the bank to regulate the amount of credit available in the economy, and thereby provide the nation with a sound currency.

The government regularly deposited its revenues in the national bank. These revenues were paid largely in bank notes (paper money) issued by state-chartered banks. If Biddle believed that a state bank had issued more notes than was safe, he presented them to that bank and demanded they be redeemed in **specie** (gold or silver). Because banks did not have enough specie reserves to back all the paper money they issued, the only way a state bank could continue to redeem its notes was to call in its loans and reduce the amount of its notes in circulation. This action had the effect of lessening the amount of credit in the economy. But if Biddle felt that a bank's credit policies were reasonable, he simply returned the state bank notes to circulation without presenting them for redemption.

Under Biddle's direction the Bank became a financial colossus with enormous power over state banks and over

specie coined money of gold or silver; also referred to as hard money or hard currency. In contrast, banknotes or notes are paper money or paper currency.

> ### . . . it was not nullification but the threat of secession that ultimately became the South's primary weapon.

Biddle and Jackson Take the Gloves Off

Can you identify this future president? What does he mean, "hit him in the breadbasket, it will make him throw up his deposits"?

This frontiersman bears the name of "Joe Tammany." The members of the original Tammany Society of New York rejected the aristocratic philosophy of the Federalist party.

The text where this cartoon appeared refers to this woman as "Mother Bank."

Port

"Old Monongahela Whiskey"

By their nature cartoons deal in visual symbols; to be accessible to their readers, the symbols cannot be subtle. For present-day viewers, however, some decoding is needed; and historians draw on their knowledge of the period to make sense of the symbols. This 1834 cartoon pits President Andrew Jackson (in black tights) against Nicholas Biddle in a bare-knuckled boxing match. Both the woman holding the bottle of port and the frontiersman (a cat on his hat, no less!) look ridiculous. But the cartoon definitely favors one of the fighters. Can you suggest several details that are tip-offs to the artist's point of view?

THINKING CRITICALLY

One key detail revolves around what the supporters are drinking. Port, an imported drink, was expensive; whiskey could be distilled in the lowliest backcountry farmhouse. Why would it matter whose supporters were drinking which one? Why draw Jackson facing the audience and Biddle with his back to us? What are the larger cultural values at the center of the cartoon's message?

the economy. Yet Biddle used this power responsibly to provide the United States a sound paper currency, which the expanding economy needed.

Although the Bank had strong support in the business community, workers complained that they were often paid in **depreciated** state bank notes that could be redeemed for only a portion of their face value, a practice that cheated them of

> **depreciated** decreased in value owing to market conditions.

their full wages. They called for a "hard money" currency of only gold and silver. Hard money advocates viewed bankers and financiers as profiteers who manipulated the paper money system to enrich themselves at the expense of honest, hardworking farmers and laborers.

The Bank Destroyed >>

Jackson's own experiences left him with a deep distrust of banks and paper money. In 1804 his Tennessee land speculations had brought him to the brink of bankruptcy, from which it took years of painful struggle to free himself. Reflecting on his personal situation, he became convinced that banks and paper money threatened to corrupt the Republic.

As president, Jackson periodically called for reform of the banking system, but Biddle refused even to consider curbing the Bank's powers. Already distracted by the nullification controversy, Jackson warned Biddle not to inject the bank issue into the 1832 campaign. When Biddle went ahead and applied for a renewal of the Bank's charter in 1832, four years early, Jackson was furious. "The Bank is trying to kill me," he stormed, "but I will kill it."

Despite the president's opposition Congress passed a recharter bill in the summer of 1832. Immediately Jackson vetoed it as unconstitutional (rejecting Marshall's earlier ruling in *McCulloch v. Maryland*). Condemning the Bank as an agent of special privilege, the president pledged to protect "the humble members of society—the farmer, mechanics, and laborers" against "the advancement of the few at the expense of the many."

When Congress failed to override Jackson's veto, the Bank became a central issue of the 1832 campaign. Jackson's opponent was Henry Clay, a National Republican who eagerly accepted the financial support of Biddle and his bank. Clay went down to defeat, and, once reelected, Jackson was determined to move boldly. He believed that as a private corporation the Bank wielded a dangerous influence over government policy and the economy, and he was justly incensed over its interference in the election.

To cripple the Bank the president simply ordered all the government's federal deposits withdrawn. Since such an act clearly violated federal law, Jackson was forced to transfer one secretary of the treasury and fire another before he finally found an ally, Roger Taney, willing to take the job and carry out the edict. Taney (pronounced "Taw-ney") gradually withdrew the government's funds while depositing new revenues in selected state banks.

Biddle fought back by deliberately precipitating a brief financial panic in 1833, but Jackson refused to budge.

Eventually Biddle had to relent, and Jackson's victory was complete. When the Bank's charter expired in 1836, no national banking system replaced it.

Jackson's Impact on the Presidency >>

Jackson approached the end of his administration in triumph. Indian removal was well on its way to completion, the nullifiers had been confounded, and the "Monster Bank" had been destroyed. In the process Jackson immeasurably enlarged the power of the presidency. "The President is the direct representative of the American people," he lectured the Senate when it opposed him. "He was elected by the people, and is responsible to them." With this declaration Jackson redefined the character of the presidential office and its relationship to the people.

> "The President is the direct representative of the American people," [Jackson] lectured the Senate when it opposed him.

Jackson also converted the veto into an effective presidential power. During his two terms in office he vetoed 12 bills, compared with only 9 for all previous presidents combined. Moreover, where his predecessors had vetoed bills only on strict constitutional grounds, Jackson felt free to block laws simply because he thought them bad policy. The threat of such action became an effective way to shape pending legislation to his liking, a tactic that fundamentally strengthened the power of the president over Congress. The development of the modern presidency began with Andrew Jackson.

"Van Ruin's" Depression >>

With the controls of the national bank removed, state banks rapidly expanded their activities, including the printing of more money. As the currency expanded, so did the number of banks: from 329 in 1829 to 788 in 1837. A spiraling **inflation** set in as prices rose 50 percent after 1830 and interest rates by half as much.

inflation increase in the overall price of goods and services over an extended period of time; or a similar decrease over time of the purchasing power of money.

As prices soared so did speculative fever. By 1836 land sales, which had been only $2.6 million four years earlier, approached $25 million. Almost all these lands were bought entirely on credit with bank notes. In July 1836 Jackson issued the Specie Circular, which decreed that the government would accept only specie for the purchase of public land. Land sales plummeted, but the speculative pressures in the economy were already too great.

During Jackson's second term, his opponents had gradually come together in a new party, the Whigs. Led by Henry Clay, they charged that "King Andrew I" had

∧ This Whig cartoon blames the Democratic party for the depression that began during Van Buren's administration. Barefoot workers go unemployed, and women and children beg and sleep in the streets. Depositors clamor for their money from a bank that has suspended specie payments, while the pawnbroker and liquor store do a thriving business and the sheriff rounds up debtors.

dangerously concentrated power in the presidency. The Whigs also embraced Clay's "American System," designed to spur national economic development through a protective tariff, a national bank, and federal aid for internal improvements. In 1836 the Democrats nominated Martin Van Buren, who triumphed over three Whig sectional candidates.

Van Buren had less than two months in office to savor his triumph before the speculative mania collapsed, and with it the economy. After a brief recovery, the bottom fell out of the international cotton market in 1839, and the country entered a serious depression. It was not until 1843 that the economy revived.

Public opinion identified hard times with the policies of the Democratic party. Since he continued to oppose a new national bank, Van Buren instead persuaded Congress in 1840 to create an Independent Treasury to hold the government's funds. Its offices were forbidden to accept paper currency, issue any bank notes, or make any loans. The government's money would be safe, as Van

Buren intended, but it would also remain unavailable to banks to make loans and stimulate the economy. Whigs, in contrast, hoped to encourage manufacturing and revive the economy by passing a protective tariff, continuing state internal improvement projects, protecting corporations, and expanding the banking and credit system.

As the depression deepened, thousands of workers were unemployed, and countless businesses failed. Nationally, wages fell 30 to 50 percent. "Business of all kinds is completely at a stand," wrote New York business and civic leader Philip Hone in 1840, "and the whole body politic sick and infirm, and calling aloud for a remedy."

The Whigs Triumph >>
For the 1840 presidential campaign the Whigs turned to William Henry Harrison, who had defeated the Shawnee Indians at Tippecanoe, to oppose Van Buren. In the midst of the worst depression of the century, Whigs employed the democratic electioneering techniques that Jackson's supporters had perfected. They

hailed Harrison as a man of the people while painting Van Buren as a dandy and an aristocrat who wore a corset, ate off gold plates with silver spoons, and used cologne. Whig rallies featured hard cider and log cabins to reinforce Harrison's image as a man of the people. Ironically, Harrison had been born into one of Virginia's most aristocratic families and was living in a 16-room mansion in Ohio. But the Whig campaign, by casting the election as a contest between aristocracy and democracy, was perfectly attuned to the prevailing national spirit.

In the campaign of 1840 Whigs also prominently involved women, urging them to become politically informed in order to morally instruct their husbands. Women attended Whig rallies, conducted meetings, made speeches, and wrote campaign pamphlets, activities previously performed solely by men. Democrats were uneasy about this innovation, yet had no choice but to follow suit. Within a few years the presence of women at party rallies was commonplace.

The election produced a record turnout, with nearly four-fifths of the eligible voters going to the polls. Although the popular vote was fairly close (Harrison led by about 150,000 votes out of 2.4 million cast), in the Electoral College he won an easy victory, 234 to 60.

The "log cabin" campaign marked the final transition from the deferential politics of the Federalist era to the egalitarian politics that had emerged in the wake of the Panic of 1819. As the *Democratic Review* conceded after the Whigs' victory in 1840, "We have taught them how to conquer us."

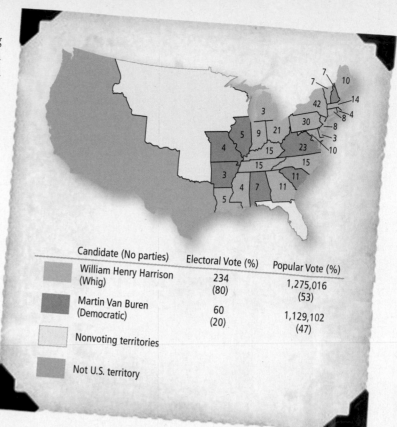

Candidate (No parties)	Electoral Vote (%)	Popular Vote (%)
William Henry Harrison (Whig)	234 (80)	1,275,016 (53)
Martin Van Buren (Democratic)	60 (20)	1,129,102 (47)
Nonvoting territories		
Not U.S. territory		

ELECTION OF 1840

 REVIEW

Why did Jackson oppose the Second Bank of the United States?

THE JACKSONIAN PARTY SYSTEM

It is easy, given the hoopla of democratic campaigning, to be distracted from the central fact that the new political system was directly shaped by the social and economic strains of an expanding nation. Whigs and Democrats held different attitudes toward the changes brought about by the market, banks, and commerce.

Democrats, Whigs, and the Market >>

The Democrats tended to view society as a continuing conflict between "the people"—farmers, planters, and workers—and a set of greedy aristocrats. They charged that this "paper money aristocracy" of bankers, stock jobbers, and investors manipulated the banking system for their own profit. For Democrats, the Bank War became a battle to restore the old Jeffersonian Republic with its values of simplicity, frugality, hard work, and independence.

Jackson understood the dangers private banks posed to a democratic society. Yet Democrats, in effect, wanted the rewards and goods that the market offered without sacrificing the features of a simple agrarian republic. They wanted the wealth that the market produced without the competitive society, the complex dealings, the dominance of urban centers, and the loss of independence that came with it.

Whigs were more comfortable with the market. They envisioned no conflict between farmers and mechanics on the one hand and businesspeople and bankers on the other. The government's responsibility was to provide a well-regulated economy that guaranteed opportunity for citizens of ability. In such an economy, banks and corporations were not only useful but necessary.

Whigs and Democrats also disagreed over how active government should be. Despite Andrew Jackson's inclination to be a strong president, Democrats as a rule believed in limited government. Government's role in the economy was to promote competition by destroying monopolies and special privileges. In keeping with this philosophy, Democrats also rejected the idea that moral beliefs were the proper sphere of government action. Religion and politics, they believed, should be kept clearly separate, and they generally opposed humanitarian legislation.

The Whigs, in contrast, viewed government power positively. They believed that it should be used to protect individual rights and public liberty, and that it had a special role where individual effort was ineffective. By regulating the economy and competition, the government could ensure equal opportunity. Indeed, for Whigs the concept of government promoting the general welfare went beyond the economy. Northern Whigs in particular also believed that government power should be used to foster the moral welfare of the country. They were much more likely to favor temperance or antislavery legislation and aid to education. Whigs portrayed themselves not only as the party of prosperity but also as the party of respectability and proper behavior.

The Social Bases of the Two Parties >>

In some ways the social makeup of the two parties was similar. To be competitive Whigs and Democrats both had to have significant support among farmers, the largest group in society, and workers. Neither party could carry an election by appealing exclusively to the rich or the poor.

The Whigs, however, enjoyed disproportionate strength among the business and commercial classes, especially following the Bank War. Whigs appealed to planters who needed credit to finance their cotton and rice trade in the world market, to farmers who were eager to sell their surpluses, and to workers who wished to improve their social position. Democrats attracted farmers isolated from the market or uncomfortable with it, workers alienated from the emerging industrial system, and rising entrepreneurs who wanted to break monopolies and open the economy to newcomers like themselves. The Whigs were strongest in the towns, cities, and rural areas that were fully integrated into the market economy, whereas Democrats dominated areas of semisubsistence farming that were more isolated and languishing economically. Attitude toward the market, rather than economic position, was more important in determining party affiliation.

Religion and ethnic identities also shaped partisanship. As the self-proclaimed "party of respectability," Whigs attracted the support of high-status native-born church groups, including Congregationalists and Unitarians in New England and Presbyterians and Episcopalians elsewhere. The party also attracted immigrant groups that most easily merged into the dominant Anglo-Protestant culture, such as the English, Welsh, and Scots. Democrats, however, recruited more Germans and Irish, whose more lenient observance of the Sabbath and (among Catholics) use of parochial schools generated native-born hostility. Democrats appealed to the lower-status Baptists and Methodists, particularly in states where they earlier had been subjected to legal disadvantages. Both parties also attracted freethinkers and the unchurched, but the Democrats had the advantage because they resisted demands for temperance and sabbatarian laws, such as the prohibition of Sunday travel. In the few states where they could vote, African Americans were solidly Whig in reaction to the Democratic party's strong racism and hostility to black rights.

✓ REVIEW

What were the major differences between the Whigs and the Democrats?

In the Americas as well as in Europe, the rise of democratic governance and the spread of market economies evolved roughly in tandem over the same half-century. Andrew Jackson's triumph was only the latest in a series of upheavals stretching back to the American and French Revolutions of the eighteenth century. Latin America, too, experienced democratic revolutions. From 1808 to 1821 Spain's American provinces declared their independence one by one, taking inspiration from the writings of Jefferson and Thomas Paine as well as the French *Declaration of the Rights of Man*. Democracy did not always root itself in the aftermath of these revolutions, but democratic ideology remained a powerful social catalyst.

In the United States the parallel growth of national markets and democratic institutions exhibited a similarly checkered history. If Jackson championed the cause of the "common people," he also led the movement to displace Indians from their lands. A poor white American might vote for "Old Hickory" at the same time that he took comfort that African Americans could never rise as high as he in an increasingly racist society. Furthermore, the advance of the market created social strains, including the increasing impoverishment of the labor force in the North and the growing gap in society between the richest and the poorest.

<< Whigs drew strongly from the business and commercial classes who were at home in the marketplace and eager to improve themselves. Especially in the North, Whigs believed that government power should be used to foster the moral welfare of the country. This sculpture by Asa Ames from the 1840s suggests the respectable, upright, middle-class outlook characteristic of many Whigs.

Still, Americans had evolved a system of democratic politics to deal with the conflicts that the new order produced. The new national parties, like the new markets, had become essential structures uniting the American nation. They advanced an ideology of equality and opportunity, competed vigorously with one another, and mobilized large numbers of ordinary Americans in the political process. Along with the market, democracy had become an integral part of American life.

CHAPTER SUMMARY

Beginning in the 1820s the United States experienced a democratic revolution that was identified with Andrew Jackson.

- The rise of democracy was stimulated by the Panic of 1819, which caused Americans to look toward both politicians and the government to address their needs.
- The new political culture of democracy included the use of conventions to make nominations, the celebration of the wisdom of the people, the adoption of white manhood suffrage, and the acceptance of political parties as essential for the working of the constitutional system.
- The new politics had distinct limits, however. Women were not given the vote, and racism intensified.
  - The eastern Indian tribes were forced to move to new lands west of the Mississippi River.
  - Free African Americans found themselves subject to increasingly harsh discrimination and exclusion.
- In politics Andrew Jackson came to personify the new democratic culture. Through his forceful leadership he significantly expanded the powers of the presidency.
  - Jackson threatened to use force against South Carolina when it tried to nullify the federal tariff using John C. Calhoun's theory of nullification—that is, that a state convention could nullify a federal law.
  - In response nationalists advanced the idea of the perpetual Union. The compromise of 1833, which gradually lowered the tariff, ended the crisis.
  - Jackson vetoed a bill to recharter the Second Bank of the United States and destroyed the Bank by removing its federal deposits.

Significant Events

| | | | | | Jackson vetoes recharter of the national bank; South Carolina nullifies tariff | Force Bill; Jackson removes deposits from the Bank of the United States |

Denmark Vesey conspiracy

| 1822 | 1825 | 1828 | 1830–1838 | 1832 | 1833 |

House elects John Quincy Adams president

Tariff of Abominations; South Carolina Exposition and Protest; Jackson elected president

Indian removal

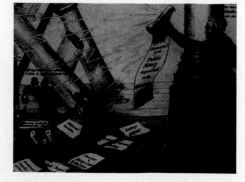

BLOW FOR BLOW.

- Under President Martin Van Buren, the nation entered a severe depression.
- Capitalizing on hard times and employing the democratic techniques pioneered by the Democrats, the Whigs gained national power in 1840.
- By 1840 the two parties had developed different ideologies.
  - The Whigs were more comfortable with the mechanisms of the market and linked commerce with progress.
  - The Democrats were uneasy about the market and favored limited government.

Additional Reading

The most comprehensive reinterpretation of antebellum political history from Jackson to Lincoln is Sean Wilentz, *The Rise of Democracy* (2005). For a broader perspective on the evolution of American political culture throughout the nineteenth century, see Glenn Altschuler and Stuart Blumin, *Rude Republic* (2000). A good interpretation of Jacksonian politics is Harry Watson, *Liberty and Power* (1990), and important discussions of party ideologies include Marvin Meyers, *The Jacksonian Persuasion* (1957); Daniel Walker Howe, *The Political Culture of American Whigs* (1979); and Lawrence Frederick Kohl, *The Politics of Individualism* (1988). For the history of the Whig party, the book to read is Michael Holt, *The Rise and Fall of the American Whig Party* (1999).

The best account of the nullification crisis is still William Freehling, *Prelude to the Civil War* (1966), and Robert Remini offers a succinct analysis of the banking controversy in *Andrew Jackson and the Bank War* (1967). Paul Goodman, *Towards a Christian Republic* (1988) is the most valuable study of Anti-Masonry. On Indian removal in the South, see John Ehle, *The Trail of Tears* (1997), and Robert Remini, *Andrew Jackson and His Indian Wars* (2001).

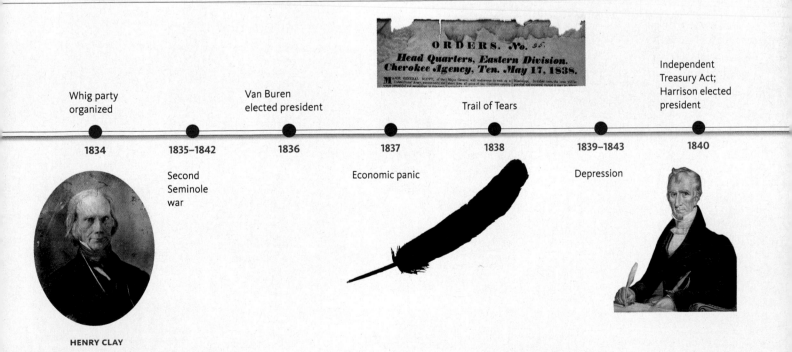

Whig party organized — 1834

Second Seminole war — 1835–1842

Van Buren elected president — 1836

Economic panic — 1837

Trail of Tears — 1838

Depression — 1839–1843

Independent Treasury Act; Harrison elected president — 1840

HENRY CLAY

⌃ Lyman Beecher (*center*) with his family in 1855. Five of his six sons, all of whom were ministers, stand in back. In front, daughters Catharine (holding his arm to steady it for the long exposure) and Isabella are on the left; Harriet, the author of Uncle *Tom's Cabin*, is at the far right.

Nor were Beecher's ambitions small. His goal was nothing less than to bring the kingdom of Christ to the nation and the world. Like many ministers Beecher had studied the intriguing final book of the New Testament, the Revelation to John. The Revelation foretold in the latter days of Earth a glorious millennium—a thousand years of peace and triumph—when the saints would rule and evil would be banished from the world. Beecher was convinced that the long-awaited millennium might well begin in the United States.

To usher in the kingdom of God entire communities and even nations would have to be swept with the fire of **millennialism.** Toward that end

millennialism belief in the thousand-year reign of Christ predicted in the New Testament's final book, the Revelation to John.

Beecher joined other Protestant ministers in supporting a host of religious reforms and missionary efforts. By 1820 they had formed voluntary organizations devoted to a wide range of activities: blanketing the United States with tracts and bibles, educating young men for the ministry, sending missionaries to every corner of the globe, promoting Sunday schools for children, ministering to sailors and the poor, reforming drunkards, and stopping business on the Sabbath. To Beecher the organizations constituting this loosely united "Benevolent Empire" were signs of the coming kingdom.

As the new pastor at Hanover Street, Beecher also directed his righteous artillery on a host of evils that seemed to be obstructing God's kingdom. With scorn he attacked Unitarians, whose liberal, rational creed rejected the divinity of Jesus. In Boston, Unitarians were mainly upper class and cultured. But he also denounced what he viewed as sinful pastimes of the lower class: playing cards, gambling, and drinking. And he denounced Roman Catholic priests and nuns as superstitious, devious agents of "Antichrist."

Beecher's efforts at "moral reform" antagonized many immigrants and other working people who enjoyed liquor or lotteries. In disdain they referred to Hanover Street Church, with its imposing stone tower, as Beecher's "stone jug." After all, it was there that its pastor drank most deeply of his religious spirits. In 1830 a blaze broke out in the basement of his church, and some of the locals had their revenge. Firefighters stood by and made jokes about "Old Beecher" and hellfire as flames cracked the stone tower from top to bottom and the splendid structure burned into ruins.

Any fire, real or spiritual, is unpredictable as it spreads from one scrap of tinder to the next. That proved to be the case with reform movements of the 1820s and 1830s as, in subsequent decades, they moved in diverging, sometimes contradictory, ways. What did it mean, after all, to make a heaven on earth? ❮❮

Lyman Beecher embodied the spirit of antebellum evangelical Protestantism. At the core of evangelicalism was the conviction that divine grace brought about a new birth, one that enabled belief in Jesus Christ. That conviction also committed the individual convert to reforming his or her own vices as well as the faults of others. But evangelicalism was changing over the course of Beecher's lifetime, and, as it changed, so did its influence on Christian believers. Early nineteenth-century evangelical leaders such as Beecher sought to convert individuals through revivals and then to turn their energies toward reforming others through the voluntary associations of the Benevolent Empire. Their conservative aim, as he expressed it, was to restore America to "the moral government of God."

But the next generation of evangelical leaders—including Beecher's own children—sought not merely to convert individuals to Christianity but also to reform the most fundamental institutions structuring American society: slavery, the family, and the political and legal subordination of women. By the 1840s they were joined by many other believers in faiths both secular and religious—Unitarians and Transcendentalists, Shakers and socialists. All were afire with the faith that they could radically remake the United States.

⌃ In *The Way of Good and Evil* devout Christians are all helped on the path (*right*) to millennial perfection by the virtues of family, religion, education, and hard work. Sinners on the left, however, take the path of disobedience, intemperance, and lying—straight to hell.

THE TRANSFORMATION OF AMERICAN EVANGELICALISM

Before about 1800, most American **evangelicals** embraced the doctrines of Calvinism (see page 31). They believed that God had determined which individuals were destined to be damned or saved and that no human effort could alter those eternal fates. But by the beginning of the nineteenth century, such propositions seemed increasingly unreasonable to the American heirs of a revolution that celebrated human equality, free will, and reason. As a result, a growing number of evangelicals moved toward an outlook that, although not denying the sinfulness of human nature and the necessity of divine grace for salvation, granted more power to free will and human effort. That more democratic belief—that all men and women might choose and win salvation, that each individual should take an active responsibility for redemption—came to characterize the religious views of most evangelicals among the ranks of Congregationalists, Presbyterians,

evangelicals Christian believers who work actively to spread the "good news" or gospel of Jesus as recounted in the New Testament of the Bible.

Baptists, and Methodists over the course of the Second Great Awakening. In turn, their more optimistic assessment of human potential fostered revivals and ambitious programs for reforming individuals and society.

Charles Grandison Finney and Modern Revivalism >>
The man who embodied this transformed evangelicalism was Charles Grandison Finney, the founder of modern revivalism. In 1821, as a young man, Finney experienced a soul-shattering conversion that led him to give up his law practice to become an itinerant minister. Eventually he was ordained in the Presbyterian Church, although he lacked any formal theological training. He first attracted national attention when in the mid-1820s and early 1830s he conducted a series of spectacular revivals in the booming port cities along the new Erie Canal.

Like George Whitefield before him Finney had an entrancing voice that carried great distances. His success also resulted from his use of special techniques—"the new measures." These new measures had been developed during the frontier revivals of the Second Great Awakening (page 176). Finney's contribution was to popularize the techniques and use them systematically. He held "protracted meetings" night after night to build up excitement. Speaking boldly and bluntly, he prayed for sinners by name, encouraged

Consumption of spirits in gallons

≈ Beginning in 1790 per capita levels of drinking steadily rose until 1830, when the temperance movement produced a sharp decline over the next two decades.

The temperance movement lasted longer and attracted many more supporters than other reforms did. Its success came partly for social reasons. Democracy necessitated sober voters; factories required sober workers. In addition, temperance attracted the upwardly mobile—professionals, small businesspeople, and skilled artisans anxious to improve their social standing. Finally, temperance advocates stressed the suffering that men inflicted on women and children, and thus the movement appealed to women as a means to defend the home and carry out their domestic mission.

Ideals of Women and the Family »

Evangelicals also contributed substantially to a new ideal of womanhood. The ideal was promoted by the clergy and female authors in sermons, advice manuals, magazine articles, and novels during the first half of the nineteenth century. Called the "cult of domesticity" or "true womanhood" or "evangelical womanhood," that ideal cast wives and mothers as the "angels" of their households. Women were singularly suited to serve as dispensers of love, comfort, and moral instruction to husbands and children. The

domesticity devotion to home life, and a woman's place at the center of that life.

premise of that new ideal was that men and women, by their very nature, inhabited separate spheres. The rough and tumble world of business and politics was the proper province of husbands and fathers, while women ruled the domestic sphere of home and family. "Love is our life our reality, business yours," Mollie Clark told one suitor.

This new ideal also held that women were by nature morally stronger and more religious than men. That view reversed the negative medieval and early modern views of women as the sinful daughters of the temptress Eve, more passionate by nature and thus less morally restrained and spiritually inclined than men. But the new ideal also held antebellum women to a higher standard of sexual purity. A man's sexual infidelity, although hardly condoned, brought no lasting shame. But a woman who engaged in sexual relations before marriage or was unfaithful afterward was threatened with everlasting disgrace. Under this new double standard women were to be pure, passionless, and passive: they were to submerge their identities in those of their husbands.

Spokespersons for the new ideal of womanhood and the notion of separate spheres directed their message mainly at elite and middle-class women. And that message found an impressionable audience among wives and daughters in the urbanizing Northeast. There the separation of the workplace from the home was most complete. As a result of industrialization, many men worked outside the home, while the rise of factories also led to a decline in part-time work such as spinning, which women had once performed to supplement family income. Home manufacturing was no longer essential, because, except on the frontier, families could easily purchase the articles that women previously had made, such as cloth, soap, and candles. This growing separation of the household from the workplace in the Northeast made it that much easier for the home to be idealized as a place of "domesticity," a haven away from the competitive, workaday world, with the mother firmly at its center.

The celebration of domesticity was not unique to the United States. Indeed, this redefinition of women's roles was more sweeping in Europe, because previously middle-class women had left the task of child-raising largely to hired nurses and governesses. By midcentury these mothers devoted much more time to domestic duties, including rearing the children. Family size also declined, both in France and in England. The middle class was most numerous in England;

Victorianism constellation of middle-class values attributed to the proper virtues of Britain's Queen.

indeed, the importance of the middle class in Britain during Queen Victoria's reign (1837–1901) gave these ideals the label **Victorianism.**

As elite and middle-class homes came to be seen as havens of moral virtue, those domestic settings developed a new structure and new set of attitudes closer in spirit to

^ As business affairs grew increasingly separate from the family in the nineteenth century, the middle-class home became a female domain. A woman's role as a wife and mother was to dispense love and moral guidance to her husband and her children. As this domestic scene makes clear, she was at the very center of the world of the family.

"FRIENDS" AND NEIGHBORS

Nineteenth-century singles in search of lodgings often rented rooms and took their meals in boardinghouses. Considerably less inviting than the apartments shared by present-day sitcom casts of twenty-somethings, antebellum boardinghouses—with their thin walls, indigestible fare, gossipy denizens, and skinflint keepers—became the butt of countless jokes. They made a tempting target in a culture that prized domesticity.

those of the modern family. The pressures to achieve success led middle-class young adults to delay marriage, since a husband was expected to have the financial means to support his wife. Smaller family size resulted, since wives, especially those among the urban middle class, began to use birth control to space children farther apart and to minimize the risks of pregnancy. In addition, it has been estimated that before 1860 one abortion was performed for every five or six live births. With smaller families, parents could tend more carefully to their children's success. Increasingly middle-class families took on the expense of additional education to prepare their sons for a career in business. They also frequently equalized inheritances rather than favoring the eldest son or favoring sons over daughters.

Expanding Public Roles for Women >>

Most women in the United States did not have time to make domesticity the center of their lives. Farmers' wives and enslaved women had to work constantly, whereas lower-class families could not get by without the wages of female members. Still, some elite and middle-class women tried to live up to the new ideals, though many found the effort confining. "The great trial is that I have nothing to do," one complained. "Here I am with abundant leisure and capable, I believe, of accomplishing some good, and yet with no object on which to expend my energies."

In response to those frustrations Lyman Beecher's eldest daughter, Catharine (who never married), made a career out of assuring women that the proper care of household and children was their sex's crucial responsibility. Like the earlier advocates of "republican motherhood," Catharine Beecher supported women's education and argued that women exercised power as moral guardians of the nation's future. She also wrote several books on efficient home management.

But many women yearned to exert moral authority outside the confines of their households. Ironically, the new host of benevolent and reform societies offered them just that opportunity. Devout wives and daughters, particularly those from middle-class families, flocked to these voluntary associations, many of which had separate women's chapters. By serving in such organizations, they gained the practical experience of holding office on governing boards, conducting meetings, drafting policy statements, organizing reform programs, and raising money.

Evangelicalism thus enabled women to enter public life and to make their voices heard in ways that were socially acceptable. After all, evangelical teachings affirmed that they were the superior sex in piety and morality, a point often invoked by those very women who devoted much of their time to benevolence and reform. They justified such public activism as merely the logical extension of their private responsibility to act as spiritual guides to their families.

Protestants and Catholics >> Women's

piety and spiritual influence were surely on the mind of Isaac Bird one Saturday morning in the autumn of 1819. A devout evangelical preparing for the ministry, he had wandered into a Roman Catholic church in Boston and now watched with rapt attention a ritual, conducted entirely in Latin, in which two women "took the veil" and became nuns. Bird often visited Boston on his vacations to proselytize its poorest inhabitants. Many were Catholics, as he noted, some of them recent Irish and German immigrants and others African American. It troubled Bird, this gathering presence of devout Catholics.

⌃ Widespread anti-Catholic sentiment among Protestants flared when Archbishop Gaetano Bedini toured the United States in 1853 and 1854. Mobs in Pittsburgh, Cincinnati, and Boston rioted, burning the archbishop in effigy, while the threat of violence in New York City forced him into hiding until he could be smuggled onto his departing ship. Bedini's opponents feared that he had come to unite Catholics in "an organization so perfect" that it would strongly influence "our future public elections."

Protestants had a long history of animosity toward Roman Catholics, especially in New England. But before the beginning of the nineteenth century, the number of Catholics had been small: by 1815 there were only 150,000 scattered throughout the United States, and they often had little access to priests or public worship.

That had begun to change by 1820. French Canadian Catholic immigrants were filtering into New England in growing numbers, and there began what would become during the 1840s and 1850s an influx of Catholic immigrants from the British Isles and German-speaking countries. By 1830 the Catholic population had jumped to 300,000, and by 1850 it accounted for 8 percent of the U.S. population—the same proportion as Presbyterians. As these newcomers settled in eastern cities and on western frontiers, there were an increasing number of priests, nuns, and churches to minister to their spiritual needs.

The differences between Roman Catholicism and Protestantism—especially evangelicalism—were substantial. Where evangelicals stressed the inward transformation of conversion as essential to salvation, Catholics emphasized the importance of outward religious observances, such as faithfully attending mass and receiving the sacraments. Where evangelicals insisted that individuals read the bible to discover God's will, Catholics urged their faithful to heed church teachings and traditions. Where Catholics believed that human suffering could be a penance paving the way toward redemption, evangelicals regarded it as an evil to be alleviated. Where evangelicals looked toward an imminent millennium, Catholics harbored no such expectation and played almost no role in antebellum benevolence and reform movements.

To Protestants many elements of Catholicism seemed superstitious and even subversive. They rejected the Catholic doctrine of transubstantiation, which held that the bread and wine consecrated by the priest during mass literally turned into the body and blood of Jesus Christ. They condemned as idolatry the Catholic veneration of the Virgin Mary and the saints. They regarded Catholic nuns and convents as threats to the new ideals of womanhood and domesticity. They found it amiss that Catholic laymen had no role in governing their own parishes and dioceses, entrusting that responsibility entirely to priests and bishops.

But the worst fears of Protestants fastened on what they saw as the political dangers posed by Catholics, especially immigrants. Alarmed as Irish and German settlers poured into the West, Lyman Beecher warned that "the world has never witnessed such a rush of dark-minded population from one country to another, as is now leaving Europe and dashing upon our shores." Beecher foresaw a sinister plot hatched by the pope to snuff out American liberty. For what else would follow in a nation overwhelmed by Catholicism, "a religion which never prospered but in alliance with despotic government, has always been and still is the inflexible enemy of liberty

↑ The Reverend Lyman Beecher's Hanover Street church—his "stone jug"—was an early example of Gothic Revival architecture, with its medieval stone battlements atop a massive tower and pointed windows. Such a church stood in stark contrast with the plain Congregational meeting houses of the Puritans. On the one hand, Beecher railed against the evils of Catholicism. On the other, he recognized the attraction of such imposing architecture. "If you want to get martins about your house," he commented, comparing his own church flock to the swallows who were so particular about where they nested, "you must put up a martin box."

of conscience and free enquiry, and at this moment is the mainstay of the battle against republican institutions?"

It was all the more appalling to evangelicals, then, that some Protestants found Catholic teachings appealing: so attractive that some 57,000 converted to Catholicism in the 30 years after 1830. In response to those defections many Protestants, believing that converts were drawn by the artistic beauties of Catholic worship, began to include in their churches recognizably Catholic elements such as the symbol of the cross, the use of candles and flowers, organ and choir music, stained glass windows, and Gothic architecture.

Other Protestants attacked Catholicism directly. Writing under the name "Maria Monk," a team of evangelical ministers produced a lurid account of life in a convent, replete with sex orgies involving priests and nuns and a cellar planted with dead babies. Published in 1836 this publication outsold every book except *Uncle Tom's Cabin* in the years before the Civil War. And with anti-Catholic sentiment running so high, predictably, there was violence. In 1834 a mob in Charlestown, Massachusetts, burned a convent to the ground. Both the sisters and their students escaped injury but, during the summer of 1844 in Philadelphia, two separate outbreaks of anti-Catholic violence left 14 people dead, as well as two churches and three dozen homes in smoldering ruins.

Most antebellum Protestants condemned violence against Catholics. But anti-Catholicism had emerged as a defining feature of American Protestant identity, and the alienation of the two groups ran deep, enduring far into the twentieth century.

 REVIEW

In what ways did Transendentalism shape the themes of writers of the American Renaissance? Who were the major communitarian reformers of the era?

VISIONARIES

Increasingly hostile to Roman Catholics, evangelicals also stood at odds with other groups in antebellum America who envisioned new ways of improving individuals and society. Although they often expressed optimism about the prospects for human betterment, these other reformers—Unitarians and Transcendentalists, socialists and communitarians—otherwise had little in common with evangelicals.

The Unitarian Contribution >> During the opening decades of the nineteenth century, the religious division among Americans that produced the fiercest debates pitted evangelicals against deists, Unitarians, and other rational Christians. A majority only in eastern Massachusetts, Unitarians denied the divinity of Jesus while affirming the ability and responsibility of humankind to follow his moral teachings. Disdainful of the emotionalism of revivals, they were also inclined to interpret the Bible broadly rather than literally. To most Americans such views were so suspect that the Presidents who adhered to Unitarianism—John Adams, Thomas Jefferson, and John Quincy Adams—did not wish to publicize their beliefs.

Despite their many differences, Unitarians shared with evangelicals an esteem for the power of human free will and a commitment to the goal of social betterment. Small though their numbers were, Unitarians made large contributions to the cause of reform. One, Boston schoolteacher Dorothea Dix, took the lead in creating state-supported asylums to treat the mentally ill, who were often chained, beaten, and kept in cages. Samuel Gridley Howe promoted education for the blind and deaf, and Horace Mann strove to give greater access to public schooling to children of poor and working-class families.

From Unitarianism to Transcendentalism >> A new philosophic outlook—transcendentalism—blossomed in the mid-1830s, when a number of Unitarian clergy such as George Ripley and Ralph Waldo Emerson resigned their pulpits, loudly protesting the church's teachings as dry, bloodless, and self-satisfied. The new "Transcendentalist Club" attracted a small following among other discontented Boston intellectuals, including Margaret Fuller, Bronson Alcott, and Orestes Brownson.

Transcendentalism emphasized feeling over reason, seeking a spiritual communion with nature. In following this

☆ In the summer of 1858 members of the cultural Saturday Club of Boston made an excursion to the Adirondacks to observe nature. In *Philosopher's Camp*, painted by William J. Stillman, who organized the expedition, a group on the left dissects a fish under the supervision of the famous scientist Louis Agassiz. Alone at the center of the painting stands Ralph Waldo Emerson, in a contemplative mood.

transcendentalism a philosophical and religious movement that embraced intuition, emotion, and the divine spark within the individual as the path to transcend, or move beyond, the material world.

course transcendentalists mirrored the beliefs of Romanticism, a European movement that arose as a reaction to the Enlightenment. As the name suggested, transcendentalists sought to go beyond or to rise above—specifically above reason and beyond the material world. As part of creation, every human being contained a spark of divinity, Emerson avowed. Transcendentalists also shared in Romanticism's glorification of the individual. "Trust thyself. Every heart vibrates to that iron string," Emerson advised. If freed from the constraints of traditional authority, the individual possessed infinite potential. Like the devout at Finney's revivals, who sought to improve themselves and society, listeners who flocked to Emerson's lectures were infused with the spirit of optimistic reform.

In extolling nature, other American writers worried that the advance of civilization, with its market economy and crowded urban centers, might destroy the natural simplicity of the land. In 1845 Henry David Thoreau built a cabin on the edge of Walden Pond in Concord, living by himself for 16 months to demonstrate the advantages of self-reliance. His experiences became the basis for *Walden* (1854), which eloquently denounced Americans' frantic competition for material goods and wealth. Only in nature, Thoreau argued, could one find true independence, liberty, equality, and happiness. Voicing the anti-institutional impulse of Romanticism, he took individualism to its antisocial extreme.

In contrast to Thoreau, who prized isolation, Walt Whitman embraced American society in its infinite variety. A journalist and laborer in the New York City area, Whitman was inspired by the common people, whose "manners, speech, dress, friendships . . . are unrhymed poetry." In taking their measure in *Leaves of Grass* (1855), he pioneered a new, modern form of poetry, unconcerned with meter and rhyme and filled with frank imagery and sexual references.

Utopian Communities ≫

Evangelicals, Unitarians, and writers such as Thoreau and Whitman focused their attention on how individuals might be saved, improved, fulfilled. But some antebellum believers, both secular and religious, sought to remake society at large by forming communities intended as examples to the rest of the world.

Even some transcendental individualists attempted a utopian venture. During the early 1840s Emerson's friend George Ripley organized Brook Farm, a community near Boston where members could live "a more wholesome and simple life than can be led amid the pressure of our competitive institutions." But predictably, these Romantic individualists could not sustain the group cooperation essential for success.

Some secular thinkers shared the transcendentalists' view that competition, inequality, and acquisitiveness were corrupting American society. Among those critics were socialists, and their goal was to defend the interests of American workers from the ravages of industrialization. The most influential was Robert Dale Owen, the unlikely founder of America's first socialist community. A Welsh industrialist who had made a fortune manufacturing textiles, Owen then turned to realizing his vision of a just society—one in which property was held in common and work equally shared. Such a benign social environment, he believed, would foster tolerant, rational human beings capable of self-government. What better place than America to make this dream come true?

Initially Owen received a warm reception. John Quincy Adams not only attended both lectures that Owen delivered at the Capitol but also displayed a model of his proposed community in the White House. A few months later about 900 volunteers flocked to Owen's community at New Harmony, Indiana. But alas, most lacked the skills and commitment to make it a success, and bitter factions soon split the settlement. Owen made matters worse by announcing that he rejected both the authenticity of the Bible and the institution of marriage. New Harmony dissolved in 1827, but Owen's principles inspired nearly 20 other short-lived experiments.

The United States was a poor proving-ground for socialist experiments. Wages were too high and land too cheap for such communities to interest most Americans. And individualism was too strong to foster a commitment to cooperative action. Communities founded by believers in religious rather than secular faiths proved far more enduring. Their common spiritual convictions muted individualism, and their charismatic leaders held divisions at bay.

Among the most successful of these religiously based communal groups were the Shakers. Ann Lee, the illiterate daughter of an English blacksmith, believed that God had a dual nature, part male and part female, and that her own life would reveal the feminine side of the divinity, just as Christ had revealed the masculine. In 1774 she led a small band of followers to America. Her followers sometimes shook in the fervent public demonstration of their faith—hence the name Shakers.

As the Second Great Awakening crested, recruits from revivals swelled Shaker ranks, and their new disciples founded about 20 villages. Members held the community's property in common, worked hard, and lived simply. Convinced that the end of the world was at hand and that there was no need to perpetuate the human race, Shakers practiced celibacy. Men and women normally worked apart, ate at separate tables in silence, entered separate doorways, and had separate living quarters. Elders typically assigned tasks by gender, with women performing household chores and men laboring in the fields, but leadership of the church was split equally between men and women.

Communities founded by believers in religious rather than secular faiths proved far more enduring.

Lacking any natural increase, membership began to decline after 1850, from a peak of about 6,000 members.

The Mormon Experience >>

The most spectacularly successful antebellum religious community—one that mushroomed into a denomination whose followers now number in the millions around the world—was The Church of Jesus Christ of Latter-day Saints. The Mormons, as they are generally known, took their rise from the visions of a young man named Joseph Smith in Palmyra, in western New York, where the religious fires of revivalism often flared. The son of a poor farmer, Smith was robust, charming, almost hypnotic in his appeal. In 1827, at the age of only 22, he announced that he had discovered and translated a set of golden tablets on which was written the Book of Mormon. The tablets told the story of a band of Hebrews who in biblical times journeyed to America, splitting into two groups, the Nephites and Lamanites. The Nephites established a Christian civilization, only to be exterminated by the Lamanites, whose descendants were said to be the Indians of the Americas. Seeking to reestablish the true church, Smith gathered a group of devoted followers.

Like nineteenth-century evangelicalism Mormonism proclaimed that salvation was available to all. Mormon culture also upheld the middle-class values of hard work, thrift, and self-control. It partook of the optimistic, materialist attitudes of American society. And by teaching that Christ would return to rule the earth, it shared in the hope of a coming millennial kingdom.

Yet Mormonism was less an outgrowth of evangelicalism than of the primitive gospel movement, which sought to reestablish the ancient church. In restoring what Smith called "the ancient order of things," he created a **theocracy** uniting church and state, reestablished biblical priesthoods and titles, and adopted temple rituals.

> **theocracy** system of government by priests or clergy claiming divine inspiration or guidance.

Like Roman Catholics, the Mormons drew bitter opposition—and armed attacks. Smith's unorthodox teachings provoked persecution wherever Smith and his followers went, first to Ohio and then to Missouri. Mob violence finally hounded him out of Missouri in 1839. Smith then established a new holy city, which he named Nauvoo, located on the Mississippi River in Illinois.

Reinforced by a steady stream of converts from Britain, Nauvoo became the largest city in Illinois, with a population

<< The Mormon temple at Nauvoo, Illinois, was adorned with this sun stone and other celestial carvings drawn from a dream vision by Joseph Smith. The image resembles some of the astronomical symbols popularized by the Masons, a fraternal order whose secret rituals and symbols were hotly debated in western New York, where Smith grew up.

of 10,000 by the mid-1840s. There Smith introduced the most distinctive features of Mormon theology, including baptism for the dead, eternal marriage, and polygamy, or plural marriage. As a result, Mormonism increasingly diverged from traditional Christianity and became a distinct new religion. To bolster his authority as a prophet Smith established a theocratic political order under which church leaders controlled political offices and governed the community, with Smith as mayor.

Neighboring residents, alarmed by the Mormons' growing political power and reports that church leaders were practicing polygamy, demanded that Nauvoo's charter be revoked and the church suppressed. In 1844, while in jail for destroying the printing press of dissident Mormons in Nauvoo, Smith was murdered by an anti-Mormon mob. In 1846 the Mormons abandoned Nauvoo, and the following year Brigham Young, Smith's successor, led them westward to Utah.

RADICAL REFORM

Late in the fall of 1834 Lyman Beecher was in the midst of his continuing efforts to "overturn and overturn" on behalf of the kingdom of God. He had left Boston for Cincinnati to assume leadership of Lane Seminary. The school had everything that an institution for training ministers to convert the West needed—everything, that is, except students. In October 1834 all but 8 of Lane's 100 scholars had departed after months of bitter fighting with Beecher and the trustees over the issue of abolition.

Beecher knew the source of his troubles: a scruffy, magnetic convert of Finney's revivals named Theodore Dwight Weld. Weld had been firing up his classmates over the need to end slavery immediately. He had been influenced by the arguments of William Lloyd Garrison, whose abolitionist writings had sent shock waves across the entire nation. Indeed, Beecher's troubles at Lane Seminary provided only one example of how the flames of reform could spread along paths not anticipated by those who had kindled them.

The Beginnings of the Abolitionist Movement >> William Lloyd Garrison symbolized the transition from a moderate antislavery movement to the more militant abolitionism of the 1830s. A sober, religious youngster deeply influenced by his Baptist mother, Garrison in the 1820s edited a newspaper sympathetic to many of the new reforms. In 1829 he was enlisted in the antislavery cause by Benjamin Lundy, a Quaker who edited a Baltimore

In 1835 abolitionists distributed over a million pamphlets through the post office to southern whites.

antislavery newspaper, *The Genius of Universal Emancipation.* Calling for a gradual end to slavery, Lundy supported colonization, hoping to overcome southern fears of emancipation by transporting free black Americans to Africa.

Garrison went to Baltimore to help edit Lundy's paper, and for the first time he encountered the opinions of free African Americans. To his surprise Garrison discovered that most of them strongly opposed the colonization movement as proslavery and antiblack. Under their influence Garrison soon developed views far more radical than Lundy's. Within a year of moving to Baltimore the young firebrand was convicted of libel and imprisoned. On his release Garrison hurried back to Boston, determined to publish a new kind of antislavery journal.

On January 1, 1831, the first issue of *The Liberator* appeared, and abolitionism was born. Repudiating gradual emancipation and embracing "immediatism," Garrison insisted that slavery end at once. He denounced colonization as a racist, antiblack movement and upheld the principle of racial equality. To those who suggested that slaveowners should be compensated for freeing their slaves, Garrison was firm. Southerners ought to be convinced by "moral suasion" to renounce slavery as a sin. Virtue was its own reward.

Garrison attracted the most attention, but other abolitionists spoke with equal conviction. Lewis Tappan and his brother Arthur, two New York City silk merchants, boldly placed their wealth behind a number of humanitarian causes, including abolitionism. Angelina and Sarah Grimké, the daughters of a South Carolina planter, left their native state to speak against the institution.

To abolitionists, slavery was a moral, not an economic, question. The institution seemed a contradiction of the principle of the American Revolution that all human beings had been created with natural rights. Abolitionists condemned slavery because of the breakup of marriages and families by sale, the harsh punishment of the lash, slaves' lack of access to education, and the sexual abuse of black women. Most of all they denounced slavery as outrageously contrary to Christian teaching. As one Ohio antislavery paper declared: "We believe slavery to be a sin, always, everywhere, and only, sin—sin, in itself." So persistent were abolitionists in their religious objections that they forced the churches to face the question of slavery head on. In the 1840s the Methodist and Baptist churches each split into northern and southern organizations over the issue.

The Spread of Abolitionism >> After helping organize the New England Anti-Slavery Society in 1832, Garrison joined with Lewis Tappan and Theodore Weld the following year to establish a national organization, the

>> Black abolitionist Frederick Douglass (*second from left at the podium*) was only one of nearly 50 runaway slaves who appeared at an abolitionist convention held in August 1850 in Cazenovia, New York. The question of whether women should be allowed to take active roles in the movement fractured antislavery advocates and sparked women reformers to speak out more strongly for women's rights.

American Anti-Slavery Society. It coordinated a loosely affiliated network of state and local societies. During the years before the Civil War, perhaps 200,000 northerners belonged to an abolitionist society.

Abolitionists were concentrated in the East, especially New England, and in areas that had been settled by New Englanders, such as western New York and northern Ohio. The movement was not strong in cities or among businesspeople and workers. Most abolitionists were young, being generally in their 20s and 30s when the movement began, and had grown up in rural areas and small towns in middle-class families. Intensely religious, many had been profoundly affected by the revivals of the Second Great Awakening.

Theodore Weld was cut from this mold. After enrolling in Lane Seminary in 1833 he promoted immediate abolitionism among his fellow students. When Lyman Beecher assumed the Lane presidency a year later, he confronted a student body dominated by committed immediatists.

The radicalism of Lane students was also made clear in their commitment to racial equality. Unlike some abolitionists, who opposed slavery but disdained blacks as inferior, Lane students mingled freely with Cincinnati's free black community. Alarmed by rumors in the summer of 1834 that the town's residents intended to demolish the school, Beecher and Lane's trustees forbade any discussion of slavery on campus, restricted contact with the black community, and ordered students to return to their studies. All except a few left the school and enrolled at Oberlin College, which agreed to their demands for guaranteeing freedom of speech and admitting black students.

Free African Americans, who made up the majority of subscribers to Garrison's *Liberator,* provided important support and leadership for the movement. Frederick Douglass assumed the greatest prominence. Having escaped from slavery in Maryland, he became an eloquent critic of its evils. Other important black abolitionists included Martin Delany, William Wells Brown, William Still, and Sojourner Truth. Aided by many other African Americans, these men and women battled against racial discrimination in the North as well as slavery in the South.

A network of antislavery sympathizers also developed in the North to convey runaway slaves to Canada and freedom. Although not as extensive or as tightly organized as contemporaries claimed, the Underground Railroad hid fugitives and transported them northward from one station to the next. Free African Americans, who were more readily trusted by wary slaves, played a leading role in the Underground Railroad. One of its most famous conductors was Harriet Tubman, an escaped slave who repeatedly returned to the South and eventually escorted to freedom more than 200 slaves.

Opponents and Divisions >> The drive for immediate abolition faced massive obstacles within American society. With slavery increasingly important to their region's economy, Southerners forced opponents of slavery to flee north. In the North, where racism was equally entrenched, abolitionism provoked bitter resistance.

On occasion northern resistance turned violent. A Boston mob seized Garrison in 1835 and paraded him with a rope around his body before he was finally rescued. And in 1837 in Alton, Illinois, Elijah Lovejoy was murdered when he tried to protect his printing press from an angry crowd. The leaders of these mobs were not from the bottom of society but, as one of their victims noted, were "gentlemen of property and standing" who reacted to the threat that abolitionists posed to their prosperity.

The antislavery cause was also hindered by divisions among reformers. Lyman Beecher conceived of sin in terms of individual immorality, not unjust social institutions. But to the abolitionists, America could never become a godly nation until slavery was abolished. Among them was Beecher's daughter, Harriet Beecher Stowe, who in the 1850s wrote the most successful piece of antislavery literature in the nation's history, *Uncle Tom's Cabin.* Yet the abolitionists themselves splintered, shaken by the opposition they encountered and unable to agree on the most effective response. More conservative reformers wanted to work within established institutions, using the churches and political action to end slavery. But for Garrison and his followers, the mob violence demonstrated that slavery was

^ In this playbill advertising a dramatic production of *Uncle Tom's Cabin*, vicious bloodhounds pursue the light-skinned runaway slave Eliza, who clutches her child as she frantically leaps to safety across the ice-choked Ohio River.

only part of a deeper national disease, whose cure required the overthrow of American institutions and values.

By the end of the decade Garrison had worked out a program for the total reform of society. He embraced perfectionism and pacifism, urged members to leave the churches, and called for an end to all government. Condemning the Constitution as proslavery—"a covenant with death and an agreement with hell"—he publicly burned a copy one July 4th. This platform was radical enough on all counts, but the final straw for Garrison's opponents was his endorsement of women's rights as an inseparable part of abolitionism.

The Women's Rights Movement >>
American women were kept out of most jobs, denied political rights, and given only limited access to education beyond the elementary grades. When a woman married, her husband became the legal representative of the marriage and gained complete control of her property. If a marriage ended in divorce, the husband was awarded custody of the children. Any unmarried woman was made the ward of a male relative.

When abolitionists divided over the issue of female participation in their societies, women found it easy to identify with the situation of slaves, since both were victims of male tyranny. Sarah and Angelina Grimké took up the cause of women's rights after they were criticized for speaking to audiences that included men as well as women. Sarah responded with *Letters on the Condition of Women and the Equality of the Sexes* (1838), arguing that women deserved the same rights as men.

Two abolitionists, Elizabeth Cady Stanton and Lucretia Mott, launched the women's rights movement after they were forced to sit behind a curtain at a world antislavery convention in London. In 1848 Stanton and Mott organized a conference in Seneca Falls, New York, that attracted about a hundred supporters. The meeting issued a Declaration of Sentiments, modeled after the Declaration of Independence, that began, "All men and women are created equal."

The Seneca Falls convention called for educational and professional opportunities for women, laws giving them control of their property, recognition of legal equality, and repeal of laws awarding the father custody of the children in divorce. The most controversial proposal, and the only resolution that did not pass unanimously, was one demanding the right to vote. The Seneca Falls convention set forth the arguments and the program for the women's rights movement for the remainder of the century.

In response, several states gave women greater control over their property, and a few made divorce easier or granted women the right to sue in courts. But disappointments and defeats outweighed these early victories. Still, many of the important leaders in the crusade for women's rights who emerged after the Civil War had already taken their places at the forefront of the movement. They included Stanton, Susan B. Anthony, Lucy Stone, and—as Lyman Beecher by now must have expected—one of his daughters, Isabella Beecher Hooker.

The Schism of 1840 >>

It was Garrison's position on women's rights that finally split antislavery ranks already divided over other aspects of his growing radicalism. The showdown came in 1840 at the national meeting of the American Anti-Slavery Society, when delegates debated whether women could hold office in the organization. By packing the convention, Garrison carried the day. His opponents, led by Lewis Tappan, resigned to found the rival American and Foreign Anti-Slavery Society.

The schism of 1840 lessened the influence of abolitionism as a reform movement. Although abolitionism heightened moral concern about slavery, it failed to convert the North to its program, and its supporters remained a tiny minority. Despite the considerable courage of its leaders, the movement lacked a realistic, long-range plan for eliminating such a deeply entrenched institution.

 REVIEW

What helped to spark the growth of an abolitionist movement? What factors caused the movement to splinter?

⚘ Elizabeth Cady Stanton, one of the instigators and guiding spirits at the Seneca Falls convention, photographed with two of her children about that time.

REFORM SHAKES THE PARTY SYSTEM

The crusading idealism of reformers inevitably collided with the hard reality that society could not be perfected by converting individuals. A growing number of frustrated reformers were abandoning the principle of voluntary persuasion and looking to government coercion to achieve their goals.

The Turn toward Politics >>

Politicians did not particularly welcome the new interest. Because the Whig and Democratic parties both drew on evangelical and nonevangelical voters, heated moral debates over the harmful effects of drink or the evils of slavery threatened to detach regular party members from their old loyalties and disrupt each party's unity. The strong opposition of German and Irish immigrants to temperance stimulated antiforeign sentiment among reformers and further divided both party coalitions, particularly the Democrats.

Because women could not vote, they felt excluded when the temperance and abolitionist movements turned to electoral action to accomplish their goals. By the 1840s female reformers increasingly demanded the right to vote as the means to change society. Nor were men blind to what was at stake: one reason they so strongly resisted female suffrage was because it would give women real power.

The political parties could resist the women's suffrage movement, because most of its advocates lacked the right to vote. Less easily put off were temperance reformers. Although drinking had significantly declined in American society by 1840, it had hardly been eliminated. In response, temperance advocates proposed state laws that would outlaw the manufacture and sale of alcoholic beverages. Their first major triumph came in 1851. The Maine Law, as it was known, authorized search and seizure of private property in that state and provided stiff penalties for selling liquor. In the next few years a number of states enacted similar laws, although most were struck down by the courts or later repealed. Prohibition remained a controversial political issue throughout the century.

Opinion

Did the status of women improve in the United States between the American Revolution and the Civil War?

Although prohibition was temporarily defeated, the issue badly disrupted the Whig and Democratic parties. It greatly increased party switching and brought to the polls a large number of new voters, including many "wets" who wanted to preserve their right to drink. By dissolving the ties between so many voters and their parties, the temperance issue played a major role in the eventual collapse of the Jacksonian party system in the 1850s.

Abolitionism and the Party System >>

Slavery proved even more divisive. In 1835 abolitionists distributed more than a million pamphlets, mostly in the South, through the Post Office. Former senator Robert Hayne led a Charleston mob that burned sacks of U.S. mail containing abolitionist literature, and postmasters in other southern cities refused to deliver the material. Andrew Jackson's administration allowed southern states to censor the mail, leading abolitionists to protest that their civil rights had been violated. In reaction, the number of antislavery societies in the North nearly tripled.

With access to the mails impaired, abolitionists began flooding Congress with petitions against slavery. Asserting that Congress had no power over the institution, angry southern representatives demanded action, and the House in response adopted the so-called gag rule in 1836. It automatically tabled without consideration any petition dealing with slavery. But southern leaders had made a tactical blunder. The gag rule allowed abolitionists not only to attack slavery but also to speak out as defenders of white civil liberties. The appeal of the antislavery movement was broadened, and in 1844 the House finally repealed the controversial rule.

Many abolitionists outside Garrison's circle began to feel that an antislavery third party offered a more effective means of attacking slavery. In 1840 these political abolitionists founded the Liberty party and nominated for president James Birney, a former slaveholder who had converted to abolitionism. Birney received only 7,000 votes, but the Liberty party was the seed from which a stronger antislavery political movement would grow. From 1840 onward abolitionism's importance would be in the political arena rather than as a voluntary reform organization.

 REVIEW

How did reform movements create instability in the political system?

The ferment of reform during the decades from 1820 to 1850 reflected a multitude of attempts to deal with transformations working through not just the United States but also Europe. Abolition was potentially the most dangerous of the trans-Atlantic reforms, because slavery was so deeply and profitably intertwined with the industrial system. Slave labor produced cotton for the textile factories of New England, Great Britain, and Europe. Plantation economies supplied the sugar, rice, tea, and coffee that were a part of European and American diets. Revolutionary France had abolished slavery in 1794, but Napoleon reinstated it, along with the slave trade. Great Britain outlawed the trade in 1808 (as did the United States) and then freed nearly 800,000 slaves in its colonies in 1834.

Any move for emancipation in the United States seemed out of the question, and as late as 1840 abolition lacked the power to threaten the political system. But the growing northern concern about slavery highlighted differences between the two sections. Despite the strength of evangelicalism in the South, the reform impulse spawned by the revivals found little support there, since reform movements were discredited by their association with abolitionism. The party system confronted the difficult

Significant Events

First Shaker commune established

Peak of revivals

New Harmony established

| 1787 | 1794 | 1824–1837 | 1824 | 1826 | 1829 | 1831 | 1833 |

African American Bethel Church organized

A BIRD'S EYE VIEW OF ONE OF THE NEW COMMUNITIES AT HARMONY. IN THE STATE OF INDIANA NORTH AMERICA. AN ASSOCIATION OF TWO THOUSAND PERSONS FORMED UPON THE PRINCIPLES PROPOUNDED BY ROBERT OWEN.

American Temperance Society founded

David Walker's *Appeal to the Colored Citizens of the World* published

The Liberator established

American Anti-Slavery Society founded

challenge of holding together sections that, although sharing much, were also diverging in important ways. To the residents of both sections, the South increasingly appeared to be a unique society with its own distinctive way of life.

CHAPTER SUMMARY

The Jacksonian era produced the greatest number of significant reform movements in American history.

- The Second Great Awakening, which preached the doctrine of salvation available to all and the coming of the millennium, encouraged revivals and reform.
- Revivals drew converts from every segment of American society and spoke to their spiritual needs.
- Women were most prominent among revival converts.
- The Second Great Awakening made evangelicals the dominant religious subculture in the United States.
- Benevolence and reform societies decisively changed drinking habits and the ideals of womanhood and the family.
- Evangelical religious fervor also fueled anti-Catholicism.
- Unitarianism and transcendentalism, which emphasized the unlimited potential of each individual, also strengthened reform.
- Utopian communities sought to establish a model society for the rest of the world to follow.
- Mormons developed a following and drew persecution.
- Abolitionism precipitated both strong support and violent opposition, and the movement split in 1840.
- Temperance, abolitionism, and women's rights movements each turned to political action to accomplish their goals.
- Although it survived, the party system was seriously weakened by these reform movements.

Additional Reading

Good introductions to antebellum evangelical religion and reform include Robert Abzug, *Cosmos Crumbling* (1994); Charles Hambrick-Stowe, *Charles G. Finney and the Spirit of American Evangelicalism* (1996); and Bertram Wyatt-Brown, *Lewis Tappan and the Evangelical War Against Slavery* (1971). For suggestive analyses of the relationship between antebellum evangelicalism and the sweeping changes in economic and political life, consult Richard Carwardine, *Evangelicals and Politics in Antebellum America* (1997); Candy Gunther Brown, *The Word in the World* (2004); and Paul Johnson and Sean Wilentz, *The Kingdom of Matthias* (1994). The best studies of the role of women in evangelical churches and reform societies are Anne Boylan, *The Origins of Women's Activism* (1988); Lori Ginzberg, *Women and the Work of Benevolence* (1990); and Nancy Hewitt, *Women's Activism and Social Change* (1984). To understand the link between reformist activism and the early women's rights movement, begin with Lori Ginzberg, *Untidy Origins* (2005), and Nancy Isenberg, *Sex and Citizenship in the United States* (1998).

Despite the dominant influence of evangelical Protestants, both Roman Catholics and Mormons attracted a growing number of adherents during the antebellum period. For a fascinating account of the origins and rise of Mormonism, see John Brooke, *The Refiner's Fire* (1996), and for a compelling account of how American Protestants responded to the growth of Roman Catholicism after the 1830s, see Ryan Smith, *Gothic Arches, Latin Crosses* (2006). To explore the reasons why a small but influential minority of nineteenth-century Americans rejected all forms of Christianity in favor of agnosticism or atheism, rely on James Turner, *Without God, Without Creed* (1985).

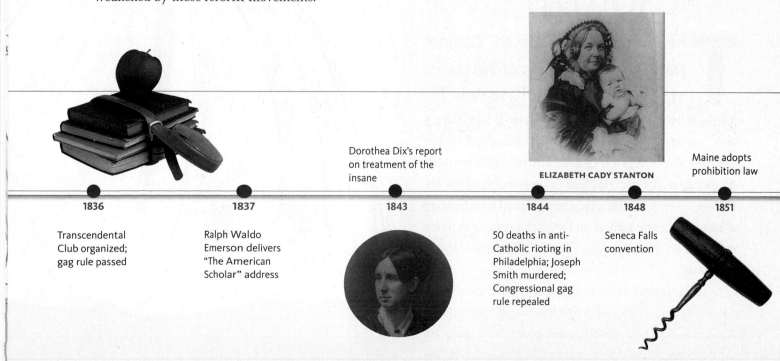

Dorothea Dix's report on treatment of the insane

ELIZABETH CADY STANTON

Maine adopts prohibition law

1836 — 1837 — 1843 — 1844 — 1848 — 1851

Transcendental Club organized; gag rule passed

Ralph Waldo Emerson delivers "The American Scholar" address

50 deaths in anti-Catholic rioting in Philadelphia; Joseph Smith murdered; Congressional gag rule repealed

Seneca Falls convention

The industrial and democratic revolutions thus transformed the South as well as the North, though in different ways. Increasingly slavery became the focus of disputes between the two sections. The industrial revolution's demand for cotton increased the demand for slave labor and the profits to be gained from it. Yet the spread of democratic ideology worldwide increased pressure to abolish slavery. France and Britain had already done so. In eastern Europe the near-slavery of feudal serfdom was being eliminated as well: in 1848 within the Hapsburg empire; in 1861 in Russia; in 1864 in Romania.

By the mid-1840s the contradictory pressures of the industrial and democratic revolutions were beginning to sharpen, as the United States embarked on a new program of westward expansion that thrust the slavery issue into the center of politics. Americans were forced to debate how much of the newly won territory should be open to slavery; and in doing so, some citizens began to question whether the Union could permanently endure, half slave and half free.

CHAPTER SUMMARY

The Old South was a complex, biracial society that increasingly diverged from the rest of the United States in the years before 1860.

- Southerners placed heavy emphasis on agriculture and upheld the superiority of the rural way of life. Few cities and towns developed.
- Southern commercial agriculture produced staple crops for sale in northern and European markets: tobacco, sugar, rice, and, above all, cotton.
- As southern agriculture expanded into the fresh lands of the Deep South, the slave population moved steadily westward and southward.
- Slavery played a major role in shaping the class structure of the Old South.
- Ownership of slaves brought privilege and status, and the largest slaveowners were extraordinarily wealthy.
- Planters on the older eastern seaboard enjoyed a more refined lifestyle than did those on the new cotton frontier.
- Most slaveowners owned only a few slaves, and the majority of southern whites were nonslave-owning yeoman farmers. Slavery hurt nonslaveholding whites economically, but class tensions were muted in the Old South because of racial fears.
- The institution of slavery was both a labor system and a social system, regulating relations between the races.
- Slaves resisted bondage in many ways, ranging from the subtle to the overt. Slave revolts, however, were rare.

Gabriel Prosser's rebellion

Denmark Vesey conspiracy trial

Agricultural reform movement in Upper South

1800

1815–1860

Spread of the cotton kingdom

1822

1830–1840

Proslavery argument developed

1830–1860

- Slaves developed their own culture, in which the family, religion, and songs played key roles in helping them cope with the pressures of bondage.
- As slavery increasingly came under attack, white southerners rallied to protect their peculiar institution. They developed a set of arguments defending slavery as a positive good.
- Many Americans, in both the North and the South, shared the same values: personal independence, social egalitarianism, evangelical Protestantism. But beginning in the mid-1840s with renewed westward expansion, the slavery issue increased sectional tensions.

Additional Reading

The reports of Frederick Law Olmsted, who traveled through the South in the 1850s, make a fascinating jumping-off point for a first look at the region. Much of Olmsted's material is conveniently collected in Lawrence Powell, ed., *The Cotton Kingdom* (1984). A contrasting approach to traveling about is to stay at one plantation, as Erskine Clarke does in his brilliant *Dwelling Place: A Plantation Epic* (2005).

Frank Owsley's *Plain Folk of the Old South* (1949), about southern yeoman farmers, is still useful and can be supplemented by Samuel C. Hyde Jr., ed., *Plain Folk of the South Revisited* (1997). The lives of upper-class southern white women and their servants are analyzed in Elizabeth Fox-Genovese, *Within the Plantation Household* (1988), whereas Victoria E. Bynum, *Unruly Women* (1992), deals with white and black women of lower status.

The best exploration of slavery as a labor system remains Kenneth M. Stampp, *The Peculiar Institution* (1956), but the most perceptive treatment of slave culture is Eugene D. Genovese, *Roll, Jordan, Roll* (1974). John Hope Franklin and Loren Schweninger, *Runaway Slaves* (1999), detail an important aspect of slave resistance. Walter Johnson, *Soul by Soul: Life Inside the Antebellum Slave Market* (1999), provides a concrete and chilling view of the trade that helped sustain the Peculiar Institution. Ira Berlin, *Slaves Without Masters* (1974), is an excellent account of southern free blacks. As for the political and ideological aspects of slavery, consult Drew Faust, *A Sacred Circle* (1977), and William J. Cooper, Jr., *The Politics of Slavery* (1978).

1831 — Nat Turner's rebellion

1832 — Virginia debate on slavery

1844 — Methodist church divides into northern and southern organizations

1845 — Baptist church divides

where the South had more power. As such, it revealed mounting sectional tensions.

Wilmot himself was hardly an abolitionist. Indeed, he hoped to keep not only slaves but all black people out of the territories. Denying any "morbid sympathy for the slave," he declared, "I would preserve for white free labor a fair country . . . where the sons of toil, of my own race and color, can live without the disgrace which association with negro slavery brings upon free labor." The Wilmot Proviso aimed not to destroy slavery in the South but to confine it to states where it already existed. Still, abolitionists had long contended that southern slaveholders—the "Slave Power"—were plotting to extend their sway over the rest of the country. The political maneuverings of slaveholders such as Tyler, and especially Polk, convinced growing numbers of northerners that the Slave Power did indeed exist.

The status of slavery in the territories became more than an abstract question once peace returned. The United States gained title to an immense territory, including all of what would become the states of California, Nevada, and Utah, nearly all of New Mexico, most of Arizona and Colorado, and parts of Wyoming, Kansas, and Oklahoma. With the United States in control of the Pacific Coast from San Diego to Puget Sound, Polk's continental vision had become a reality. But slavery would once again dominate national politics.

WITNESS

In the Gold Diggings

"We selected a poor spot for a location and staked all on it, and it has proved worth nothing . . . I was in hopes to have sent home a good pile of money before this time, but I am not able to at present . . . I am of the opinion that the gold will soon be gathered from these washings and then will come the hardest part of this gold fever . . . But were I to be unfortunate in all my business here and arrive at last at home without *one cent*, I should ever be glad that I have taken the trip to California."

—J. S. Holliday, Letter, April 15, 1850

 REVIEW

What factors best explain the cause and the outcome of the U.S.-Mexican War?

NEW SOCIETIES IN THE WEST

As Hispanic, Asian, Anglo-American, and dozens of different native cultures interacted, the patterns of development along the frontier varied widely. Some newcomers recreated the farm economies and small towns of the Anglo-American East; others continued the cattle ranching life of the Hispanic West. In California the new settlements were overwhelmingly shaped by the rush for gold after 1848. And in the Great Basin around Salt Lake, the Mormons established a society whose sense of religious mission was as strong as that of the Puritans.

Farming in the West >> The overlanders expected to replicate the societies they had left behind.

When a wagon train arrived at its destination, members had usually exhausted their resources and thus quickly scattered in search of employment or a good farm site. "Friday, October 27.—Arrived at Oregon City at the falls of the Willamette," read one pioneer diary. "Saturday, October 28.—Went to work."

In a process repeated over and over, settlers in a new area set up the machinery of government. Although violence was common on the frontier, farming communities tended to resolve problems by traditional means. Churches took longer to establish, because ministers were hard to recruit and congregations were often not large enough to support a church. As the population grew, however, a more conventional society evolved. Towns and a middle class developed, the proportion of women increased, schools were established, and the residents became less mobile.

Although opportunity was greater on the frontier and early arrivals had a special advantage, more and more the agricultural frontier of the West resembled the older society of the East. With the development of markets and transportation, wealth became concentrated, some families fell to the lower rungs of society, and those who were less successful left, seeking yet another fresh start.

The Gold Rush >> In January 1848, while constructing a sawmill along the American River, James Marshall noticed gold flecks in the millrace. More discoveries followed, and when the news reached the East, it spread like wildfire. The following spring some 55,000 emigrants jammed the Overland Trail as "forty-niners" on the way to California. Another 25,000 traveled by boat. In only two

^ San Francisco in 1850. In this daguerrotype, the masts of hundreds of sailing ships along the wharves appear like a forest, hemming in the chaos and overcrowding of a city thrown up over a space of many months.

years, from 1848 to the end of 1849, California's population jumped from 14,000 to 100,000. By 1860 it stood at 380,000.

Among those who joined the rush was William Swain, a 27-year-old farmer in western New York. Bidding good-bye to his wife and daughter in 1849, he set off for the gold fields to make his fortune. On his arrival he entered a partnership and staked a claim along the Feather River, but months of back-breaking work in icy waters led only to the discovery that his claim was "worth nothing." He sold out and joined another company, but early rains soon forced a halt to the work. In October 1850, after less than a year in the diggings, Swain returned home, only a few hundred dollars richer. He counted himself one of the vast majority of miners who had seen "their bright day-dreams of golden wealth vanish like the dreams of night."

Predictably, mining the miners offered a more reliable road to prosperity. Perhaps half the inhabitants of a mining town were shopkeepers, businesspeople, and professionals who provided services for prospectors. Also conspicuous were gamblers, card sharks, and other outcasts, all bent on separating the miner from his riches.

More than 80 percent of the prospectors who poured into the gold country were Americans, including free blacks. Mexicans, Australians, Argentinians, Hawaiians, Chinese, French, English, and Irish also came. Observers praised the diggings' democratic spirit. Yet such assertions overlooked strongly held nativist prejudices: when frustrated by a lack of success, American miners directed their hostility toward foreigners. The miners ruthlessly exterminated the Indians in the area, sometimes hunting them for sport. Mob violence drove Mexicans out of nearly every camp, and the Chinese were confined to claims abandoned by Americans as unprofitable. The state eventually enacted a foreign miners' tax that fell largely on the Chinese. Free African Americans felt the sting of discrimination as well, both in the camps and in state law. White American miners proclaimed that "colored men were not privileged to work in a country intended only for American citizens."

Only about 5 percent of gold rush emigrants were women or children; given this relative scarcity, men were willing to pay top dollar for women's domestic skills. Women supported themselves by cooking, sewing, and washing, as well as by running hotels and boardinghouses. "A smart woman can do very well in this country," one woman informed a friend in the East. "It is the only country I ever was in where a woman received anything like a just compensation for work." Women went to the mining frontier to be with their husbands, to make money, or to find adventure. But the class most frequently seen in the diggings was prostitutes, who numbered perhaps 20 percent of female Californians in 1850.

Before long the most easily worked claims had been played out, and large corporations moved in heavy equipment to get at hidden ore. Such techniques caused lasting environmental damage. Abandoned prospect holes and diggings pockmarked the gold fields and created piles of debris that heavy rains would wash down the valley, choking streams and ruining lands below. Excavation of hillsides, construction of dams to divert rivers, and the destruction of the forest cover to meet the heavy demand for lumber and firewood caused serious erosion of the soil and spring floods.

Instant City: San Francisco >>
When the United States assumed control of California, San Francisco had a population of perhaps 200. But thousands of emigrants took the water route west, passing through San Francisco's harbor on their way to the diggings. By 1856 the city's population had jumped to an astonishing 50,000. In a mere 8 years the city had attained the size New York had taken 190 years to reach.

by a small number of plants cultivated as commodities. Domesticated grasses replaced native grasses in pastures for making hay.

Western farmers altered the landscape by reducing the annual fires, often set by Indians, that had kept the prairie free from trees. In the fires' absence, trees reappeared on land not in cultivation and, if undisturbed, eventually formed wood lots. The earlier unbroken landscape gave way to independent farms, each fenced in the precise checkerboard pattern established by the Northwest Ordinance. It was an artificial ecosystem of animals, wood lots, and crops whose large, uniform layout made western farms more efficient than the more irregular farms in the East.

Railroads and the Urban Environment »

Railroads transformed the urban environment as well. Communities soon recognized that their economic survival depended on creating rail links to the countryside and to major urban markets. Large cities feared they would be left behind in the struggle to be the dominant city in the region, and smaller communities saw their very survival at stake in the battle for rail connections.

Communities that obtained rail links found the new technology difficult to adjust to. Merchants in Jacksonville, Illinois, complained about the noise, dirt, and billowing smoke produced by the new locomotives passing through their business district. "The public square was filled with teams [of horses]," one resident recalled, "and whenever the engine steamed into the square making all the noise possible, there was such a stampede." After a few years the tracks were relocated to the outskirts of town. Increasingly communities kept railroads away from fashionable neighborhoods and shopping areas. As the tracks became a physical marker of social and economic divisions in the town, the notion of living "on the wrong side of the tracks" became a way of defining the urban landscape.

Rising Industrialization » The expansion

of commercial agriculture, along with the shift from water power to steam, spurred the growth of industry. Out of the 10 leading American industries, 8 processed raw materials produced by agriculture, including flour milling and the manufacture of textiles, shoes, and woolens. (The only exceptions were iron and machinery.)

Most important, the factory system of organizing labor and the technology of interchangeable parts spread to other areas of the economy during the 1850s. Isaac Singer began using interchangeable parts in 1851 to mass-produce sewing machines, which made possible the ready-made clothing industry, while workers who assembled farm implements performed a single step in the process over and over again. By 1860 the United States had nearly

a billion dollars invested in manufacturing, almost twice as much as in 1849. And for the first time, less than half the workers in the North were employed in agriculture.

Immigration » The surge of industry depended

on a large factory labor force. Natural increase helped swell the nation's population to more than 30 million by 1860, but only in part, since the birthrate had begun to decline. It was the beginning of mass immigration to America during the mid-1840s that kept population growth soaring.

In the 20 years from 1820 to 1840 about 700,000 newcomers had entered the United States. That figure jumped to 1.7 million in the 1840s, then to 2.6 million in the 1850s. Though even greater numbers arrived after the Civil War, as a percentage of the nation's total population, the wave from 1845 to 1854 was the largest influx of immigrants in American history. The great majority of newcomers were in the prime of life, between 10 and 40 years old. Certainly the booming economy and the lure of freedom drew immigrants, but they were also pushed by deteriorating conditions in Europe. In Ireland a potato blight beginning in 1845 created a *Gorta Mór*—"Great Famine"—leaving potatoes rotting in the fields. The blight may well have spread from the United States and Canada, and it also infected Europe generally. But Ireland suffered more, because nearly a third of its population depended almost entirely on the potato for food. "They are all gone—clean gone," wrote a priest in the Irish town of Galway. "If travelling by night, you would know when a potato field was near by the smell." Out of a population of 9 million, as many as a million people perished, while a million and a half more emigrated, two-thirds to the United States.

The Irish tended to be poorer than other immigrant groups of the day. Although the Protestant Scots-Irish continued to emigrate, as so many had during the eighteenth century, the decided majority of the Irish who came after 1845 were Catholic. Because they were poor and unskilled, the Irish congregated in the cities, where the women performed domestic service and took factory jobs and the men did manual labor.

Germans and Scandinavians also had economic reasons for leaving Europe. They included small farmers whose lands had become marginal or who had been displaced by landlords, and skilled workers thrown out of work by industrialization. Some fled political and social oppression and came to live under the free institutions of the United States. Since arriving in America, wrote a Swede who settled in Iowa in 1850, "I have not been compelled to pay a penny for the privilege of living. Neither is my cap worn out from lifting it in the presence of gentlemen."

Unprecedented unrest and upheaval prevailed in Europe in 1848, the so-called year of revolutions. The famine that had driven so many Irish out of their country was part of a larger food shortage caused by a series of poor harvests. In this situation, middle-class reformers,

^ "Conditions of famine across Ireland led many to buy passage on ships like this one, departing for the United States. New York was the major port of entry for immigrants who surged into the United States during the 1840s and 1850s.

who wanted civil liberty and a more representative government, joined forces with lower-class workers to overthrow several regimes. France, Austria, Hungary, Italy, and Prussia all witnessed popular uprisings. Yet though these revolts gained temporary success, they were all quashed by the forces of the old order. Liberal hopes for a more open, democratic society suffered a severe setback.

In the aftermath of this failure a number of hard-pressed German workers and farmers as well as disillusioned radicals and reformers emigrated to the United States, the symbol of democratic liberalism in the world. They were joined by the first significant migration from Asia, as thousands of Chinese joined the gold rush to California and other strikes (page 277). This migration was part of a century-long phenomenon, as approximately fifty million Europeans, largely from rural areas, would migrate to the Western Hemisphere.

Although many Germans and Scandinavians arrived in modest straits, few were truly impoverished, and many could afford to buy a farm or start a business. Unlike the Irish, Germans tended to emigrate as families, and wherever they settled, they formed social, religious, and cultural organizations to maintain their language and customs. Whereas the Scandinavians, Dutch, and English immigrants were Protestant, half or more of the Germans were Catholic.

Factories came more and more to depend on immigrant labor, including children, since newcomers would work for lower wages and were less likely to protest harsh working conditions. The shift to an immigrant workforce could be seen most clearly in the textile industry, where by 1860 over half the workers in New England mills were foreign-born.

The sizable foreign-born population in many American cities severely strained urban resources. Immigrants who could barely make ends meet were forced to live in overcrowded, unheated tenement houses, damp cellars, and even shacks. Urban slums became notorious for crime and drinking, which took a heavy toll on families and the poor. In the eyes of many native-born Americans, immigrants were to blame for driving down factory wages and pushing American workers out of jobs. Overshadowing these complaints was a fear that America might not be able to **assimilate** the new groups, with their unfamiliar languages and customs. These fears precipitated an outburst of political **nativism** in the mid-1850s.

> **assimilate** to absorb a culturally distinct group into the dominant culture.
>
> **nativism** outlook championing the supremacy of "native" cultural traits and political rights over those of immigrants from different backgrounds.

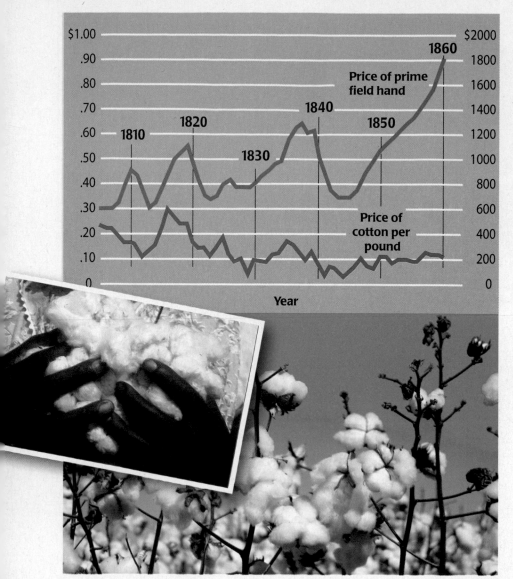

PRICES OF COTTON AND SLAVES

From 1815 to 1850 cotton and slave prices generally moved together, as southerners plowed their profits from growing cotton into buying more land and slaves. During the 1850s, however, the booming southern economy and bumper cotton crops drove the price of slaves steeply upward compared to cotton prices, squeezing slaveowners' profit margins and heightening southern anxieties about the future.

Chart labels: $1.00, .90, .80, .70, .60, .50, .40, .30, .20, .10, 0 (left axis); $2000, 1800, 1600, 1400, 1200, 1000, 800, 600, 400, 200, 0 (right axis); years 1810, 1820, 1830, 1840, 1850, 1860; "Price of prime field hand"; "Price of cotton per pound"; "Year"

for economic development, which they were convinced would enrich the North at southern expense. This attitude further weakened the South's political alliance with the West, which needed federal aid for transportation.

White southerners also feared that the new tide of immigration would shift the sectional balance of power. Most immigrants shunned the South, not wanting to compete with cheap slave labor. The lack of industry and the limited demand for skilled labor also shunted immigrants northward. As a result, the North surged even further ahead of the South in population, thereby strengthening its control of the House of Representatives and heightening southern concern that the North would rapidly settle the western territories.

Southern Complaints >> With British and northern factories buying cotton in large quantities, southern planters prospered in the 1850s. But instead of investing in machinery as northern commercial farmers had, white southerners invested in slaves. During the 1850s, the price of prime field hands reached record levels.

Despite southern prosperity the section's leaders repeatedly complained that the North had used its power over banking and commerce to convert the South into a colony. Storage and shipping charges, insurance, port fees, and commissions, which added some 20 percent to the cost of cotton and other commodities, went into the pockets of northern merchants, shippers, and bankers. The idea that the South was a colony of the North was inaccurate, but southern whites found it a convincing explanation of the North's growing wealth. More important, it reinforced their resistance to federal aid

✓ **REVIEW**

How did the new railroads affect urban and prairie environments? How did they increase sectional tensions?

THE POLITICAL REALIGNMENT OF THE 1850S

When Franklin Pierce (he pronounced it "Purse") assumed the presidency in 1853, he was only 48 years old, the youngest man yet to be elected president. He was also a supporter of the "Young America" movement of the Democratic party, which enthusiastically looked to spread democracy around the globe and annex additional territory to the United States.

The believers in Young America felt it idle to argue about slavery when the nation could be developing new resources. In 1853 Pierce did manage to conclude the Gadsden Purchase, thereby gaining control of about 45,000 square miles of Mexican desert, which contained the most practical southern route for a transcontinental railroad. He had no success with his major goal, acquiring Cuba, the rich sugar-producing island where slavery had once been important. In any case, he soon had his hands full with the proposals of another Democrat of the Young America stamp, Senator Stephen A. Douglas of Illinois.

The Kansas-Nebraska Act >> Known as the Little Giant, Douglas was ambitious, bursting with energy, and impatient to get things done. As chairman of the Senate's Committee on Territories, he hoped to organize federal lands west of Missouri as part of his program for economic development. And as a citizen of Illinois, he wanted Chicago selected as the eastern terminus of the proposed transcontinental railroad. To do so, the rest of the Louisiana Purchase

would have to be organized into territories, since any northern rail route would run through that region.

Under the terms of the Missouri Compromise of 1820 slavery was prohibited in this portion of the Louisiana Purchase (pages 182–183). Douglas had tried once to organize the area while keeping a ban on slavery—only to have his bill voted down by southern opposition in the Senate. In January 1854 he reintroduced the measure. This time, to obtain southern support, he omitted the prohibition on slavery that had been in effect for 34 years.

The bill created two territories: Kansas, directly west of Missouri, and a much larger Nebraska Territory, located west of Iowa and the Minnesota Territory. The Missouri Compromise was explicitly repealed. Instead, Douglas's doctrine of popular sovereignty was to determine the status of slavery in both territories, though it was left unclear whether residents of Kansas and Nebraska could prohibit slavery at any time or only at the time of statehood, as southerners insisted. It was widely assumed that Kansas would be a slave state and Nebraska a free state.

The Kansas-Nebraska Act outraged northern Democrats, Whigs, and Free Soilers alike. Critics rejected Douglas's contention that popular sovereignty would keep the

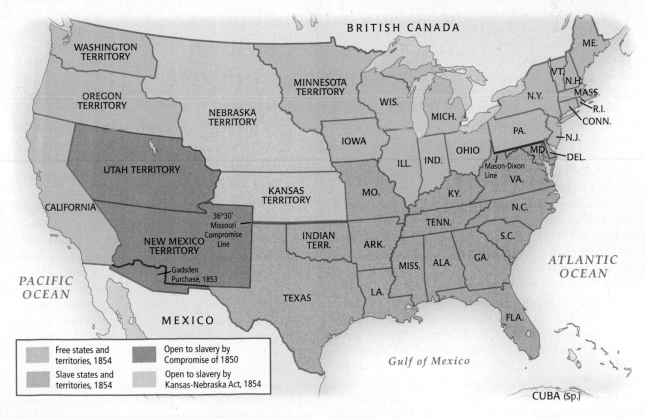

THE KANSAS-NEBRASKA ACT

When the Kansas-Nebraska Act of 1854 opened the remaining portion of the Louisiana Purchase to slavery under the doctrine of popular sovereignty, conflict between the two sections focused on control of Kansas, directly west of the slave state of Missouri.

territories free. The bill, they charged, was meant to give slaveholders—the "Slave Power"—territory previously consecrated to freedom. Most northern opponents of the bill focused on the expansion of slavery and the political threat of a Slave Power rather than the moral evil of slavery. Indignation swept the North, but the Senate passed the bill easily. The real fight came in the House, where the North held a large majority. President Pierce put intense pressure on his fellow northern Democrats to come along, and finally the bill passed by a narrow margin, 113 to 100. Pierce signed it on May 30, 1854.

The Collapse of the Second American Party System >> The furor over the Kansas-Nebraska Act laid bare the underlying tensions that had developed between the North and the South. These tensions put mounting pressure on the political parties, and in the 1850s the Jacksonian party system collapsed. Voters who had been loyal to one party for years, even decades, began switching allegiances. By the time the process of realignment was completed, a new party system had emerged, divided this time along clearly sectional lines.

In part, the old party system decayed because new problems had replaced the traditional economic issues of both Whigs and Democrats. The Whigs alienated many of their traditional Protestant supporters by openly seeking the support of Catholics and recent immigrants. Then, too, the growing agitation for the prohibition of alcohol divided both parties, especially the Whigs. Finally, both the Whigs and the Democrats were increasingly perceived as little more than corrupt engines of plunder. Many voters became disillusioned.

Thus the party system was already weak when the Kansas-Nebraska Act divided the two major parties along sectional lines. In such an unstable atmosphere, independent parties flourished. Antislavery veterans, who had earlier sparked the Liberty and Free Soil parties, united with Whigs and anti-Nebraska Democrats in the new antislavery Republican party. Their calculations were derailed, however, when another new party capitalized on fears aroused by the recent flood of immigrants.

The Know-Nothings >> In 1854 the American party, a secret nativist organization whose members were called Know-Nothings, suddenly emerged as a potent political force. (Its members, sworn to secrecy, had

been instructed to answer inquiries by replying, "I know nothing.") Taking as their slogan "Americans should rule America," Know-Nothings denounced illegal voting by immigrants, the rising crime and disorder in urban areas, and immigrants' heavy drinking. They were also strongly anti-Catholic and were convinced that the church's "undemocratic" hierarchy of bishops and archbishops was conspiring to undermine American democracy. Know-Nothings advocated lengthening the residency period for naturalization and ousting from office corrupt politicians who openly bid for foreign and Catholic votes.

The Know-Nothings won a series of remarkable victories in the 1854 elections. Their showing spelled doom for the Whigs, as party members deserted in droves to the Know-Nothings. With perhaps a million voters enrolled in its lodges in every state of the Union, Know-Nothing leaders confidently predicted in 1855 that they would elect the next president.

Yet only a year later—by the end of 1856—the party had collapsed as quickly as it had risen. Inexperienced leaders failed to enact the party's reform platform; but in the end, rising sectional tensions destroyed the party when it adopted a proslavery platform for the elections of 1856. Northern party members then flocked to the other new party, the Republicans. This party, unlike the Know-Nothings, had no base in the South. It intended to elect a president by sweeping the free states, which controlled a majority of the electoral votes.

> **Stephen Douglas's idea of popular sovereignty transformed the settlement of Kansas into a referendum on slavery in the territories. A race developed between northerners and southerners to settle Kansas first.**

The Republicans and Bleeding Kansas >>
At first, the Republican party made little headway in the North. Although it attracted a variety of Whigs, anti-Nebraska Democrats, and Free Soilers, many moderate Whigs and Democrats viewed the party as too radical.

Those attitudes changed on the heels of the alarming developments in Kansas. Most early settlers migrated to Kansas for the same reason other white Americans headed west: the chance to prosper in a new land. But Douglas's idea of popular sovereignty transformed the new settlement into a referendum on slavery in the territories. A race soon developed between northerners and southerners to settle Kansas first. To the proslavery residents of neighboring Missouri, free state communities like Lawrence seemed ominous threats. "We are playing for a mighty stake," former senator David Rice Atchison of Missouri insisted. "If we win, we carry slavery to the Pacific Ocean; if we fail we lose Missouri, Arkansas and Texas and all the territories; the game must be played boldly."

When the first Kansas elections were held in 1854 and 1855, Missourians poured over the border, seized the polls, and stuffed the ballot boxes. This massive fraud tarnished popular sovereignty at the outset and greatly aroused public opinion in the North. It also provided proslavery forces with a commanding majority in the Kansas legislature, where they enacted a strict legal code designed to intimidate antislavery settlers. This Kansas Code limited such time-honored rights as freedom of speech, impartial juries, and fair elections. Mobilized into action, the free-staters in the fall of 1855 organized a separate government, drafted a state constitution prohibiting slavery, and asked Congress to admit Kansas as a free state. In such a polarized situation, violence quickly broke out between the two factions, which culminated in the raid on Lawrence in May 1856 (see the chapter introduction).

The Caning of Charles Sumner >> Only
a few days before the proslavery attack on Lawrence, Republican senator Charles Sumner of Massachusetts delivered a scathing speech, "The Crime against Kansas." Sumner passionately condemned slavery and deliberately insulted the state of South Carolina and one of its senators. Preston S. Brooks, a member of Congress from South Carolina, was outraged that Sumner had insulted his relative and mocked his state.

Several days later, on May 22, Brooks strode into the Senate after it had adjourned, went up to Sumner, who was

seated at his desk, and proceeded to beat him over the head with a cane. The cane shattered into three pieces from the violence of the attack, but Brooks, swept up in the emotion of the moment, furiously continued hitting Sumner until the senator collapsed unconscious, drenched in blood.

Northerners were electrified to learn that a senator of the United States had been beaten unconscious in the Senate chamber. What caused them even greater consternation was southern reaction—for in his own region, Preston Brooks was lionized as a hero. Instantly, the Sumner caning breathed life into the fledgling Republican party. Its claims about "Bleeding Kansas" and the Slave Power now seemed credible.

The Election of 1856 >> In the face of the storm
over Kansas, the Democrats turned to James Buchanan of Pennsylvania as their presidential nominee. Buchanan's supreme qualification was having the good fortune to have been out of the country as minister to England when the Kansas-Nebraska Act was passed. The American party, split badly by the Kansas issue, nominated former president Millard Fillmore.

The Republicans chose John C. Frémont, a western explorer who had helped liberate California during the Mexican War. The party's platform denounced slavery as a "relic of barbarism" and demanded that Kansas be admitted as a free state. Throughout the summer the party hammered away on Bleeding Sumner and Bleeding Kansas.

A number of basic principles guided the Republican party, one of which was the ideal of free labor. Slavery degraded labor, Republicans argued, and would inevitably drive free labor out of the territories. Condemning the South as a stagnant, hierarchical, and economically backward region, Republicans praised the North as a fluid society of widespread opportunity where enterprising individuals could improve their lot. Stopping the expansion of slavery, in Republican eyes, would preserve this heritage of opportunity and economic independence for white Americans. Republicans also appealed to former Know-Nothings by criticizing the Catholic Church, particularly its political activity, and by being much more favorable to temperance.

SOUTHERN CHIVALRY — ARGUMENT versus CLUB'S.

⌃ The caning of Senator Charles Sumner of Massachusetts by Representative Preston S. Brooks of South Carolina inflamed public opinion. In this northern cartoon the fallen Sumner, a martyr to free speech, raises his pen against Brooks's club. Rushing to capitalize on the furor, printmakers did not know what the obscure Brooks looked like and thus had to devise ingenious ways of portraying the incident. In this print, Brooks's face is hidden by his raised arm.

Also important was the moral opposition to slavery, strengthened by such works as Harriet Beecher Stowe's *Uncle Tom's Cabin.* Republican speakers and editors stressed that slavery was a moral wrong, that it was incompatible with the ideals of the Republic and Christianity. "Never forget," Republican leader Abraham Lincoln declared on one occasion, "that we have before us this whole matter of the right and wrong of slavery in this Union, though the immediate question is as to its spreading out into new Territories and States."

More negatively, Republicans gained support by shifting their attacks from slavery itself to the Slave Power, or the political influence of the planter class. Pointing to the Sumner assault and the incidents in Kansas, Republicans contended that the Slave Power had set out to destroy the liberties of white northerners. Just as the nation's founders had battled against tyranny, aristocracy, and minority rule in the Revolution, so the North confronted the unrepublican Slave Power. "If our government, for the sake of Slavery, is to be perpetually the representative of a minority," argued the *Cincinnati Commercial,* "it may continue republican in form, but the substance of its republicanism has departed."

In the election Buchanan all but swept the South (losing only Maryland to Fillmore) and won enough free states to push him over the top. Still, the violence in Kansas and Sumner's caning nearly lofted Frémont into the presidency. Had he carried Pennsylvania plus one more free state, he would have been elected. For the first time in American history, an antislavery party based entirely in the North threatened to elect a president and snap the bonds of union.

 REVIEW

What events led the political realignment of the 1850s to favor the Know-Nothings at first? What events led the Republicans to emerge as the more powerful party?

THE WORSENING CRISIS

James Buchanan was one of the most experienced men ever elected president: he had served in Congress, in the cabinet, and in the foreign service. Moderates in both sections hoped that the new president would thwart Republicans in the North and secessionists of the Deep South, popularly known as "fire-eaters." Throughout his career, however, Buchanan had taken the southern position on sectional matters, and he proved insensitive to the concerns of northern Democrats. Moreover, on March 6,

1857, only two days after Buchanan's inauguration, the Supreme Court rendered one of the most controversial decisions in its history.

The Dred Scott Decision >> The owner of
a Missouri slave named Dred Scott had taken him to live for several years in Illinois, a free state, and in what is now Minnesota, where slavery had been banned by the Missouri Compromise. Eventually the owner returned with Scott to Missouri. Scott sued for his freedom on the grounds that his residence in a free state and a free territory had made him free, and his case ultimately went to the Supreme Court. Two northern justices joined all five southern members in ruling 7 to 2 that Scott remained a slave. The majority opinion was written by Chief Justice Roger Taney of Maryland.

Wanting to strengthen the judicial protection of slavery, Taney ruled that African Americans could not be and never had been citizens of the United States. Instead, he insisted that they were "regarded as beings of an inferior order" at the time the Constitution was adopted, "so far inferior that they had no rights which the white man was bound to respect." In addition, the Court ruled that the Missouri Compromise was unconstitutional. Congress, it declared, had no power to ban slavery from any territory of the United States.

While southerners rejoiced at this result Republicans denounced the Court for rejecting their party's main principle, that Congress should prohibit slavery in all territories. "We know the court . . . has often over-ruled its own decisions," Abraham Lincoln observed, "and we shall do what we can to have it over-rule this." For Republicans, the decision foreshadowed the spread of slavery throughout the West and even the nation.

But the decision also was a blow to Douglas's moderate solution of popular sovereignty. If Congress had no power to prohibit slavery in a territory, how could it authorize a territorial legislature to do so? Although the Court did not rule on this point, the clear implication of the Dred Scott decision was that popular sovereignty was also unconstitutional. The Court, in effect, had endorsed John C. Calhoun's radical view that slavery was legal in all the territories. In so doing, the Court, which had intended to settle the question of slavery in the territories, instead pushed the political debate toward new extremes.

Although the nation grappled with the Dred Scott decision, an economic depression aggravated sectional conflict. The Panic of 1857 was nowhere near as severe as the depression of 1839–1843. But the psychological results were far-reaching, for the South remained relatively untouched. With the price of cotton and other southern commodities still high, southern secessionists hailed the panic as proof that an independent southern nation could survive economically. Insisting that cotton sustained the international economy, James Henry Hammond, a senator from South Carolina, boasted: "No, you dare not make war on cotton. No power on earth dares to make war on it. Cotton is king."

The Lecompton Constitution >>
Although the Dred Scott decision and economic depression weakened the bonds of the Union, Kansas remained at the center of the political stage. In June 1857, when the territory elected delegates to draft a state constitution, free-staters boycotted the election, giving proslavery forces control of the convention that met in Lecompton. The delegates promptly drafted a constitution that made slavery legal. Even more boldly, they scheduled a referendum in which voters could not vote against either the constitution or slavery. Once again, free-staters boycotted the election, and the Lecompton constitution was approved.

President Buchanan had pledged earlier that there would be a free and fair vote on the Lecompton constitution. But the outcome offered Buchanan the unexpected opportunity to create one additional slave state and thereby satisfy his southern supporters by pushing the Lecompton constitution through Congress. This was too much for Douglas, who broke party ranks and denounced the Lecompton constitution as a fraud. Although the administration prevailed in the Senate without Douglas's support, the House rejected the constitution. In a compromise, Congress returned the constitution to Kansas for another vote. This time it was decisively defeated, 11,300 to 1788. No doubt remained that as soon as Kansas had sufficient population, it would come into the Union as a free state.

The attempt to force slavery on the people of Kansas drove many conservative northerners into the Republican party. And Douglas now found himself assailed by the southern wing of his party. On top of that, in the summer of 1858, he faced a desperate fight for reelection to the Senate in his race against Republican Abraham Lincoln.

The Lincoln-Douglas Debates >>
"He is the strong man of his party . . . and the best stump speaker, with his droll ways and dry jokes, in the West," Douglas commented when he learned of Lincoln's nomination to oppose him. "He is as honest as he is shrewd, and if I beat him my victory will be hardly won." Tall (6 feet, 4 inches) and gangly, Lincoln had an awkward manner as he spoke, yet his logic and sincerity carried the audience with him. His sentences had none of the oratorical flourishes common in that day. "If we could first know *where* we are, and *whither* we are tending, we could then better judge *what* to do, and *how* to do it," Lincoln began, in accepting his party's

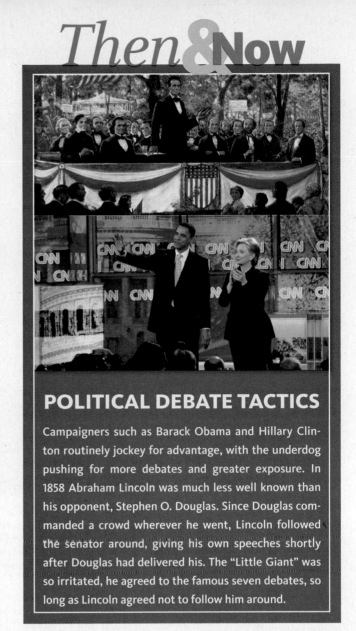

POLITICAL DEBATE TACTICS

Campaigners such as Barack Obama and Hillary Clinton routinely jockey for advantage, with the underdog pushing for more debates and greater exposure. In 1858 Abraham Lincoln was much less well known than his opponent, Stephen O. Douglas. Since Douglas commanded a crowd wherever he went, Lincoln followed the senator around, giving his own speeches shortly after Douglas had delivered his. The "Little Giant" was so irritated, he agreed to the famous seven debates, so long as Lincoln agreed not to follow him around.

nomination for senator in 1858. He then commented on a proverb from the Bible:

> "A house divided against itself cannot stand."
> I believe this government cannot endure, permanently half *slave* and half *free*.
> I do not expect the Union to be *dissolved*—
> I do not expect the house to *fall*—but I *do* expect it will cease to be divided.
> It will become *all* one thing, or *all* the other.
> Either the *opponents* of slavery, will arrest the further spread of it, and place it where the public mind shall rest in the belief that it is in the course of ultimate extinction; or its *advocates* will push it forward, till it shall become alike lawful in all the States, *old* as well as *new*—*North* as well as *South*.

The message echoed through the hall and across the pages of the national press.

Born in the slave state of Kentucky, Lincoln had grown up mostly in southern Indiana and central Illinois. Yet his intense ambition lifted him above the backwoods from which he came. He compensated for a lack of schooling through disciplined self-education, and he became a shrewd courtroom lawyer of respectable social standing. Known for his sense of humor, he was nonetheless subject to fits of acute depression.

Lincoln's first love was always politics. A fervent admirer of Henry Clay and his economic program, he became a Whig and then, after the party's collapse, joined the Republicans and became one of their key leaders in Illinois. Lincoln challenged Douglas to discuss the issues of slavery and the sectional controversy in a series of seven debates.

In the campaign Douglas sought to portray Lincoln as a radical who preached sectional warfare. The nation *could* endure half slave and half free, Douglas declared, as long as states and territories were left alone to regulate their own affairs. Lincoln countered by insisting that the spread of slavery was a blight on the Republic. Even though Douglas had voted against the Lecompton constitution, he could not be counted on to oppose slavery's expansion, for he admitted that he didn't care whether slavery was voted "down or up."

In the debate held at Freeport, Illinois, Lincoln asked Douglas how under the Dred Scott decision the people of a territory could lawfully exclude slavery before statehood. Douglas answered, with what became known as the **Freeport**

Freeport Doctrine Stephen A. Douglas's response to Lincoln (at Freeport, Illinois) that even though the Dred Scott decision forbade Congress from banning slavery in any territory, a territorial government might effectively do so by refusing to pass a slave code.

Doctrine, that slaveowners would never bring their slaves into an area where slavery was not legally protected. Therefore, Douglas explained, if the people of a territory refused to pass a slave code, slavery would never be established there.

In a close race, the legislature elected Douglas to another term in the Senate.[1] But on the national scene,

⌃ Superb debaters, Douglas (*left*) and Lincoln (*right*) nevertheless had very different speaking styles. The deep-voiced Douglas was constantly on the attack, drawing on his remarkable memory and showering points like buckshot in all directions. Lincoln, who had a high-pitched voice, developed his arguments more carefully and methodically, and he relied on his sense of humor and unmatched ability as a storyteller to drive his points home to the audience.

southern Democrats angrily repudiated him and condemned the Freeport Doctrine. And although Lincoln lost, his impressive performance marked him as a possible presidential contender for 1860.

The Beleaguered South >> While northerners increasingly feared that the Slave Power was conspiring to extend slavery into the free states, southerners worried that the "Black Republicans" would hem them in and undermine their political power.

The very factors that brought prosperity during the 1850s stimulated the South's sense of crisis. As the price of slaves rose sharply the proportion of southerners who owned slaves had dropped almost a third since 1830. At the same time California and Kansas had been closed to southern slaveholders—unfairly, in their eyes. Finally, Douglas's clever claim that a territory could effectively outlaw slavery using the Freeport Doctrine seemed to negate the Dred Scott decision that slavery was legal in all the territories.

Several possible solutions to the South's internal crisis had failed. Agricultural reform to restore worn-out lands

[1] State legislatures elected senators until 1913, when the Seventeenth Amendment was adopted. Although Lincoln and Douglas both campaigned for the office, Illinois voters actually voted for candidates for the legislature who were pledged to one of the senatorial candidates.

THE ROAD TO WAR

In 1857 John Brown—the abolitionist firebrand—had returned to the East from Kansas, consumed with the idea of attacking slavery in the South itself. Financed by a number of prominent northern reformers, Brown gathered 21 followers, including 5 free blacks, in hope of fomenting a slave insurrection. On the night of October 16, 1859, his band seized the unguarded federal armory at Harpers Ferry in Virginia. But no slaves rallied to Brown's standard: few lived in the area to begin with. Before long the raiders found themselves surrounded and holed up in the town. Charging with bayonets fixed, federal troops commanded by Colonel Robert E. Lee soon captured Brown and his raiders. On December 2, 1859, Virginia hanged Brown for treason.

Brown's raid at Harpers Ferry was yet another blow weakening the forces of compromise within the nation. Although the invasion itself was a dismal failure, the old man knew how to bear himself with a martyr's dignity. Republicans made haste to denounce Brown's raid, lest they be tarred as radicals, but other northerners were less cautious. Ralph Waldo Emerson described Brown as a "saint, whose martyrdom will make the gallows as glorious as the cross." While only a minority of northerners endorsed Brown, southerners were shocked by such displays of sympathy. "I have always been a fervid Union man," one North Carolina resident wrote, "but I confess the endorsement of the Harpers Ferry outrage has shaken my fidelity and I am willing to take the chances of every probable evil that may arise from disunion, sooner than submit any longer to Northern insolence and Northern outrage."

had made significant headway only in Virginia and Maryland. Elsewhere the rewards of a single-crop economy were too great to persuade southern farmers to adopt new methods. Another alternative—bringing industry to the South—had also failed to take root. Finally, private military expeditions in Latin America, which were designed to strengthen the South by adding slave territory to the United States, came to naught.

The South's growing sense of isolation made this crisis more acute. By the 1850s slavery had been abolished throughout most of the Americas, and in the United States the South's political power was steadily shrinking. Only the expansion of slavery and the admission of new slave states held any promise of preserving the South's political power and protecting its way of life. "The truth is," fumed one Alabama politician, ". . . the South is excluded from the common territories of the Union. The right of expansion claimed to be a necessity of her continued existence, is practically and effectively denied the South."

✔ REVIEW

How did the Dred Scott decision and Stephen A. Douglas's Freeport Doctrine affect the debate over whether slavery could exist in the territories?

Opinion

Was the Civil War an "irresistible conflict," as Senator William Seward of New York insisted, or could it have been avoided?

A Sectional Election >> When Congress convened in December, there were ominous signs everywhere of the growing sectional rift. Intent on destroying Douglas's Freeport Doctrine, southern radicals demanded a congressional slave code to protect slavery in the territories. To northern Democrats such a platform spelled political death. As one Indiana Democrat put it, "We cannot carry a single congressional district on that doctrine in the state."

At the Democratic convention in April, southern radicals boldly pressed their demand for a federal slave code. Instead the convention adopted the Douglas

⌄ The Civil War was the first conflict whose major battles routinely involved more than 100,000 troops, and casualties soared beyond the scale Americans experienced in the U.S.–Mexican War. The battle of Antietam, fought in 1862, produced almost 23,000 casualties, the bloodiest single day of the war. A group of Confederate soldiers are shown where they fell along the Hagerstown Pike. Said one Union officer of the fighting: "Men, I cannot say fell; they were knocked out of the ranks by dozens."

The arrival of fresh troops, however, enabled the Confederates to regroup. Among the reinforcements who rushed to Henry Hill was 19-year-old Randolph McKim of Baltimore. A student at the University of Virginia, McKim joined the First Maryland Infantry as a private when Abraham Lincoln imposed martial law in his home state. "The cause of the South had become identified with liberty itself," he explained. The arrival of the First Maryland and other reinforcements in the late afternoon turned the tide of battle. The faltering Confederate line held, and Union troops began to withdraw.

But with retreat came confusion. Discipline dissolved and the army degenerated into a stampeding mob. As they fled, terrified troops threw away their equipment, shoved aside officers who tried to stop them, and raced frantically past the wagons and artillery pieces that clogged the road. All the next day in a drizzling rain, mud-spattered troops straggled into the capital in complete disorder. William Russell, an English reporter, asked one pale officer where they were coming from. "Well, sir, I guess we're all coming out of Virginny as far as we can, and pretty well whipped too," he replied. Joining the stampede was Jim Tinkham, who confessed he would have continued on to Boston if he had not been stopped by a guard in Washington.

The rout at Bull Run sobered the North. Gone were dreams of ending the war with one glorious battle. Gone was the illusion that 75,000 volunteers serving three months would be sufficient. As one perceptive observer noted, "We have undertaken to make war without in the least knowing how." Having cast off his earlier misconceptions, a newly determined Jim Tinkham reenlisted for a three-year hitch.

Still, it was not surprising that both sides underestimated the magnitude of the conflict. Warfare as it had evolved in Europe consisted largely of maneuverings that took relatively few lives, respected private property, and left civilians largely unharmed. The Civil War, however, was the first war whose major battles routinely involved more than 100,000 troops. So many combatants could be equipped only through the use of factory-produced weaponry, they could be moved and supplied only with the help of railroads, and they could be sustained only through the concerted efforts of civilian society as a whole. The morale of the population, the quality of political leadership, and the use of industrial and economic might were all critical to the outcome. Quite simply, the Civil War was the first total war in history. «

THE DEMANDS OF TOTAL WAR

When the war began the North had an enormous advantage in manpower and industrial capacity. The Union's population was 2.5 times larger; it contained more railroad track and rolling stock and possessed more than 10 times the industrial capacity.

From a modern perspective the South's attempt to resist against such odds seems hopeless. Yet this view indicates how much the conception of war has changed. European observers, who knew the strength and resources of the two sides, believed that the Confederacy could never be conquered. Indeed, the South enjoyed definite strategic advantages. To be victorious it did not need to invade the North—only to defend its own land and prevent the North from destroying its armies. Southern soldiers knew the topography of their home country better, and

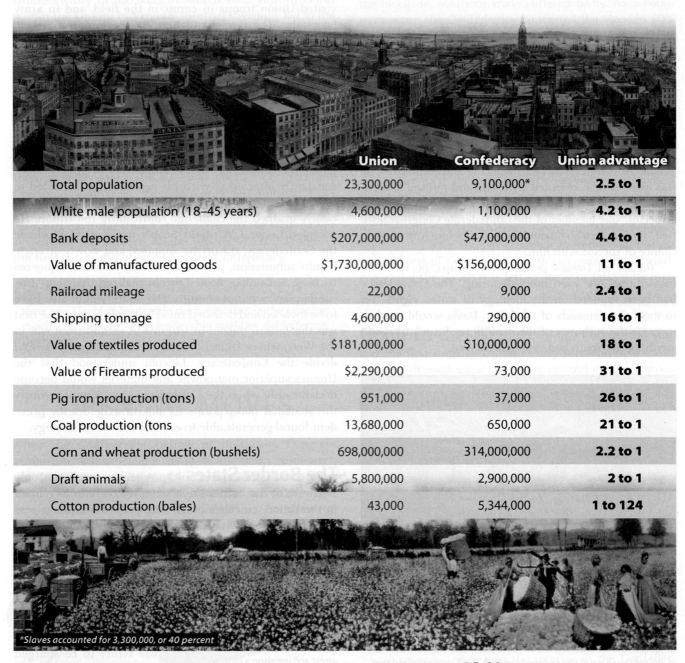

	Union	Confederacy	Union advantage
Total population	23,300,000	9,100,000*	**2.5 to 1**
White male population (18–45 years)	4,600,000	1,100,000	**4.2 to 1**
Bank deposits	$207,000,000	$47,000,000	**4.4 to 1**
Value of manufactured goods	$1,730,000,000	$156,000,000	**11 to 1**
Railroad mileage	22,000	9,000	**2.4 to 1**
Shipping tonnage	4,600,000	290,000	**16 to 1**
Value of textiles produced	$181,000,000	$10,000,000	**18 to 1**
Value of Firearms produced	$2,290,000	73,000	**31 to 1**
Pig iron production (tons)	951,000	37,000	**26 to 1**
Coal production (tons	13,680,000	650,000	**21 to 1**
Corn and wheat production (bushels)	698,000,000	314,000,000	**2.2 to 1**
Draft animals	5,800,000	2,900,000	**2 to 1**
Cotton production (bales)	43,000	5,344,000	**1 to 124**

*Slaves accounted for 3,300,000, or 40 percent

RESOURCES OF THE UNION AND THE CONFEDERACY, 1861

(Source: U.S. Census 1860 and E. B. Long, *The Civil War Day by Day* [New York: Doubleday, 1971], p. 723.)

Face Value?

"Act of Feby 25, 1862"

Why is Alexander Hamilton on the bill?

"Confederate States of America will pay to the bearer on demand"

Why is this man on the bill? (Hint: Chapter 14 includes his photograph.)

Hand-signed and hand-numbered

A government at war can survive only if it maintains its credit—not only with its bankers but with its citizens. Both the Union and the Confederacy issued paper money to finance the war, and by examining the bills' designs, historians can appreciate the efforts to portray the issuers as creditworthy. The Union note uses Alexander Hamilton to vouch for its reliability—the republic's first treasury secretary, who during the 1790s stabilized the nation's shaky finances. It announces the act of Congress that allows the government to issue the notes: the Legal Tender Act,

passed February 25, 1862. And the intricate engraving and red treasury seal made the bill harder to counterfeit. The Confederacy had more difficulty issuing bills because few skilled engravers lived in the South. To help prevent counterfeiting, the Confederacy followed the older tradition of signing each bill individually, employing as many as 200 secretaries to do the tedious work. (The Union's signatures were printed.) But by war's end so many Confederate notes had been issued that they were carted about in wheelbarrows to pay the hugely inflated prices for goods.

In the end mere symbols of credit could not obliterate the realities on the ground.

THINKING CRITICALLY

The fine print located above the Confederate promise to "pay on demand" reads "Six months after a ratification of a Treaty of Peace between The Confederate States & The United States of America." What effect does this condition have? Who are the people portrayed at the center of the Confederate bill? Why choose to include them?

Confederate Finance and Government >>

The most serious domestic problem the Confederate government faced was finance, for which officials at Richmond never developed a satisfactory program. Only in 1863 did the government begin levying a **graduated income tax** (from 1 to 15 percent) and a series of excise taxes. Most controversial, the government resorted to a tax-in-kind on farmers that, after exempting a certain portion, took one-tenth of their crops. Even more unpopular was the policy of impressment, which allowed the army to seize private property for its own use, often with little or no compensation.

graduated income tax tax based on a percentage of an individual's income, the percentage increasing as total income increases.

Above all, the Confederacy financed the war effort simply by printing paper money not backed by specie, some $1.5 billion, which amounted to three times more than the federal government issued. The result was runaway inflation, so that by 1865 a Confederate dollar was worth only 1.7 cents in gold and prices had soared to 92 times their prewar base. Prices were highest in Richmond, where flour sold for $275 a barrel by early 1864 and coats for $350 each.

In politics even more than finance, the Confederacy exercised far greater powers than those of the federal government before 1861. Indeed, Jefferson Davis strove to meet the demands of total war by transforming the South into a centralized, national state. He sought to limit state authority over military units, and in April 1862 the

Confederacy passed the first national **conscription** law in American history. The same year, the Confederate Congress authorized Davis to invoke martial law and suspend the writ of habeas corpus.

> **conscription** act of compulsory enrollment for military service, as opposed to a voluntary enlistment.

Critics protested that Davis was destroying states' rights, the driving principle of the Confederacy. Intent on preserving states' traditional powers, Confederate governors obstructed the draft and retained military supplies. When President Davis suspended the writ of habeas corpus, his own vice president, Alexander H. Stephens, accused him of aiming at a dictatorship. Davis used those powers for a limited time and only with the permission of Congress, yet in practice it made little difference whether the writ was suspended or not. With disloyalty a greater problem than in the Union, the Confederate army arrested thousands of civilians.

But the Confederate draft, more than any other measure, produced an outcry. As one Georgia leader complained, "It's a notorious fact if a man has influential friends—or a little money to spare he will never be enrolled." Most controversially, the draft exempted from service one white man on every plantation with 20 or more slaves (later reduced to 15). This law was designed to preserve control of the slave population, but more and more nonslaveholders complained that it was a rich man's war and a poor man's fight.

Hardship and Suffering >>

By 1864 food shortages had become so severe that southerners concocted various substitutes: parched corn in place of coffee, strained blackberries in place of vinegar. Scarcity bred speculation, hoarding, and spiraling prices. The high prices and food shortages led to riots, most seriously in Richmond in April 1863, when about 300 women and children chanting "Bread!" looted stores.

As always, war corroded the discipline and the order of society. Speculation was rampant, gambling halls were crowded with revelers seeking relief, and many southerners spent money in frenzied haste. Even in the army theft became common, and in Richmond, the House of Representatives was robbed and Jefferson Davis's favorite horse stolen.

The frantic effort to escape war's grim reality led to a forced cheer among southern civilians. "The cities are gayer than before the war," one refugee reported, "—parties every night in Richmond, suppers costing ten and twenty thousand dollars." Walking home at night after spending several hours at the bedside of a dying soldier, Judith McGuire passed a house echoing with laughter, music, and dancing. "The revulsion was sickening," she wrote in her diary. "I . . . felt shocked that our own Virginians, at such a time, should remind me of scenes which we were wont to think only belonged to . . . foreign society." The war was a cancer that ate away not only at southern society but at the southern soul itself.

 REVIEW

In what ways did the Confederacy, which championed states' rights, become a more centralized, national government?

THE UNION HOME FRONT

Since the war was fought mostly on southern soil, northern civilians rarely felt its effects directly. Yet to be effective, the North's economic resources had to be organized and mobilized.

Government Finances and the Economy >>

To begin with, the North required a comprehensive system to finance its massive campaign. Taxing the populace was one obvious means, and taxes paid for 21 percent of Union war expenses, compared with only 1 percent of the Confederacy's. In August 1861 Congress levied the first federal income tax, of 3 percent on all incomes over $800 a year. When that, along with increased tariff duties, proved insufficient, Congress enacted a comprehensive tax law in 1862 that for the first time brought the tax collector into every northern household.

The government also borrowed heavily, through the sale of $2.2 billion in **bonds.** It financed the rest of the war's cost by issuing paper money. In all, the Union printed $431 million in greenbacks (so named because of their color on one side). Congress also instituted a national banking system, allowing nationally chartered banks to issue notes backed by U.S. bonds. By taxing state bank notes out of circulation, Congress for the first time created a uniform national currency.

> **bonds** certificates of debt issued by a government or corporation promising to repay the buyers of the bonds their original investment, plus interest, by a specified date of maturity.

During the war the Republican-controlled Congress encouraged economic development. Tariffs to protect industry from foreign competition rose to an average rate of 47 percent, compared to 19 percent in 1860. To encourage development of the West, the Homestead Act of 1862 granted 160 acres of public land—the size of the traditional American family farm—to anyone (including women) who settled and improved the land for five years. In addition, the Land Grant College Act of 1862 donated the proceeds from certain land sales to finance public colleges and universities. This aid was especially crucial in promoting higher education in the West.

A Rich Man's War >>

Over the course of the war the government purchased more than $1 billion worth of goods and services. In response to this heavy demand, the economy boomed and business and agriculture prospered. Since prices rose faster than wages, workers' real income dropped almost 30 percent, which meant that the working class paid a disproportionate share of financing the war.

The Republican belief that government should play a major role in the economy also fostered a cozy relationship between business and politics. In the rush to profit from government contracts, some suppliers succumbed to the temptation to sell inferior goods at inflated prices. Uniforms made of "shoddy"— bits of unused thread and recycled cloth—were fobbed off in such numbers that the word became an adjective describing inferior quality.

Stocks and dividends rose with the economy, speculation during the last two years of the war became particularly feverish, and the fortunes made went toward the purchase of showy luxuries. Like Richmond, Washington became the symbol of this moral decay. Prostitution, drinking, and corruption reached epidemic proportions in the capital, and social festivities became the means to shut out the numbing horror of the casualty lists.

> Uniforms made of "shoddy"— bits of unused thread and recycled cloth—were fobbed off in such numbers that the word became an adjective describing inferior quality.

Women and the Workforce >>

Even more than in the South, the war opened new opportunities for northern women. Countless wives ran farms while their husbands were away at war. One traveler in Iowa reported, "I met more women driving teams on the road and saw more at work in the fields than men." The war also stimulated the shift to mechanization: by 1865 three times as many reapers and harvesters were in use as in 1861. Beyond the farm, women filled approximately 100,000 new jobs in industry. As in the South they also worked as clerks in the expanding government bureaucracy.

The war also allowed women to enter and eventually dominate the profession of nursing. Led by Drs. Emily and Elizabeth Blackwell, Dorothea Dix, and Mary Ann Bickerdyke, women fought the bureaucratic inefficiency of the army medical corps. Their service in the hospital wards reduced the hostility to women in medicine.

One nurse was Clara Barton, who later founded the Red Cross. During the battle of Fredericksburg, she worked in a battlefield hospital. She later recalled that as she rose from the side of one soldier, "I wrung the blood from the bottom of my clothing, before I could step, for the weight about my feet." She steeled herself at the sight of amputated arms and legs casually tossed in piles outside the front door as the surgeons cut away. Sleeping in a tent nearby, she drove herself to the brink of exhaustion until the last patients were transferred to permanent hospitals.

Civil Liberties and Dissent >>

In mobilizing the northern war effort, Lincoln did not hesitate to curb dissenters. Shortly after the firing on Fort Sumter, he suspended the writ of habeas corpus in specified areas, which allowed the indefinite detention of anyone suspected of disloyalty or activity against the war. Although the Constitution permitted such suspension in time of rebellion or invasion, Lincoln did so without consulting Congress (unlike President Davis), and he used his power far more broadly, expanding it in 1862 to cover the entire North for cases involving antiwar activities. The president also decreed that those arrested under its provisions could be tried in a military court. Eventually more than 20,000 individuals were arrested, most of whom were never brought to trial.

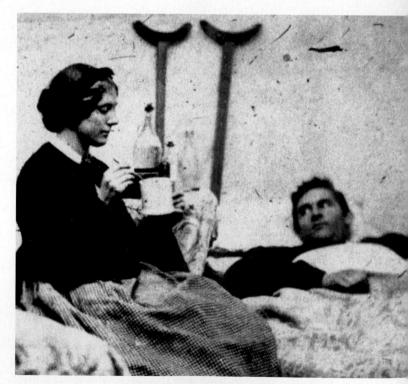

⚑ A nurse tends a wounded Union soldier in a military hospital in Nashville, Tennessee. Despite the opposition of army doctors, hundreds of female volunteers worked in army hospitals for each side.

HOW FREE BALLOT IS PROTECTED!

⌃ This anti-Republican cartoon from Philadelphia expresses the fears of many Copperhead Democrats that the war for the Union had been subverted by becoming a war on slavery. A caricatured black soldier tries to prevent a legless Union veteran from voting for General McClellan, Lincoln's opponent in the election of 1864. The election clerk beside the stuffed ballot box is told to "pretend you see nothing" of the ballot stuffing.

Democrats attacked Lincoln as a tyrant bent on destroying the Constitution. After the war the Supreme Court, in *Ex parte Milligan* (1866), struck down the military conviction of a civilian accused of plotting to free Confederate prisoners of war. The Court ruled that as long as the regular courts were open, civilians could not be tried by military tribunals.

Republicans labeled those who opposed the war **Copperheads**, conjuring up the image of a venomous snake waiting to strike the Union. Copperheads constituted the extreme peace wing of the Democratic party. They condemned the draft as an attack on individual freedom and an instrument of special privilege.

> **Copperhead** derogatory term used by Republicans to label northern Democrats who opposed the war policies of the Lincoln administration and advocated a negotiated peace.

According to the provisions enacted in 1863 a person would be exempt from the present draft by paying a commutation fee of $300, about a year's wages for a worker or an ordinary farmer. Or those drafted could hire a substitute, the cost of which was beyond the reach of all but the wealthy. In July 1863 largely Irish workers in New York City rose in anger against the draft. By the time order was restored four days later, at least 105 people had been killed, the worst loss of life from any riot in American history.

✔ **REVIEW**

How did the war affect women in the workforce? How were civil liberties compromised?

GONE TO BE A SOLDIER

Marcus Spiegel, the son of a rabbi, came to the United States after the German revolution of 1848 failed. A naturalized citizen when the war began, Spiegel considered it his

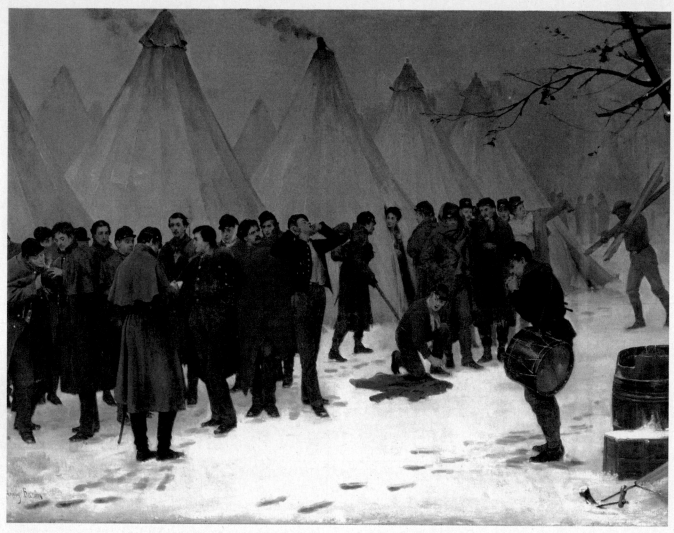

^ Reveille rouses drowsy Union soldiers on a wintry morning as a drummer boy warms his hands. Instead of the glory they expected, reveille, roll call, and drill constituted Civil War soldiers' usual camp routine. A hired black laborer is already at work as the troops awaken.

duty to preserve the Union for his children, so he enlisted and eventually rose to the rank of colonel. He did not go to war to end slavery and flatly proclaimed that black people were not "worth fighting for." But after seeing slavery first hand, his views changed, and by 1864 he was "in favor of doing away with the institution of Slavery." He assured his wife that "this is no hasty conclusion but a deep conviction." A few weeks later Spiegel died while fighting in Louisiana.

By war's end about two million men had served the Union cause and another million the Confederate. They were mostly young, with almost 40 percent of entering soldiers 21 years of age or younger. They were not drawn disproportionately from the poor, and in both North and South, farmers and farm laborers accounted for the largest number of recruits.

Discipline >> The near-holiday atmosphere of the war's early months soon gave way to dull routine. Men from rural areas, accustomed to the freedom of the farm,

complained about the endless recurrence of reveille, roll call, and drill. "When this war is over," one Rebel promised, "I will whip the man that says 'fall in' to me." Troops in neither army cared for the spit and polish of regular army men. "They keep us very strict here," noted one Illinois soldier. "It is the most like a prison of any place I ever saw."

By modern standards training was minimal and discipline lax in both armies. Troops from rural families found it harder to adjust to army routine than did urban soldiers, especially factory workers, who were more familiar with impersonal organizations and used to greater social control. Many southerners were "not used to control of any sort," one Rebel noted, "and were not disposed to obey anyone except for good and sufficient reason given." Manifesting strong feelings of equality that clashed with military hierarchy, Yanks and Rebs alike complained about officers' privileges and had no special respect for rank. "The boys recognized no superiors, except in the line of legitimate duty," an Indiana private explained. The Union discontinued the election of lower officers, but this tradition was retained in the Confederate army, further undermining discipline, since those known as strict disciplinarians were eventually defeated.

Camp Life >>

On average, soldiers spent 50 days in camp for every day in battle. Camp life was often unhealthy as well as unpleasant. Poor sanitation, miserable food, exposure, and primitive medical care contributed to widespread sickness and disease. It was a common belief that if a fellow went to the hospital, "you might as well say good bye." Conditions were even worse in the Confederate hospitals, for the Union blockade produced a shortage of medical supplies. Twice as many soldiers died from dysentery, typhoid, and other diseases as from wounds.

The boredom of camp life, the horrors of battle, and the influence of an all-male society all corrupted morals. Swearing and heavy drinking were common and gambling was pervasive, especially immediately after payday. Prostitutes flooded the camps of both armies. Yet with death so near, some soldiers also sought solace in religion, especially in Confederate camps. A wave of revivals swept their ranks during the last two winters of the war, producing between 100,000 and 200,000 conversions. Significantly, the first major revivals occurred after the South's twin defeats at Vicksburg and Gettysburg. Then, too, as battle after battle thinned Confederate ranks, the prospect of death loomed increasingly large.

The Environment of Battle >>

As in all modern wars, technology revolutionized the conditions under which Civil War soldiers fought. Smoothbore muskets, which at first served as the basic infantry weapon, gave way to the rifle, so named because of the grooves etched into the barrel to give a bullet spin. The percussion cap rendered a rifle serviceable in wet weather. More important, the new weapon had an effective range of 400 yards—five times greater than that of the old musket. As a result, soldiers fought each other from greater distances and battles produced many more casualties. Under such conditions, the defense became a good deal stronger than the offense. Although larger artillery pieces were too inaccurate to effectively support attacking troops, they proved deadly when fired at close range against advancing infantry.

The face of war left gashes on the landscape as well. As armies of a hundred thousand marched and massed, they dug trenches, threw up breastworks, fouled streams and fields with waste, plundered nearby farms for supplies, ripped down fences for firewood. At battle sites such as The Wilderness, fires often burned out of control. Wounded soldiers, unable to move, were roasted alive. Cities under siege, such as Vicksburg, Atlanta, Charleston, and Richmond, were bombarded and burned. Animals died in great numbers (perhaps a million and a half horses alone), not only from bullets and bombs but also from disease and overwork. In the South, not only armies devoured hogs but a cholera epidemic decimated many herds.

As the haze of gunfire covered the land and the spray of bullets mimicked rain pattering through the trees, soldiers lost any of their romantic notions about war. Men witnessed horrors they had never envisioned and choked from the stench of decaying flesh. They knew their efforts to convey to those back home the gruesome truth of combat were inadequate. "No tongue can tell, no mind can conceive, no pen portray the horrible sights I witnessed this morning," a Union soldier wrote after Antietam. And yet they tried.

An Ohio soldier at Antietam (23,000 casualties), two days after the fighting: "The smell was offul . . . there was about 5 or 6,000 dead bodes decaying over the field . . . I could have walked on the boddees all most from one end too the other." A Georgian, the day after Chancellorsville (30,000 casualties): "It looked more like a slaughter pen than anything else. . . . The shrieks and groans of the wounded . . . was heart rending beyond all description." A Maine soldier who fought at Gettysburg (50,000 casualties): "I have Seen . . . men rolling in their own blood, Some Shot in one place, Some another. . . . our dead lay in the road and the Rebels in their hast to leave dragged both their baggage wagons and artillery over them and they lay mangled and torn to pieces so that Even friends could not tell them. You can form no idea of a battle field."

Hardening Attitudes >>

Throughout the war Civil War soldiers continued to commend traditional ideals of duty, honor, and patriotism. Nevertheless, military service profoundly changed them. The early volunteers of 1861 expected to fight a restrained war that upheld their moral code. They admired the courage of the foe and considered it pointless to kill an isolated soldier.

By 1864 the nature of war had been transformed. Soldiers discovered the futility of mass frontal assaults, and under the rain of fire on the battlefield, they sought to kill enemy soldiers any way they could in order to hasten the war's end. At the same time, they became indifferent to death and suffering. Amid "the daily sight of blood and mangled bodies," combatants began taking personal property from the dead and wounded and even prisoners after a battle.

Increasingly alienated from civilians back home, soldiers on both sides developed a stronger sense of comradeship with their adversaries, based on their belief that only other soldiers could understand what they had gone through and why they acted the way they did. In the face of what Charles Francis Adams, Jr., termed "the carnival of death," soldiers braced themselves with a grim determination to see the war through to the end.

 REVIEW

How did the experience of battle evolve during the war?

THE WAR IN THE EAST, 1863–1865

Lee won his most brilliant victory at Chancellorsville, then launched a second invasion of the North, which ended in defeat at Gettysburg. In 1864 Grant delivered a series of blows against Lee's outnumbered forces in Virginia. Despite staggering losses, Grant pressed on in a ruthless demonstration of total war. (Note the casualties listed from mid-May to mid-June of 1864; Grant lost nearly 60,000 men, equal to Lee's total strength.) In April 1865, too weak to defend Richmond any longer, Lee surrendered at Appomattox Courthouse.

THE UNION'S TRIUMPH

In the spring of 1863 matters still looked promising for Robert E. Lee, the general who had so ably led the Confederates in Virginia. At the battle of Chancellorsville, he won another brilliant victory. But during the fighting Stonewall Jackson was accidentally shot by his own men, and he died a few days later—a grievous setback for the Confederacy. Determined to invade the North and take the offensive, Lee invaded Pennsylvania in June with an army of 75,000. Lincoln's newest general, George Gordon Meade, warily shadowed the Confederates. On the first of July, advance parties from the two armies accidentally collided at the town of Gettysburg, and the war's greatest battle ensued.

For once it was Lee who had the extended supply lines and was forced to fight on ground chosen by his opponent. After two days of assaults failed to break the Union left or right, Lee made the greatest mistake of his career, sending 14,000 men under General George Pickett in a charge up the center of the Union line. "Pickett's division just seemed to melt away in the blue musketry smoke which now covered the hill," one Confederate officer wrote. "Nothing but stragglers came back." With the loss

THE WAR IN THE WEST, 1863–1865

The Union continued its war of mobility in the western theater, bringing more Confederate territory under its control. After Grant captured Vicksburg, the entire Mississippi River lay in Union hands. His victories at Lookout Mountain and Missionary Ridge, near Chattanooga, ended the Confederate threat to Tennessee. In 1864 Sherman divided the Confederacy by seizing Atlanta and marching across Georgia; then he turned north. When Joseph Johnston surrendered, several weeks after Lee's capitulation at Appomattox, the war was effectively over.

of more than a third of his troops, Lee was never again able to assume the offensive.

Lincoln Finds His General >>

To the west, Grant had been trying for months to capture Vicksburg, a Rebel stronghold on the Mississippi. In a daring maneuver, he left behind his supply lines and marched inland, feeding his army from the produce of Confederate farms. These were the tactics of total war, and seldom had they been tried before. On July 4 the city surrendered. With the fall of Port Hudson, Louisiana, four days later, the Mississippi was completely in Union hands, thus dividing the Confederacy.

Grant followed up this victory by rescuing Union forces holed up in Chattanooga. His performance confirmed Lincoln's earlier judgment that "Grant is my man,

and I am his the rest of the war." In March 1864 Lincoln brought Grant east and placed him in command of all the Union armies.

Grant recognized that in the past Union forces had "acted independently and without concert, like a balky team, no two ever pulling together." He intended to change that. While he launched a major offensive against Lee in Virginia, William Tecumseh Sherman, who replaced Grant as commander of the western army, would drive a diagonal wedge through the Confederacy from Tennessee across Georgia. Grant instructed Sherman to "get into the interior of the enemy's country so far as you can, inflicting all the damage you can against their war resources."

In May and June 1864 Grant tried to maneuver Lee out of the trenches and into an open battle. But Lee was too

U.S. Gunboat Cimerone

U.S. TROOPS BURNING "The COLE HOUSE" and PLANTATION. OPPOSITE HARRISON'S LANDING JAMES RIVER on the night of 1st August 1862

Steamers landing troops from Harrison

⌃ General William Sherman demonstrated the tactics of total war in the autumn of 1864. "Destroyed all we could not eat . . . burned their cotton and gins . . . burned and twisted their railroads . . .," wrote one of Sherman's soldiers. This drawing, done by a Union private, depicts a similar destructive raid on a plantation along Virginia's James River in 1862, and by the spring of 1865 Confederate armies were increasingly unable to resist Union might.

weak to win head-on, so he opted for a strategy of attrition, hoping to inflict such heavy losses that the northern will would break. It was a strategy that nearly worked, for Union casualties were staggering. In a month of fierce fighting, the Army of the Potomac lost 60,000 men. Yet at the end of the campaign Grant's reinforced army was larger than when it started, whereas Lee's was significantly weaker.

Unable to break Lee's lines, Grant settled into a siege of Petersburg, which guarded Richmond's last remaining rail link to the south. In the west, meanwhile, the gaunt and grizzled Sherman fought his way by July to the outskirts of Atlanta, which was heavily defended and gave no sign of capitulating. "Our all depends on that army at Atlanta," wrote Mary Chesnut in August, based on her conversations with Confederate leaders in Richmond. "If that fails us, the game is up."

War in the Balance ›› As the Union war machine swept more and more northerners south to their death, and with Grant and Sherman bogged down in Virginia and Georgia, Lincoln's chances for reelection in 1864 seemed slim. Yet the president rejected any suggestion to postpone the election, an act that he believed would be

to lose democracy itself. At the Republican convention he made certain that the Republican platform called for adoption of a constitutional amendment abolishing slavery. To balance the ticket he selected Andrew Johnson, the military governor of Tennessee and a prowar Democrat, as his running mate. The two men ran under the label of the "Union" party.

The Democrats nominated George McClellan, the former Union commander. Their platform called for an armistice and a peace conference. Warned that a cessation of fighting would lead to disunion, McClellan partially repudiated this position, insisting that "the Union is the one condition of peace—we ask no more." In private he made it clear that if elected he intended to restore slavery. Late in August, Lincoln was still gloomy about his prospects, as well as those of the Union. But Admiral David Farragut won a dramatic victory at Mobile Bay, and in early September, Sherman captured Atlanta. As Secretary of State Seward gleefully noted, "Sherman and Farragut have knocked the bottom out of the Chicago [Democratic] nominations."

Polling an impressive 55 percent of the popular vote, Lincoln won 212 electoral votes to McClellan's 21. Eighteen states allowed soldiers to vote in the field, and Lincoln received nearly 80 percent of their ballots. One

The Twilight of the Confederacy >>

For the Confederacy the outcome of the 1864 election had a terrible finality. In March 1865 the Confederate Congress authorized recruiting 300,000 slaves for military service. When he signed the bill, Davis announced that freedom would be given to those who volunteered and to their families. That same month he offered through a special envoy to abolish slavery in exchange for British diplomatic recognition. A Mississippi paper denounced this proposal as "a total abandonment of the chief object of this war." The British rejected the offer, and the war ended before any slaves were mustered into the Confederate army, but the demands of total war had forced Confederate leaders to forsake the Old South's most important values and institutions.

In the wake of Lincoln's reelection the Confederate will to resist disintegrated. As Sherman pushed deeper into the Confederacy, the war came home to southern civilians as never before.

⌃ The war's greatest generals, Ulysses S. Grant (*left*) and Robert E. Lee (*right*), confronted each other in the eastern theater during the last year of the war. A member of a distinguished Virginia family, the tall, impeccably dressed Lee was every inch the aristocratic gentleman. Grant, a short, slouched figure with a stubby beard, dressed indifferently, but his determination is readily apparent in this picture, taken at his field headquarters in 1864.

lifelong Democrat described the sentiment in the army: "I had rather stay out here a lifetime (much as I dislike it) than consent to a division of our country." Jefferson Davis remained defiant, but the last hope of a Confederate victory was gone.

Equally important, the election of 1864 ended any doubt that slavery would be abolished in the reconstructed Union. The Emancipation Proclamation had not put an end to the question, for its legal status remained unclear. Lincoln argued that as a war measure, it would have no standing once peace returned; and in any case, it had not freed slaves in the border states or those parts of the Confederacy already under Union control.

In 1864 the Senate approved an amendment to the Constitution that freed all slaves without compensating their owners. The measure passed the House on January 31, 1865. By December enough states had ratified the Thirteenth Amendment to make it part of the Constitution.

"We haven't got nothing in the house to eat but a little bit o meal," wrote the wife of one Alabama soldier in December 1864. ". . . Try to get off and come home and fix us all up some and then you can go back. . . . If you put off a-coming, 'twont be no use to come, for we'll all . . . [be] in the grave yard." He deserted. In the last months of the fighting, over half the Confederacy's soldiers were absent without leave.

After the fall of Atlanta Sherman gave a frightening demonstration of the meaning of total war. He imitated Grant's strategy by abandoning his supply lines for an audacious 300-mile march to the sea. The goal was to deprive Lee's army of the supplies it desperately needed to continue and to break the southern will to resist. Or as he bluntly put it, "to whip the Rebels, to humble their pride, to follow them to their recesses, and make them fear and dread us."

Moving in four columns, Sherman's army covered about 10 miles a day, cutting a path of destruction 50 miles wide. Sherman estimated that his men did $100 million in damage, of which $20 million was necessary to supply his army and the rest was wanton destruction. After he captured Savannah, he turned north and wreaked even greater havoc in South Carolina.

By December the interior of the Confederacy was essentially conquered. Only Lee's army remained, entrenched around Petersburg. As Grant extended his lines, Lee's troops were forced to evacuate Richmond. Westward Grant doggedly pursued the Army of Northern Virginia, until the weary gentleman from Virginia finally asked for terms. On April 9, 1865, Lee surrendered at Appomattox Courthouse. As the vanquished foe mounted his horse, Grant saluted by raising his hat; Lee raised his respectfully and rode off at a slow trot. The guns were quiet.

Remaining resistance throughout the Confederacy collapsed within a matter of weeks. Visiting the captured city of Richmond on April 4, Lincoln was enthusiastically greeted by the black population. He looked "pale, haggard, utterly worn out," noted one observer. The lines in his face showed how much the war had aged him in only four years. Often his friends had counseled rest, but Lincoln had observed that "the tired part of me is inside and out

of reach." The burden, he confessed, was almost too much to bear.

Back in Washington the president received news of Lee's surrender with relief. The evening of April 14, Lincoln, seeking a welcome escape, went to a comedy at Ford's Theater. In the midst of the performance John Wilkes Booth, a famous actor and Confederate sympathizer, slipped into the presidential box and shot him. Lincoln died the next morning. As he had called on his fellow citizens to do in his Gettysburg Address, the sixteenth president had given his "last full measure of devotion" to the Republic.

 REVIEW

What decisions by Grant and Lincoln led the Union to victory?

> # The assassination left a tiredness in the nation's bones—a tiredness "inside" and not easily within reach.

The assassination left a tiredness in the nation's bones—a tiredness "inside" and not easily within reach. In every way the conflict had produced fundamental changes. There was, of course, the carnage. Approximately 620,000 men on both sides lost their lives, almost as many as in all the other wars the nation has fought from the Revolution through Vietnam combined. In material terms, the conflict cost an estimated $20 billion, more than 11 times the total amount spent by the federal government from 1789 to 1861. Even without adding the market value of freed slaves, southern wealth declined 43 percent, transforming what had been the richest section in the nation (on a white per capita basis) into the poorest.

The Civil War reordered not only the national economy but also economic relations worldwide. Manufacturers were forced to supply the army on an unprecedented scale over great distances. One consequence was the creation of truly national industries in flour milling, meat packing, clothing and shoe manufacture, and machinery making.

People across the globe felt the effects of the war, particularly because of changes in the cotton trade. In 1860 the South was supplying more than three-quarters of all cotton imported by Britain, France, Germany, and Russia. When the war cut off that supply, India, Egypt, and Brazil all opened new cotton fields. The effect of the trade on Egypt was so great, historians of that nation rank the American Civil War along with the construction of the Suez Canal as the most crucial events in its nineteenth-century history.

WITNESS

A Georgia Plantation Mistress in Sherman's Path

"Oh God, the time of trial has come! . . . To my smoke-house, my dairy, pantry, kitchen, and cellar, like famished wolves they come, breaking locks and whatever is in their way . . . they tore down my garden palings, made a road through my back yard and lot field, driving their stock and riding through, tearing down my fences and desolating my home—wantonly doing it when there was no necessity for it."

— Dolly Lunt, *A Woman's Wartime Journal*, September 19, 1864

⌃ Lincoln's funeral procession.

Politically, the war dramatically changed the balance of power. The South lost its substantial influence, as did the Democratic party, while the Republicans emerged in a dominant position. The Union's military victory also signaled the triumph of nationalism. The war destroyed the idea that the Union was a voluntary confederacy of sovereign states, which theorists like John C. Calhoun had argued, and that the states had the right to secede.

In the short run, the price was disillusionment and bitterness. The war's corrosive effect on morals corrupted American life and politics, destroyed idealism, and severely crippled humanitarian reform. Millennialism and perfectionism were victims of the war's appalling slaughter, forsaken for a new emphasis on practicality, order, materialism, and science.

The remorseless logic of war did push to the fore one ideal of the previous decades: the abolition of slavery. In 1865 the United States joined the ranks of those nations that had embraced emancipation: Britain in 1833, Portugal (1836), Sweden (1847), Denmark and France (1848), and Holland in 1863. (Spain did not relent until 1886.) Without war to force the issue, slavery in the United States might have continued for decades.

George Ticknor, a prominent critic of the day, reflected on the changes that had shaken the nation. The war, it seemed to him, had left "a great gulf between what happened before it in our century and what has happened since. . . . It does not seem to me as if I were living in the country in which I was born."

CHAPTER SUMMARY

As the first total war in history, the Civil War's outcome depended not just on armies but also on the mobilization of society's human, economic, and intellectual resources.

- Confederate president Jefferson Davis's policy of concentrating power in the government at Richmond, along with the resort to a draft and impressment of private property, provoked strong protests from many southerners.
- Abraham Lincoln's suspension of habeas corpus and interference with civil liberties were equally controversial, but Lincoln skillfully kept the border states in the Union.

- Lincoln at first resisted pressure to make emancipation a Union war aim, but he eventually issued the Emancipation Proclamation, which transformed the meaning of the war.
- African Americans helped undermine slavery and contributed vitally to the Union's military victory.
- On the home front, women confronted new responsibilities and enjoyed new occupational opportunities.
- Confederate financial and tax policies and the tightening Union blockade increased hardships within the Confederacy.
- Technology, particularly the use of rifles and rifled artillery, revolutionized the tactics of warfare.
- The Union victory at Gettysburg and Lincoln's choice of Grant to lead Union forces marked the turning point of the war. Union success relied in part on the strategy of attacking the civilian population of South.

Significant Events

Border states remain in the Union;
Battle of Bull Run

1861

1862

Forts Henry and Donelson captured; Battle of Shiloh; New Orleans captured; McClellan's Peninsula campaign fails; Battle of Antietam; Lincoln suspends writ of habeas corpus throughout the Union; Battle of Fredericksburg

Additional Reading

A good single-volume history of the Civil War remains James M. McPherson's *Battle Cry of Freedom* (1988). Some historians have questioned whether the conflict should be considered a "total war"; McPherson (who does) discusses the debate in *Drawn with the Sword* (1996). An interesting example that traces the evolution of the Union's strategy toward southern civilians is Mark Grimsley, *The Hard Hand of War* (1995).

The best biography of Lincoln is David Donald, *Lincoln* (1995). William E. Gienapp, *Abraham Lincoln and Civil War America* (2002), is concise and focuses on the presidential years. Much longer, but vividly written, is Doris Kearns Goodwin's *Team of Rivals: The Political Genius of Abraham Lincoln* (2005). Mark E. Neely has written two innovative studies of civil liberties in wartime: *The Fate of Liberty* (1991) examines the Union, and *Southern Rights* (1999) deals with the Confederacy. The fullest discussion of southern politics is George C. Rable, *The Confederate Republic* (1994). After years of relative neglect, historians have turned their attention to the vital home front. Drew Faust, *Mothers of Invention* (1996), is an imaginative study of slaveholding women; Daniel Sutherland, *Seasons of War* (1995), and William Blair, *Virginia's Private War* (1998), explore several Virginian counties in the war; and Stephen V. Ash, *When the Yankees Came* (1995), examines southerners under Union occupation. For the northern home front, see J. Matthew Gallman, *The North Fights the Civil War* (1994). Leon Litwack, *Been in the Storm So Long* (1979), is a graceful account of African Americans' experiences, and James L. Roark's *Masters without Slaves* (1977) discusses the collapse of the southern slaveholders' world. Chandra Manning, in *What This Cruel War Was Over* (2007), argues that Union rank-and-file widely believed in emancipation as early as the end of 1861. Drew Gilpin Faust, *This Republic of Suffering* (2008), explores how death, grieving, and belief were changed by this most deadly of wars.

Emancipation Proclamation issued; Union institutes conscription; Confederacy enacts general tax laws, initiates impressment; bread riots in the Confederacy; Battle of Gettysburg; Vicksburg captured; New York City draft riots

1863

Grant becomes Union general in chief; Grant's Virginia offensive; siege of Petersburg; fall of Atlanta; Lincoln reelected; Sherman's march to the sea

1864

Sherman's march through the Carolinas; Lee surrenders; Lincoln assassinated; Thirteenth Amendment ratified

1865

their masters." After serving in Congress and as military governor of Tennessee following its occupation by Union forces, Johnson, a Democrat, was tapped by Lincoln in 1864 as his running mate on the rechristened "Union" ticket.

The Radicals expected Johnson to uphold their views on Reconstruction, and on assuming the presidency he spoke of trying Confederate leaders and breaking up planters' estates. Unlike most Republicans, however, Johnson strongly supported states' rights, and his political shortcomings sparked conflicts almost immediately. Scarred by his humble origins, he became tactless and inflexible when challenged or criticized, alienating even those who sought to work with him.

Johnson moved to return the southern states to the Union quickly. He prescribed a loyalty oath that most white southerners would have to take to regain their civil and political rights and to have their property, except for slaves, restored. High Confederate officials and those with property worth over $20,000 had to apply for individual pardons. Once a state drafted a new constitution and elected state officers and members of Congress, Johnson promised to revoke martial law and recognize the new state government. Suffrage was limited to white citizens who had taken the loyalty oath. This plan was similar to Lincoln's, though more lenient. Only informally did Johnson stipulate that the southern states were to renounce their ordinances of secession, repudiate the Confederate debt, and ratify the Thirteenth Amendment abolishing slavery, which had been passed by Congress in January 1865 and was in the process of being ratified by the states. (It became part of the Constitution in December.)

The Failure of Johnson's Program >>

The southern delegates who met to construct new governments were in no mood to follow Johnson's recommendations. Several states merely repealed instead of repudiating their ordinances of secession, rejected the Thirteenth Amendment, or refused to repudiate the Confederate debt.

Nor did the new governments allow African Americans any political rights or provide in any effective way for black education. In addition, each state passed a series of laws, often modeled on its old slave code, that applied only to African Americans. These "black codes" did give African Americans some rights that had not been granted to slaves. They legalized marriages from slavery and allowed black southerners to hold and sell property and to sue and be sued in state courts. Yet their primary intent was to keep African Americans as propertyless agricultural laborers with inferior legal rights. The new freedpeople could not serve on juries, testify against whites, or work as they pleased. Mississippi prohibited them from buying or renting farmland, and most states ominously provided that black people who were vagrants could be arrested and hired out to landowners. Many northerners were incensed by the restrictive black codes, which violated their conception of freedom.

black codes laws passed by southern states in 1865 and 1866, modeled on the slave codes in effect before the Civil War. The codes did grant African Americans some rights not enjoyed by slaves, but their primary purpose was to keep African Americans as propertyless agricultural laborers.

Southern voters under Johnson's plan also defiantly elected prominent Confederate military and political leaders to office. At this point, Johnson could have called for new elections or admitted that a different program of Reconstruction was needed. Instead he caved in. For all his harsh rhetoric, he shrank from the prospect of social upheaval, and as the lines of ex-Confederates waiting to see him lengthened, he began issuing special pardons almost as fast as they could be printed. Publicly Johnson put on a bold face, announcing that Reconstruction had been successfully completed. But many members of Congress were deeply alarmed, and the stage was set for a serious confrontation.

⌃ Andrew Johnson was a staunch Unionist, but his contentious personality and inflexibility masked a deep-seated insecurity, which was rooted in his humble background. As a young man, he worked and lived in this rude tailor shop in Greeneville, Tennessee.

Johnson's Break with Congress >> The

new Congress was by no means of one mind. A small number of Democrats and a few conservative Republicans backed the president's program of immediate and unconditional restoration. At the other end of the spectrum, a larger group of Radical Republicans, led by Thaddeus Stevens, Charles Sumner, Benjamin Wade, and others, was bent on remaking southern society in the image of the North. Reconstruction must "revolutionize Southern institutions, habits, and manners," insisted Representative Stevens, ". . . or all our blood and treasure have been spent in vain."

As a minority the Radicals needed the aid of the moderate Republicans, the largest bloc in Congress. Led by William Pitt Fessenden and Lyman Trumbull, the moderates had no desire to foster social revolution or promote racial equality in the South. But they wanted to keep Confederate leaders from reassuming power, and they were convinced that the former slaves needed federal protection. Otherwise, Trumbull declared, the freedpeople would "be tyrannized over, abused, and virtually reenslaved."

The central issue dividing Johnson and the Radicals was the place of African Americans in American society. Johnson accused his opponents of seeking "to Africanize the southern half of our country," while the Radicals championed civil and political rights for African Americans. The only way to maintain loyal governments and develop a Republican party in the South, Radicals argued, was to give black men the ballot. Moderates agreed that the new southern governments were too harsh toward African Americans, but they feared that too great an emphasis on black civil rights would alienate northern voters.

In December 1865, when southern representatives to Congress appeared in Washington, a majority in Congress voted to exclude them. Congress also appointed a joint committee, chaired by Senator Fessenden, to look into Reconstruction.

The growing split with the president became clearer when Congress passed a bill extending the life of the Freedmen's Bureau. Created in March 1865, the bureau provided emergency food, clothing, and medical care to war refugees (including white southerners) and took charge of settling freedpeople on abandoned lands. The new bill gave the bureau the added responsibilities of supervising special courts to resolve disputes involving freedpeople and establishing schools for black southerners. Although this bill passed with virtually unanimous Republican support, Johnson vetoed it.

Johnson also vetoed a civil rights bill designed to overturn the more flagrant provisions of the black codes. The law made

⌃ Thaddeus Stevens, Radical leader in the House.

African Americans citizens of the United States and granted them the right to own property, make contracts, and have access to courts as parties and witnesses. For most Republicans Johnson's action was the last straw, and in April 1866 Congress overrode his veto. Congress then approved a slightly revised Freedmen's Bureau bill in July and promptly overrode the president's veto. Johnson's refusal to compromise drove the moderates into the arms of the Radicals.

The Fourteenth Amendment >> To pre-

vent unrepentant Confederates from taking over the reconstructed state governments and denying African Americans basic freedoms, the Joint Committee on Reconstruction proposed an amendment to the Constitution, which passed both houses of Congress with the necessary two-thirds vote in June 1866.

The amendment guaranteed repayment of the national war debt and prohibited repayment of the Confederate debt. To counteract the president's wholesale pardons, it disqualified prominent Confederates from holding office. Because moderates balked at giving the vote to African Americans, the amendment merely gave Congress the right to reduce the representation of any state that did not have impartial male suffrage. The practical effect of this provision, which Radicals labeled a "swindle," was to allow northern states to retain white suffrage, since unlike southern states they had few African Americans in their populations and thus would not be penalized.

The amendment's most important provision, Section 1, defined an American citizen as anyone born in the United States or naturalized, thereby automatically making African Americans citizens. Section 1 also prohibited states from abridging "the privileges or immunities" of citizens, depriving "any person of life, liberty, or property, without due process of law," or denying "any person . . . equal protection of the laws." The framers of the amendment probably intended to prohibit laws that applied to one race only, such as the black codes, or that made certain acts felonies when committed by black but not white people, or that decreed different penalties for the same crime when committed by white and black lawbreakers. The framers probably did not intend to prevent segregation (the legal separation of the races) in schools and public places.

Johnson denounced the amendment and urged southern states not to ratify it. Ironically, of the seceded states only the president's own state ratified the amendment, and Congress readmitted Tennessee with no further restrictions. The telegram sent to Congress by

<< This politician is literally "waving the bloody shirt"—using the bitter memories of the Civil War to rouse voters to side with Republicans.

Voters soundly repudiated Johnson, as the Republicans won more than a two-thirds majority in both houses of Congress. The Radicals had reached the height of their power, propelled by genuine alarm among northerners that Johnson's policies would lose the fruits of the Union's victory. Johnson was a president virtually without a party.

✔ REVIEW

What were Lincoln's and Andrew Johnson's approaches to Reconstruction, and why did Congress reject Johnson's approach?

a longtime foe of Johnson officially announcing Tennessee's approval ended: "Give my respects to the dead dog in the White House."

The Election of 1866 >>

When Congress blocked his policies Johnson undertook a speaking tour of the East and Midwest in the fall of 1866 to drum up popular support. But the president found it difficult to convince northern audiences that white southerners were fully repentant. Only months earlier white mobs in Memphis and New Orleans had attacked black residents and killed nearly 100 in two major race riots. "The negroes now know, to their sorrow, that it is best not to arouse the fury of the white man," boasted one Memphis newspaper. When the president encountered hostile audiences during his northern campaign, he made matters only worse by trading insults and proclaiming that the Radicals were traitors.

Not to be outdone, the Radicals vilified Johnson as a traitor aiming to turn the country over to former rebels. Resorting to the tactic of "waving the **bloody shirt**," they appealed to voters by reviving bitter memories of the war. In a classic example of such rhetoric, Governor Oliver Morton of Indiana proclaimed that "every bounty jumper, every deserter, every sneak who ran away from the draft" was a Democrat; every "New York rioter in 1863 who burned up little children in colored asylums called himself a Democrat. In short, the Democratic party may be described as a common sewer."

bloody shirt political campaign tactic of "waving the bloody shirt," used by Republicans against Democrats; it invoked the deaths and casualties from the Civil War as a reason to vote for Republicans as the party of the Union, rather than the Democrats, who had often opposed the war.

CONGRESSIONAL RECONSTRUCTION

With a clear mandate in hand congressional Republicans passed their own program of Reconstruction, beginning with the first Reconstruction Act in March 1867. Like all later pieces of Reconstruction legislation, it was repassed over Johnson's veto.

Placing the 10 unreconstructed states under military commanders, the act provided that in enrolling voters, officials were to include black adult males but not former Confederates, who were barred from holding office under the Fourteenth Amendment. Delegates to the state conventions were to frame constitutions that provided for black suffrage and disqualified prominent ex-Confederates from office. The first state legislatures to meet under the new constitution were required to ratify the Fourteenth Amendment. Once these steps were completed and Congress approved the new state constitution, a state could send representatives to Congress.

White southerners found these requirements so obnoxious that officials took no steps to register voters. Congress then enacted a second Reconstruction Act, also in March, ordering the local military commanders to put the machinery of Reconstruction into motion. Johnson's efforts to limit the power of military commanders produced a third act, passed in July, that upheld their

Opinion

If the North won the war, how well did it win the peace?

superiority in all matters. When the first election was held in Alabama to ratify the new state constitution, whites boycotted it in sufficient numbers to prevent a majority of voters from participating. Undaunted, Congress passed the fourth Reconstruction Act (March 1868), which required ratification of the constitution by only a majority of those voting rather than those who were registered.

By June 1868 Congress had readmitted the representatives of seven states. Texas, Virginia, and Mississippi did not complete the process until 1869. Georgia finally followed in 1870.

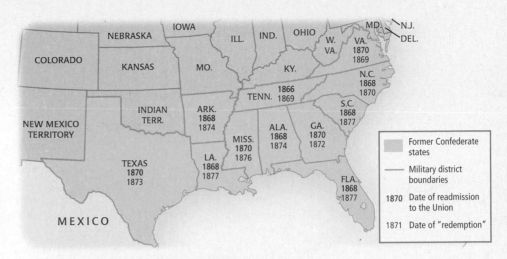

THE SOUTHERN STATES DURING RECONSTRUCTION

Post-Emancipation Societies in the Americas >>

With the exception of Haiti's revolution (1791–1804), the United States was the only society in the Americas in which the destruction of slavery was accomplished by violence. But the United States, uniquely among these societies, enfranchised former slaves almost immediately after the emancipation. Thus in the United States former masters and slaves battled for control of the state in ways that did not occur in other post-emancipation societies. In most of the Caribbean, property requirements for voting left the planters in political control. Jamaica, for example, with a population of 500,000 in the 1860s, had only 3,000 voters.

Moreover, in reaction to political efforts to mobilize disfranchised black peasants, Jamaican planters dissolved the assembly and reverted to being a Crown colony governed from London. Of the sugar islands, all but Barbados adopted the same policy, thereby blocking the potential for any future black peasant democracy. Nor did any of these societies have the counterparts of the Radical Republicans, a group of outsiders with political power that promoted the fundamental transformation of the post-emancipation South. These comparisons highlight the radicalism of Reconstruction in the United States, which alone saw an effort to forge an interracial democracy.

The Land Issue >>

While the political process of Reconstruction proceeded, Congress debated whether land should be given to former slaves to foster economic

independence. At a meeting with Secretary of War Edwin Stanton near the end of the war, African American leaders declared: "The way we can best take care of ourselves is to have land, and till it by our own labor." The Second Confiscation Act of 1862 had authorized the government to seize and sell the property of supporters of the rebellion. In June 1866, however, President Johnson ruled that confiscation laws applied only to wartime.

After more than a year of debate Congress rejected all proposals to give land to former slaves. Given Americans' strong belief in self-reliance, little sympathy existed for the idea that government should support any group. In addition, land redistribution represented an attack on property rights, another cherished American value. "A division of rich men's lands amongst the landless," argued the *Nation,* a Radical journal, "would give a shock to our whole social and political system from which it would hardly recover without the loss of liberty." By 1867 land reform was dead.

> ## After more than a year of debate, Congress rejected all proposals to give land to former slaves.

Impeachment >>

Throughout 1867 Congress routinely overrode Johnson's vetoes, but the president undercut congressional Reconstruction in other ways. He interpreted the new laws narrowly and removed military commanders who vigorously enforced them. Congress responded by restricting his power to issue orders to military commanders in the South. It also passed the Tenure of Office Act, which forbade Johnson to remove any member of the cabinet without the Senate's consent. The intention of this law was to

GEORGIA PLANTATION AFTER THE WAR

After emancipation, sharecropping became the dominant form of agricultural labor in the South. Black families no longer lived in the old slave quarters but dispersed to separate plots of land that they farmed themselves. At the end of the year each sharecropper turned over part of the crop to the white landowner.

prevent him from firing Secretary of War Edwin Stanton, the only remaining Radical in the cabinet.

When Johnson tried to dismiss Stanton in February 1868, the House of Representatives angrily approved articles of impeachment. The articles focused on the violation of the Tenure of Office Act, but the charge with the most substance was that Johnson had acted to systematically obstruct Reconstruction legislation. In the trial before the Senate, his lawyers argued that a president could be impeached only for an indictable crime, which Johnson clearly had not committed. The Radicals countered that impeachment applied to political offenses and not merely criminal acts. In May 1868 the Senate voted 35 to 19 to convict, one vote short of the two-thirds majority needed. The seven Republicans who joined the Democrats in voting for acquittal were uneasy about using impeachment as a political weapon.

 REVIEW

What was Congress's approach to Reconstruction, and why did it not include a provision for giving land to former slaves?

RECONSTRUCTION IN THE SOUTH

As the power of the Radicals in Congress waned, the fate of Reconstruction increasingly hinged on developments in the southern states themselves. Power in these states rested with the new Republican parties, representing a coalition of black and white southerners and transplanted northerners.

Black and White Republicans >> Once

African Americans received the right to vote, black men constituted as much as 80 percent of the Republican voters in the South. They steadfastly opposed the Democratic party with its appeal to white supremacy. But during Reconstruction African Americans never held office in proportion to their voting strength. No African American was ever elected governor. And only in South Carolina, where more than 60 percent of the population was black, did they control even one house of the legislature. Between 15 and 20 percent of the state officers and 6 percent of members of Congress (2 senators and 15 representatives) were black. Only in South Carolina did black officeholders approach their proportion of the population.

Those who held office came from the top levels of African American society. Among state and federal officeholders, perhaps 80 percent were literate, and over a quarter had been free before the war, both marks of distinction in the black community. Their occupations also set them apart: many were professionals (mostly clergy), and of the third who were farmers, nearly all owned land. In their political and social values, African American leaders were more conservative than the rural black population, and they showed little interest in land reform.

Black citizens were a majority of the voters only in South Carolina, Mississippi, and Louisiana. Thus in most of the South the Republican party had to secure white votes to stay in power. Opponents scornfully labeled white southerners who allied with the Republican party **scalawags**, yet an estimated quarter of white southerners at one time voted Republican. They were primarily Unionists from the upland counties and hill areas and largely yeoman farmers. Such voters were attracted by Republican promises to rebuild the South, restore prosperity, create public schools, and open isolated areas to the market with railroads.

> **scalawags** white southerners who supported the Republican party.

The other group of white Republicans in the South were known as **carpetbaggers.** Originally from the North, they allegedly had arrived with all their worldly possessions stuffed in a carpetbag, ready to loot and plunder the defeated South. Some did, certainly, but northerners moved south for a variety of reasons. Though carpetbaggers made up only a small percentage of Republican voters, they controlled almost a third of the offices. More than half of all southern Republican governors and nearly half of Republican members of Congress were originally northerners.

> **carpetbaggers** northern white Republicans who came to live in the South after the Civil War. Most were veterans of the Union army; many were teachers, Freedman's Bureau agents or investors in cotton plantations.

The Republican party in the South had difficulty maintaining unity. Scalawags were especially susceptible to the race issue and social pressure. "Even my own kinspeople have turned the cold shoulder to me because I hold office under a Republican administration," testified a Mississippi white Republican. As black southerners pressed for greater recognition, white southerners increasingly defected to the Democrats. Carpetbaggers, in contrast, were less sensitive to race, although most felt that their black allies should be content with minor offices. The animosity between scalawags and carpetbaggers, which grew out of their rivalry for party honors, was particularly intense.

Reforms under the New State Governments >>
The new southern state constitutions enacted several significant reforms. They devised fairer systems of legislative representation and made many previously appointive offices elective. The Radical state governments also assumed some responsibility for social welfare and established the first statewide systems of public schools in the South.

All the new constitutions proclaimed the principle of equality and granted black adult males the right to vote. On social relations they were much more cautious. No state outlawed segregation, and South Carolina and Louisiana were the only ones that required integration in public schools (a mandate that was almost universally ignored). Sensitive to status, mulattoes pushed for prohibition of social discrimination, but white Republicans refused to adopt such a radical policy.

Economic Issues and Corruption >>
With the southern economy in ruins at the end of the war, problems of economic reconstruction were severe. The new Republican governments encouraged industrial development by providing subsidies, loans, and even temporary exemptions from taxes. These governments also largely rebuilt the southern railroad system, offering lavish aid to railroad corporations. In the two decades after 1860, the region doubled its manufacturing establishments, yet the South steadily slipped further behind the booming industrial economy of the North.

The expansion of government services offered temptations for corruption. Southern officials regularly received bribes and kickbacks for awarding railroad charters, franchises, and other contracts. The railroad grants and new social services such as schools also left state governments in debt, even though taxes rose in the 1870s to four times the rate in 1860.

Corruption, however, was not only a southern problem but a national one. During these years, the Democratic Tweed Ring in New York City alone stole more money than all the southern Radical governments combined. Moreover, corruption was hardly limited to southern Republicans: many Democrats and white business leaders participated. Louisiana governor Henry Warmoth, a carpetbagger, told a congressional committee: "Everybody is demoralizing down here. Corruption is the fashion."

Corruption in Radical governments existed, but southern Democrats exaggerated its extent for partisan purposes. They opposed honest Radical regimes just as bitterly as notoriously corrupt ones. In the eyes of most white southerners, the real crime of the Radical governments was that they allowed black citizens to hold some offices and tried to protect the civil rights of black Americans. Race was white conservatives' greatest weapon. And it would prove the most effective means to undermine Republican power in the South.

 REVIEW

What roles did African Americans, southern whites, and northern whites play in the Reconstruction governments of the South?

BLACK ASPIRATIONS

Emancipation came to slaves in different ways and at different times. Betty Jones's grandmother was told about the Emancipation Proclamation by another slave while they were hoeing corn. Mary Anderson received the news from her master near the end of the war when Sherman's army invaded North Carolina. Whatever the timing, freedom meant a host of precious blessings to people who had been in bondage all their lives.

Experiencing Freedom >>

The first impulse was to think of freedom as a contrast to slavery. Emancipation immediately released slaves from the most oppressive aspects of bondage—the whippings, the breakup of families, the sexual exploitation. Freedom also meant movement, the right to travel without a pass or white permission. Above all, freedom meant that African Americans' labor would be for their own benefit. One Arkansas freedman, who earned his first dollar working on a railroad, recalled that when he was paid, "I felt like the richest man in the world."

Freedom included finding a new place to work. Changing jobs was one concrete way to break the psychological ties of slavery. Even planters with reputations for kindness sometimes saw most of their former hands depart. The cook who left a South Carolina family, despite the offer of higher wages than her new job's, explained: "I must go. If I stays here I'll never know I'm free."

Symbolically, freedom meant having a full name. African Americans now adopted last names, most commonly the name of the first master in the family's oral history as far back as it could be recalled. Most, however, retained their first name, especially if the name had

SAML. DOVE wishes to know of the whereabouts of his mother, Areno, his sisters Maria, Neziah, and Peggy, and his brother Edmond, who were owned by Geo. Dove, of Rockingham county, Shenandoah Valley, Va. Sold in Richmond, after which Saml. and Edmond were taken to Nashville, Tenn., by Joe Mick; Areno was left at the Eagle Tavern, Richmond
Respectfully yours,
SAML. DOVE.
Utica, New York, Aug. 5, 1865–3m

⌃ During the decades before the Civil War many slave families were split when individual slaves were sold to new masters. This Tennessee newspaper advertisement shows one way that freed people sought to deal with the consequences.

been given to them by their parents (as most often had been the case). Whatever the name, black Americans insisted on making the decision themselves.

The Black Family >>

African Americans also sought to strengthen the family in freedom. Since slave marriages had not been recognized as legal, thousands of former slaves insisted on being married again by proper authorities, even though this was not required by law. Those who had been forcibly separated in slavery and later remarried confronted the dilemma of which spouse to take. Laura Spicer, whose husband had been sold away in slavery, wrote him after the war seeking to resume their marriage. In a series of wrenching letters, he explained that he had thought her dead, had remarried, and had a new family. "You know it never was our wishes to be separated from each other, and it never was our fault. I had rather anything to had happened to me most than ever have been parted from you and the children," he wrote. "As I am, I do not know which I love best, you or Anna." Declining to return, he closed, "Laura, truly, I have got another wife, and I am very sorry."

As in white families, black husbands deemed themselves the head of the family and acted legally for their wives. They often insisted that their wives would not work in the fields as they had in slavery. "The [black] women say they never mean to do any more outdoor work," one planter reported, "that white men support their wives and they mean that their husbands shall support them." In negotiating contracts, a father also demanded the right to control his children and their labor. All these changes were designed to insulate the black family from white control.

The Schoolhouse and the Church >>

In freedom, the schoolhouse and the black church became essential institutions in the black community. "My Lord, Ma'am, what a great thing learning is!" a South Carolina freedman told a northern teacher. "White folks can do what they likes, for they know so much more than we." At first, northern churches and missionaries, working with the Freedmen's Bureau, set up black schools in the South. Tuition at these schools represented 10 percent or more of a laborer's monthly wages, yet these schools were full. Eventually, states established public school systems, which by 1867 enrolled 40 percent of African American children.

Black adults, who often attended night classes, had good reasons for seeking literacy. They wanted to be able to read the Bible, to defend their newly gained civil and political rights, and to protect themselves from being cheated. Both races saw that education would undermine the servility that slavery had fostered.

The teachers in the Freedmen's Bureau schools were primarily northern middle-class white women sent south by northern missionary societies. "I feel that it is a precious privilege," Esther Douglass wrote, "to be allowed to do something for these poor people." Many saw themselves as peacetime soldiers, struggling to make emancipation a reality. Indeed, hostile white southerners sometimes destroyed black schools and threatened and even murdered white teachers. Then there were the everyday challenges: low pay, run-down buildings, few books, classes of 100 or more children. By 1869 most teachers in these Freedmen's Bureau schools were black, trained by the bureau.

Most slaves had attended white churches or services supervised by whites. Once free, African Americans quickly established their own congregations led by black preachers. Mostly Methodist and Baptist, black churches were the only major organizations in the African American community controlled by blacks themselves. A white missionary reported that "the Ebony preacher who promises perfect independence from White control and direction carried the colored heart at once." Just as in slavery, religion offered African Americans a place of refuge in a hostile white world and provided them with hope, comfort, and a means of self-identification.

�findA After living for years in a society in which teaching slaves to read and write was usually illegal, freedpeople viewed literacy as a key to securing their newfound freedom. Blacks were not merely "anxious to learn," a school official in Virginia reported, they were "crazy to learn."

New Working Conditions >> As a largely propertyless class, blacks in the postwar South had no choice but to work for white landowners. Except for paying wages, whites wanted to retain the old system of labor, including close supervision, gang labor, and physical punishment. Determined to remove all emblems of servitude, African Americans refused to work under these conditions, and they demanded time off to devote to their own interests. Because of shorter hours and the withdrawal of children and women from the fields, blacks' output declined by an estimated 35 percent in freedom. They also refused to live in the old slave quarters located near the master's house and instead erected cabins on distant parts of the plantation. Wages initially were $5 or $6 a month plus provisions and a cabin; by 1867, they had risen to an average of $10 a month.

These changes eventually led to the rise of sharecropping. Under this arrangement African American families farmed separate plots of land and then at the end of the year divided the crop, normally on an equal basis, with the white landowner. Sharecropping had higher status and offered greater personal freedom than being a wage laborer. "I am not working for wages," one black farmer declared in defending his right to leave the plantation at will, "but am part owner of the crop and as [such,] I have all the rights that you or any other man has." Although black per capita agricultural income increased 40 percent in freedom, sharecropping was a harshly exploitative system in which black families often sank into perpetual debt.

The task of supervising the transition from slavery to freedom on southern plantations fell to the Freedmen's Bureau, a unique experiment in social policy supported by the federal government. Assigned the task of protecting freedpeople's economic rights, approximately 550 local agents regulated working conditions in southern agriculture after the war. The racial attitudes of Bureau agents varied widely, as did their commitment and competence.

Most agents required written contracts between white planters and black laborers, specifying wages and the conditions of employment. Although agents sometimes intervened to protect freedpeople from unfair treatment, they also provided important help to planters. They insisted that black laborers not leave at harvest-time, they arrested those who violated their contracts or refused to sign new ones at the beginning of the year, and they preached the need to be orderly and respectful.

Because of such attitudes, freedpeople increasingly complained that Bureau agents were mere tools of the planter class. One observer reported: "Doing justice seems to mean seeing that the blacks don't break contracts and compelling them to submit cheerfully."

The primary means of enforcing working conditions were the Freedmen's Courts, which Congress created in 1866 in order to avoid the discrimination African Americans received in state courts. These new courts functioned as military tribunals, and often the agent was the entire court. The sympathy black laborers received varied from state to state. But since Congress was opposed to creating any permanent welfare agency, it shut down the Bureau, and by 1872 it had gone out of business. Despite its mixed record, it was the most effective agency in protecting blacks' civil and political rights. Its disbanding signaled the beginning of the northern retreat from Reconstruction.

Planters and a New Way of Life

Planters and a New Way of Life >> Planters and other white southerners faced emancipation with dread. "All the traditions and habits of both races had been suddenly overthrown," a Tennessee planter recalled, "and neither knew just what to do, or how to accommodate themselves to the new situation." Slavery had been a complex institution that welded black and white southerners together in intimate relationships. The old ideal of a paternalistic planter, which required blacks to act subservient and grateful, gave way to an emphasis on strictly economic relationships. Only with time did planters develop new norms to judge black behavior.

After the war, however, planters increasingly embraced the ideology of segregation. Since emancipation significantly reduced the social distance between the races, white southerners sought psychological separation and kept dealings with African Americans to a minimum. By the time Reconstruction ended, white planters had developed a new way of life based on the institutions of sharecropping and segregation, and undergirded by a militant white supremacy.

While most planters kept their land, they did not regain the economic prosperity of the prewar years. Cotton prices began a long decline, and southern per capita income suffered as a result. By 1880 the value of southern farms had slid 33 percent below the level of 1860.

> "All the traditions and habits of both races had been suddenly overthrown," a Tennessee planter recalled, "and neither knew just what to do, or how to accommodate themselves to the new situation."

REVIEW

In what ways were the church and the school central to African American hopes after the Civil War?

THE ABANDONMENT OF RECONSTRUCTION

On Christmas Day 1875 a white acquaintance approached Charles Caldwell in Clinton, Mississippi, and invited him to have a drink. A former slave, Caldwell was a state senator and the leader of the Republican party in Hinds County. But the black leader's fearlessness made him a marked man. Only two months earlier, Caldwell had fled the county to escape an armed white mob. Despite threats against him, he had returned home to vote in the November state election. Now, as Caldwell and his "friend" raised their glasses in a holiday toast, a gunshot exploded through the window and Caldwell collapsed, mortally wounded. He was taken outside, where his assassins riddled his body with bullets. He died alone in the street.

Charles Caldwell shared the fate of a number of black Republican leaders in the South during Reconstruction. Resorting to violence and terror, southern whites challenged the commitment of the federal government to sustaining Reconstruction. After Andrew Johnson was acquitted in May 1868 at his impeachment trial, the crusading idealism of the Republican party began to wane. Ulysses S. Grant was hardly the cause of this change, but he certainly came to symbolize it.

The Grant Administration >> In 1868 Grant was elected president—and Republicans were shocked. Their candidate, a great war hero, had won by a margin of only 300,000 votes. Furthermore, with an estimated 450,000 black Republican votes cast in the South, a majority of whites had voted Democratic. The election helped convince Republican leaders that an amendment securing black suffrage throughout the nation was necessary.

THE FIFTEENTH AMENDMENT.

CELEBRATED MAY 19T 1870.

⌃ The Fifteenth Amendment, ratified in 1870, secured the right of African American males to vote as free citizens. In New York, black citizens paraded in support of Ulysses S. Grant for president (*center*). But citizenship was only one component of what African Americans insisted were central aspects of their freedom. What other features of a free life does the poster champion?

In February 1869 Congress sent the Fifteenth Amendment to the states for ratification. It forbade any state to deny the right to vote on grounds of race, color, or previous condition of servitude. It did not forbid literacy and property requirements, as some Radicals wanted, because the moderates feared that only a conservative version of the amendment could be ratified. As a result, when the amendment was ratified in March 1870, loopholes remained that eventually allowed southern states to **disfranchise** African Americans.

> **disfranchisement** denial of a citizen's right to vote.

Advocates of women's suffrage were bitterly disappointed when Congress refused to outlaw voting discrimination on the basis of sex as well as race. The Women's Loyal League, led by Elizabeth Cady Stanton and Susan B. Anthony, had pressed for first the Fourteenth and then the Fifteenth Amendment to recognize that women had

a civic right to vote. But even most Radicals were unwilling to back women's suffrage, contending that black rights had to be ensured first. As a result, the Fifteenth Amendment divided the feminist movement. Although disappointed that women were not included in its provisions, Lucy Stone and the American Woman Suffrage Association urged ratification. Stanton and Anthony, however, denounced the amendment and organized the National Woman Suffrage Association to work for passage of a new amendment giving women the ballot. The division hampered the women's rights movement for decades to come.

When Ulysses S. Grant was a general his quiet manner and well known resolution served him well. As president he proved much less certain of his goals and therefore less effective at corralling politicians than at maneuvering troops.

>> Grant swings from a trapeze while supporting a number of associates accused of corruption. Among those holding on are Secretary of the Navy George M. Robeson (*top center*), who was accused of accepting bribes for awarding Navy contracts; Secretary of War William W. Belknap (*top right*), who was forced to resign for selling Indian post traderships; and the president's private secretary, Orville Babcock (*bottom right*), who was implicated in the Whiskey Ring scandal. Although not personally involved in the scandals during his administration, Grant was reluctant to dismiss from office supporters accused of wrongdoing.

A series of scandals wracked his administration, so much so that "Grantism" soon became a code word in American politics for corruption, cronyism, and venality. Although Grant did not profit personally, he remained loyal to his friends and displayed little zeal to root out wrongdoing. Nor was Congress immune from the lowered tone of public life. In such a climate ruthless state machines, led by men who favored the status quo, came to dominate the party.

As corruption in both the North and the South worsened, reformers became more interested in cleaning up government than in protecting black rights. Congress in 1872 passed an amnesty act, allowing many more ex-Confederates to serve in southern governments. That same year liberal Republicans broke with the Republican party and nominated for president Horace Greeley, the editor of the New York *Tribune.* A one-time Radical, Greeley had become disillusioned with Reconstruction and urged a restoration of home rule in the South as well as adoption of civil service reform. Democrats decided to back the Liberal Republican ticket. The Republicans renominated Grant, who, despite the defection of a number of prominent Radicals, won an easy victory.

Growing Northern Disillusionment >>

During Grant's second term Congress passed the Civil Rights Act of 1875, the last major piece of Reconstruction legislation. This law prohibited racial discrimination in public accommodations, transportation, places of amusement, and juries. At the same time Congress rejected a ban on segregation in public schools, which was almost universally practiced in the North as well as the South. The federal government made little attempt to enforce the law, however, and in 1883 the Supreme Court struck down its provisions, except the one relating to juries.

Despite passage of the Civil Rights Act many northerners were growing disillusioned with Reconstruction. They were repelled by the corruption of the southern governments, they were tired of the violence and disorder that accompanied elections in the South, and they had little faith in black Americans. William Dodge, a wealthy New York capitalist and an influential Republican, wrote in 1875 that the South could never develop its resources "till confidence in her state governments can be restored, and this will never be done by federal bayonets." It had been a mistake, he went on, to make black southerners feel "that the United States government was their special friend, rather than those . . . among whom they must live and for whom they must work. We have tried this long enough," he concluded. "Now let the South alone."

As the agony of the war became more distant, the Panic of 1873, which precipitated a severe four-year depression, diverted public attention to economic issues. Battered by the panic and the corruption issue, the Republicans lost a shocking 77 seats in Congress in the 1874 elections, and along with them control of the House of Representatives for the first time since 1861.

"The truth is our people are tired out with the worn out cry of 'Southern outrages'!!" one Republican concluded. "Hard times and heavy taxes make them wish the 'ever lasting nigger' were in hell or Africa." More and more, Republicans spoke about cutting loose the unpopular southern governments.

The Triumph of White Supremacy >>

Meanwhile, southern Democrats set out to overthrow the remaining Radical governments. Already white Republicans in the South felt heavy pressure to desert their party. To poor white southerners who lacked social standing, the Democratic appeal to racial solidarity offered special comfort. The large landowners and other wealthy groups that led southern Democrats objected less to black southerners voting, since they were confident that if outside influences were removed, they could control the black vote.

Democrats also resorted to economic pressure to undermine Republican power. In heavily black counties, newspapers published the names of black residents who cast Republican ballots and urged planters to discharge

<< "Brute Might Makes Right. Shoot Suffrage to Death," reads the sign above the figure. By the time this cartoon appeared in 1879, terror tactics had "redeemed" the South for white Democrats.

them. But terror and violence provided the most effective means to overthrow the radical regimes. A number of paramilitary organizations broke up Republican meetings, terrorized white and black Republicans, assassinated Republican leaders, and prevented black citizens from voting. The most notorious of these organizations was the Ku Klux Klan, which along with similar groups functioned as an unofficial arm of the Democratic party.

In the war for supremacy, contesting control of the night was paramount to both southern whites and blacks. Before emancipation masters regulated the nighttime hours, with a system of passes and patrols that chased slaves who went hunting or tried to sneak a visit to a family member at a neighboring plantation. For slaves the night provided precious free time: to read, to meet for worship, school or dancing. During Reconstruction African Americans actively took back the night for a host of activities, including torchlight political parades and meetings of such organizations as the Union League. Part of the Klan's mission was to recoup this contested ground and to limit the ability of African Americans to use the night as they pleased. When indirect threats of violence were not enough (galloping through black neighborhoods rattling fences with lances), beatings and executions were undertaken—again, facilitated by the dark of night.

What became known as the Mississippi Plan was inaugurated in 1875, when Democrats decided to use as much violence as necessary to carry the state election. Local papers trumpeted, "Carry the election peaceably if we can, forcibly if we must." Recognizing that

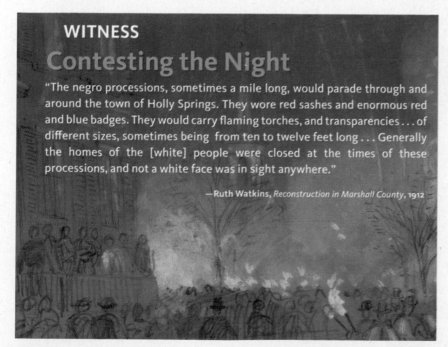

WITNESS
Contesting the Night

"The negro processions, sometimes a mile long, would parade through and around the town of Holly Springs. They wore red sashes and enormous red and blue badges. They would carry flaming torches, and transparencies . . . of different sizes, sometimes being from ten to twelve feet long . . . Generally the homes of the [white] people were closed at the times of these processions, and not a white face was in sight anywhere."

—Ruth Watkins, *Reconstruction in Marshall County*, 1912

northern public opinion had grown sick of repeated federal intervention in southern elections, the Grant administration rejected the request of Republican governor Adelbert Ames for troops to stop the violence. Bolstered by terrorism, the Democrats swept the election in Mississippi. Violence and intimidation prevented as many as 60,000 black and white Republicans from voting, converting the normal Republican majority into a Democratic majority of 30,000. Mississippi had been "redeemed."

> ## Even under redeemer governments, African Americans did not return to the social position they had occupied before the war.

The Disputed Election of 1876 >>

The 1876 presidential election was crucial to the final overthrow of Reconstruction. The Republicans nominated Ohio governor Rutherford B. Hayes to oppose Samuel Tilden of New York. Once again violence prevented an estimated quarter of a million Republican votes from being cast in the South. Tilden had a clear majority of 250,000 in the popular vote, but the outcome in the Electoral College was in doubt

because both parties claimed South Carolina, Florida, and Louisiana, the only reconstructed states still in Republican hands.

To arbitrate the disputed returns Congress established a 15-member electoral commission. By a straight party vote of 8 to 7, the commission awarded the disputed electoral votes—and the presidency—to Hayes.

When angry Democrats threatened a filibuster to prevent the electoral votes from being counted, key Republicans met with southern Democrats and reached an informal understanding, later known as the Compromise of 1877. Hayes's supporters agreed to withdraw federal troops from the South and not oppose the new Democratic state governments. For their part, southern Democrats dropped their opposition to Hayes's election and pledged to respect African Americans' rights.

Redeemers southerners who came to power in southern state governments from 1875 to 1877, claiming to have "redeemed" the South from Reconstruction. The Redeemers looked to undo many of the changes wrought by the Civil War.

Without federal support, the last Republican southern governments collapsed, and Democrats took control of the remaining states of the Confederacy. By 1877, the entire South was in the hands of the **Redeemers,** as they called themselves. Reconstruction and Republican rule had come to an end.

Racism and the Failure of Reconstruction >>

Reconstruction failed for a multitude of reasons. The reforming impulse behind the Republican party of the 1850s had been battered and worn down by the war. The new materialism of industrial America inspired a jaded cynicism in many Americans. In the South, African American voters and leaders inevitably lacked a certain amount of education and experience; elsewhere, Republicans were divided over policies and options.

Yet beyond these obstacles, the sad fact remains that the ideals of Reconstruction were most clearly defeated by a deep-seated racism that permeated American life. Racism stimulated white southern resistance, undercut northern support for black rights, and eventually made northerners willing to write off Reconstruction, and with it the welfare of African Americans. Although Congress could pass a constitutional amendment abolishing slavery, it could not overturn at a stroke the social habits of two centuries.

Candidate (Party)	Electoral Vote (%)	Popular Vote (%)
Rutherford B. Hayes (Republican)	185 (50)	4,034,311 (48)
Samuel J. Tilden (Democrat)	184 (50)	4,288,546 (51)
Minor parties	–	93,895 (1)
Nonvoting territories		

ELECTION OF 1876

REVIEW

What factors in the North and the South led the federal government to abandon Reconstruction in the South?

With the overthrow of Reconstruction, the white South had won back some of the power it had lost in 1865—but not all. In the longer term, the political equations of power had been changed. Even under redeemer governments, African Americans did not return to the social position they had occupied before the war. They were no longer slaves, and black southerners who walked dusty roads in search of family members, sent their children to school, or worshiped in their own black churches knew what a momentous change this was. Even under the exploitative sharecropping system, black income rose significantly in freedom. Then, too, the guarantees of "equal protection" and "due process of law" had been written into the Constitution and would be available for later generations to use in championing once again the Radicals' goal of racial equality.

But this was a struggle left to future reformers. For the time being, the clear trend was away from change or hope—especially for former slaves like Benjamin Montgomery and his sons, the owners of the old Davis plantations in Mississippi. In the 1870s bad crops, lower cotton prices, and falling land values undermined the Montgomerys' financial position, and in 1875 Jefferson Davis sued to have the sale of Brierfield invalidated. Following the overthrow of Mississippi's Radical government, a white conservative majority of the court awarded Brierfield to Davis in 1878. The Montgomerys lost Hurricane as well.

The waning days of Reconstruction were times filled with such ironies: of governments "redeemed" by violence, of Fourteenth Amendment rights being used by conservative courts to protect not black people but giant corporations, of reformers taking up other causes. Increasingly, the industrial North focused on an economic task: integrating both the South and the West into the Union. In the case of both regions, northern factories sought to use southern and western raw materials to produce goods and to find national markets for those products. Indeed, during the coming decades European nations also scrambled to acquire natural resources and markets. In the onrushing age of imperialism, Western nations would seek to dominate newly acquired colonies in Africa and Asia, with the same disregard for their "subject peoples" that was seen with African Americans, Latinos, and Indians in the United States.

Disowned by its northern supporters and unmourned by public opinion, Reconstruction was over.

CHAPTER SUMMARY

Presidents Abraham Lincoln and Andrew Johnson and the Republican-dominated Congress each developed a program of Reconstruction to quickly restore the Confederate states to the Union.

- Lincoln's 10 percent plan required that 10 percent of qualified voters from 1860 swear an oath of loyalty to begin organizing a state government.
- Following Lincoln's assassination, Andrew Johnson changed Lincoln's terms and lessened Reconstruction's requirements.
- The more radical Congress repudiated Johnson's state governments and eventually enacted its own program of Reconstruction, which included the principle of black suffrage.
  - Congress passed the Fourteenth and Fifteenth Amendments and also extended the life of the Freedmen's Bureau, a unique experiment in social welfare.
  - Congress rejected land reform, however, which would have provided the freedpeople with a greater economic stake.
  - The effort to remove Johnson from office through impeachment failed.
- The Radical governments in the South, led by black and white southerners and transplanted northerners, compiled a mixed record on matters such as racial equality, education, economic issues, and corruption.
- Reconstruction was a time of both joy and frustration for former slaves.
  - Former slaves took steps to reunite their families and establish black-controlled churches.
  - They evidenced a widespread desire for land and education.
  - Black resistance to the old system of labor led to the adoption of sharecropping.
  - The Freedmen's Bureau fostered these new working arrangements and also the beginnings of black education in the South.
- Northern public opinion became disillusioned with Reconstruction during the presidency of Ulysses S. Grant.
- Southern whites used violence, economic coercion, and racism to overthrow the Republican state governments.
- In 1877 Republican leaders agreed to end Reconstruction in exchange for Rutherford B. Hayes's election as president.
- Racism played a key role in the eventual failure of Reconstruction.

Additional Reading

Historians' views of Reconstruction have dramatically changed over the past half century. Modern studies offer a more sympathetic assessment of Reconstruction and the experience of African Americans. Indicative of this trend is Eric Foner, *Reconstruction* (1988), and his briefer treatment (with photographic essays by Joshua Brown) *Forever Free: the Story of Emancipation and Reconstruction* (2005). Michael Les Benedict treats the clash between Andrew Johnson and Congress in *The Impeachment and Trial of Andrew Johnson* (1973). Political affairs in the South during Reconstruction are examined in Dan T. Carter, *When the War Was Over* (1985), and Thomas Holt, *Black over White* (1977), an imaginative study of black political leadership in South Carolina. Hans Trefousse, *Thaddeus Stevens: Nineteenth-Century Egalitarian* (1997), provides a sympathetic reassessment of the influential Radical Republican.

Leon Litwack, *Been in the Storm So Long* (1979), sensitively analyzes the transition of enslaved African Americans to freedom. Heather Andrea Williams, *Self-Taught: African American Education in Slavery and Freedom* (2005), illustrates the black drive for literacy and education. James L. Roark, *Masters without Slaves* (1977), discusses former slaveholders' adjustment to the end of slavery. The dialectic of black-white relations is charted from the antebellum years through Reconstruction and beyond in Steven Hahn, *A Nation under Our Feet: Black*

Significant Events

1864	1865–1866	1865	1866	1867–1868
Louisiana, Arkansas, and Tennessee establish governments under Lincoln's Reconstruction Plan		Freedmen's Bureau established; Johnson becomes president; presidential Reconstruction completed; Thirteenth Amendment ratified		
	Black codes enacted		Civil rights bill passed over Johnson's veto; Memphis and New Orleans riots; Ku Klux Klan organized	Constitutional conventions in the South; Blacks vote in southern elections

Political Struggles in the Rural South from Slavery to the Great Migration (2003). Two excellent studies of changing labor relations in southern agriculture are Julie Saville, *The Work of Reconstruction* (1995), and John C. Rodrigue, *Reconstruction in the Cane Fields* (2001). For contrasting views of the Freedman's Bureau see George R. Bentley, *A History of the Freedman's Bureau* (1955)—favorable—and Donald Nieman, *To Set the Law in Motion* (1979)—more critical. William Gillette, *Retreat from Reconstruction, 1869–1879* (1980), focuses on national politics and the end of Reconstruction, while Michael Perman, *The Road to Redemption* (1984), looks at developments in the South.

Johnson impeached but acquitted; Fourteenth Amendment ratified; Grant elected president

Disputed Hayes-Tilden election

Compromise of 1877; Hayes declared winner of electoral vote; last Republican governments in South fall

1867   1868   1870   1875   1876   1877

Congressional Reconstruction enacted; Tenure of Office Act passed

Fifteenth Amendment ratified

Civil Rights Act; Mississippi Plan

Appendix

- **The Declaration of Independence**

- **The Constitution of the United States of America**

The Declaration of Independence

IN CONGRESS, JULY 4, 1776

The Unanimous Declaration of the Thirteen United States of America

When, in the course of human events, it becomes necessary for one people to dissolve the political bands which have connected them with another, and to assume, among the powers of the earth, the separate and equal station to which the laws of nature and of nature's God entitle them, a decent respect to the opinions of mankind requires that they should declare the causes which impel them to the separation.

We hold these truths to be self-evident, that all men are created equal; that they are endowed by their Creator with certain unalienable rights; that among these, are life, liberty, and the pursuit of happiness. That, to secure these rights, governments are instituted among men, deriving their just powers from the consent of the governed; that, whenever any form of government becomes destructive of these ends, it is the right of the people to alter or to abolish it, and to institute a new government, laying its foundation on such principles, and organizing its powers in such form, as to them shall seem most likely to effect their safety and happiness. Prudence, indeed, will dictate that governments long established, should not be changed for light and transient causes; and, accordingly, all experience hath shown, that mankind are more disposed to suffer, while evils are sufferable, than to right themselves by abolishing the forms to which they are accustomed. But, when a long train of abuses and usurpations, pursuing invariably the same object, evinces a design to reduce them under absolute despotism, it is their right, it is their duty, to throw off such government and to provide new guards for their future security. Such has been the patient sufferance of these colonies, and such is now the necessity which constrains them to alter their former systems of government. The history of the present King of Great Britain is a history of repeated injuries and usurpations, all having, in direct object, the establishment of an absolute tyranny over these States. To prove this, let facts be submitted to a candid world:

He has refused his assent to laws the most wholesome and necessary for the public good.

He has forbidden his governors to pass laws of immediate and pressing importance, unless suspended in their operation till his assent should be obtained; and, when so suspended, he has utterly neglected to attend to them.

He has refused to pass other laws for the accommodation of large districts of people, unless those people would relinquish the right of representation in the legislature; a right inestimable to them, and formidable to tyrants only.

He has called together legislative bodies at places unusual, uncomfortable, and distant from the depository of their public records, for the sole purpose of fatiguing them into compliance with his measures.

He has dissolved representative houses repeatedly for opposing, with manly firmness, his invasions on the rights of the people.

He has refused, for a long time after such dissolutions, to cause others to be elected; whereby the legislative powers, incapable of annihilation, have returned to the people at large for their exercise; the state remaining, in the meantime, exposed to all the danger of invasion from without, and convulsions within.

He has endeavored to prevent the population of these States; for that purpose, obstructing the laws for naturalization of foreigners, refusing to pass others to encourage their migration hither, and raising the conditions of new appropriations of lands.

He had obstructed the administration of justice, by refusing his assent to laws for establishing judiciary powers. He has made judges dependent on his will alone, for the tenure of their offices, and the amount and payment of their salaries.

He has erected a multitude of new offices, and sent hither swarms of officers to harass our people, and eat out their substance.

He has kept among us, in time of peace, standing armies, without the consent of our legislatures.

He has affected to render the military independent of, and superior to, the civil power.

He has combined, with others, to subject us to a jurisdiction foreign to our Constitution, and unacknowledged by our laws; giving his assent to their acts of pretended legislation:

For quartering large bodies of armed troops among us:

For protecting them by a mock trial, from punishment, for any murders which they should commit on the inhabitants of these States:

For cutting off our trade with all parts of the world:

For imposing taxes on us without our consent:

For depriving us, in many cases, of the benefit of trial by jury:

For transporting us beyond seas to be tried for pretended offences:

For abolishing the free system of English laws in a neighboring province, establishing therein an arbitrary government, and enlarging its boundaries, so as to render it at once an example and fit instrument for introducing the same absolute rule into these colonies:

For taking away our charters, abolishing our most valuable laws, and altering, fundamentally, the powers of our governments:

For suspending our own legislatures, and declaring themselves invested with power to legislate for us in all cases whatsoever.

He has abdicated government here, by declaring us out of his protection, and waging war against us.

He has plundered our seas, ravaged our coasts, burnt our towns, and destroyed the lives of our people.

He is, at this time, transporting large armies of foreign mercenaries to complete the works of death, desolation, and tyranny, already begun, with circumstances of cruelty and perfidy scarcely paralleled in the most barbarous ages, and totally unworthy the head of a civilized nation.

He has constrained our fellow citizens, taken captive on the high seas, to bear arms against their country, to become the executioners of their friends, and brethren, or to fall themselves by their hands.

He has excited domestic insurrections amongst us, and has endeavored to bring on the inhabitants of our frontiers, the merciless Indian savages, whose known rule of warfare is an undistinguished destruction of all ages, sexes, and conditions.

In every stage of these oppressions, we have petitioned for redress, in the most humble terms; our repeated petitions have been answered only by repeated injury. A prince, whose character is thus marked by every act which may define a tyrant, is unfit to be the ruler of a free people.

Nor have we been wanting in attention to our British brethren. We have warned them, from time to time, of attempts made by their legislature to extend an unwarrantable jurisdiction over us. We have reminded them of the circumstances of our emigration and settlement here. We have appealed to their native justice and magnanimity, and we have conjured them, by the ties of our common kindred, to disavow these usurpations, which would inevitably interrupt our connections and correspondence. They, too, have been deaf to the voice of justice and consanguinity. We must, therefore, acquiesce in the necessity which denounces our separation, and hold them as we hold the rest of mankind, enemies in war, in peace, friends.

We, therefore, the representatives of the United States of America, in general Congress assembled, appealing to the Supreme Judge of the world for the rectitude of our intentions, do, in the name, and by the authority of the good people of these colonies, solemnly publish and declare, that these united colonies are, and of right ought to be, free and independent states: that they are absolved from all allegiance to the British Crown, and that all political connection between them and the state of Great Britain is, and ought to be, totally dissolved; and that, as free and independent states, they have full power to levy war, conclude peace, contract alliances, establish commerce, and to do all other acts and things which independent states may of right do. And, for the support of this declaration, with a firm reliance on the protection of Divine Providence, we mutually pledge to each other our lives, our fortunes, and our sacred honor.

The foregoing Declaration was, by order of Congress, engrossed, and signed by the following members:

New Hampshire	Massachusetts Bay	Rhode Island	Connecticut
New York	New Jersey	Pennsylvania	John Morton
Delaware	Maryland	Virginia	Benjamin Harrison
North Carolina	South Carolina	Georgia	Roger Sherman
Josiah Bartlett	Samuel Adams	Stephen Hopkins	George Clymer
William Floyd	Richard Stockton	Robert Morris	Thomas Nelson, Jr.
Caesar Rodney	Samuel Chase	George Wythe	Samuel Huntington
William Hooper	Edward Rutledge	Button Gwinnett	James Smith
William Whipple	John Adams	William Ellery	Francis Lightfoot Lee
Philip Livingston	John Witherspoon	Benjamin Rush	William Williams
George Read	William Paca	Richard Henry Lee	George Taylor
Joseph Hewes	Thomas Heyward, Jr.	Lyman Hall	Carter Braxton
Matthew Thornton	Robert Treat Paine	Benjamin Franklin	Oliver Wolcott
Francis Lewis	Francis Hopkinson	Thomas Jefferson	James Wilson
Thomas M'Kean	Thomas Stone	George Walton	George Ross
John Penn	Thomas Lynch, Jr.		
Lewis Morris	Elbridge Gerry		
	John Hart		
	Charles Carroll,		
	of Carrollton		
	Arthur Middleton		
	Abraham Clark		

Resolved, That copies of the Declaration be sent to the several assemblies, conventions, and committees, or counsils of safety, and to the several commanding officers of the continental troops; that it be proclaimed in each of the United States, at the head of the army.

The Constitution of the United States of America[1]

We the People of the United States, in Order to form a more perfect Union, establish Justice, insure domestic Tranquility, provide for the common defence, promote the general Welfare, and secure the Blessings of Liberty to ourselves and our Posterity, do ordain and establish this CONSTITUTION for the United States of America.

ARTICLE I

SECTION 1. All legislative Powers herein granted shall be vested in a Congress of the United States, which shall consist of a Senate and House of Representatives.

SECTION 2. The House of Representatives shall be composed of Members chosen every second Year by the People of the several States, and the Electors in each State shall have the Qualifications requisite for Electors of the most numerous Branch of the State Legislature. No Person shall be a Representative who shall not have attained to the Age of twenty-five Years, and been seven Years a Citizen of the United States, and who shall not, when elected, be an Inhabitant of that State in which he shall be chosen.

[Representatives and direct Taxes[2] shall be apportioned among the several States which may be included within this Union, according to their respective Numbers, which shall be determined by adding to the whole Number of free Persons, including those bound to Service for a Term of Years, and excluding Indians not taxed, three fifths of all other Persons.][3] The actual Enumeration shall be made within three Years after the first Meeting of the Congress of the United States, and within every subsequent Term of ten Years, in such Manner as they shall by Law direct. The Number of Representatives shall not exceed one for every thirty Thousand, but each State shall have at Least one Representative; and until such enumeration shall be made, the State of New Hampshire shall be entitled to chuse three, Massachusetts eight, Rhode- Island and Providence Plantations one, Connecticut five, New York six, New Jersey four, Pennsylvania eight, Delaware one, Maryland six, Virginia ten, North Carolina five, South Carolina five, and Georgia three. When vacancies happen in the Representation from any State, the Executive Authority thereof shall issue Writs of Election to fill such Vacancies. The House of Representatives shall chuse their Speaker and other Officers; and shall have the sole Power of Impeachment.

SECTION 3. The Senate of the United States shall be composed of two Senators from each State, chosen by the Legislature thereof, for six Years; and each Senator shall have one Vote.

Immediately after they shall be assembled in Consequence of the first Election, they shall be divided as equally as may be into three Classes. The Seats of the Senators of the first Class shall be vacated at the Expiration of the second Year, of the second Class at the Expiration of the fourth Year, and of the third Class at the Expiration of the sixth Year, so that one-third may be chosen every second Year; and if Vacancies happen by Resignation, or otherwise, during the Recess of the Legislature of any State, the Executive thereof may make temporary Appointments until the next Meeting of the Legislature, which shall then fill such Vacancies. No Person shall be a Senator who shall not have attained to the Age of thirty Years, and been nine Years a Citizen of the United States, and who shall not, when elected, be an Inhabitant of that State for which he shall be chosen.

The Vice President of the United States shall be President of the Senate, but shall have no vote, unless they be equally divided.

The Senate shall chuse their other Officers, and also a President pro tempore, in the absence of the Vice President, or when he shall exercise the Office of President of the United States.

The Senate shall have the sole Power to try all Impeachments. When sitting for that purpose they shall be on Oath or Affirmation. When the President of the United States is tried, the Chief Justice shall preside: And no person shall be convicted without the Concurrence of two thirds of the Members present.

Judgment in Cases of Impeachment shall not extend further than to removal from Office, and disqualification to hold and enjoy any Office of honor, Trust, or Profit under the United States: but the Party convicted shall nevertheless be liable and subject to Indictment, Trial, Judgment, and Punishment, according to Law.

---

1 This version follows the original Constitution in capitalization and spelling. It is adapted from the text published by the United States Department of the Interior, Office of Education.

2 Altered by the Sixteenth Amendment.

3 Negated by the Fourteenth Amendment.

SECTION 4. The Times, Places and Manner of holding Elections for Senators and Representatives, shall be prescribed in each State by the Legislature thereof; but the Congress may at any time by Law make or alter such Regulations, except as to the Places of Chusing Senators. The Congress shall assemble at least once in every Year, and such Meeting shall be on the first Monday in December, unless they shall by Law appoint a different Day.

SECTION 5. Each House shall be the Judge of the Elections, Returns and Qualifications of its own Members, and a Majority of each shall constitute a Quorum to do Business; but a smaller number may adjourn from day to day, and may be authorized to compel the Attendance of absent Members, in such Manner, and under such Penalties, as each House may provide.

Each House may determine the Rules of its Proceedings, punish its Members for disorderly Behaviour, and, with the Concurrence of two thirds, expel a Member. Each House shall keep a Journal of its Proceedings, and from time to time publish the same, excepting such Parts as may in their Judgment require Secrecy; and the Yeas and Nays of the Members of either House on any question shall, at the Desire of one fifth of those Present, be entered on the Journal.

Neither House, during the Session of Congress, shall, without the Consent of the other, adjourn for more than three days, nor to any other Place than that in which the two Houses shall be sitting.

SECTION 6. The Senators and Representatives shall receive a Compensation for their Services, to be ascertained by Law, and paid out of the Treasury of the United States. They shall in all Cases, except Treason, Felony, and Breach of the Peace, be privileged from Arrest during their Attendance at the Session of their respective Houses, and in going to and returning from the same; and for any Speech or Debate in either House, they shall not be questioned in any other Place.

No Senator or Representative shall, during the Time for which he was elected, be appointed to any civil Office under the Authority of the United States, which shall have been created, or the Emoluments whereof shall have been increased, during such time; and no Person holding any Office under the United States shall be a Member of either House during his continuance in Office.

SECTION 7. All Bills for raising Revenue shall originate in the House of Representatives; but the Senate may propose or concur with Amendments as on other bills. Every Bill which shall have passed the House of Representatives and the Senate, shall, before it become a Law, be presented to the President of the United States; If he approve he shall sign it, but if not he shall return it, with his Objections, to that House in which it shall have originated,

who shall enter the Objections at large on their Journal, and proceed to reconsider it. If after such Reconsideration two thirds of that House shall agree to pass the bill, it shall be sent, together with the objections, to the other House, by which it shall likewise be reconsidered, and if approved by two thirds of that House, it shall become a Law. But in all such Cases the Votes of both Houses shall be determined by Yeas and Nays, and the Names of the Persons voting for and against the Bill shall be entered on the Journal of each House respectively. If any Bill shall not be returned by the President within ten Days (Sundays excepted) after it shall have been presented to him, the Same shall be a Law, in like Manner as if he had signed it, unless the Congress by their Adjournment prevent its Return, in which Case it shall not be a Law. Every Order, Resolution, or Vote to which the Concurrence of the Senate and House of Representatives may be necessary (except on a question of Adjournment) shall be presented to the President of the United States; and before the Same shall take Effect, shall be approved by him, or being disapproved by him, shall be repassed by two thirds of the Senate and House of Representatives, according to the Rules and Limitations prescribed in the Case of a Bill.

SECTION 8. The Congress shall have Power To lay and collect Taxes, Duties, Imposts and Excises, to pay the Debts and provide for the common Defence and general Welfare of the United States; but all Duties, Imposts and Excises shall be uniform throughout the United States;

To borrow money on the credit of the United States;

To regulate Commerce with foreign Nations, and among the several States, and with the Indian Tribes;

To establish an uniform rule of Naturalization, and uniform Laws on the subject of Bankruptcies throughout the United States; To coin Money, regulate the Value thereof, and of foreign Coin, and fix the Standard of Weights and Measures;

To provide for the Punishment of counterfeiting the Securities and current Coin of the United States;

To establish Post Offices and post Roads; To promote the Progress of Science and useful Arts, by securing for limited Times to Authors and Inventors the exclusive Right to their respective Writings and Discoveries;

To constitute Tribunals inferior to the Supreme Court;

To define and punish Piracies and Felonies committed on the high Seas, and Offenses against the Law of Nations;

To declare War, grant Letters of Marque and Reprisal, and make Rules concerning Captures on Land and Water;

To raise and support Armies, but no Appropriation of Money to that Use shall be for a longer Term than two Years;

To provide and maintain a Navy;

To make Rules for the Government and Regulation of the land and naval forces;

To provide for calling forth the Militia to execute the Laws of the Union, suppress Insurrections and repel Invasions;

To provide for organizing, arming, and disciplining the Militia, and for government such Part of them as may be employed in the Service of the United States, reserving to the States respectively, the Appointment of the Officers, and the Authority of training the Militia according to the discipline prescribed by Congress;

To exercise exclusive Legislation in all Cases whatsoever, over such District (not exceeding ten Miles square) as may, by Cession of particular States, and the acceptance of Congress, become the Seat of the Government of the United States, and to exercise like Authority over all Places purchased by the Consent of the Legislature of the State in which the Same shall be, for the Erection of Forts, Magazines, Arsenals, Dock-yards, and other needful Buildings;—And

To make all Laws which shall be necessary and proper for carrying into Execution the foregoing Powers, and all other Powers vested by this Constitution in the Government of the United States, or in any Department or Officer thereof.

SECTION 9.   The Migration or Importation of such Persons as any of the States now existing shall think proper to admit, shall not be prohibited by the Congress prior to the Year one thousand eight hundred and eight, but a tax or duty may be imposed on such Importation, not exceeding ten dollars for each Person.

The privilege of the Writ of Habeas Corpus shall not be suspended, unless when in Cases of Rebellion or Invasion the public Safety may require it.

No bill of Attainder or ex post facto Law shall be passed.

No capitation, or other direct, Tax shall be laid unless in Proportion to the Census or Enumeration herein before directed to be taken.

No Tax or Duty shall be laid on Articles exported from any State.

No Preference shall be given by any Regulation of Commerce or Revenue to the Ports of one State over those of another: nor shall Vessels bound to, or from, one State, be obliged to enter, clear, or pay Duties in another.

No Money shall be drawn from the Treasury, but in Consequence of Appropriations made by Law; and a regular Statement and Account of the Receipts and Expenditures of all public Money shall be published from time to time.

No Title of Nobility shall be granted by the United States: And no Person holding any Office of Profit or Trust under them, shall, without the Consent of the Congress, accept of any present, Emolument, Office, or Title, of any kind whatever, from any King, Prince, or foreign State.

SECTION 10.   No State shall enter into any Treaty, Alliance, or Confederation; grant Letters of Marque and Reprisal; coin Money; emit Bills of Credit; make any Thing but gold and silver Coin a Tender in Payment of Debts; pass any Bill of Attainder, ex post facto Law, or Law impairing the Obligation of Contracts, or grant any Title of Nobility.

No State shall, without the Consent of the Congress, lay any Imposts or Duties on Imports or Exports, except what may be absolutely necessary for executing its inspection Laws; and the net Produce of all Duties and Imposts, laid by any State on Imports or Exports, shall be for the use of the Treasury of the United States; and all such Laws shall be subject to the Revision and Control of the Congress.

No state shall, without the Consent of Congress, lay any duty of Tonnage, keep Troops, or Ships of War in time of Peace, enter into any Agreement or Compact with another State, or with a foreign Power, or engage in War, unless actually invaded, or in such imminent Danger as will not admit of delay.

ARTICLE II

SECTION 1.   The executive Power shall be vested in a President of the United States of America. He shall hold his Office during the Term of four years, and, together with the Vice President, chosen for the same Term, be elected, as follows:

Each State shall appoint, in such Manner as the Legislature thereof may direct, a Number of Electors, equal to the whole Number of Senators and Representatives to which the State may be entitled in the Congress: but no Senator or Representative, or Person holding an Office of Trust or Profit under the United States, shall be appointed an Elector.

[The Electors shall meet in their respective States, and vote by Ballot for two persons, of whom one at least shall not be an Inhabitant of the same State with themselves. And they shall make a List of all the Persons voted for, and of the Number of Votes for each; which List they shall sign and certify, and transmit sealed to the Seat of the Government of the United States, directed to the President of the Senate. The President of the Senate shall, in the Presence of the Senate and House of Representatives, open all the Certificates, and the Votes shall then be counted. The Person having the greatest Number of Votes shall be the President, if such Number be a Majority of the whole Number of Electors appointed; and if there be more than one who have such Majority, and have an equal Number of Votes, then the House of Representatives shall immediately chuse by Ballot one of them for President; and if no Person have a Majority, then from the five highest on the List the said House shall in like Manner chuse the President. But in chusing the President, the Votes shall be taken by States, the Representation from each State having one Vote; a quorum for this Purpose shall consist of a Member or Members from two-thirds of the States, and a Majority of all the States shall be necessary to a Choice. In every Case, after the Choice of the President, the Person having the greatest Number of Votes of the Electors shall be the Vice President. But if there should remain two or more who have equal votes, the Senate shall chuse from them by Ballot the Vice President.][4]

The Congress may determine the Time of chusing the Electors, and the Day on which they shall give their Votes; which Day shall be the same throughout the United States.

No person except a natural-born Citizen, or a Citizen of the United States, at the time of the Adoption of this Constitution, shall be eligible to the Office of President; neither shall any Person be eligible to that Office who shall not have attained to the Age of thirty-five years, and been fourteen Years a Resident within the United States.

In Case of the Removal of the President from Office, or of his Death, Resignation, or Inability to discharge the Powers and Duties of the said Office, the same shall devolve on the Vice President, and the Congress may by Law provide for the Case of Removal, Death, Resignation, or Inability, both of the President and Vice President, declaring what Officer shall then act as President, and such Officer shall act accordingly, until the disability be removed, or a President shall be elected.

The President shall, at stated Times, receive for his Services a Compensation, which shall neither be increased nor diminished during the Period for which he shall have been elected, and he shall not receive within that Period any other Emolument from the United States, or any of them.

Before he enter on the execution of his Office, he shall take the following Oath or Affirmation:—"I do solemnly swear (or affirm) that I will faithfully execute the Office of President of the United States, and will, to the best of my Ability, preserve, protect, and defend the Constitution of the United States."

SECTION 2. The President shall be Commander in Chief of the Army and Navy of the United States, and of the Militia of the several States, when called into the actual Service of the United States; he may require the Opinion, in writing, of the principal Officer in each of the executive Departments, upon any subject relating to the Duties of their respective Offices, and he shall have Power to Grant Reprieves and Pardons for Offenses against the United States, except in Cases of Impeachment.

He shall have Power, by and with the Advice and Consent of the Senate, to make Treaties, provided two-thirds of the Senators present concur; and he shall nominate, and by and with the Advice and Consent of the Senate, shall appoint Ambassadors, other public Ministers and Consuls, Judges of the supreme Court, and all other Officers of the United States, whose Appointments are not herein otherwise provided for, and which shall be established by Law: but the Congress may by Law vest the Appointment of such inferior Officers, as they think proper, in the President alone, in the Courts of Law, or in the Heads of Departments.

The President shall have Power to fill up all Vacancies that may happen during the Recess of the Senate, by granting Commissions which shall expire at the End of their next Session.

SECTION 3. He shall from time to time give to the Congress Information of the State of the Union, and recommend to their Consideration such Measures as he shall judge necessary and expedient; he may, on extraordinary occasions, convene both Houses, or either of them, and in Case of Disagreement between them, with respect to the Time of Adjournment, he may adjourn them to such Time as he shall think proper; he shall receive Ambassadors and other public Ministers; he shall take care that the Laws be faithfully executed, and shall Commission all the Officers of the United States.

SECTION 4. The President, Vice President and all civil Officers of the United States, shall be removed from Office on Impeachment for, and Conviction of, Treason, Bribery, or other high Crimes and Misdemeanors.

ARTICLE III

SECTION 1. The judicial Power of the United States, shall be vested in one supreme Court, and in such inferior Courts as the Congress may from time to time ordain and establish. The Judges, both of the supreme and inferior Courts, shall hold their Offices during good Behaviour, and shall, at stated Times, receive for their Services, a Compensation, which shall not be diminished during their Continuance in Office.

SECTION 2. The judicial Power shall extend to all Cases, in Law and Equity, arising under this Constitution, the Laws of the United States, and Treaties made, or which shall be made, under their Authority;—to all Cases affecting ambassadors, other public ministers and consuls;—to all cases of admiralty and maritime Jurisdiction;— to Controversies to which the United States shall be a Party;—to Controversies between two or more States;—between a State and Citizens of another State;[5] —between Citizens of different States—between Citizens of the same State claiming Lands under Grants of different States, and between a State, or the Citizens thereof, and foreign States, Citizens, or Subjects. In all Cases affecting Ambassadors, other public Ministers and Consuls, and those in which a State shall be Party, the supreme Court shall have original Jurisdiction. In all the other Cases before mentioned, the

---

4 Revised by the Twelfth Amendment.

5 Qualified by the Eleventh Amendment.

supreme Court shall have appellate Jurisdiction, both as to Law and Fact, with such Exceptions, and under such Regulations as the Congress shall make.

The trial of all Crimes, except in Cases of Impeachment, shall be by Jury; and such Trial shall be held in the State where the said Crimes shall have been committed; but when not committed within any State, the Trial shall be at such Place or Places as the Congress may by Law have directed.

SECTION 3. Treason against the United States, shall consist only in levying War against them, or in adhering to their Enemies, giving them Aid and Comfort. No Person shall be convicted of Treason unless on the Testimony of two Witnesses to the same overt Act, or on Confession in open Court.

The Congress shall have power to declare the Punishment of Treason, but no Attainder of Treason shall work Corruption of Blood, or Forfeiture except during the Life of the Person attainted.

ARTICLE IV

SECTION 1. Full Faith and Credit shall be given in each State to the public Acts, Records, and judicial Proceedings of every other State. And the Congress may by general Laws prescribe the Manner in which such Acts, Records and Proceedings shall be proved, and the Effect thereof.

SECTION 2. The Citizens of each State shall be entitled to all Privileges and Immunities of Citizens in the several States.

A Person charged in any State with Treason, Felony, or other Crime, who shall flee from Justice, and be found in another State, shall on demand of the executive Authority of the State from which he fled, be delivered up, to be removed to the State having Jurisdiction of the crime. No Person held to Service or Labour in one State, under the Laws thereof, escaping into another, shall, in Consequence of any Law or Regulation therein, be discharged from such Service or Labour, but shall be delivered up on Claim of the Party to whom such Service or Labour may be due.

SECTION 3. New States may be admitted by the Congress into this Union; but no new State shall be formed or erected within the Jurisdiction of any other State; nor any State be formed by the Junction of two or more States, or parts of States, without the Consent of the Legislatures of the States concerned as well as of the Congress. The Congress shall have Power to dispose of and make all needful Rules and Regulations respecting

the Territory or other Property belonging to the United States; and nothing in this Constitution shall be so construed as to Prejudice any Claims of the United States, or of any particular State.

SECTION 4. The United States shall guarantee to every State in this Union a Republican Form of Government, and shall protect each of them against Invasion; and on Application of the Legislature, or of the Executive (when the Legislature cannot be convened) against domestic Violence.

ARTICLE V

The Congress, whenever two-thirds of both Houses shall deem it necessary, shall propose Amendments to this Constitution, or, on the Application of the Legislatures of two-thirds of the several States, shall call a Convention for proposing Amendments, which, in either Case, shall be valid to all Intents and Purposes, as part of this Constitution, when ratified by the Legislatures of three-fourths of the several States, or by Conventions in three-fourths thereof, as the one or the other Mode of Ratification may be proposed by the Congress; Provided that no Amendment which may be made prior to the Year One thousand eight hundred and eight shall in any Manner affect the first and fourth Clauses in the Ninth Section of the first Article; and that no State, without its Consent, shall be deprived of its equal Suffrage in the Senate.

ARTICLE VI

All Debts contracted and Engagements entered into, before the Adoption of this Constitution, shall be as valid against the United States under this Constitution, as under the Confederation.

This Constitution, and the Laws of the United States which shall be made in Pursuance thereof; and all Treaties made, or which shall be made, under the Authority of the United States, shall be the supreme Law of the Land; and the Judges in every State shall be bound thereby, any Thing in the Constitution or Laws of any State to the Contrary notwithstanding.

The Senators and Representatives before mentioned, and the Members of the several State Legislatures, and all executive and judicial Officers, both of the United States and of the several States, shall be bound by Oath or Affirmation to support this Constitution; but no religious Tests shall ever be required as a qualification to any Office or public Trust under the United States.

ARTICLE VII

The Ratification of the Conventions of nine States shall be sufficient for the Establishment of this Constitution between the States so ratifying the same.

Done in Convention by the Unanimous Consent of the States present the Seventeenth Day of September in the Year of our Lord one thousand seven hundred and Eighty seven, and of the Independence of the United States of America the Twelfth. In Witness whereof We have hereunto subscribed our Names.[6]

GEORGE WASHINGTON
PRESIDENT AND DEPUTY FROM VIRGINIA

| **New Hampshire**
New Jersey
Delaware
North Carolina
John Langdon
William Livingston
George Read
William Blount
Nicholas Gilman
David Brearley
Gunning Bedford, Jr.
Richard Dobbs Spaight
William Paterson
John Dickinson
Hugh Williamson
Jonathan Dayton
Richard Bassett
Jacob Broom | **Massachusetts**
Pennsylvania
Maryland
South Carolina
Nathaniel Gorham
Benjamin Franklin
James McHenry
John Rutledge
Rufus King
Thomas Mifflin
Daniel of St. Thomas Jenifer
Charles Cotesworth Pinckney
Robert Morris
Daniel Carroll
Charles Pinckney | **Connecticut**
George Clymer
Pierce Butler
William Samuel Johnson
Thomas FitzSimons

Virginia
Roger Sherman
Jared Ingersoll
John Blair | **Georgia**
James Wilson
James Madison, Jr.
William Few

New York
Gouverneur Morris
Abraham Baldwin
Alexander Hamilton |

Articles in Addition to, and Amendment of, the Constitution of the United States of America, Proposed by Congress, and Ratified by the Legislatures of the Several States, Pursuant to the Fifth Article of the Original Constitution[7]

[AMENDMENT I]

Congress shall make no law respecting an establishment of religion, or prohibiting the free exercise thereof; or abridging the freedom of speech, or of the press; or the right of the people peaceably to assemble, and to petition the Government for a redress of grievances.

[AMENDMENT II]

A well regulated Militia, being necessary to the security of a free State, the right of the people to keep and bear Arms shall not be infringed.

[AMENDMENT III]

No Soldier shall, in time of peace, be quartered in any house, without the consent of the Owner, nor in time of war, but in a manner to be prescribed by law.

6 These are the full names of the signers, which in some cases are not the signatures on the document.

7 This heading appears only in the joint resolution submitting the first ten amendments, known as the Bill of Rights.

[AMENDMENT IV]

The right of the people to be secure in their persons, houses, papers, and effects, against unreasonable searches and seizures, shall not be violated, and no Warrants shall issue, but upon probable cause, supported by Oath or affirmation, and particularly describing the place to be searched, and the persons or things to be seized.

[AMENDMENT V]

No person shall be held to answer for a capital or otherwise infamous crime, unless on a presentment or indictment of a Grand Jury, except in cases arising in the land or naval forces, or in the Militia, when in actual service in time of War or public danger; nor shall any person be subject for the same offence to be twice put in jeopardy of life or limb; nor shall be compelled in any criminal case to be a witness against himself, nor be deprived of life, liberty, or property, without due process of law; nor shall private property be taken for public use, without just compensation.

[AMENDMENT VI]

In all criminal prosecutions, the accused shall enjoy the right to a speedy and public trial, by an impartial jury of the State and district wherein the crime shall have been committed, which district shall have been previously ascertained by law, and to be informed of the nature and cause of the accusation; to be confronted with the witnesses against him; to have compulsory process for obtaining witnesses in his favour, and to have the Assistance of Counsel for his defence.

[AMENDMENT VII]

In suits at common law, where the value in controversy shall exceed twenty dollars, the right of trial by jury shall be preserved, and no fact tried by a jury, shall be otherwise reexamined in any Court of the United States, than according to the rules of the common law.

[AMENDMENT VIII]

Excessive bail shall not be required, nor excessive fines imposed, nor cruel and unusual punishments inflicted.

[AMENDMENT IX]

The enumeration of the Constitution, of certain rights, shall not be construed to deny or disparage others retained by the people.

[AMENDMENT X]

The powers not delegated to the United States by the Constitution, nor prohibited by it to the States, are reserved to the States respectively, or to the people. [Amendments I-X, in force 1791.]

[AMENDMENT XI] [8]

The Judicial power of the United States shall not be construed to extend to any suit in law or equity, commenced or prosecuted against one of the United States by Citizens of another State, or by Citizens or Subjects of any Foreign State.

[AMENDMENT XII] [9]

The Electors shall meet in their respective States and vote by ballot for President and Vice-President, one of whom, at least, shall not be an inhabitant of the same State with themselves; they shall name in their ballots the person voted for as President, and in distinct ballots the person voted for as Vice-President, and they shall make distinct lists of all persons voted for as President, and of all persons voted for as Vice-President, and of the number of votes for each, which lists they shall sign and certify, and transmit sealed to the seat of the government of the United States, directed to the President of the Senate;—The President of the Senate shall, in the presence of the Senate and House of Representatives, open all the certificates and the votes shall then be counted;—The person having the greatest number of votes for President, shall be the President, if such number be a majority of the whole number of Electors appointed; and if no person have such majority, then from the persons having the highest numbers not exceeding three on the list of those voted for as President, the House of Representatives shall choose immediately, by ballot, the President. But in choosing the President, the votes shall be taken by states, the representation from each state having one vote; a quorum for

8 Adopted in 1798.
9 Adopted in 1804.

this purpose shall consist of a member or members from two-thirds of the states, and a majority of all the states shall be necessary to a choice. And if the House of Representatives shall not choose a President whenever the right of choice shall devolve upon them, before the fourth day of March next following, then the Vice-President shall act as President, as in the case of the death or other constitutional disability of the President.—The person having the greatest number of votes as Vice-President, shall be the Vice-President, if such number be a majority of the whole number of Electors appointed, and if no person have a majority, then from the two highest numbers on the list, the Senate shall choose the Vice-President; a quorum for the purpose shall consist of two-thirds of the whole number of Senators, and a majority of the whole number shall be necessary to a choice. But no person constitutionally ineligible to the office of President shall be eligible to that of Vice-President of the United States.

[AMENDMENT XIII][10]

SECTION 1. Neither slavery nor involuntary servitude, except as a punishment for crime whereof the party shall have been duly convicted, shall exist within the United States, or any place subject to their jurisdiction.

SECTION 2. Congress shall have power to enforce this article by appropriate legislation.

[AMENDMENT XIV][11]

SECTION 1. All persons born or naturalized in the United States, and subject to the jurisdiction thereof, are citizens of the United States and of the State wherein they reside. No State shall abridge the privileges or immunities of citizens of the United States; nor shall any State deprive any person of life, liberty, or property, without due process of law; nor deny to any person within its jurisdiction the equal protection of the laws.

SECTION 2. Representatives shall be apportioned among the several States according to their respective numbers, counting the whole number of persons in each State, excluding Indians not taxed. But when the right to vote at any election for the choice of electors for President and Vice-President of the United States, Representatives in Congress, the Executive and Judicial officers of a State, or the members of the Legislature thereof, is denied to any of the male inhabitants of such State, being twentyone years of age, and citizens of the United States, or in any way abridged, except for participation in rebellion, or other crime, the basis of representation therein shall be reduced in the proportion which the number of such male citizens shall bear to the whole number of male citizens twenty-one years of age in such State.

SECTION 3. No person shall be a Senator or Representative in Congress, or elector of President and Vice- President, or hold any office, civil or military, under the United States, or under any State, who, having previously taken an oath, as a member of Congress, or as an officer of the United States, or as a member of any State legislature, or as an executive or judicial officer of any State, to support the Constitution of the United States, shall have engaged in insurrection or rebellion against the same, or given aid or comfort to the enemies thereof. But Congress may by a vote of two-thirds of each House, remove such disability.

SECTION 4. The validity of the public debt of the United States, authorized by law, including debts incurred for payment of pensions and bounties for services in suppressing insurrection or rebellion, shall not be questioned. But neither the United States nor any State shall assume or pay any debts or obligation incurred in aid of insurrection or rebellion against the United States, or any claim for the loss or emancipation of any slave; but all such debts, obligations, and claims shall be held illegal and void.

SECTION 5. The Congress shall have the power to enforce, by appropriate legislation, the provisions of this article.

[AMENDMENT XV][12]

SECTION 1. The right of citizens of the United States to vote shall not be denied or abridged by the United States or by any State on account of race, color, or previous condition of servitude—

SECTION 2. The Congress shall have power to enforce this article by appropriate legislation.

[AMENDMENT XVI][13]

The Congress shall have power to lay and collect taxes on incomes, from whatever source derived, without apportionment among the several States, and without regard to any census or enumeration.

10 Adopted in 1865.

11 Adopted in 1868.

12 Adopted in 1870.

13 Adopted in 1913.

[AMENDMENT XVII][14]

The Senate of the United States shall be composed of two Senators from each State, elected by the people thereof, for six years; and each Senator shall have one vote. The electors in each State shall have the qualifications requisite for electors of the most numerous branch of the State legislatures.

When vacancies happen in the representation of any State in the Senate, the executive authority of such State shall issue writs of election to fill such vacancies: Provided, That the legislature of any State may empower the executive thereof to make temporary appointments until the people fill the vacancies by election as the legislature may direct. This amendment shall not be so construed as to affect the election or term of any Senator chosen before it becomes valid as part of the Constitution.

[AMENDMENT XVIII][15]

SECTION 1. After one year from the ratification of this article the manufacture, sale, or transportation of intoxicating liquors within, the importation thereof into, or the exportation thereof from the United States and all territory subject to the jurisdiction thereof for beverage purposes is hereby prohibited.

SECTION 2. The Congress and the several States shall have concurrent power to enforce this article by appropriate legislation.

SECTION 3. This article shall be inoperative unless it shall have been ratified as an amendment to the Constitution by the legislatures of the several States, as provided in the Constitution, within seven years from the date of the submission hereof to the States by the Congress.

[AMENDMENT XIX][16]

The right of citizens of the United States to vote shall not be denied or abridged by the United States or by any State on account of sex.

Congress shall have power to enforce this article by appropriate legislation.

14 Adopted in 1913.

15 Adopted in 1918.

16 Adopted in 1920.

[AMENDMENT XX][17]

SECTION 1. The terms of the President and Vice-President shall end at noon on the 20th day of January, and the terms of Senators and Representatives at noon on the 3d day of January, of the years in which such terms would have ended if this article had not been ratified; and the terms of their successors shall then begin.

SECTION 2. The Congress shall assemble at least once in every year, and such meeting shall begin at noon on the 3d day of January, unless they shall by law appoint a different day.

SECTION 3. If, at the time fixed for the beginning of the term of the President, the President elect shall have died, the Vice-President elect shall become President. If a President shall not have been chosen before the time fixed for the beginning of his term or if the President elect shall have failed to qualify, then the Vice-President elect shall act as President until a President shall have qualified; and the Congress may by law provide for the case wherein neither a President elect nor a Vice-President elect shall have qualified, declaring who shall then act as President, or the manner in which one who is to act shall be selected, and such person shall act accordingly until a President or Vice-President shall have qualified.

SECTION 4. The Congress may by law provide for the case of the death of any of the persons from whom the House of Representatives may choose a President whenever the right of choice shall have devolved upon them, and for the case of the death of any of the persons from whom the Senate may choose a Vice-President whenever the right of choice shall have devolved upon them.

SECTION 5. Sections 1 and 2 shall take effect on the 15th day of October following the ratification of this article.

SECTION 6. This article shall be inoperative unless it shall have been ratified as an amendment to the Constitution by the legislatures of three-fourths of the several States within seven years from the date of its submission.

17 Adopted in 1933.

[AMENDMENT XXI]¹⁸

SECTION 1. The eighteenth article of amendment to the Constitution of the United States is hereby repealed.

SECTION 2. The transportation or importation into any State, Territory, or possession of the United States for delivery or use therein of intoxicating liquors, in violation of the laws thereof, is hereby prohibited.

SECTION 3. This article shall be inoperative unless it shall have been ratified as an amendment to the Constitution by conventions in the several States, as provided in the Constitution, within seven years from the date of the submission hereof to the States by the Congress.

[AMENDMENT XXII]¹⁹

No person shall be elected to the office of the President more than twice, and no person who has held the office of President, or acted as President, for more than two years of a term to which some other person was elected President shall be elected to the office of the President more than once.

But this Article shall not apply to any person holding the office of President when this Article was proposed by the Congress, and shall not prevent any person who may be holding the office of President, or acting as President, during the term within which this Article becomes operative from holding the office of President or acting as President during the remainder of such term.

This article shall be inoperative unless it shall have been ratified as an amendment to the Constitution by the legislatures of three-fourths of the several states within seven years from the date of its submission to the states by the Congress.

[AMENDMENT XXIII]²⁰

SECTION 1. The District constituting the seat of Government of the United States shall appoint in such manner as the Congress may direct:

A number of electors of President and Vice-President equal to the whole number of Senators and Representatives in Congress to which the District would be entitled if it were a State, but in no event more than the least populous State; they shall be in addition to those appointed by the States, but they shall be considered, for the purpose of the election of President and Vice-President, to be electors appointed by a State; and they shall meet in the District and perform such duties as provided by the twelfth article of amendment.

SECTION 2. The Congress shall have power to enforce this article by appropriate legislation.

[AMENDMENT XXIV]²¹

SECTION 1. The right of citizens of the United States to vote in any primary or other election for President or Vice- President, for electors for President or Vice-President, or for Senator or Representative in Congress, shall not be denied or abridged by the United States or any state by reason of failure to pay any poll tax or other tax.

SECTION 2. The Congress shall have the power to enforce this article by appropriate legislation.

[AMENDMENT XXV]²²

SECTION 1. In case of the removal of the President from office or of his death or resignation, the Vice-President shall become President.

SECTION 2. Whenever there is a vacancy in the office of the Vice President, the President shall nominate a Vice President who shall take office upon confirmation by a majority vote of both Houses of Congress.

SECTION 3. Whenever the President transmits to the President Pro Tempore of the Senate and the Speaker of the House of Representatives his written declaration that he is unable to discharge the powers and duties of his office, and until he transmits to them a written declaration to the contrary, such powers and duties shall be discharged by the Vice-President as Acting President.

SECTION 4. Whenever the Vice-President and a majority of either the principal officers of the executive departments or of such other body as Congress may by law provide, transmit to the President Pro Tempore of the Senate and the Speaker of the House of Representatives their written declaration that the President is unable to discharge the powers and duties of his office, the Vice

18 Adopted in 1933.

19 Adopted in 1951.

20 Adopted in 1961.

21 Adopted in 1964.

22 Adopted in 1967.

President shall immediately assume the powers and duties of the office as Acting President.

Thereafter, when the President transmits to the President Pro Tempore of the Senate and the Speaker of the House of Representatives his written declaration that no inability exists, he shall resume the powers and duties of his office unless the Vice President and a majority of either the principal officers of the executive departments or of such other body as Congress may by law provide, transmit within four days to the President Pro Tempore of the Senate and the Speaker of the House of Representatives their written declaration that the President is unable to discharge the powers and duties of his office. Thereupon Congress shall decide the issue, assembling within forty-eight hours for that purpose if not in session. If the Congress, within twenty-one days after receipt of the latter written declaration, or, if Congress is not in session, within twenty-one days after Congress is required to assemble, determines by two-thirds vote of both Houses that the President is unable to discharge the powers and duties of his office, the Vice President shall continue to discharge the same as Acting President; otherwise, the President shall resume the powers and duties of his office.

[AMENDMENT XXVI][23]

SECTION 1. The right of citizens of the United States, who are eighteen years of age or older, to vote shall not be denied or abridged by the United States or by any State on account of age.

SECTION 1. The Congress shall have power to enforce this article by appropriate legislation.

[AMENDMENT XXVII][24]

No law, varying the compensation for the services of the Senators and Representatives, shall take effect, until an election of Representatives shall have intervened.

23 Adopted in 1971.
24 Adopted in 1992.

Credits

Photo Credits

Page 2–3: © Richard A. Cooke/Corbis; 4: Gift of Clara S. Peck/Buffalo Bill Historical Center, Cody, Wyoming/21.69.16/The Art Archive; 6 T: Photo Courtesy of The Newberry Library, Chicago; 7: Muench Photography, Inc.; 10: Service Historique de la Marine, Vincennes, France, Giraudon/The Bridgeman Art Library International; 11: © Raymond Gehman/Corbis; 12: Free Library, Philadelphia/The Bridgeman Art Library International; 16 BL: ©Photodisc/Age Fotostock; 16 BR: © Steve Cole/Getty Images; 17 TL: ©Adalberto Rios Szalay/Getty Images; 17 BL: © PhotoLink/Getty Images; 17 TR: ©Brand X Pictures/PunchStock; 17 BR: Princeton University Art Museum. Museum purchase, Fowler McCormick, Class of 1921, Fund, in honor of Gillett G. Griffin on his seventieth birthday. Photo: Bruce M. White, © Trustees of Princeton University; 18–19: *A Ship Sailing Past Rocks in a Rough Sea*, c. 1620, by Cornelisz Verbeec. © National Maritime Museum, Greenwich, London; 21 T, B: Unknown English Pendant: Skull, 1600's. Enamel on gold, gemstones 1.4 x 1.2 x 3.4 cm. Thomson Collection. © 2008 Art Gallery of Ontario; 22 L: © Geffrye Museum, London, UK/The Bridgeman Art Library International; 22 R: Courtesy of Dr. Alan Massey, Loughborough University, England; 23: The Granger Collection, New York; 27 L: Document sur l'Aperreamiento, ca. 1540, ms. mex. 374. Bibliothèque Nationale, Paris; 27 R: Library of Congress; 31: Bildarchiv Preussischer Kulturbesitz/Art Resource, NY; 33: Private Collection/The Bridgeman Art Library International; 36 BL: © Digital Vision/Getty Images; 36 BC: Library of Congress (LC-USZC2-1687); 36 T: ©Pixtal/AGE Fotostock; 36 BR: ©Stockbyte/Getty Images; 37 BL: Library of Congress (mhhe015508); 37 BR: Library of Congress (LC-USZ62-37993); 37 T: © Harnett/Hanzon/Getty Images; 38–39: © MedioImages/Corbis; 41 L: Library of Congress (LC-USZC4-8104); 41 R: © Walt Disney Pictures/Photofest; 42 T: © Kevin Fleming/Corbis; 42 B: Service Historique de la Marine, Vincennes, France, Lauros/Giraudon/The Bridgeman Art Library International; 45: Art Resource, NY; 46: Courtesy of APVA Preservation Virginia; 50 T: Foto Marburg/Art Resource, NY; 50 B: The Granger Collection, New York; 51 T: Musée du Chateau des ducs de Bretagne Cliché: P. Jean Ville de Nantes; 51 BL: John Gabriel Stedman, Narrative of a Five Years Expedition, Plate 53. The New York Public Library/Art Resource, NY; 51 BR: *Blacks working on the James River* by Benjamin Henry Latrobe, 1798–99. Courtesy of The Library of Virginia; 52: Image copyright © The Metropolitan Museum of Art/Art Resource, NY; 56: *View of Mulberry, House and Street*, 1805 by Thomas Coram (American, 1756–1811), Oil on paper. Gibbes Museum of Art/Carolina Art Association, 1968.18.01.; 58 TL: ©Creatas/PunchStock; 58 BL: Library of Congress (LC-USZC4-4961); 58 TR: ©Stockbyte; 58 BR: Library of Congress ; 59 TL: © Steve Cole/Getty Images; 59 BL: Library of Congress (LC-USZ62-61966); 59 TR: Jacques Cornell/McGraw-Hill Companies; 59 BR: © Ingram Publishing/Alamy; 60–61: The Granger Collection, NY; 62: The New York Public Library, Astor, Lenox and Tilden Foundation. Print Division, Phillip Stokes Collection of American Historical Prints.; 63: Museé Marguerite-Bourgeoys; 64 T: The Granger Collection, New York; 64 B: National Library of Medicine; 67: By permission of the Folger Shakespeare Library, Washington, D.C.; 68: © Massachusetts Historical Society, Boston, MA, USA/The Bridgeman Art Library International; 71: Royalty-Free/Corbis; 73: Library of Congress (cph3b42346); 75: Prints Collection, Miriam and Ira D. Wallach Division of Arts, Prints and Photographs, New York Public Library, Astor, Lenox and Tilden Foundations; 77: © Bristol City Museum and Art Gallery, UK/The Bridgeman Art Library International ; 78 L: The Granger Collection, New York; 78 T: Library of Congress; 78 R: © Photodisc/Getty Images; 79 L: Dennis Lyall, Illustrator/McGraw-Hill Companies; 79 R: Library of Congress; 80–81: Segesser II. Courtesy Palace of Governors (MNM/DCA) 158345.; 84: © Gilcrease Museum, Tulsa, Oklahoma (4016–336.7); 85: Courtesy of the Private Collection of Mrs. Janis Lyon and the Phoenix Art Museum; 86: National Library of Australia; 87: The Maryland Historical Society (1960.108.1.14.17); 90 B: The Library Company of Philadelphia (#603); 91: From the Collection of the Henry Ford (THF6826_36.17.1); 93: Abby Aldrich Rockefeller Folk Art Museum, Williamsburg, VA; 95 L: Harvard Art Museums, Fogg Art Museum, Harvard University Portrait Collection Bequest of Dr. John Collins Warren, 1856, (H47). Photo: Katya Kallsen © President and Fellows of Harvard College; 95 R: The Granger Collection, New York; 96: British Museum, London, UK/ The Bridgeman Art Library International; 98 L: © Pixtal /AGE Fotostock; 98 T: © Ingram Publishing/Alamy; 98 R: C Squared Studios/Getty Images; 99 L: Library of Congress; 99 B: Library of Congress; 99 R: Library of Congress; 100–101 B: Fort Necessity Battlefield, National Park Service; 100 inset: The Granger Collection, New York; 104 L: (detail) © National Gallery of Scotland (PG2190); 104 R: Library of Congress; 108: Library of Congress (LC-USZ62-242); 110 T: Massachusetts Historical Society; 110 B: Collection of The New-York Historical Society (49494); 111: © V&A Images/Victoria and Albert Museum, London; 113 T: © Bettmann/Corbis; 114: Library of Congress (LC-USZC4-4617); 117: The Art Archive/Laurie Platt Winfrey/Picture Desk; 118 L: © Brand X Pictures/PunchStock; 118 BL: Library of Congress (LC-USZ62-48404); 118 T: © Ingram Publishing/Alamy; 118 BR: Library of Congress (LC-USZ62-21637); 119 L: Library of Congress; 119 B: PhotoObjects.net/JupiterImages; 119 R: Library of Congress (LC-USZCN4-5); 120–121: The Granger Collection, New York; 123: © Atwater Kent Museum of Philadelphia/Courtesy of Historical Society of Pennsylvania Collection/The Bridgeman Art Library International; 128 T: The Dietrich American Foundation; 129: Image copyright © The Metropolitan Museum of Art/Art Resource, NY; 132: ©The Board of Trustees of the Armouries/HIP/The Image Works; 134: Photo by MPI/Getty Images; 135: The Historical Society of Pennsylvania, Bb612 R2997; 136 L: Library of Congress (LC-USZC4-4970); 136 T: © Brand X Pictures/Alamy; 136 R: The Palma Collection/Getty Images; 137 L, T: Library of Congress; 137 R: National Archives; 138–139: © Collection of the New-York Historical Society, USA/The Bridgeman Art Library International; 141: Miriam & Ira D. Wallach Division of Arts, Prints and Photographs. New York Public Library. Astor, Lenox and Tilden Foundations.; 142: Library of Congress, 144 L: University of Virginia Library Special Collections/Thomas Jefferson Foundation.; 144 R: José Luis Guttiérez/iStockPhoto; 146: The Library Company of Philadelphia (W26); 149: Winterthur Museum (1954.0093.001); 152: Private Collection, Peter Newark American Pictures/The Bridgeman Art Library International; 154: ©Derek Damman/iStockphoto; 156 L: National Archives; 156 T, R: Library of Congress; 157 TL: C Squared Studios/Getty Images; 157 BL: Library of Congress (LC-USZC4-6423); 157 TR: Library of Congress (LC-DIG-pga-01404); 157 BR: Photodisc; 158–159: Collection of New-York Historical Society/The Bridgeman Art Library International; 160: The Granger Collection, New York; 164: Private Collection; 166: *Alexander Hamilton*, c. 1972, (detail) by John Trumbull. Oil on canvas, 30 1/4 x 24 1/8 in. Gift of Avalon Foundation, © 2000 Board of Trustees, National Gallery of Art, Washington, DC.; 167: Private Collection/Archives Charmet/The Bridgeman Art Library International; 171: *The Procession of Victuallers*, 1821, by Joseph Yeager. Philadelphia Museum of Art. (1961-7-17); 173: Independence National Historical Park; 176: The Granger Collection, New York; 179: © CMCD/Getty Images; 180: The Granger Collection, New York; 182 L: Special Collections and College Archives, Skillman Library, Lafayette College; 182 R: Collection of The New-York Historical Society (1937.714); 184 L: Ken Cavanagh/McGraw-Hill Companies; 184 T: Library of Congress (LC-USZ62-13002); 184 R: National Archives; 185 TL: Library of Congress (LC-USZ62-20214); 185 TC: Library of Congress (LC-USZ62-10609); 185 BL: Library of Congress (LC-USZ64-3616); 185 TR: Library of Congress (LC-USZO4-3675); 185 BR: Library of Congress; 186–187: Munson-Williams-Proctor Arts Institute/Art Resource, NY; 188: Library of Congress (USZC 4-4161); 192: Beinecke Rare Book and Manuscript Library, Yale University, New Haven; 193: Library of Congress; 194: Missouri Historical Society (Neg # CT SS831); 196 T: American Textile History Museum, Lowell MA.; 196 B: Library of Congress (LC-USZC2-4831); 198: Pawtucket Falls, Rhode Island by Jacques Gerard Milbert, 1828–29. Lithograph on India paper, The New York Public Library/Art Resource, NY; 199: *Calculating*, 1844, by Thomas Hicks, American (1823–1890). Oil on canvas, 13 5/8 x 17 in. Gift of Maxim Karolik for the M. and M. Karolik Collection of American Paintings, 1815–1865, 62.273. © 2011 Museum of Fine Arts, Boston. All Rights Reserved; 201: Library of Congress (LC-USZ62-89594); 202 BL: Library of Congress (LC-USZC4-12270); 202 BC: Library of Congress; 202 TL: Library of Congress (LC-USZ62-1342); 202 TR: © StockByte/PunchStock; 202 BR: Hulton Archive/Getty Images; 203 BL: The Granger Collection, New York; 203 BR: Library of Congress (LC-USZC4-12948); 203 T: © CMCD/Getty Images; 204–205: *The Verdict of the People*, by George Caleb Bingham, 1854–55. Saint Louis Art Museum, Gift of Bank of America.; 206: Tennessee State Museum Collection. Photography by June Dorman; 207: Nicolino Calyo, *The Butcher*, c. 1840–44. Museum of the City of New York, Gift of Mrs. Francis P. Garvan in memory of Francis P. Garvan.; 209: The Granger Collection, New York; 210 L: 1858.11, Collection of the The New-York Historical Society; 210 R: Library of Congress (3b53144u); 214: Courtesy of the J. Paul Getty Museum, Los Angeles, 84.XT.441.3; 217: The Library Company of Philadelphia (Cartoon 1834-6/P.8464.5); 219: Museum of the City of New York, The J. Clarence Davies Collection; 221: Fenimore Art Museum, Cooperstown, NY. Photograph by Richard Walker. (No402.1955); 222 BL: Library of Congress (LC-USZC4-2523); 222 T: Library of Congress (LC-USZC2-2753); 222 BR: Library of Congress; 223 BL: Library of Congress; 223 BC: © Brand X Pictures/Punchstock; 223 T: Library of Congress; 223 BR: Library of Congress (LC-USZC2-3178);

Photo Credits (Design Elements)

Index